CHASING DRAGONS

Canada has received significant attention of late for initiating a government-sponsored medical marijuana program and for its flirtation with marijuana decriminalization. These initiatives have contributed to Canada being seen by Washington as a reluctant ally or even as a potential threat. The result of this impression is increasing American pressure on Canada to adopt more robust domestic security policies. At the same time, the Canadian public sees itself as upholding values that differ from those held by its neighbour to the south. These values are supposedly reflected in a distinctive security outlook that reasonably responds to potential threats, in sharp contrast to the overreactions of the United States.

Chasing Dragons challenges these assumptions of difference and exposes the politics of security in Canada and the policy that they make possible. Focusing on the issues surrounding illicit drugs, Kyle Grayson examines how the discourses and practices of security policy in fact contribute to the construction of Canadian national and cultural identity. This analysis is also relevant beyond Canada. A crucial contribution of this book is to identify the dangers of underestimating the centrality of race and geopolitics to civic conceptions of nationality in liberal societies.

Chasing Dragons reconsiders the meaning of security and discusses avenues for resisting the insecurity produced by liberal states in the post-9/11 world. This critical approach reveals the pervasiveness of power in contemporary Canadian society, how this power is hidden, and the consequences for progressive social politics.

KYLE GRAYSON is a lecturer in International Politics at Newcastle University.

KYLE GRAYSON

Chasing Dragons

Security, Identity, and Illicit Drugs in Canada

UNIVERSITY OF TORONTO PRESS
Toronto   Buffalo   London

© University of Toronto Press Incorporated 2008
Toronto Buffalo London
www.utppublishing.com
Printed in Canada

ISBN 978-0-8020-9287-8 (cloth)
ISBN 978-0-8020-9479-7 (paper)

Printed on acid-free paper

Library and Archives Canada Cataloguing in Publication

Grayson, Kyle
Chasing dragons : security, identity, and illicit drugs in Canada / Kyle
Grayson.

Includes bibliographical references and index.
ISBN 978-0-8020-9287-8 (bound). – ISBN 978-0-8020-9479-7 (pbk.)

1. Drug control – Canada.   2. National security – Social aspects – Canada.
3. Internal security – Social aspects – Canada.   4. Nationalism – Canada.
5. Marginality, Social – Political aspects – Canada.   6. Drug abuse – Canada.
I. Title.

HV5840.C3C39 2008   363.450971   C2007-906681-X

This book has been published with the help of a grant from the Canadian
Federation for the Humanities and Social Sciences, through the Aid to
Scholarly Publications Programme, using funds provided by the Social
Sciences and Humanities Research Council of Canada.

The University of Toronto Press acknowledges the financial assistance to its
publishing program of the Canada Council for the Arts and the Ontario Arts
Council.

University of Toronto Press acknowledges the financial support for its
publishing activities of the Government of Canada through the
Book Publishing Industry Development Program (BPIDP).

Contents

Acknowledgments

This monograph has been published with the help of a grant from the Canadian Federation for the Humanities and Social Sciences, through the Aid to Scholarly Publications Program, using funds provided by the Social Sciences and Humanities Research Council of Canada. I am appreciative of the three anonymous reviewers whose close readings and helpful suggestions as a part of this process enhanced the breadth and depth of this manuscript. Of course any errors or omissions remain my own responsibility.

While at York University, I was blessed to have received tremendous support, encouragement, and intellectual guidance from Margaret Beare, Daniel Drache, David Dewitt, and David Mutimer. In particular, each of these individuals displayed both intellectual honesty and a willingness to mentor, qualities that helped foster my own professional development. I am also deeply appreciative of the intellectual safe havens provided by the York Centre for International and Security Studies, the Nathanson Centre for the Study of Organized Crime and Corruption, and the Robarts Centre for Canadian Studies, and for the efforts of their staff, including Joan Broussard, Sarah Whitaker, Laura Taman, and Joan Shields.

A number of my colleagues, including Samantha Arnold, J. Marshall Beier, Collen Bell, Ryerson Christie, Elizabeth Dauphinée, Mark Heeler, Alison Howell, Tina Managhan, and Cristina Masters, participated in intellectual engagements that greatly contributed to my growth as an academic; they also added the requisite level of wit necessary to survive the banalities that define contemporary life. I have the continuing good fortune of great colleagues at the University of Newcastle Upon Tyne in the United Kingdom. In particular, I am thankful to Jocelyn Mawdsley, Simon Philpott, and Nick Randall for going well beyond the call of duty to make me feel welcome in my new home and for helping me acculturate into a new environment.

I appreciate all of the support that my family and friends have given me. To my parents, thank you for always having my best interests at heart. To my grandparents, thank you for instilling the importance of obtaining an education.

Finally, there are two people to whom I owe an impossible debt. To my wonderful wife, Denise, who has been exceptionally understanding of the peculiarities of academic life and extremely forgiving of all the disruptions these can cause, I could not have done this without you. To my daughter, Elle, you are my world and my inspiration. I love you both very much.

Kyle Grayson
Newcastle Upon Tyne
September 2007

Preface

Security is the trap that has ensnared Canadian politics. Security has become a preferred means of appropriating space available for political contestation, and it has recklessly encroached on the most minute aspects of our everyday lives. We live in an era of *securitization*, a time in which growing legions of issues are being placed above politics, allowing for established rules to be broken and emergency measures to be taken in order to make populations 'secure.' Cameras are now everywhere. Our transactions are monitored. Banal activities are recorded and analysed for deviance and danger. We can be detained without charge and without ever gaining access to the evidence that portrays us as a risk. There is a growing list of threats: weapons of mass destruction, illegal immigrants, small arms, teenagers, the poor, sexual deviants, AIDS, illicit drugs, identity theft, organized crime, environmental degradation, cultural contamination, and terrorism. We are supposed to be afraid.

In this context, security and its constitutive concept of fear have stunted political imagination in lieu of techno-strategic salvation; security is no longer considered to be a political matter but rather has become a policy domain devoid of ethico-political reflection. Security deploys strategies, tactics, and technologies to confront political uncertainties as well as claims that its prescriptions are self-evident. Security is everywhere and it is nowhere; the government can provide security, but according to the governmental security discourse there are no secure spaces in the new geopolitical environment. Since threats can manifest themselves anywhere, it is important to always be on guard.

Most important, security has narrowed the boundaries of political possibility. Liberty and security are now to be considered an economy. For the sake of freedom and security, we are being asked to give up some freedoms and the security that these provide. We are told that we should not be concerned; only those engaged in prohibited activities need be wary. Within this labyrinthine world, security is both consistent and contradictory, omnipresent and absent, simple and complex.

Despite the centrality of security in contemporary politics, there has been a marked absence of any real political debate about how dominant understandings of security and the policies those understandings make possible are shaping Canadian society. In particular, the ways in which security is imbricated within wider understandings of what it might mean to be 'Canadian' have been assumed rather than interrogated. Although 'Canadians are peacekeepers not war makers' is a common refrain, the specifics of Canadian security policy are rarely examined. In particular, the ways in which security has shaped (inter)national representations of Canada and the ways in which Canada represents itself (inter)nationally have escaped sustained public scrutiny. Inspired by this lack of reflection, this monograph examines how one security issue has fit into the construction of dominant discursive representations of Canada.

Over the past century, various substances referred to as illicit drugs have played an important though relatively overlooked role in constructing Canadian (inter)national identities through the security discourses and practices that have been mobilized to respond to them. In this capacity, illicit drugs have served as a focal point for discussions of health and sickness, normalcy and deviancy, opportunity and threat, civilization and barbarity, tolerance and intolerance, progression and tradition. These discussions, furthermore, have been utilized to make claims about what it means to *be* 'Canadian.'

As such, the central theme that weaves throughout this monograph is that by examining illicit drug issues in Canada from a perspective that is sensitive to the *political* dimensions of both security and identity (rather than just their politics), a set of observations can be made that challenge dominant conceptualizations of what Canada *is*, including the contention that Canadian identity exists independently of political processes. Thus, all of the case studies analysed will demonstrate that Canadian discourses of security centred on illicit drugs, including their constitutive parts such as discourses of race, medicine, policing, and fear, have been central to and a reflection of relations of power that have produced particular definitions of 'Canadian' as well as the body politic that Canada has been said to represent. The case studies will also reveal how these discourses have made certain kinds of responses to illicit drugs possible while precluding others, and how the possible responses have all been mobilized to reaffirm dominant understandings of Canadian (inter)national identity in a variety of historical contexts.

The approach taken in this work is unapologetically critical in its orientation. This critique spans from dissatisfaction with the discourses and practices of Canadian security policy, to the limited scope available for questioning and analysis under the traditional theories and methodologies of the social sciences. As such, this exploration will utilize forms of inquiry that have recently been pioneered by a range of social theorists in the arts, humanities, and social sciences. This constitutes a deliberate strategy on my part to reveal and highlight the contours of security, identity, and illicit drugs – contours that either have been positioned as being beyond scrutiny (i.e., as *common sense*) or that have remained hidden from vigorous interrogation in the Canadian context.

The position of illicit drugs as security threats has everything to do with what these substances are said to represent across a spectrum of interwoven discursive formations rather than what are understood to be their direct material characteristics. Facts never speak for themselves; 'facts' are always selected from a suite of contending 'facts,' and 'facts' are always interpreted. Thus, the goal of this study is not to correct dominant representations or to replace these with better representations through an appeal to 'facts' in order to provide a gateway to 'truth,' but rather to show that *any* representation and *any* essential claim always embodies normative considerations that not only reflect particular power/relations but also provide a venue for these power/relations to operate. The analytic focal point of this study is how it has become possible for some substances, people, places, and things to be interpreted in certain ways and not others, and how these interpretations change (or do not change) over time based on shifting appeals to, and interpretations of 'facts.'

This monograph, then, will challenge whatever certainties readers may have had about what defines security, the importance of identity, the threats posed by illicit drugs, and even what it may mean to be 'Canadian.' If security is to be reigned in and the political reconstituted in Canada, it will be necessary to confront commonsense (inter)-national mythologies and sacred understandings on a much grander scale than is undertaken here. Although difficult, such an endeavour is a struggle certainly worthy of pursuit.

CHASING DRAGONS

Words are, of course, the most powerful drug used by mankind.

– Rudyard Kipling

1 Introduction

Already one must conclude that the concept of drugs is a non-scientific concept, that it is instituted on the basis of moral or political evaluations: it carries in itself norm or prohibition, and allows no possibility of description or certification – it is a decree, a buzz word [*mot d'ordre*] ... As soon as one utters the 'drugs,' even before any 'addiction,' a prescriptive or normative 'diction' is already at work, performatively whether one likes it or not (Derrida 1995, 229).

Drug Pushing and the Simulation of Canadian Identity

In the late spring of 2003, Absolut Country of Sweden Vodka launched its 'Absolut Canada.' (full stop in original) advertising campaign to coincide with that year's Canada Day celebrations. According to the advertising copy, the colourful, double-sided, full-page magazine inserts had been developed to form 'a series of individual snapshots that combine to describe the truly unique Canadian experience.' Incorporating what could be conceived as popular elements of Canadian national identity into its own already highly successful marketing strategy, one of the primary goals of the campaign seemed to be to affiliate the brand image of Absolut Vodka with *the* official and hegemonic brand of Canadian nationalism. Each side of the insert was divided into four postcards with the following images:

- [upper left-hand quadrant of the first page]: 'Absolut Canada' appears in large-font white lettering on a black background.
- [upper right-hand quadrant]: A reproduction of the famous Fathers of Confederation painting is accurately depicted, save for

one of the windows looking out onto the Atlantic Ocean, which has been changed into the shape of an Absolut Vodka bottle. The accompanying caption reads 'Absolut Birthday.'
- [bottom left-hand quadrant]: An artist's rendition of a Group of Seven painting that shows an Arctic mountain range covered in ice caps. The outline of a bottle of Absolut Vodka has been textured into the contours of the snow at the base with a caption reading 'Absolut Seven.'
- [bottom right-hand quadrant]: A 'photograph' of Canada geese flying south for the winter in the formation of an Absolut Vodka bottle. The caption below reads 'Absolut Vacation.'
- [upper left-hand quadrant, second page]: A picture of what appears to be an Inuksuk constructed in the shape of an Absolut Vodka bottle. The tag line is 'Absolut Guidance,' in reference to the important role these structures play in Inuit navigation.
- [upper right-hand quadrant, second page]: An aerial photograph of Niagara Falls that has been altered so that the falls and the Niagara River take the shape of an Absolut Vodka bottle. The text below reads 'Absolut Rush.'
- [lower left-hand corner, second page]: Another pseudo-photograph of several tractors ploughing a field on the prairies. The upturned soil is, of course, in the shape of an Absolut Vodka bottle with the caption 'Absolut Backbone' nestled underneath.
- [lower right-hand corner, second page]: A photograph of a telephone pole in a generic urban setting plastered with flyers for language lessons in Japanese and French, Spanish and Ukrainian dancing lessons, Chinese food, and an African art exhibit, all of which combine to form the silhouette of an Absolut Vodka bottle. The tag line accompanying this picture is 'Absolut Mosaic.'[1]

In the Canadian context, harnessing nationalist sentiment to sell alcohol was not totally original. For example, a direct appeal to notions of Canadian identity had been made two years previously in a campaign for Molson Canadian Lager; this television commercial featured a prototypically white, heterosexual male named 'Joe Canadian.' Titled 'The Rant,' the spot featured Joe in front of a microphone on a stage, with images of 'Canada' appearing on cue in the background while he delivered a monologue on the inherent differences between Canadians and Americans to a hidden but clearly appreciative, audience. The rant went as follows:

Hey, I'm not a lumberjack, or a fur trader ... I don't live in an igloo or eat blubber, or own a dogsled ... and I don't know Jimmy, Sally, or Suzy from Canada, although I'm certain they're really nice. I have a Prime Minister, not a President. I speak English and French, not American. And I pronounce it 'about,' not ' a boot.' I can proudly sew my country's flag on my backpack. I believe in peacekeeping, not policing, diversity, not assimilation, and that the beaver is a truly proud and noble animal. A tocque is a hat, a chesterfield is a couch, and it is pronounced 'zed' not 'zee,' 'zed'!!! Canada is the second largest land mass! The first nation of hockey! And the best part of North America!!! My name is Joe!!! And I am Canadian!!!! Thank you.

What was ingenious about the Absolut campaign was the use of piggyback branding to coalesce Absolut Vodka and Canadian national identity in order to help sell a drug that was being manufactured and distributed by a foreign producer. What was interesting was how the Absolut product, despite the well-known dangers of alcohol and alcohol consumption, was able to represent itself, and find room to be accepted, as a celebrated part of the Canadian experience to an extent that other recreational drugs from outside Canada could not.[2] Drinking vodka, even if it was 'Swedish,' had been inscribed with 'Canadianess.'

Many other intoxicating substances that have not been able to present themselves as 'Canadian,' and an opaque and ever-shifting apparatus of adjudication has been put in place to constantly evaluate such claims. While it is typically presumed that security considerations regarding the legality or illegality of intoxicants have been based on the scientific analysis of their physiological and social consequences, these decisions have been *political* decisions determined largely by the security dictates of establishing a distinct Canadian identity. As such, state practices that have ostensibly been undertaken to physically secure the Canadian body politic and Canadian territoriality within various historical contexts should also be seen as moves that have secured *the* hegemonic conception of Canada and of 'Canadianess.'

The guiding question, then, is how have competing ideas of security and Canadian identity managed to code particular practices as un-Canadian, thereby making it possible to pursue various forms of prohibition towards illicit drugs?

The term 'illicit drug' is used quite deliberately throughout this study rather than alternatives such as illicit narcotics, illegal narcotics, illegal drugs, or simply narcotics/drugs. The term 'illicit' signifies that a particular activity or thing is forbidden, though this prohibition may not necessarily be codified by law; this potentially includes, then, more than the term 'illegal,' and also acknowledges that social behaviour can be disciplined in ways that extend beyond legal norms. Illicit also draws attention to the different ways in which drugs are represented outside of their legal status: some are considered inherently more problematic than others.

'Drug' is being deployed because the term covers the entire spectrum of substances that introduce pharmacological agents into the body. Though the word narcotic is often used by the law enforcement community, it properly only refers to those substances that produce stupors, drowsiness, or sleep, from the Greek roots *narkōtikos*/narkō-sis/narkoō (to benumb). As such, illicit drugs will be used as shorthand for a range of substances such as heroin, cocaine, marijuana, LSD, MDMA, methamphetamine, khat, and opium. 'Drugs discourse' will be used as a signifier to describe the constellation of discourses that construct knowledge of illicit and licit drugs and those involved in their production, distribution, and consumption.

Even though alcohol consumption is legal in Canada and has remained largely removed from the drugs discourse, the ability of Absolut to position itself as a *natural* part of the Canadian body politic is quite remarkable, given the politics of interpretation that has surrounded intoxicants for the past hundred years, particularly when they have been classified as 'foreign.' Since the passage of the Opium Act in 1908, a growing range of pharmaceutical substances have been incorporated into popular Canadian understandings of what should legitimately be considered security threats to the body politic and its unique 'way of life.' The project of combatting the social scourges represented as naturally emanating from the chemical properties of these drugs, and from those said to have used them, has been able to commandeer vast amounts of resources, energies, and time. Because of the seriousness of what have been seen as associated dangers, efforts have long been made to eliminate the production, distribution, and consumption of illicit drugs in Canadian society. Thus, within these processes of combatting illicit drugs, both individual bodies and the Canadian body politic have been made subject to technologies of discipline and social control. As such, this book provides a map of how these actions have influenced dominant perceptions of Canadian identity and how have they shaped practices of political marginalization.

Chasing Dragons/Chasing Canada

Since as human beings we are all vulnerable to a plethora of risks from getting hit by lightning to succumbing to degenerative illness, the discursive construction of some person/place/thing as a *security threat* is primarily an interpretative assessment that draws from subjective classificatory criteria shaped by a multitude of contextual factors, including our cultural, social, economic, and political circumstances. The ways in which we understand our relationships both with respect to and within these circumstances contribute to who we think we are (the Self) by juxtaposing ourselves with that which we claim we are not (the Other). Very often, what is perceived as difference is interpreted primarily as a threat to who we claim to be, and the subjective criteria utilized in making these judgements are *naturalized* in order to provide an objective grounding for our definitional claims. However, there are also always possibilities to *not* feel threatened by difference, to move beyond liberal acts of toleration that still betray a wish for redeeming change into sameness, and to find security in intersubjective differences. While this process is not easy and is fraught with difficulties and dilemmas, acknowledgment of the shared vulnerabilities and interdependencies that constitute (human) lived experience does offer the potential to foster a world less capricious in the deployment of violence in the name of security.

The crucial aspect of the interpretative exercise that is central to defining threats as well as to engendering the subjectively produced understandings that make these meanings possible is the binary of Self and Other. In these risk assessment situations, the intersubjective relationship reproduces a hierarchy that reifies the superiority of the 'Us' with respect to a 'Them.' Security and identity are therefore mutually constitutive in the processes through which the Self is distinguished from its Others and given an ontological foundation, a foundation that is not 'natural' but rather which is produced through discourse. Similarly, the security threats that are said to emanate from illicit drugs in Canada owing to their chemical properties or their effects on the body (politic) have not acquired an ontological status within security discourses prior to being interpreted as security concerns. The security implications are not 'facts' to be discovered, facts whose meanings are innate and unquestionably objective; rather, security threats have arisen from what are concurrently understood to be acceptable claims about what illicit drugs represent and the meanings read from them in terms of the ever present dynamic relationship between Self and Other.

Meanings made possible in the relationship between Self and Other, including the categories of Self and Other themselves, are never self-evident, though they are often presented within dominant discourses as incontestable; however, all meanings are without a centre – that is, without some objective/neutral point of observation that can validate a particular interpretation based on how it corresponds to a predetermined and objectively knowable 'reality' (Derrida 1978, 1982). The process of interpretation is one in which all potential and/or competing understandings are made intelligible through culture, 'the context within which people give meanings to their actions and experiences and make sense of their lives' (Tomlinson 1991, 7, in Weldes et al., 1999, 1). Yet as Weldes and her colleagues argue, culture is 'composed of potentially contested codes and representations ... a field on which are fought battles over meaning' (1999, 2). As such, culture becomes a social filter for discourse, always in a state of flux and contestation, through which understandings of (in)security, and subjects, and objects such as illicit drugs, are 'produced, reproduced, and transformed' by political communities (ibid., 2). The central role of culture in the composition of Canadian security and identity, which includes the performative enactment of a subjectivity that is named 'the Canadian people,' should therefore not be overlooked.[3]

Within the ongoing interactions among cultures, discourses of security/insecurity, and representations of Self and Other within the field of illicit drugs in Canada, it is instructive to draw from the metaphor 'chasing the dragon,' a slang term for using opium. In Eastern mythology the dragon is considered the grandest of creatures, one that embodies wisdom, strength, and good fortune (Nigg 1995, 105). Having emerged from the terrestrial confines of the earth to occupy the limitless spaciousness of the heavens, the dragon is most commonly portrayed as a form of pure energy, swirling, circling, and laughing in the air above (ibid., 120). The dragon is routinely illustrated playing with a ball of light, referred to as the 'sacred pearl' (usually a bluish-white, gold, or red in colour), that is symbolic of the power of thunder, the sun, and the moon. This ball is also sometimes described as a 'cosmic egg' or as 'the pearl of truth' (ibid., 121). In Chinese folklore, dragons ruled over the earth, the sea, the sky, and all of their associated elements. It was said that dragons created clouds and rain with their breath and winds, thunder and lightning with their movement (ibid., 121). Thus dragons were said to control the awesome forces of nature and to rule over all of those who were subject to them.

From this description, it is easier to see how 'chasing the dragon' may have come to be used as a term signifying opium use. Metaphorically, it harkens images of being freed from the limiting confines of human existence, fuelled by the psychotropic effects of the narcotic to explore an ethereal world of pleasure, possibility, and potential spiritual enlightenment. To use opium would be to partake in the pursuit of this noblest of creatures. Moreover, the fleeting effects of the drug itself, and the tendency to build up a resistance to it, speak to the Sisyphusian task of grabbing hold of the ever-elusive dragon and fully realizing the power and scope of its otherworldly gifts.

However, 'chasing dragons' as a metaphor for responses to (or towards) illicit drugs in Canada has a double-meaning that represents the position that has been historically taken by the Canadian state in response to the use of opium, as well as other drugs deemed to be illicit. In Western mythology, the dragon was originally presented in the ancient world as a creature of great wisdom but also with a propensity for heinous acts of violence. In the Middle Ages, the dragon began to be seen as a being of pure evil who preyed on humankind through activities such as defiling women and accumulating treasure, and who provided opportunities for acts of hypermasculinity by engaging in life-or-death duels with knights. As a creature that supposedly had primordial origins, a dragon was thought to engulf sinners 'among the fiery legions of the Devil ... stalk[ing] the righteous, roaring at the edge of dream' (ibid., 105). In response to these fears, there developed a long tradition of dragon slaying in Western folklore, including the story of St George, the patron saint of England. As such, the dragon has been revered both for its strength and for serving as a rite of passage in the realization of the Christian determination to triumph over the temptations of sex, wealth, and pleasure – temptations that are portrayed as defining the dark side of corporeal existence.

Besides playing a significant role in Western mythology, dragons have loomed large in the practices of Western cartography. Pictures of dragons accompanied by the Latin words 'Cave! hic dragones!' ('Beware! here be dragons!') were used on the edges of old maps, in reference to remote, unexplored areas and to oceans at the limits of the earth (ibid., 109). These were regions both unknown and uncertain, regions considered foreign in the extreme. In the natural sciences, dragons appeared in zoological encyclopaedias beginning in ancient Greece and continuing well into the Renaissance as actual creatures that could be found in exotic locales (Smith 1977). Described as deadly, devastating in their appetites, and ferocious, dragons became a common element in descriptions of wildlife contained in travel literature.

The roles that dragons have occupied in the popular Western imagination are similar to ones that illicit drug users have played in Canada. That is, the drug user over the past hundred years has been seen as dangerous, evil, crafty, manipulative, tempting, violent, and – perhaps most important – foreign to the principled ethos of Canadian society. Like the dragon, the illicit drug user is contaminated with a degree of sin that is impossible to fully expiate except through elimination. The locations where drug use has allegedly taken place, such as opium dens, ethnic neighbourhoods, and raves, are coded as exotic foreign enclaves within the secure boundaries of the domestic sphere, as zones one must delineate and take steps against in order to stem the proliferation of immorality, violence, and chaos.

Ironically, in much the same way that opium users futilely pursue the pleasures of the dragon, the apparatus of the Canadian state charged with responding to illicit drug use – or to continue with the metaphor, the task of 'dragon slaying' – finds success elusive. As with the Hydra of Greek mythology, it is claimed that the slaying of one dragon does little more than spawn several more with an ever increasing power to corrupt. As such, Canadian society has consistently struggled to navigate the elements of foreignness, uncertainty, peril, and threat that are claimed to originate with illicit drug users and the lairs they are said to inhabit. Policy has traversed a continuum ranging from elimination to concealment, management, and incorporation in order to preserve what have been constructed as the vital characteristics of the Canadian Self.

In examining this quest for security, it becomes important to deconstruct not only the dragon but also the dragon slayer. While identity can be read through dominant constructions of illicit drugs as security threats, it is equally important to navigate how conceptions of national identity are imbricated in the ways that Canada claims to be responding to them. As reflected in the Absolut Vodka advertising campaign, how Canadians wish to see themselves can be discerned through Canadian drugs discourses and policy. By highlighting the origins of Canadian Confederation, Canadian high culture, nature, geography, technology, and ethnic diversity, the Absolut Vodka campaign reaffirmed dominant Canadian narratives about Canada and Canadian identity. It transformed the 'imagined' of the Canadian 'imagined community' into something real and tangible. It grounded national identity in elements that were unquestionably perceived by the audience as inherently Canadian. In this respect, the grammatical full stop that follows each tag line (e.g., 'Absolute Mosaic.') can be read as an attempt to dissuade any reflection on these characteristics by the audience.

Ultimately, though, despite claims read through vodka ads or illicit drug policies, identity is an ephemeral social phenomenon. There is no natural or inherent basis to any identity, which is always subject to interpretation. Thus, in Jean Baudrillard's terminology, the signifiers preceded the signified in the reproduction of a hyperreal (i.e., an overly real yet not grounded in 'reality') Canadian identity through both discursive performatives and physical performances, be they articulated in the Absolut Vodka and Molson Canadian campaigns or through the conduits of Canada's Drug Strategy. The argument, though, is not that anything goes in terms of performatively constructing identities. Judith Butler, borrowing from Derrida, makes the point that the power of the performative to convince is not a function of an originating will, but rather it is a derivative of ideas, signifiers, or modes of representation (i.e., what Derrida refers to as iterable utterances) already present in relevant discursive formations (Butler 1999, 239–40). Instead, the point is that discursive performatives and physical performances should be seen as simulations that produce truth effects that hide the non-existence of *the* 'truth' of Canadian identity (Ó Tuathail 1996, 247). Therefore, the goal of this study is not to discover *the* truth of Canadian identity but to demonstrate the ways in which its contingency – the ultimate inability to *know* Canada – requires that performatives (i.e., utterances that inscribe Canada with particular characteristics) and performances (i.e., playing the role[s] made possible by specific performatives) be undertaken.

This argument is anathema to the best-known views on Canadian culture, which have essentialized characteristics that supposedly define Canadian identity and character at the individual and collective levels. These views embrace categorizations from past historical contexts as well as the modern day such as loyalist, law-abiding, strong, communal, tolerant, multicultural, resourceful, middle-power, liberal, peacekeeper, the helpful fixer, the good international citizen, and, most important, *not* American.[4] Also, Canadian researchers have undertaken quantitative work to gauge the differences between Canadians and Americans and to provide an ontological grounding and fixedness to them (Adams 1997).

While there may indeed be attitudinal differences and divergences in the perceptions of the national Self, these are not the direct result of the natural essences of respective populations and/or material interests; instead, they reflect differences in the ways that national identity and characteristics have been socially constructed and discursively reproduced in the Canadian and American contexts through a series of performatives and performances. Rather than reflecting 'natural' characteristics, identity arises through contingencies generated by the interactions of a constellation of sociopolitical forces that once established can be both articulated and managed through public policy actions that extend beyond the explicit promotion of national culture. In particular, national identity is read through Canadian security policy with respect to illicit drugs.

The social signifiers contributing to hegemonic Canadian conceptualizations of the Self that are of greatest interest here are the ideas of enlightened tolerance, multiculturalism, and non-Americaness – ideas that pervade most nationalist discourses. How have these been utilized in the process of securitizing particular drugs and drug users? The following chapters will demonstrate how those elements have been modified in practice, how they evade potential tensions with dominant security discourses, and how these reconciliations have been reproduced in Canadian responses to the issue of illicit drugs. The overarching argument is that tolerance, multiculturalism, and non-Americanness are contradictorily and arbitrarily invoked in official Canadian drug discourses and practices. As such, I am interested in the discursive relations surrounding illicit drugs in Canada that have securitized these substances and in the accompanying regimes of truth that contribute to the reproduction of *a* Canadian identity.

Discourse and Power/Relations

Given that the Canadian state has identified illicit drugs as a security threat, has implemented a national drug control strategy with medical and criminal components, and continues to engage in practices to maintain social taboos against these substances, research has focused on *why* the government has responded to the drug issue in this fashion. Yet, even if done from a critical perspective, asking *why* limits examination to the official rationales and/or reasons for policy decisions and whether they are appropriate given what are presented as the *objectively* definable circumstances of a particular situation. Instead of promoting alternatives, these approaches constrict them by remaining faithful to epistemic realism, 'a logic of explanation whereby it is the purpose of analysis [and political argument] to identify ... self-evident things and material causes so that actors can accommodate themselves to the realm of necessity that they engender' (Campbell 1993, 7–8).

Unfortunately, such analyses miss the key point. While there *may* be objectively definable circumstances and situations such as an increase in the consumption of illicit drugs, an important aspect of study is what kind(s) of meaning(s) are ascribed to those drugs in discourse. What kinds of meanings have been assigned to illicit drugs, illicit drug users, and those charged with protecting the Canadian body politic from them? The strategy, then, is to read how discursive representations of illicit drugs construct and reflect dominant understandings of Canadian identity.

Traditionally, discourse has been used primarily to describe a practice of signifying a domain of knowledge or experience from perspectives with shared foci, such as criminological discourse, security discourse, and the illicit drugs discourse (Fairclough 1992, 215). But as Michael J. Shapiro (1989) notes, discourse is much more than a 'transparent communication between subjects about things, a view within which the value of a statement of a discourse is wholly absorbed in a statement's truth value' (1989, 17). Similarly, Michel Foucault (1972) has distinguished between language and discursive analyses in the following way: 'The question posed by the language analysis of some discursive fact or other is always: according to what rules could other similar statements be made? The description of the events of discourse poses quite a different question: how is it that one particular statement appeared rather than another?' (1972, 27).

In other words, discourse is the terrain on which divergent interpretations of the world compete to define our 'commonsense' beliefs about 'reality.' As such, discourse becomes a site for political analysis; it does so by exploring the power/relations that encourage particular articulations, while precluding others, in the construction of categories of classification that are able to produce 'concrete and significant, material effects' (Weldes et al. 1999, 16–17).

This does not necessarily mean that discourse is just another site where competing interests do battle. Most of the time, discourse cannot be manipulated or transformed. This is because we talk about people, places, and things in ways that make logical and interpretive sense to us; discourse is what we draw from in order to describe the world as we believe it to be. This is where the power of discourse lies: in its ability to shape interpretative dispositions and frame descriptions that make action possible. To achieve political transformation thus requires more than changing the language or words that constitute a discourse. It requires nothing less than a transformation of the modes of thinking that constitute the discursive formations we draw upon in sociopolitical activity.

By breaking away from the traditional analytical dichotomy that establishes an independent external reality and our thoughts about it, we can view discourse as a social process that produces relations between subjects, between subjects and objects, and among objects that would not otherwise exist as subjects and/or objects prior to discourse. This is not to say that objects/subjects do not exist in the absence of discourse. Rather, the point is that they do not exist as *meaningful* entities (in a social/political sense) outside of discourse.[5] In *The Archaeology of Knowledge* (1972), Foucault argues that 'discursive relations are at the limit of discourse: they offer it objects of which it can speak, or rather they determine the group of relations that discourse must establish in order to speak of this or that object, in order to deal with them, name them, analyse them, classify them, et cetera. These relations characterise not the language used by discourse, nor the circumstances in which it is deployed, but discourse itself as a practice' (1972, 46).

Discourse, then, is not mere rhetoric; it imbues subjects, objects, and the relationships among them with meaning. Therefore, 'it would be quite wrong to see discourse as a place where previously established objects are laid one after the other like words on a page' (ibid., 43).

Instead, discourse should be seen as a site where these objects are made *meaningful* through an ongoing series of interpretations.

This suggests that discourse itself is a politicized space open to questioning, reexamination, and transformation. Bradley Klein (1987) has argued that 'to be engaged in a discourse is to be engaged in the making and remaking of meaningful conditions of existence. A discourse then is not a way of learning "about" something out there in the "real world"; it is rather a way of producing that something as real, as identifiable, classifiable, knowable, and therefore, meaningful. Discourse creates the conditions of knowing' (1987, 4, in George 1994, 30).

In creating the 'conditions of knowing' and the theoretical filters through which we interpret the world, discourse highlights the multi-directional relationship between theory and practice. Primarily, discursive analyses open the potential to see that theory *is* practice and that practice *is* theory, or what we can call theory/practice. Moreover, theory does not necessarily have to be thought of in a formal sense here (e.g., realism, liberalism, Marxism) but also includes the *common-sense* propositions we utilize in navigating our social worlds. Thus, far from merely describing the world as it is, the ways in which we are able to talk about the world shape the ways in which we are able to see the world (i.e., theory), which in turn contributes to shaping the ways we (re)act to (and in) the world (i.e., practice). The converse relationship also holds: the ways we (re)act to (and in) the world shape the way we see the world, which in turn, contributes to the ways we are able to think about the world. Therefore, theory constitutes our perceptions of the real or material.

Once our awareness is heightened of the role of theory/practice in social activity, discourse and the discursive formations that surround subject areas become central to our understanding of how power/relations are exercised.[6] Power, though, is being conceptualized here not as a force that fills a vacuum but rather as a relationship that

> must be understood in the first instance as the multiplicity of force relations imminent in the sphere in which they operate and which constitute their own organization; as the process which, through ceaseless struggles and confrontations, transforms, strengthens, or reverses them; as the support which these force relations find in one another, thus forming a chain or a system, or on the contrary, the disjunctions and contradictions, which isolate them from one another; and lastly, as the strategies in which

they take effect, whose general design or institutional crystallization is embodied in the state apparatus, in the formulation of the law, in the various social hegemonies. (Foucault 1990, 92–3)

Therefore, rather than conceptualizing power as a unidirectional coercive force that is defined by a strict case of ruler and ruled, a Foucauldian perspective conceives of power as a diffuse multidirectional *relationship* that permeates all social connections.[7] As such, power/relations depend on points of resistance (ibid., 93–5). Close attention must therefore be paid to the political, social, and economic conditions in question, for, as Norman Fairclough (1992) argues, 'how texts are produced and interpreted, and therefore how genres and discourses are drawn upon and combined, depends upon the nature of the social context' (1992, 213). In other words, 'social relations are the key to all ideas and hence to whatever reality a culture constructs' (Hollis and Smith 1990, 83).

Contrary to the traditional analytic dichotomy, power/relations are integral to processes of knowledge accumulation, for they must produce knowledge in order to become fully realized in practice as legitimate networks. Thus, 'there is no power relation without the correlative constitution of a field of knowledge, nor any knowledge that does not presuppose and constitute at the same time power relations' (Foucault 1984a, 175). In *The History of Sexuality* (1990), Foucault spoke of the power–knowledge–pleasure nexus that shapes who is allowed to speak, from what positions and viewpoints they may speak, the institutions that prompt people to speak, and the institutions that store and distribute what they have to say (1990, 11). Thus, rather than marking some pure space of unadulterated verity, 'truth is not outside of power or lacking in power ... truth is a thing of this world: it is produced only by virtue of multiple forms of constraint. And it induces regular effects of power' (Foucault 1977b, 131). Therefore, in order to be able to establish what is true, 'each society has its regime of truth, its general politics of truth: that is the types of discourse which it accepts and makes function as true; the mechanisms and instances which enable one to distinguish true and false statements, the means by which each is sanctioned; the techniques and procedures accorded value in the acquisition of truth; the status of those who are charged with saying what counts as true' (ibid., 131).

The analytic goal, though, is not to judge from a 'neutral' position how closely these competing understandings correspond to some objectively verifiable reality but rather to ascertain the ethico-political implications of adopting one method of interpretation over others, and the series of (dominant) representations that are thus made possible. This discursive mode of analysis eschews what Jacques Derrida has referred to as *logocentrism*, which Gearoid Ó Tuathail (1996) describes as 'the dependence on theories of thought, discourse, or ... meaning on a metaphysical authority (*Logos*) that is considered external to them and whose truth and validity they express' (1996, 65). Jim George (1994) has highlighted the ways in which the logocentric process excludes anything that is not considered to respond to the 'logo' in order to create 'identity, unity, and universalized meanings' that demarcate the 'real' from the 'unreal' (1994, 30). As such, one of focuses of any analysis should be to identify who is speaking, from what institutional sites, what position(s) are being occupied by this person in relation to various social domains and/or groups of objects, and what kinds of politics do the representations embodied by their preferred discursive formations (or logos) make possible.

Neo-Parrhesia and the Discourse of Drugs in Canada

What, then, are the roles of those who are identified as having access to truth, such as the expert, the witness, the authority, and the critic? What claims can they put forward, and why are their statements accepted as truthful? In *Fearless Speech* (2001), Foucault examines the dynamic history of these questions in the Western tradition, with an emphasis on how the social positions and discourses of legitimacy for those who have claimed to speak truth have radically shifted over time. To understand how processes of truth adjudication have been dramatically transformed, he focuses on the concept of *parrhesia*. In the Greek experience, the coincidence of belief and truth occurred in verbal activity (i.e., *parrhesia*). As a consequence, the literal ancient Greek meaning of *parrhesia* is incapable of being inserted into modern epistemological frameworks (2001, 14).

In its most literal translation from ancient Greek, *parrhesia* means 'free speech.' To best reflect the meanings in its own context, *parrhesia* should be thought of as 'true speech': the *parrhesiastes* is the one who speaks the truth (ibid., 11). *Parrhesia* required that the speaker use the most direct words and expressions possible in order to make it clear that whatever he might be saying was his *own* opinion. As a 'speech activity,' *parrhesia* was largely limited to male citizens. It often took the form of 'I am the one who thinks ... ' and adopted what today appears to be a rather tautological claim to truth: that something was to be considered true by others because the speaker himself knew it to be true. Therefore, the question raised at the time was how could one know that an individual was a truth teller?

A claim to *parrhesia* required that the speaker be taking some kind of risk in speaking, whether it be in terms of personal popularity, friendship, or even mortality; danger for the *parrhesiastes* always arose from the fact that the spoken truth was capable of hurting or angering the audience. Foucault's genealogy of the practice in ancient Greece and Rome uncovered that despite the dangers of speaking the truth, those who engaged in *parrhesia* did so out of the belief that the activity was a duty that *had* to be undertaken. It was a form of criticism that arose in a situation defined by a speaker who occupied a subordinate position with respect to the audience. By definition, a king, a tyrant, or a majority could not be a *parrhesiastes*, for in making a truth claim, they risked absolutely nothing. In this sense, then, it was possible to interpret *parrhesia* as a means to separate the guardianship of 'truth' from the corridors of political power.[8] It was a counter-hegemonic exercise that sought to transform standard modes of being by exposing them to *the* truth in order to improve them.

Sensitivity to the challenges posed by *parrhesia* unravels a critical set of questions for the contemporary study of power/knowledge and illicit drugs in Canada. Instead of trying to provide an answer to the question of 'what is true' about illicit drugs and their effects, the focus shifts to who is able to tell the truth, about what, with what consequences, and with what relation to power in processes that have been touted as marking a slow liberal transformation in Canadian drug policy (ibid., 170).

To be clear, *parrhesia* has dramatically changed in contemporary society, and the concept as understood in ancient Greece has been thoroughly reconfigured. No longer is the separation between truth and power starkly delineated. Those who hold certain occupations in contemporary society, or who have received particular types of training that contribute to a dominant standing in social relations with others, are better positioned to make truth claims that will be accepted by an audience, especially when these claims are evoked for the purposes of securitization. As such, effects are produced that reverberate beyond the initial sphere of public and/or private life that made a particular configuration of power/relations possible. Moreover, power is consti-tutive of itself in the sense that power and societal power/relations cannot be understood apart from each other. In this way, knowledge and/or truth must be understood and analysed not as ontological cer-tainties that can be objectively verified, but rather as social phenomena that create subjects and objects that are imbued with particular mean-ings. In turn, commonly accepted meanings make possible various forms of hegemony.

As such, power/knowledge and truth form a mutually constitutive nexus of meaning and order: power/relations help define knowledge and truth, while truth and knowledge help to regularize relations of power. For example, Foucault (1984a) argued that 'there is no power relation without the correlative constitution of a field of knowledge, nor any knowledge that does not presuppose and constitute at the same time power relations' (1984a, 175). No longer, then, is truth telling primarily a risky activity taken out of a sense of duty by a sub-ordinate element in an asymmetrical power relationship in order to initiate a transformation of the status quo.[9] Instead truth telling serves as a means to cement the ontological foundations and the asymmetries of power/relations by stabilizing the hierarchical positions designated to the various assortment of subjects and objects that constitute them. *Parrhesia* is a hollow shell of its original form, but its importance to political discourse remains. Contemporary *parrhesia*, or what is better classified as an ersatz *neo-parrhesia*, is now a means by which ontolog-ical security can be obtained.

This is not to say that the truth-telling actions of authorities and experts do not go unchallenged. Within the confines of the drugs dis-course itself, there are numerous claims made about those actions from a variety of sites. However, the scope of these claims must be policed by the boundaries of recognized iteration, or what can be understood by others to be possible within an already established realm of poten-tial truth. Moreover, the position of neutral arbitrator needs to be con-structed, some system that can judge the merit of individual truth claims or adjudicate between those in competition while having its claim of objectivity accepted. And once constructed, some social prac-tice must fulfil this role.

Within the contemporary Canadian drugs discourse, the discipline of science and its particular knowledge-producing practices have been appealed to to perform these duties. But this has not always been the case: the performance of science as the iteration police and neutral arbitrator has been uneven, a consequence both endogenous and exogenous to science itself. Science as a knowledge-producing practice is often conspicuously absent from the construction of representations of drugs and drug users. Conversely, claims to scientific knowledge are sometimes harnessed by authorities to bolster *commonsense* assertions and the representational practices they foster.

Second, despite the claims of its adherents and the representation in popular discourses, science is never a completely neutral enterprise. Science, like any other knowledge-producing institution, can feed into existing gender, racial, and cultural hierarchies (Tuhiwai Smith 1999, 59–64). It can be used to perpetuate existing power/relations, not just in the nihilistic sense that in challenging power one is also recognizing its authority, but because of what science values: control, prediction, the separation of mind and body, and what it finds difficult to quantify: emotion, faith, and the interconnectedness of mind and body. Additionally, scientific knowledge has shown total comfort with being used for the purposes of control, for example, with respect to harnessing natural forces, as a part of its wider raison d'être: liberation from myth (Tickner 1992b, 101–5).

This relationship with control spans the entire scientific enterprise. While there are clear instances of poor science and sound science (based on the criteria with which the field chooses to evaluate itself), especially within the area of research on illicit drugs, all forms of science are a deployable form of contextualized knowledge that is both a manifestation of relations of power in a society as well as a venue for these power/relations to operate. Thus even sound science creates authorities and hierarchies, though these may be more agreeable than those formed by poor science, which shape the social environment through our (scientific) understandings of it.

The limitations of contemporary science as a knowledge-producing technology have been identified by other positions within philosophy, including those that wish to contest the claims of the essential neutrality of the scientific method (i.e., positivism) as a form of inquiry. In particular, critical realism has raised challenges about the ability of the scientific method to accurately decipher the underlying essence of reality (both material and social) while advancing its own post-positivist methodology to unite the study of the natural and social sciences. My own position differs from critical realism in that I do not share the belief that the meaning of 'reality' exists independently of our thoughts about it. Again, this does not mean that I deny the existence of the material and/or social world in the absence of discourse, but rather that the material and/or social world has no inherent (ethico-political) meaning outside of discourse and the specific narrative used to describe it (Campbell 1999, 319–20). These contending meanings and their corresponding outlooks become important because ultimately, they make possible various and often discrete types of responses. Once established as *common sense*, particular interpretative dispositions are concretized as the best, or even the only way, of producing 'facts.' Moreover, the status of the framework of inquiry as an *interpretative* framework among many other reasonable possibilities, rather than as *the* only framework capable of discovering 'facts,' is often quickly forgotten.

What, then, are the questions raised by the modern practices of *neo-parrhesia* in Canada? In particular, how have the law enforcement and medical communities played a central role in producing representations of illicit drug users that are taken by the public audience as *the* truth? To be clear, these questions are not formulated to inspire a history of Canadian drug legislation nor an analysis of the legal intricacies of drug law.[10] Instead, the tack taken is to embark on a genealogy of how the body of the drug user has been represented by various domains in the Canadian drugs discourse and how this has contributed to a politics of the possible. In this way, I am interested in what Roxanne Doty (1996) has referred to as *power as productive* of meanings that are attached to social subjects and objects, thus 'constituting particular interpretative dispositions that create certain possibilities and preclude others' (1996, 4).

Methodology and Method

Security analysts have long treated identity as epiphenomenal and as reflective of underlying objective material factors such as power.[11] Kenneth Waltz's (1979) discipline-dominating neorealism in the field of global security was almost completely non-social, save for his discussion of the need for states to mimic the successful survival strategies of other states. John Ruggie (1998) has remarked that even liberal analysts were so restricted by an ontological privileging of the material over the social that the views of advocates, such as Robert Keohane, left almost no room for liberty and rights, the very characteristics that differentiate liberalism from other political ideologies (1998, 883). Given this neglect, questions about and analyses of social phenomena like identity were largely absent from this field of inquiry.

Constructivism has experienced a meteoric rise in terms of its popularity, to the point where its mainstream variant has been recognized as one of the three legitimate theoretical approaches to the study of global politics (Katzenstein, Keohane, and Krasner 1998; Walt 1999). Within this growing body of work, identity has been taken on as a variable that should be examined in order to provide richer *explanations* of the practices of international relations. Yet despite its potential to provide a more social account of global politics, the claimed merging of postmaterialist ontology with positivist epistemology into a *via media* has unduly limited the scope of inquiry into the relationship between security and identity (Wendt 1999).

In contrast to these highly bounded notions, William Connolly (1989) has remarked that the study of identity in global politics can be thought of in two dimensions, with serious political implications that follow from how we conceive of its spatiality:

> First, it might be tightly or loosely demarcated in the dimension of its breadth ... [Second], an identity can also vary along the dimension of depth because it construes itself to be the bearer of a fundamental truth that it knows to be true; it might have faith in its truth and look forward to a day when the faith is translated into knowledge; it might conclude that it must always be founded on a contestable faith in its truth; or it might conclude that it is both crucial to its individual and collective bearers but historically contingent in its formation and ungrounded ontologically in its truth – ungrounded, not because it alone in the world of identities has no ground, but because it treats as true the proposition that no identity is grounded in ontological truth; no identity is the true identity because every identity is particular and contingent. (1989, 331)

The major problem with many contemporary constructivist accounts of security and identity is that both security and identity are conceptualized as true objects that produce clear causal effects. In this way, ideational and discursive elements are transposed onto the material realm and given firm objective foundations in order to ground analysis on some objectively verifiable factor. This sleight of hand is necessary because mainstream constructivists still desire to be perceived as social *scientists* and thus have remained bound to only analysing those factors which have materially measurable characteristics.

For example, the recent work of Alexander Wendt (1992, 1999), which has enjoyed tremendous academic recognition, theorizes identity as an intervening variable (sometimes) that can influence (sometimes) the objective interests that arise from the need for survival in an anarchical global system. Typically, then, constructivist research undertaken on how identity and state security policy intersect has proceeded in the following fashion. The first move is to examine the characteristics that, according to the experts, define the object of study (e.g., characteristics that distinguish a particular political community, usually a nation-state). The second is to compile this list of plausible characteristics and rename it *identity*. The third move is to treat this interpretation as a series of objective facts. The final move is to show how identity (the objectively verifiable fact) has influenced (or *caused*) practice, particularly in instances when the object of study appears to have acted in a way that cannot be derived from *the* rational calculation of its *interests*. As such, much of the literature on security and the state has been preoccupied with mapping out functional understandings of the *causal* relationship constituted by identity, norms, and state behaviour.[12]

By taking an approach that favours systemic explanations for practical outcomes, constructivists like Wendt try to compartmentalize and separate the sites within which identity formation is taking place. The focus is on the interstate level (and above), where – he argues – Self and Other come into contact and develop intersubjective understandings of who they are. However, the so-called levels of analysis are not as watertight as Wendt, and the social sciences more generally, have assumed them to be. Interactions between Self and Other that may contribute to state or national identity in contrast to what is perceived as foreign also arise in what has been assumed to be, for analytic *or* political ease, a homogenous domestic realm. Particularly in the case of Canada, the domestic realm has never been homogenous by any stretch of the imagination, and thus the invocation of a Canadian national identity has been largely influenced by how Self and Other have been constructed within the confines of Canadian territory (and have even constructed what territory can be considered Canadian).

The Wendtian constructivist framework also limits analysis by giving all actors a pre-existing identity that refuses to acknowledge that the agency of actors is what gives rise to these identities, and that these actors are not necessarily states. The depoliticization of identity is unproblematic for many constructivists like Wendt: they argue via epistemic realism that there are simply certain facts that are true regardless of our thoughts about them, such as 'pigs cannot fly.' However, this elides the crucial question: What has come to be understood as a pig in a particular social context? For example, many police forces have now procured helicopters that are used for surveillance and to apprehend suspects. Therefore, 'pigs' do sometimes fly if one defines 'pig' in this manner.[13] Thus, the reading of critical realism operationalized by mainstream constructivism is unable to adequately navigate either inter- or intra-subjective difference and must gloss over ambiguities by appealing to a naturalized 'reality' that cannot be legitimately questioned. In the end, it wishes to depoliticize politics in order to maintain its analytic coherence.

When identity is not taken as a given and is denaturalized, we can see it as the tenuous political outcome of performativity rather than as an innate characteristic(s) of an agent. The failure of *via media* approaches to ask the kinds of questions that seek to discover how particular identities have been socially constructed has given rise to a very limited vision of the role of narratives and discourses in global politics. In addition, Wendt tries to subsume discourse under the 'ideational' category, a move that is problematic because 'the relative autonomy of discourse cannot be reduced to the intentions, motivations, interests, etc. of those human beings who do the speaking, writing, and other acts of signification' (Doty 2000, 138). Moreover, the influence of ideas is confined to interactions between already existing actors in an already existing system, one in which identities are depoliticized and potentially ahistorical.

Identity, then, in this body of work becomes something that should be analysed as a static objective material factor that can be used to *explain* the securitization of political issues. Identity is sometimes posited as another way of recognizing interest; in other cases it is incorporated as structure itself (McSweeny 1999). The analytic focus centres on explaining agent-initiated changes to structure through the exercise of interest, which is also to be treated as structure, rather than understanding how actors may actually perceive themselves. The common conceptual thread that runs through constructivist accounts is that for something to be analytically useful and to have ontological relevance, it needs to be material or treated as a material object. This is the move, recognized by Connolly, that attempts to convert *faith* in an identity into *knowledge* of an identity.

From a political standpoint, these approaches want to take far too much for granted; moreover, they do not problematize how it becomes possible for particular discourses, practices, and resulting constellations of power to be dominant. Identity and security are dynamic intersubjective processes that are contextually contingent; they are more than an analytic category that can explain shared understandings for the benefit of the outside observer (Kulbálková 2001, 75). They are constantly being negotiated, rethought, and challenged not just within the global system but perhaps more important, within social groups themselves. Other interpretations are therefore *always* a possibility. To not look at how this intersubjective process is understood by actors themselves and to not problematize the identities and security postures that are made possible by this process reveals a willingness to commit the same transgressions that Richard K. Ashley (1986) raised about neorealism's thin account of (state) actors more than two decades ago.

The theoretical and methodological approaches undertaken in this study lead to a very different research problematic. Canadian identity will be read through security practices and discourses. In turn, the limits of these practices and discourses, demarcated by the ways in which Canadian identity has been constructed within them, will also be analysed. These approaches are self-reflectively post-positivist and therefore move away from *determining the causes* of effects in the social world towards trying to *understand the meanings* these phenomena have for the inhabitants. To this end, post-positivist social science stresses that people find meaning in their experience, that language and linguistic meaning are a 'crucial component of social life,' that social context is important, and that 'ideas have meaning for social actors' (Hollis and Smith 1990, 68–70).

In moving towards an understanding of the meanings assigned to security and identity within the security practices charged with managing illicit drugs in Canada, deconstruction – of both the representational practices of the illicit drugs discourse, and the concepts that make them possible – has been used as an analytic guide, bearing in mind that 'deconstruction in its Derridean sense raises the question of whether deconstruction can be thought of in terms of method ... because it is impossible to give the usual methodological or logical intra-orbitary assurances' (Gasché 1986, 122).

Although Derrida himself has declared that 'deconstruction is not a method and cannot be transformed into one,' Richard Beardsworth

(1996) argues that this must be understood in terms of the following reasoning: 'A thinker with a method has already decided *how* to proceed, is unable to give him or herself up to the matter of thought in hand, is a functionary of the criteria which structure his or her conceptual gestures. For Derrida ... this is irresponsibility itself' (1996, 4; in Royle 2000, 4).

As an antimethod, deconstruction allows for flexible means of analytic interpretation whose common ethos is a 'questioning of the "is," a concern with what remains to be thought, with what cannot be thought within the present' (ibid., 7). Rodolphe Gasché (1986) has argued that while deconstruction is the deconstruction of method, both scientific and philosophical, it 'is not a non-method, an invitation to wild and crazy lucubrations' (1986, 123). The point is that unlike other methodological positions, deconstruction explicitly aims to undermine its own methodological authority by refusing to provide evidence that it is 'right.' While this is certainly disconcerting, and for some even annoying, it is no more problematic than traditional methodological positions, whose rationales for analytic rigour are tautologies that bare no logic independent of their own epistemological foundations.

One of the advantages of deconstruction is that it draws attention to how 'concepts [and representations] are always ... inscribed within systems or conceptual chains in which they constantly relate to a plurality of other concepts and conceptual oppositions from which they receive their meaning' (ibid., 129). As such, it becomes important to discern whether these traces are acknowledged. If not, by which processes and practices are they masked? Nicholas Royle (2000) has argued that 'deconstruction [also] has to do with what is *not* present, for example with what makes every identity at once itself and different from itself, haunted, contaminated, set beside itself' (2000, 10). By embracing the non-assurances of deconstruction, one leaves the traditional world of strict delineation and enters a counterintuitive zone where lines blur 'since concepts are produced within a discursive network of differences, they not only are what they are by virtue of other concepts, but they also, in a fundamental way, inscribe that Otherness within themselves' (Gasché 1986, 128).

Thus there lies within *every* concept, *every* representation, *every* discursive formation, and *every* discourse a logic of destabilization. The difficulty is that this logic is not static: it is in a constant state of transformation (Royle 2000, 11). For example, one can consider Derrida's (cryptic) discussion of what he calls *différance* that 'exceeds the order of truth at a certain precise point, but without dissimulating itself as something, as mysterious being, in the occult of non-knowledge or in a whole with indeterminable borders' (Derrida 1982, 6). Thus, in sharp contrast to the standard theoretical perception that construes contradictions and aporias as detriments because they undermine the consistency of discourses/concepts/representations, those elements that unsettle should be seen as useful in that they are constitutive of the realization of an insight that results only after the 'discrepancies and inconsistencies of philosophy's mise en scène' are revealed (Gasché 1986, 127). Primarily, deconstruction offers an awareness to the cruel irony that even in contestation, most contemporary alternative interpretative frameworks 'slip into the form, the logic, and implicit postulations' of that which is constructed as their opposite (Derrida 1978, 280).

When applied to positions that extend beyond philosophical considerations, deconstruction makes it possible to map the ethico-political content that permeates the discourses, concepts, and representations that make political practice possible. To these ends, 'deconstruction begins with demonstrating ... inequalities within concepts or texts, but it aims as little as the texts themselves at an annulment of that which is in opposition ... the contradictions, oppositions, and dyadic structures of concepts, texts, and their multiple argumentational levels are never symmetrical ... We are not dealing with the peaceful coexistence vis à vis, but rather with a violent hierarchy' (Gasché 1986, 137).

In this light, binaries should be seen as infused with judgment as to which element must be considered normal, primary, and most desirable. Tragically, then, because of the inability to come to terms to the codependency of dualistic 'oppositions,' contemporary politics has been constituted by a series of practices that survey, classify, categorize, and naturalize threats said to manifest themselves through disparate modes of being. So, one of the primary tasks of political prac tice – especially practices of security – has been to dispose of, both discretely and indiscretely, the subordinate, the ambiguous, and the different. However, in 'affirm[ing] the play of the positive *and* the negative,' deconstructive interpretations are able to 'ward off the ethical temptation to liquidate negativity and difference' by leaving the desire for total separation behind (ibid., 154).[14] Thus, as philosophical and political practice, deconstruction makes it possible for us to open ourselves to our Others (ibid., 176).

Typically, political practice is conceptualized as the area of social life inhabited by elections, governments, parties, policies, and institutions. But as Jenny Edkins (2002) notes, contemporary power/relations have depoliticized these sites through processes of bureaucratization, routinization, and fixation, which discipline our imaginations in terms of the limits of what can be considered possible or doable (2002, 256). Certain conditions such as poverty, violence, and inequality are naturalized as unpleasant but inevitable parts of contemporary modes of being whose effects at best can be mitigated but certainly not overcome. Edkins argues that this notion of politics should be juxtaposed with '"the political" – the arena where the setting up of particular systems of power and their maintenance on a day to day basis is contested' (ibid., 256). Yet both these domains are implicated in creating the conditions of possibility within each other.

In this context, Foucault (2003d) has argued that a critique 'does not consist in saying that things aren't good the way they are. It consists in seeing on what type of assumptions, of familiar notions, of established, unexamined ways of thinking the accepted practices are based ... Criticism consists in ... showing that things are not as obvious as people believe, making it so that what is taken for granted is no longer taken for granted' (2003d, 172).

Deconstruction offers the ability to critique both politics and 'the political' in the Canadian context with regard to illicit drugs. It allows for a rigorous examination of the productive capacities of power to create, define, and address all aspects of our daily lives while remaining hidden from our critical gaze. It also pushes the Foucauldian critical ethos so that one can present discourses to show how they have shaped the ways in which issues are represented while having a method in place to demonstrate the lack of a natural and unambiguous 'foundation' for key elements of the discourse itself.

Genealogy and Illicit Drugs

Leading examinations of the emergence of Canadian drug law all fall prey to one of the fundamental epistemological shortcomings of historical analysis: the teleological search for origins (Foucault 1984b, 78). All of these accounts assume that there is some sort of pure essence behind events, a purposeful procession towards some predestined goal. An outcome, such as drug laws, is presented as almost inevitable, and the contributing factors made the outcome the only possible one.[15] However, if one peers beneath this veneer, 'there is something altogether different behind things: not a timeless and essential secret, but the secret that [drug laws] have no essence or that this essence was fabricated in a piecemeal fashion from alien forms' (Foucault 1984b, 78). So to gain a greater appreciation and understanding of responses to illicit drugs in Canada, one must identify accidents, deviations, reversals in meaning, errors, false appraisals, and miscalculations 'that gave birth to those things that continue to exist and have a value for us' in order to discover 'that truth or being does not lie at the root of what we know and what we are, but the exteriority of accidents' (ibid., 81).

Methodologically, then, this project is also engaged in a 'history of the present' that begins with 'an incitement from the present – an acute manifestation of a ritual of power' and proceeds to genealogically map how these came to be, the shapes they have taken, the development of their 'legitimacy,' and how they have shaped the boundaries of political possibility (Campbell 1998, 5–6). To this end, one will find that most chapters begin with a brief story or example that serves as a catalyst for investigation. But this exercise is not a search for root causes, as 'a genealogy of values, morality, asceticism, and knowledge will never confuse itself with a quest for their "origins," will never neglect as inaccessible the vicissitudes of history. On the contrary, it will cultivate the details and accidents that accompany any beginning; it will be scrupulously attentive to their petty malice; it will await their emergence, once unmasked as the face of the other' (Foucault 1984b, 80).

This unpacking of the lineage of the Canadian illicit drugs discourse does not seek to shore up the foundations of contemporary political practices; instead, it concerns itself with deconstructing them, undermining what has been considered unitary, universal, and internally consistent. The role of genealogy is to record the history of interpretation that has made possible contemporary understandings of politics, the political, morality, and ethics (ibid., 82, 86). Foucault has argued that interpretation can be thought of as 'the violent or surreptitious appropriation of a system of rules, which in itself has no essential meaning, in order to impose a direction, to bend it to a new will, to force its participation in a different game, and to subject it to secondary rules' (ibid., 86). The history of interpretation therefore should be conceived as a series of competing representational practices – that is, processes that define subjects, objects, and their inherent characteristics – most of which (be they hegemonic or counterhegemonic) seek to create a fixedness of meaning that ultimately is impossible (Doty 1996, 8).

As such, I am partaking in a deconstruction of the representational practices that have comprised the history of interpretation within the Canadian drugs discourse. This involves a three-pronged strategy. The first is to challenge the binaries that have been deployed to distinguish licit and illicit drugs, the Canadian Self from its Others, security from insecurity, science from myth, and tolerance from intolerance. The second is to expose the aporias contained within dominant understandings of why illicit drugs are a security threat. The third is to map the congruencies between hegemonic constructions of illicit drugs as a security threat and those that claim to offer counterhegemonic alternatives. Each of these endeavours, in turn, will help to reveal the contingent construction of threat and to underscore the mutually constitutive relationship between security and identity in the Canadian political context.

In examining the interplay of formal academic discourses, practical policy discourses, and popular discourses that contribute to perceptions of security and identity, the public record becomes a significant area for study because of the ways in which public statements, policy documents, and newspaper reports are constitutive of commonsense interpretations and understandings of issues. These are the battlefields for contending interpretative dispositions and their machinations of power. The public record is the site where power demonstrates its productive capacities to control our conceptions of the politically possible, all the while remaining hidden from a direct appraisal of its legitimacy.

The most productive way to move towards an effective interpretation of Canadian responses to illicit drugs is to pay greater attention to the discursive formation that established the parameters of legitimate discussion regarding drugs, drug use, and drug users in the Canadian context. Most existing accounts do make note of what was said at the time by influential individuals and the media; however, they treat these statements as outcomes or indicators of some other intentional process such as racism or medical interests. In trying to answer 'how possible' questions, it is much more fruitful to examine these statements as both reflections of and contributions to the attitudes, beliefs, values, representations, and meanings that constructed drug use as a social problem. It then becomes possible to see how predominant discourses constricted the number of viable interpretations of and responses to illicit drugs in Canada. An examination of the emergence of central aspects of the drugs discourse in the Canadian context makes it clear that Canadian securitizations were not the result of some teleological progression with solid medical, legal, and social foundations but rather the mixed result of instabilities and accidents within these realms that created particular and mutually constitutive constellations of meaning. Of utmost importance is how a set of discourses intermingled with and intertwined around the body of the drug user and how these dynamics changed, transforming the drug user from a pathetic but benign object of pity into a threatening, fiendish, and, most important, foreign contagion who 'lurked in the gutter of the criminal world' (Green 1979, 62).

The genealogical analysis that follows will not be utilizing the notion of 'moral panics' to explain when and why legislation was implemented – a strategy that runs through previous examinations of Canada and illicit drugs.[16] Moral panics are the proverbial red herrings when it comes to making sense of the power/relations at play: they are *a* reflection of the conditions of possibility produced by entrenched discourses at a given time. They are not inevitable even when the possibility exists that one will be generated; they always arise among many other possible modes of interpretation. Even in times of moral panic, legal controls are but one possibility in the spectrum of responses. Furthermore, analyses that have utilized moral panic as an explanatory concept presuppose the existence of some previously articulated morality that all members of society draw from and interpret in a uniform manner – a precarious assumption even in the most homogenous of social environments. Thus, the moral panic explanation neglects the fundamental question that is raised when the approach taken is sensitive to the politics of *securitization*: What factor(s) made it possible for an audience to accept the interpretation of some phenomena as an existential threat requiring emergency actions that break free of existing limits on state conduct?

In exploring this question, this study draws from researched data and follows standard rules of evidence. At times, arguments based on empirical data will be provided that counter what are considered by authorities to be conventional 'facts'; at other times, alternative interpretations of conventional 'facts' are offered. Some may want to argue that, given the discussion about the productive role of discourse made above, the presentation of evidence in this manner is at best dubious (i.e., it does not clearly define its ontological basis), or at worst, intellectually unsustainable and contradictory. Such charges, though, project onto this project the traditional aim of (social) science as the search for truth; they neglect to recognize that no such truth claims are being made here.

This is a very different kind of study. Instead of solely utilizing epistemology and ontology to make appeals to what are claimed to be the 'time-space events' of a situation (i.e., the historical record) in order to assess competing interpretations, I examine the narratives that emerge when these events are made meaningful through discourse (Campbell 1999, 319). In the following substantive chapters, these narratives are mapped and assessed based on their representational practices, their ethico-political content, and the kinds of politics they make possible.

Structure

Deconstructing hegemonic understandings of *the* Canadian identity through a critical reading of responses to illicit drugs in Canada opens up the possibility to pose questions that might otherwise seem specious and unworthy of examination. Canada as an open, pluralist, tolerant, multicultural, and therefore *not*-American society is quite ingrained into Canadian discourses. Although few would argue that Canada is perfect, moving around or beyond stories of its 'enlightened' capacity for tolerance is both difficult and disconcerting.

While illicit drugs and responses to them serve as sites where encounters between Self and Other transpire, it is important to note the contemporary demographic context that is constitutive of these relationships. In particular, contemporary discussions of identity in Canada in nationalist and multicultural discourses coalesce around a shared understanding that whatever Canada is (or may be), it is certainly not what it was prior to the end of the Second World War because of specific transformations in demography and immigration patterns. The point is not that current changes to demography make social conflict inevitable, nor is the implicit point that a more homogenous society would not have to grapple with how to negotiate difference. Rather, the demographic data are presented below in order to give some insight into the figures that social authorities and commentators in Canada draw from when offering their various interpretations of the imperatives that derive from the imagined diversity of contemporary Canadian society.

According to the 2001 census, with 18.4 per cent of the population having been born outside the country, Canada is experiencing the highest proportion of foreign born residents since 1931, second in the world only to Australia (22.2 per cent) and well ahead of the United States (11 per cent) (Statistics Canada 2003, 5). The same year, 13.4 per cent of the Canadian population identified themselves as visible minorities (compared to 4.7 per cent in 1981) and more than two hundred different ethnic origins were reported (ibid., 10, 12). The City of Toronto has taken nearly three times greater than its share of New Canadians over the preceding decade (43 per cent of the total number of immigrants to Canada during the 1990s), with the most recent data showing that 44 per cent of Torontonians were born outside Canada (ibid., 7, 24). This ratio of foreign born is higher than in Miami (40 per cent), Sydney (31 per cent), Los Angeles (31 per cent), and New York (24 per cent) (ibid., 25). Moreover, 36.8 per cent of Torontonians self-identify as visible minorities (ibid., 25).

Although the demographic data have no inherent meaning in and of themselves, they have been interpreted in Canada as marking a dramatic demographic shift towards the de-Europeanization of the country. Before 1961, Europe was the source region of 90.5 per cent of immigrants in Canada. By 1991–2001, this had shrunk to 19.5 per cent. In contrast, Asia (3.2 per cent), Africa (0.5 per cent), and the Caribbean and Central and South America (1.4 per cent) accounted for 5.3 per cent of Canada's immigrant population prior to 1961. From 1991 to 2001, Asian immigrants represented 58.2 per cent, Africans 7.6 per cent, and Caribbeans and Central and South Americans 10.9 per cent, for a combined 76.7 per cent of the total number of New Canadians (ibid., 39). Although the federal government still officially promotes multiculturalism, there is a heightened sensitivity among many self-described 'Canadian Canadians' towards any perceived loss of 'Western' cultural character and national identity in the accommodation of New Canadians. In this climate of fluctuating levels of distress and hostility, geographic spaces that embody high levels of diversity such as Toronto become important locations for the exercise of power/relations between the Canadian Self and Other. In this sense, these contested spaces serve as border areas in which a series of encounters with difference take place and affect notions of culture, identity, and security.

Normally, understandings of Canadian culture consider aspects of social life such as art, language, museums, national celebrations, flags, and how 'Canadian Canadians' respond to the identity politics inherent in these domains. A central claim here is that Canadian security policies and discourses are reflective and constitutive of national culture and national identity and their performatives. Therefore, security needs to be considered a cultural practice.[17] The following chapters, then, take a critical look at the discursive relations that transect discourses of race, ethnicity, culture, identity, health, science, law, criminology, and security. The representations that emerge from these relationships constitute the power/knowledge that has reproduced a regime of truth that frames specific drugs as requiring prohibition and illicit drugs in Canada as a security issue writ large. In sum, by focusing on illicit drugs – an area of public security policy that is constructed as above politics – this analysis will demonstrate clearly the interconnections between security and identity in Canada by critically evaluating the performatives and performances of threat, the forms of marginalization that these make possible, and their ethico-political ramifications for the Canadian body politic.

Chapter 2 is a theoretical exploration of the relationship(s) between security and identity. Its purpose is to set the analytic stage for the case studies that follow. As such, it is argued that turning to performative accounts of security and identity that are sensitive to their performances is conducive to a critical exploration of the issues raised by illicit drugs in Canada.

Chapter 3 analyses Canada–U.S. relations through the prism of (inter)national drug control and how those relations have been constitutive of performatives of Canadian (inter)national identity. The recent notion of 'geonarcotics' is deconstructed to account for what has been forgotten in terms of Canada's contributions, in tandem with the United States, to the global drug control regime. This is then linked to the contemporary politics of the possible, which has seen increasing strains in the security relationship between Canada and the United States, particularly with regard to illicit drugs. The central argument is that what has been interpreted as American extremism with regard to a variety of social issues more broadly, and security more narrowly, has been discursively deployed *in Canada* to shore up performatives of Canada as a tolerant, reasoned, and civilized political entity.

Building on the performatives of Canadian identity as 'not-American,' chapter 4 looks at how discourses of race and discourses of security have interplayed in the creation and implementation of Canadian drug policy practices that have aided in the disciplining of the limits of cultural diversity. Contemporary issues surrounding the use of khat by Somali Canadians are juxtaposed with racialized discourses at the turn of the twentieth century that produced opium use by Chinese Canadians as a pressing social concern. The importance of discourses of race, nationality, religion, and social transformation in the constitution of Canadian biopolitics is examined to show how it became possible to interpret illicit drug use as a security threat to the Canadian body politic, and how the discursive formation of Othering has been dynamically reproduced in vastly different social contexts.

Chapters 5 and 6 construct a genealogical account of the body of the illicit drug user in Canada to provide a rich context in which to locate the *Marihuana Medical Access Regulations* (*MMAR*). They then move towards the decriminalization of marijuana possession. Discourses centred on illicit drug use are examined to map the spectrum of understandings that constituted the pathologies, abnormalities, and dangers that have made possible particular reactions to illicit drug use by Canadians. Instead of interpreting recent policies as the logical outcome of a clear progression in an increasingly liberalized drug outlook, the analyses highlight the long-standing struggle between the medical community and the law enforcement community over control of the bodies of illicit drug users. From this perspective, the power/relations constitutive of medical marijuana and decriminalization are not representative of a loosening of social regulation in Canada; instead, they should be seen as a productive reconfiguration in their technologies of control.

Chapter 7 examines the securitization of Canadian rave subculture through the deployment of a series of representational practices that inextricably tied the space of rave to illicit drug use. In particular, the rise and fall of rave in Toronto is discussed with reference to the social context generated after a high-profile overdose death at an event in the autumn of 1999. Competing interpretations of threat from both the law enforcement and rave communities in this context are presented. These contending interpretations are juxtaposed with the actions taken to eliminate rave from Toronto and the strategies of resistance initiated by ravers themselves. While Toronto's rave community succeeded at first in generating popular support for its cause and overturning a municipal ban on the events, this analysis demonstrates how the terms of discourse and the discursive representations utilized made it possible for a de facto prohibition to be initiated. This result has not only contributed to the further marginalization of rave culture, but also left ravers exposed to the targeted drug pushing of alcohol and tobacco companies.

The conclusion returns to questions of security, Canadian identity, Otherness, and the United States that form a powerful intertext in the proceeding discussions of illicit drugs. Reflections are given on the categorization of Canadian illicit drug policy as progressive, the reproduction of power/relations in Canadian society, the kind of politics that these make possible, and prospects for transformation. The point is to highlight the centrality of identity to Canadian security policy and how identity frames the ways in which the Canadian Self responds to its Others beyond issues related directly to illicit drugs.

2 The Theory/Practice of Security and Identity

Introduction: (Re)Thinking Security

At a time when the country is focused on issues like terrorism, under-development, weapons of mass destruction, and illegal migration, we need to (re)think what it means to classify social phenomena as security issues in the Canadian context by looking at how security and identity form a nexus that produces meanings and representations that have important political consequences. In trying to (re)think security, Rob Walker (1997) has commented that the process must both engage with attempts to theorize the locations and characteristics of the political beyond – what has been framed as 'international relations' – and respond to questions about 'whose security is being assumed and under what conditions' (1997, 69).[1]

These are not questions that are generally asked, even at a time when traditional definitions of security, which usually concern themselves with 'the absence of military threat or the protection of the nation[-state] from external overthrow and attack,' are limiting (Krasna 1999, 47). The simultaneous move made by traditionalists and policy makers has not been to (re)think security in the manner outlined by Walker above, but rather to try to show how issues that do not fall directly within the military realm – such as drug trafficking, environmental degradation, and poverty – when left unaddressed, can transform themselves into military dangers that threaten the nation-state.[2]

Moreover, this trend towards broadening the scope of security issues while retaining a militarized vision of what security means has been accelerated by the events of 11 September 2001. This is now manifest in both popular discourses (e.g., the 'Clash of Civilizations' thesis) and official policy discourses in North America. Simon Dalby (1997) warned about this outcome throughout the 1990s in his discussions of the dangers of adding environmental issues to security agendas without rethinking the concept of security itself. Thus, James Der Derian's (1995) contention that we have inherited an *'ontotheology* of security ... an *a priori* that proves the existence and necessity of only one form of security because there happens to be a widespread metaphysical belief in it,' provides a compelling interpretation of the contemporary conceptual environment (1995, 25).

In common terminology, security is about being protected, being free from danger, and feeling safe from threat. From Der Derian's genealogy of the term, what becomes clear, though, is that security has always been an essentially contested concept with competing and often contradictory meanings. For example, during the sixteenth, seventeenth, and eighteenth centuries, security could be defined as an overconfidence in what one is or what can be called one's sense of Self (ibid., 28). The irony, of course, is that contemporary security practices have been based on boosting this confidence through 'the normalization or extirpation' of difference rather than through the appreciation and promotion of variance (ibid., 27–8). However, in contrast to common perceptions, Lene Hansen (1997) has argued that security as homogeneity and insecurity as heterogeneity are not binary opposites, for 'security can only be thought by incorporating the trace of insecurity in the very articulation of security itself' (1997, 377).

Popular definitions of security that are couched as expressions of military necessity should be understood as means of positing alterity, which is assumed to originate outside the Self as a danger that needs to be protected against in order to feel 'safe' and 'secure.' Therefore, while it may go unacknowledged by many within the discipline at large, Bradley Klein (1997) argues that 'security ... was never simply about preparing against military threats "out there." It was always intended as a way of defending common ways of life. It was an inherently cultural practice that was always about more than just the deployment of weapons systems' (1997, 362).

Thus, a broader interpretation of security and security practices than is typically found in contemporary discussions of global politics needs to be taken. 'Broader' not so much in terms of the focus of analysis (e.g., illicit drugs and identity) but rather in terms of an approach that examines what is being rendered secure, the perceptions of threats to these referent objects, how these perceptions have contributed to what is thought of as the best available means and practices of securing these objects, and how these perceptions have shifted over time. The argument that will be put forward is that Canada's illicit drug problems are the result of the reflexive security practices of the Canadian state and society, rather than a consequence of their introduction into 'timeless social structures' (Williams and Krause 1997, 49–50).

Security and Securitization

Security theory and security practice are always reflexive in that they are not separate domains; rather, they feed back into each other. Thus, the security discourse surrounding the issue of illicit drugs defines what can be considered legitimate approaches to illicit drugs and drug users by constructing the very objects it speaks of as security issues. Ken Booth (1997) has remarked that humans are a 'meanings-making species' (1997, 91). The reverse also holds, in that the ways in which the issue of illicit drugs is thought about in Canada are at the root of the meanings that Canadians may have of security (ibid.). This reflects the overall dynamics of security: it is intersubjective, it is relational among subjects as well as objects, and it is 'what we want it to be,' in terms of both what is seen as threatening and what is seen as the policy end goal. Security threats do not exist as security threats a priori; they have to undergo processes of 'securitization' to be considered as security issues.

According to Barry Buzan and other members of the Copenhagen School (1998), an issue becomes securitized when it is presented as an existential threat that requires emergency measures and that justifies actions outside the bounds of normal political procedure (Buzan, Waever, and de Wilde 1998, 23–4).[3] Within this framework, security is not a condition to be strived for; rather, it 'is the move that takes politics beyond the established rules of the game and frames the issue as a special kind of politics or as above politics' (ibid., 23). Thus the meaning of security is not wrapped up in how people define it but rather in the ways the word itself is utilized – both explicitly and implicitly – to frame the discussion of some issues and not others. Security issues are considered security issues because a claim has been made *and* accepted that these issues are of the utmost importance and need to take priority. More often than not, security issues centre on the survival of something, be it the physical well-being of a group or their way of life (ibid., 24).

For the Copenhagen School, 'security is ... a self-referential practice, because it is in this practice that the issue becomes a security issue – not necessarily because a real existential threat exists but because the issue is presented as such a threat' (ibid., 24). By this view, threats are not objectively definable; the authors refer to a strongly 'radical constructivism' that underlies this position. The consequences of this are that one cannot make claims about security based on appeals to *'the truth'* (e.g., the claim that something *is* or *is not* objectively a security issue); however, this does not preclude discussions about *the ethics* of framing something as a security concern, nor does it prevent one from examining the ethico-political consequences of treating, or not treating, an issue as a security issue.

For an analyst who is attempting to understand security, 'the task is not to assess some objective threats that "really" endanger some object to be defended or secured; rather it is to understand the process of constructing a shared understanding of what it is to be considered and collectively responded to as a threat' (ibid., 26). This opens the space for security policy to be discussed in terms of *ethics* based on the political, social, and economic consequences of policy; such policy need no longer be seen as a scientific and technical enterprise divorced from normative considerations, with success measured in terms of (primarily) military objectives. With this radical departure, militarized measures or responses become failures of security policy, rather than its raison d'être.

Above all else, securitization should be viewed as a speech act, the communicative process that constitutes the parameters of what is considered to be a security issue and what is not: 'it does not refer to something more real; the act is in the mere utterance' (ibid., 26). The use of the concept 'speech act' in security studies can be traced back to the rules-based constructivism of Nicholas Onuf and Friedrich Kratochwil, who were greatly influenced by the work of J.L. Austin (1962). Kratochwil (1993) argues that speech act theory shows that when we speak, we are not just describing an action but are also performing it (e.g., saying 'I promise ... '). It follows that language *'does not mirror action by sticking a descriptive label on the activity: it is the action'* (1993, 76). Therefore, as a speech act, 'the exact *definition* and *criteria* of securitization is constituted by the intersubjective establishment of an existential threat with a saliency sufficient to have substantial political effects' (Buzan et al. 1998, 25). This does not mean that a situation becomes a security issue just because some person defines it as such. Rather, an issue is securitized only if and when the audience, be it the voting public, influential state officials, or global civil society, accepts it as such (ibid., 25). The key question, therefore, that highlights the role of power in security policy is, 'Who has been vested with the legitimacy and/or expertise to be able to perform the act of securitization within a given society?'

For the necessary level of acceptance for a successful securitization to be achieved, what has been represented as an existential threat has to be agreed on and 'gain enough resonance for a platform to be made from which it is possible to legitimize emergency measures or other steps that would not have been possible had the discourse not taken the form of existential threats, point of no return, and necessity' (ibid., 25). This is made possible through the exhibition of three characteristics: the identification of existential threats, emergency action, and effects on interunit relations by breaking free of rules. Thus securitization should be seen as a series of processes (i.e., speech acts within a discourse) that take what would ordinarily be political issues open to contestation from a wide variety of viewpoints and transport them to a realm above politics (ibid., 26).

The capacity to foreclose the possibility of discussion about the reasonableness of defining something as a security threat may increase our efficiency in responding to it; however, Buzan and his colleagues caution that we have to curb the tendency, particularly in the post–Cold War world, to treat an increasing range of phenomena as security issues: 'Security should be seen as negative, as a failure to deal with issues as normal politics; *desecuritization is the optimal long-range option* since it means not to have issues phrased as "threats against which we have no counter-measures" but to move them out of this threat–defence sequence and into the ordinary public sphere' (ibid., 29; italics added).

Yet securitization continues to proliferate in contemporary Canadian society; and more important, it has been able to do so in ways that mask its scope. Because I agree that security is a negative – that it is a social process that eliminates the capacity to accept difference and to cooperate/cohabit with Others in significant ways – I will explore in subsequent chapters how utilizing different frameworks and representational practices can potentially produce discursive shifts that could promote desecuritization with respect to illicit drug issues.

Securitization and Criminalization

Within the security literature, particularly in post-9/11 discussions of how to respond to terrorism, criminalization is presented as an alternative policy process separate from the traditional security architecture. Yet criminalization rests on much the same conceptual foundations as securitization: it requires the identification of existential threats that must be confronted (e.g., drug dealers); it requires emergency actions (e.g., increased surveillance, police raids); and it affects interagent relations by breaking free of existing rules of behaviour (e.g., asset forfeiture, violence, or imprisonment) that establish the boundaries of legitimate state encroachment in society, at least rhetorically in societies that claim to be operating under the rule of law. Of course, criminalization is not limited to intrastate or intrasociety contexts; with the proliferation of international law, it can also be defined in terms of relationships between global society and the state, global society and collectivities, global society and individuals, and so forth.

One might argue that contra securitization, criminalization is always constrained by law in terms of what states or individuals can do when reacting to activities defined as criminal, especially at the domestic level. However, this argument is based on claims that security practices are devoid of any consideration of norms, which is highly problematic. Moreover, for criminalization to be constrained, everyone – regardless of race, class, gender, creed, religion, and so on – needs to treated equally under the law both in theory and in practice. Yet as Giorgio Agamben (1999) has shown with respect to modern forms of governance, limits on the powers of a sovereign (e.g., the state) concurrently define the instances when there are *no* limits to this power (1999, 15–70). Responding to crime is one of those areas in which there are limits on state behaviour; yet at the same time, the sovereign and/or its agents are able to legitimately commit acts such as physical violence that ordinarily would not be permissible. Thus, criminalization in extreme cases contributes to the production of *homo sacer*, a human who can be killed but not murdered by actions undertaken by the security apparatus with the consent of the sovereign.

Securitization/desecuritization, then, should be seen as a policy spectrum, a bandwidth of potential responses whose length of possibility is shaped by social context. The differences along the bandwidth are often found less in terms of characteristic responses than in the intensity of these responses. As such, criminalization can be viewed as a *covert* form of securitization in that it *does* securitize an issue, but it does this by directly appealing to legal principles so as to try to mask the securitization and to occlude the powers vested in the securing agent, which is permitted to respond in ways that would otherwise be considered illegitimate. With covert securitization, the general public and even many elites may not necessarily be aware that a securitization has taken place. Laws, rules, or codes of conduct are changed so that previously proscribed behaviours on the part of the state are no longer prohibited, or issues are publicly framed in ways that do not highlight the extraordinary measures that are being taken in response. From this perspective, the parallels between the 'war on drugs' and the 'war on terror' move beyond mere invocations of the war metaphor, to touch on the ways both 'wars' sanction and mask intense moments of violence that are otherwise unacceptable, all in the name of security.

The act of securitization, in each of its forms, is also much more expansive than initially conceptualized by the Copenhagen School, for its effects go beyond the actual speech act itself; securitization is also a discursive practice that 'produces the subjectivities which then form the basis for what can be articulated as threat and threatened' (Hansen 2000, 306). This means that we must pay attention to discourses that exist prior to the moments of securitization in order to discern how these may be influenced, (re)constructed, and made amenable or resistant to the processes of securitization. In doing so, we can develop compelling answers to the question, 'How did it become possible to securitize a certain issue?'

Still, security issues are not black boxes that can be separated from issues of politics or, more narrowly, issues of identity. These are all mutually constitutive, and the reproduction of identity is a central component of security policy.

Identity and Security: Moving beyond the *Via Media*

In undertaking this exploration of security and identity, I am primarily concerned with *understanding* how identity as an infinite performative manifests itself in Canadian drug discourses and policy; the political consequences (i.e., the associated power/relations) of the ways in which it is invoked; and how these invocations try to reinforce (and hide) the contestable foundations of performativity itself. As noted in the introductory chapter, identity is not being treated as a 'thing' that can be known and that provides an anchor around which to ground policy analysis. Furthermore, identity is not being treated as an exogenous variable to explain the behaviour of social actors. Instead, this project has self-consciously positioned itself to engage in an *understanding* of how key social actors perceive the issues at hand and the political dimensions of those perceptions; it is not an attempt to *explain* with scientific certainty why particular events transpired. This does not entail an attempt on my part to replicate a split between the material and understandings of the material that are communicated in discourse. Instead I want to demonstrate how this post-material approach to security brings an awareness that 'it is through discourses that the material and the ideational is represented for us and by us' (Hansen 1997, 382).

Issues of identity, therefore, are a fundamental dimension of the practices that constitute the foreign policies of contemporary nation-states like Canada. In *Writing Security: United States Foreign Policy and the Politics of Identity* (1998), David Campbell examines the ways 'in which the identity of the (United States of) America has been written and rewritten through foreign policies operating in its name'; how, through the 'inscription of foreignness,' U.S. foreign policy helps produce and reproduce the political identity of the 'doer behind the deed'; how 'foreign policy seeks to contain contingency and domesticate challenges to the dominant identity of the period'; and how 'the domains of inside/outside, self/other, and domestic/foreign (those moral spaces made possible by the ethical borders of identity as much as by the territorial boundaries of states) are constituted through the writing of threat' (1998, x). Moreover, cartographic, ethnographic, and historico–political narratives that arise both within and outside the national Self contribute to the formation of identity and the territorialization of danger, as Ronald B. Inden (2001) and Thongchai Winichakul (1994) have shown with respect to the imagined communities of India and Thailand.

The central argument here is that much like what happens in the United States, India, and Thailand, identity issues in Canada interplay with foreign policy concerns; moreover, the two mutually constitute each other through security discourses and the practices these discourses make possible. This does not mean that structural and material conditions must be removed from the analysis. Rather, structures, the material, and the meanings that are read into them will all be treated as *conditional*.

This move represents the Foucauldian thrust of this approach to security and identity. It also points to how the post-materialist move has been misunderstood in the social sciences, even by other constructivists. It does not demand that one eliminate structure from any analysis. Rather, it treats claims about the *naturalness* of structure with a necessary degree of scepticism. Thus what distinguishes post-materialist accounts is how they are able to show how discourses which describe the ideas, subjects, *and* structures that constitute current social conditions also create those very ideas, subjects, *and* structures by giving them meaning(s). This view imbues humanity with the ability to transform them. Yet structure is still important, because without it we are denied the possibility of intersubjectivity, and are left with an empty void and with no ability to derive meaning. Human beings, as social creatures, do not inhabit such a place.

Security and Identity as Performative and Performance

Traditionally in security analyses, dangers and threats are seen as having objective characteristics or qualities that make it absolutely clear that they will be detrimental to our physical well-being or our *interests* unless we take prudent action(s). Nuclear proliferation, rogue states, terrorism, illegal migration, and the international drug trade are among those phenomena that today find themselves framed within the discipline – but more important, within popular political discourses – as 'real and present dangers' that necessitate special responses – most often militarized actions – if we are to guard ourselves against their harmful effects.

However, the designation of threat or danger 'is an act of interpretation; it bears no essential, necessary, or unproblematic relation to the action or event from which it is said to derive' (Campbell 1998, 2). This is not to say that nothing is potentially a risk to our safety; it *is* to say that ultimately, dangers 'come to be ascribed as such only through an interpretation of their various dimensions of dangerousness' (ibid.). For example, people living in North America are far more likely to be killed as a result of a car accident than by a terrorist attack. Yet the discourses of danger surrounding these two issues are constructed and interpreted in vastly different ways. Terrorism is considered to be a genuine security threat that requires a heightened level of vigilance and particular sorts of preventative and reactive security actions. By contrast, car accidents are generally seen as an unpleasant but inevitable part of modern life in North American societies. We take precautions – for example, we limit our night driving, avoid travel during inclement weather, drive defensively, and wear seat belts, and the state invests in policing and safer motorways – but car accidents are not represented in the same way as terrorist attacks, nor are they presented as a security danger (Grayson 2003b, 338).

We generally think of threats and dangers in relation to our physical safety, as the above example illustrates; but there is also a strong ideational element to our individual and collective threat radars, as a result of which dangers are tagged to our ontological security and Self-identity (or identities). Often, though, ontological threats are represented as threats to survival. For example, cultural differences between immigrants and their host societies are often couched in language that emphasizes threats to physical safety (e.g., disease, crime); and these threats are seen as being in tandem with difference (Wald 2000). Disturbingly, especially in a world in which homogeny should no longer be taken as a given, 'the mere existence of an alternate mode of being, the presence of which exemplifies that different identities are possible and thus denaturalizes the claim of a particular identity to be *the* true identity, is sometimes enough to produce the understanding of a threat' (Campbell 1998, 3).

The label *danger* results not from drawing upon the objective characteristics of the material environment out there but rather 'from the calculation of a threat that objectifies events, disciplines relations, and sequesters an ideal of identity of the people said to be at risk' (ibid., 3).[4] This points to a view of security practices that is radically different from those traditionally espoused by security analysts.

Far from being a tangential factor that may help explain behaviour that would otherwise be seen as counter-intuitive in traditional theoretical paradigms, identity is central to the study of security if one acknowledges that the practice of security itself is a conduit for the (re)production of identity and difference: 'Identity is an inescapable dimension of being. No body could be without it ... It is not fixed by nature, given by God, or planned by intentional behaviour. Rather identity is constituted in relation to difference. But neither is difference fixed by nature, given by God, or planned by intentional behaviour. Difference is constituted in relation to identity' (ibid., 9).

Yet these classifications with serious ontological repercussions are extremely contentious, as 'the problematic of identity/difference contains ... no foundations that are prior to, or outside of, its operation' (ibid.). Identity, then, is *performatively* constituted through 'the reiterative and citational practice by which discourse produces the effects that it names'; such practice inscribes boundaries that seek to distinguish clearly between Self and Other by making choices about whether to incorporate or banish/reject what is perceived to be different (Butler, in Weber 1998, 81). At the same time, identity is also constituted and reinforced through its performance and what the performance is claimed to represent. Performance, 'a singular or deliberate act,' whether it be language, custom, or a specific policy orientation, always projects a sense of Self and underscores a far larger geo-ontological mapping of the world and one's position in it (Butler, in ibid.).

But difference is not something that is clearly delineated between Self and Other, nor is it objectively apparent. Campbell (1998), borrowing from the work of Judith Butler, argues that 'the border between the internal and external is tenuously maintained by taking elements that were originally part of identity and repackaging them into a "defiling otherness"' (1998, 9). This performative that (re)produces the borders between the Self and the Other is amplified in both importance and effect by the lack of a 'sovereign presence that inhabits a prediscursive domain which provides these markers with naturalized and unproblematic qualities' (ibid.).[5] Therefore, understanding identity as a performative means that it has 'no ontological status apart from the various acts that constitute its reality ... Identities are neither true nor false, nor normal or abnormal in and of themselves ... They are produced as "truth effects of a discourse of primary and stable identity"' (ibid.). In other words, we create identities in the absence of any neutral ground to adjudicate their accuracy. As such, the formation and categorization of identity are *political* rather than descriptive acts.

As Butler's work is primarily concerned with individual 'Selves,' it is important to draw out the implications of performativity for human collectives.[6] The orthodox view is that states are the primary actors in the global system and that their ontological status, if not self-evident, is certainly objectively verifiable. What is important to remember here is that the conceptualization of performativity argues that there is not a preconstituted Self that exists prior to the performative expressions of its characteristics in discourse (Weber 1998, 80). There is no 'independent' higher authority to help define the identity characteristics of an actor and to reassure subjects of the correctness of these boundaries. Nor is there an objective blueprint mapping a 'pure' Self that can be used as a guide for this process.

The implications of performativity are that we should see the state as having 'no ontological status apart from the various acts which constitute its reality'; that its status as a sovereign presence in world politics is produced by a 'discourse of primary and stable identity'; and that the identity of any particular state should be understood as 'tenuously constituted in time ... through a *stylized repetition of acts,*' and achieved *'not* [through] *a founding act, but rather a regulated process of repetition'* (Campbell 1998, 10; italics in original).

This makes the performative of identity by the Self all the more necessary, because it is the performative that constitutes identity rather than being the product of a fixed pre-existing identity that can be appealed to for evidential support (Hansen 2000, 301–2). It follows that in states like Canada and the United States, foreign policy (in all of its guises, including security) is the vehicle through which discursive articulations of the nation-state (and society) as 'Self' take place in the form of attempts to fix the boundaries around which protective barriers must be built to prevent the intrusion of Otherness.

But it is important not to view this process as apolitical or power neutral. These claims are necessarily infused with power/relations. Not every actor in global politics has the capacity to shape the iterative to the same extent as others, or to have its voice heard and taken into account. Moreover, identity claims, in order to sustain themselves, sometimes rely as much on opposition as they do on acceptance. Yet even for states, which are still among the most powerful actors in global politics, there is an inevitable vulnerability when it comes to identity, a tangible albeit largely unacknowledged sense that all is not quite secure.

To mask this uncertainty, the identity of being a 'state' and a state's 'identity' must be constantly performed through the 'repeated, yet, varied' discursive articulation of these characteristics (Weber 1998, 80). Thus power occupies another position in this dynamic as a productive force. Power makes it possible for specific performances to be under-taken, performances that can then be drawn from in the discur-sive articulation of identity claims that implicitly reflect existing power/relations. Thus contentious political claims are hidden behind what are presented as self-evident categorizations to a targeted audi-ence that shares similar ontological norms. We can currently see this multidirectional dynamic at play in the United States. There is the offi-cial foreign policy discourse, which stresses the privileged American position at the top of the global hierarchy as 'the brightest beacon for freedom and opportunity in the world' and which places Others within the 'Axis of Evil.'[7] This in turn has been operationalized and reaffirmed through the enactment of specific policies dealing with ter-rorism and Iraq.

But as Butler (1999) reminds us, 'performativity is ... not a single act for it is always a reiteration of a norm or set of norms, and to the extent that it acquires an act-like status in the present, it conceals or dissimu-lates the conventions of which it is a repetition' (1999, 241). Thus, to understand how current U.S. discourses and policies have become possible, one must consider where they have been derived from and what makes them able to be reiterated, understood, and accepted (ibid., 241).

Foreign policy should thus be thought of as comprising two interre-lated aspects. The first is as 'foreign policy,' which refers to 'all prac-tices of differentiation or modes of exclusion (possibly figured as rela-tionships to Otherness) that constitute their objects as "foreign" in the process of dealing with them' (Campbell 1998, 68–9). These do not necessarily have to deal directly with the nation-state; they may be taken from any confrontation that arises between a Self and an Other at sites localized around race, gender, ethnicity, geography, or class and within discourses centred on crime, security, policing, culture, and so forth (ibid.).

The constructions of meaning and identity that result from these interactions are 'always the consequence of a relationship between the self and the other that emerges through the imposition of an interpre-tation, rather than being the product of uncovering an exclusive domain with its own preestablished identity' (ibid., 23). In turn, these constructions establish 'conventional dispositions in which a particu-lar set of representational practices serves as the resource from which are drawn the modes of interpretation employed to handle new instances of ambiguity or contingency' (ibid., 69). Formal, practical, and popular discourses that underpin these interpretations then emerge to serve as code books for making sense of social worlds and of difference. They allow the reiterative aspects of performativity to be understood.

The second aspect is what Campbell calls 'Foreign Policy,' or what are usually considered to be the traditional practices of interstate relationships. Instead of constituting identity by itself, Foreign Policy reproduces the constitution of identity made possible by 'foreign policy' and its 'conventional matrix of interpretation' (ibid.). Foreign Policy is thus a (para)site that feeds on the modes of representation performatively constructed by the discourses of foreign policy. Furthermore, Foreign Policy also helps contain challenges to the resulting identity by existentially performing it (ibid.). Campbell notes that 'whichever Foreign Policy practices are implemented, they always have to overcome or neutralize other practices that might instantiate alternative possibilities for identity; and the intensive and extensive nature of the "internal" and "external" political contestation that this presupposes means the efficacy of one particular practice will more often than not be sharpened by the representation of danger' (ibid., 71).

Therefore, utilizing the terminological distinction first developed by Butler, we can understand foreign policy as the performative and Foreign Policy as the performance.

From this conceptualization of foreign policy/Foreign Policy, it follows that 'states are never finished as entities; the tension between the demands of identity and the practices that constitute it can never be fully resolved, because the performative nature of identity can never be revealed. This paradox inherent to their being renders states in a permanent need of reproduction: with no ontological status apart from the many and varied practices that constitute their reality, states are (and have to be) always in a process of becoming' (ibid., 12).

Thus states such as Canada find themselves compelled to replicate the performative of identity and the corresponding performances, while leaving enough ambiguity to necessitate further re-enactments of this identity, in order to remain teleologically grounded as the security provider par excellence. To fail to do so is to risk losing control of the power/knowledge of danger (i.e., the ability to securitize) and the political legitimacy that extends from being *the* authority on security issues.

To repeat, the identities that arise from the performative of foreign policy and the performances of Foreign Policy are not stable on their own terms. Securing identity in the form of the nation-state 'requires an emphasis on the unfinished and endangered nature of the world' by amplifying the dangers posed by difference (ibid., 48). Difference is predicated on a fear of the unknown, of things that are foreign to the Self defined by an understanding of the nation-state as a specific kind of social community. Fear is based on the belief that these foreign elements are capable of destabilizing the solid social and interpersonal foundations that give rise to the Self (i.e., ontological security), thus erasing the uniqueness, familiarity, and assurance of current conditions both internal and external to the state.

Paradoxically, as noted earlier, no notion of the Self can arise in the absence of these perceived dangers, for it is these dangers that provide the basis for Self-identification of the nation-state (e.g., 'We are not' ...). In turn, identity, who or what a nation-state *is*, should be seen as a marker that provides the basis for recognizing dangers/threats and what it is that must be secured against those dangers/threats. Campbell argues that 'discourses of danger are central to discourses of the state and discourses of man. In place of the spiritual certainties which underpinned Christian kingdoms in the West, the state requires discourses of danger to provide a whole new theology of truth about who and what "we" are by highlighting who or what "we" are not, and what "we" have to fear' (ibid.).

It is through the discourses and practices of foreign policy/Foreign Policy, particularly security policy, that states like Canada have created a 'new evangelism of fear' based on a specific set of temporal dangers (ibid., 49). The key, though, is that both the threats and the nodal identity that is to be protected are not static; rather, they undergo various rearticulations. Thus, the borderlines of a national identity are subject to (re)drawing, yet they are presented in such a way that their contingent and unstable nature has been rendered more permanent (ibid., 31). Moreover, (re)drawing does not necessarily imply a change in meaning, though such changes are always possible.

The Significance of Security and Identity

What, then, does all of this mean? What is the primary significance of taking this view of identity, foreign policy, security, threat, and danger?

Perhaps the most immediate effect is that one is left with a vastly different view of the ethos of foreign policy/Foreign Policy practices. In general, we view (if only metaphorically) Foreign Policy and the study of global politics as endeavours that attempt to bring together nations, states, and people who are different and to find ways in which they can coexist. In other words, Foreign Policy is often seen as a bridge-building enterprise.

However, in analysing its mutually constitutive performatives and the practices these make possible, we should see Foreign Policy as a *'boundary producing political performance.'* Metaphorically, it is not about bringing people together, it's about keeping them apart (ibid., 62; italics in original). The paradox is that the clearly and neatly delimited parameters that can accomplish the task of keeping the Self free from the contamination of the outside world are never available. Thus, the 'differences, discontinuities, and conflicts that might be found *within* all places and times must be converted into an absolute difference *between* a domain of domestic society, understood as an identity, and a domain of anarchy, understood as at once ambiguous, indeterminate, and dangerous' (ibid., 63; italics in original).

Power/relations then become an essential aspect of inventing, orchestrating, and resisting the violences that accompany attempts to appropriate and discount characteristics in the construction of matrices of risk and hierarchies of threat classification.

Conceptualizing foreign policy and the practices of Foreign Policy in this manner provides an opportunity to problematize the locations where they can be said to be operating. The social sciences have confined the practices of Foreign Policy to those relationships which are found among states. Walker (1992) has argued that the significance of this point has been that '[this] distinction ... has been the silent condition permitting the construction of received understandings of social and political theory. The affirmation ironically seems to challenge not only the myth of a tradition of international relations theory but also and more crucially the myth of a tradition of political theory as the story of life, liberty, and the pursuit of happiness/property in the bounded polis/state' (1992, 197). From this perspective, there is much to gained analytically not just by challenging the levels of analysis and their implications through Walker's emphasis on erasing the inside/outside distinction that limits the possibility of progress to the 'bounded polis/state,' but also by critically examining how foreign policy/Foreign Policy as security practices try to *constrain* transformation, *limit* who can be said to legitimately belong to the 'bounded ·polis/state' even while residing in it, and *delineate* what are to be considered acceptable behaviours for citizens of a specific 'bounded polis/state.'

The third significant implication of this approach is that policy and practice are not to be conceptualized as outcomes of deliberate interest(s). Practice is shaped by the way we view the world and by what we believe our role is within it, as outlined in formal, practical, and popular discourses. This speaks to how our representations of 'reality' can lead to particular actions not because those actions are in our (objectively definable) interest but because we think that given who *we* are, and who *they* are, they are (among) the only legitimate actions that can be taken (Doty 2000). Dominant discourses may be beneficial to the material interests of particular social actors, but this is secondary to the fact that they are seen as the natural and truthful expression of our understanding of ourselves and our world(s). To move beyond them would be to deconstruct our own ontological groundings to the point of extinction, which is fearfully interpreted as leaving nothing but an undeterminable void of incomprehension and paralysis.

To be clear, the argument is not that radical change can be easily achieved if people are simply prepared to rethink the representational practices that help define contemporary security discourses. As Hansen (1997) argues, the transformative task is in practice very difficult, for one must always operate within dominant discourses in order to be understood, while trying at the same to expose their contingent character (1997, 386). Thus, even if we are doomed by our own prejudices to always have an Other, 'the distance to it can vary and we do have a choice as to how we enact our "responsibility to the Other"' by the ways in which we construct security policy/Security Policy (ibid., 391).

Understanding the Politics of Security and Identity

By infusing security policy practice with agency both in terms of the scope of possible action but even more importantly in terms of the meanings that are constitutive of these actions, performative accounts of the security/identity nexus bring much needed attention to our understandings of security that allow us to navigate our worlds. Navigation, though, is codependent on the ways in which the world is written by us as a text. Yet the paradox is that to feel grounded, this process of (con)textualization must not be revealed as a subjective act; it must be treated as an objective reality.

To understand security and security practices, it also is instructive to abandon the traditional philosophical dichotomy that separates interpretations from facts, a dichotomy that resonates because it is so ingrained in contemporary modes of thought. Facts themselves are always interpretations that carry considerable ethico-political implications, all of which contain varying degrees of legitimacy depending on one's own values. However, within the Western tradition this undermines the sense of ontological security (i.e., the security that comes from knowing with certainty that some things exist); it also expands the political to a dimension beyond the easy control of current matrices of power. Many strategies, both material and discursive, have been deployed to transform interpretations into tangible items. Thus, one of the most important acts in politics relates to that moment when we can convince ourselves that our interpretations *are* facts that provide *the* one accurate and true description of the world.

Our interpretations of facts delineate the possibilities and limits of social action by constructing the context in which decisions are made. The irony, of course, is that we often forget both the interpretative acts we have carried out to establish memories as facts in discourse, as well as alternative interpretative options that are available both at the instant when they are discursively constructed and when we draw meaning from them afterwards. This is crucially relevant to the study of foreign policy/Foreign Policy and security practices when one stresses the importance of the performative construction of Self and threat. What do we choose to give the status of fact? And what significance does this have for the contours of politics? Conversely, what has been denied the status of fact and thus been forgotten? Most importantly, what are the political consequences of having no memory of them or of the processes through which they were constructed?

States such as Canada cannot afford to contemplate these important questions, as to do so would be to open the possibility of undermining established notions of Canadian identity and of the social order that identity fosters. Instead, efforts must performatively (re)create ongoing problems, hazards, and threats through discourses of danger that (re)produce an evangelism of fear, so that *external* worlds can be navigated and their differences made coherent. Drawing on the discussion of foreign policy via Campbell (i.e., the ways in which we understand and negotiate difference and then apply these matrices to Foreign Policy), as well as the dragon metaphor that underpins this project, *external* worlds are also found within the supposed internal territory of sovereign states like Canada. Thus, to stop performatives of threat and identity, and their associated performances, would disrupt the state's ability to exist as a functioning unit. The performatives we undertake (i.e., the characteristics we assert as being naturally ours) are derived from choices we make about how we want to see (our)Self, how we wish to be seen by Others, and how we want to see *our* Others. In this way, while it may be difficult to do so, we are able to shape the scripts through which we read the world and through which we want the world to read us.

Finally, an ethos of critique can be taken from reading security and identity as a mutually constituted dynamic produced by complex sets of power/relations. Above all else, this position illustrates the importance of asking, 'How have we come to be a particular way in the present?' or perhaps more precisely, 'How have we come to represent ourselves in a specific fashion in the present?' By examining the dominant narratives of the discourse of danger surrounding illicit drugs, and how those narratives have been utilized in securitizing this issue in the Canadian context, we can arrive at answers to these questions.

Thus, by being prepared to ask 'how possible' questions, we can expose the subjectivity of identity and security. These questions also bring to light the instabilities of identity by requiring us to examine how the foundations of the Self may shift over time, thereby opening the possibility that both what *was* and what *is* do not necessarily have to *be*. In the process, we come face to face with our own personal dragons. Whether we see these as reptilian demons or as guardians of spiritual wisdom depends on choices we make – choices in which we must exercise great integrity, ethical responsibility, and accountability to ourselves and also towards our Others. The following substantive chapters address these fundamental issues through the prism of illicit drugs in Canada.

3 Situating Canadian Geonarcotics: Canada, the United States, and the Performatives of Canadian Identity

On 30 July 2003, an op-ed appeared in the *Pittsburgh Post-Gazette* titled 'It's Not Just the Weather That's Cooler in Canada.' It began with the following passage: 'You live next door to a clean-cut, quiet guy. He never plays loud music or throws raucous parties. He doesn't gossip over the fence, just smiles politely and offers you some tomatoes. His lawn is cared for, his house is neat as a pin and you get the feeling he doesn't always lock his front door. He wears Dockers. You hardly know he's there. And then one day you discover that he has pot in his basement, spends his weekends at peace marches and that guy you've seen mowing the yard is his spouse. Allow me to introduce Canada' (Bennett 2003).

Bennett went on to list the *real* variations between Canada and the United States, including Canada's refusal to join the coalition of the willing in Iraq, Canada's proposed decriminalization of marijuana, strict Canadian gun control laws, declining Canadian crime rates, the legal recognition of same-sex marriages in Canada, less religiosity in Canadian politics, Canada's signing of the Kyoto Protocol, a lower Canadian drinking age, a higher level of urbanization in Canada, and a larger number of immigrants in relation to the general population compared to the United States (ibid.).

The author argued that all of these factors could lead to but one overwhelming conclusion in terms of the respective abilities of Canada and the United States to negotiate difference: 'Like teenagers we [Americans] fiercely idolize individual freedom but really demand that everyone be the same. But the Canadians seem more adult – more secure. They aren't afraid of foreigners. They aren't afraid of homosexuality. Most of all, they're not afraid of each other. I wonder if America will ever be that cool?' (ibid.).

While the delivery was comedic in tone, the underlying message that Canada is not only 'cool' but 'cooler' than the United States was a significant contributor to popular discourses of nationalism and Canadian identity within Canada. The editorial was picked up by Canadian newspapers, distributed by e-mail, and made the topic for radio call-in shows.

Many Canadians were quick to embrace these notions of 'coolness' when it came to performatives of Canadian (inter)national identity that were bound up with performances said to exhibit tolerance and political moderation. Yet this masked much of the internal dissension against many of the policy positions highlighted in the editorial. Especially divisive were the issues inextricably tied to biopolitics, including same-sex marriage and marijuana decriminalization, with Canadian traditionalists of various stripes vehemently opposed to these changes in law and social mores. The Roman Catholic Church, for example, mounted an aggressive campaign against same-sex marriages, claiming that homosexual unions would defile the sanctity of the holy relationship between man and woman while providing encouragement for other 'deviant' sexual practices such as bestiality. Neoconservative moralists and the law enforcement establishment publicly expressed fears that marijuana decriminalization would send the wrong message to young people about the negative consequences of illicit drug use.

What makes the editorial remarkable is that the musings of a reporter for a mid-sized American paper were able to launch a renewal of Canadian nationalist sentiment. It was able to resonate in the discourses of Canadian identity and nationalism because it echoed dominant domestic representations of a distinctive Canadian national identity reflected in Canada's approach to social policy issues. This portrayal of Canada as tolerant, moderate, cosmopolitan, and hip reaffirmed the long-standing suspicion held by many Canadians that Canada is inherently superior to the United States. Thus, the divergences in social policy were portrayed as the natural outcome of vastly different political cultures. Eva Mackey (2002) has noted that 'ironically, while one of Canada's defining and supposedly essential characteristics is tolerance to difference, one of the major socially acceptable forms of overt *intolerance* has been that directed at the United States' (2002, 145).

Within popular discourses of Canadian nationalism, a statement of an American yearning for 'Canadianization' contributed to a new geopolitical mapping of the world based on performatives of identity that placed Canada within the locus of 'civilized' states (if not at the epicentre) and the United States on the margins as a 'pseudo-civilized' entity rife with religious fundamentalism, crime, violence, and paranoia. Canadians no longer had to be jealous of American exceptionalism and wealth and needed not be reserved in expressing their rejection of the United States as a hegemon and a guardian of *the* global social standard. The desire for 'Canadianization' also played against type in terms of the traditional prognosis for the region. Typically, Canadians have worried to varying degrees that the United States, emboldened by its wealth and power, might try to act on the notion of 'manifest destiny' and subordinate Canada as a political entity. Now, the *problematique* seemed to be reversed, with segments of the United States wishing to be part of Canada.

Although the sentiments expressed in Bennett's piece were presented in Canada as emblematic of American envy towards its northern neighbour, this was not the view held in the White House. Six months earlier, George W. Bush, in the text of Presidential Determination No. 2003-14, engaged in his own geopolitical mapping of the world with the publication of the results of the annual U.S. Government National Certification Process for Illicit Narcotics. Bush argued:

> Although the United States enjoys an excellent level of bilateral cooperation with Canada, the United States Government is concerned that Canada is a primary source of pseudoephedrine and an increasing source of high potency marijuana, which are exported to the United States. Over the past few years there has been an alarming increase in the amount of pseudoephedrine diverted from Canadian sources to clandestine laboratories in the United States, where it is used to make methamphetamine. The Government of Canada, for the most part, has not regulated the sale and distribution of precursor chemicals. The regulations to restrict the availability of pseudoephedrine, which the Government of Canada has just promulgated, should be stronger. Notwithstanding Canada's inadequate control of illicit diversion of precursor chemicals, I commend Canadian law enforcement agencies, which continue to work energetically to support our joint law enforcement efforts. (White House 2003)

The statement may seem innocuous to some because it recognized the efforts of Canadian law enforcement and acknowledged the two countries' history of bilateral cooperation. Yet it marked an escalation in the American determination to geopolitically reposition Canada within the global community as a major player in the production and transport of illicit drugs unless it stopped straying from U.S. legislative demands stemming from its own 'war on drugs' and the 'war on terror.'[1] While U.S. government complaints about illicit drug production in Canada and its distribution into the United States had been voiced at various times over the previous decades, this was the first time that disapproval with Canadian illicit drug policy had been forcefully articulated to the global community in an American policy statement.

Previous concerns had been addressed through bilateral channels. Now, Canada found itself being criticized in the summary of a document that included it among major drug transit and/or producing countries like Afghanistan, the Bahamas, Bolivia, Brazil, Burma, China, Colombia, Dominican Republic, Ecuador, Guatemala, Haiti, India, Jamaica, Laos, Mexico, Nigeria, Pakistan, Panama, Paraguay, Peru, Thailand, Venezuela, and Vietnam.[2] Association with this grouping of countries had the potential to undermine popular performatives of Canadian (inter)national identity as 'the good international citizen' based on an adherence to international law and democratic governance in combination with advanced economic development. In the terminology of Gerrit W. Gong (1984), Canada was in danger of falling outside the 'standard of civilization' of proper international society as defined by the United States, with all of the attendant dangers, including economic costs and overt political marginalization.

In resorting to Gong's term 'standard of civilization,' I am not implying that major drug-producing and transit countries are 'uncivilized.' Rather, I am drawing attention to practices within the dominant representational politics of contemporary international relations that place these countries outside of this privileged community. They are represented in dominant Western discourses as politically, socially, and economically underdeveloped – traits attributed to the failure to culturally modernize. This makes it possible for most countries that have been identified as major drug transit/producing states to continue to be politically marginalized in the international community as a part of a long-standing historical trend.

This chapter explores a critical theoretical understanding of geopolitics in order to reflect on how issues related to illicit drugs have shaped the contours of identity in the Canada–U.S. bilateral relationship as well as (inter)national performatives of Canadian identity. The central argument is that geopolitics or, more appropriately, *geonarcotics*, should be considered not as an area of objectively verifiable knowledge but rather as an active political practice that inscribes particular spatial entities with meaning(s) that help to shape the spectrum of legitimate policy possibility.[3] The influence of geonarcotic power–knowledge has been more pressing in Canada than is generally perceived. The pressure to remain 'on-side' with U.S. global security policy in general, and drug policy in particular, means that Canada's capacity to (re)produce performatives of Canadian national identity based on assertions of naturalized policy differences must be negotiated.

Geopolitics

Kennan Ferguson (1996) has argued that the instability of geographic identities, the plurality of histories, and having national character tied to a method of thought rather than to an ideologically secure territory have long provoked a strong need to map the world into divisions based on subjectively chosen criteria of difference (1996, 167). In his discussion of Deleuze and Guattari, he notes that they argue that the earth is always coded in terms of subjectively derived meanings rather than objectively determined characteristics (ibid., 168). 'Territorialization' for them becomes mainly a process of creating and separating different classifications of people (ibid.).[4] Thus, within these processes of territorialization, the geographic mapping of the world is imbricated with a far broader set of power/relations. Gearóid Ó Tuathail (1996) argues that since its inception as a word in European languages, geography has been about power, for it 'is not something already possessed by the earth but *an active writing of the earth by an expanding, centralizing imperial state. It was not a noun but a verb, a geo-graphing*, and earth writing by ambitious endocolonizing and exocolonizing states who sought to seize space and organize it to fit their own cultural visions and material interests' (1996, 1–2; italics in original). In this way, space is always being (re)produced, making geography not a 'natural given but a power/knowledge relationship' (ibid., 5, 10).

Production here is being used in the Baudrillardian sense, not in terms of being able to materially manufacture an area but in terms of being able to 'render visible' and 'make appear' (ibid., 29). In this sense, geography is a technology through which particular discursive representations can be materialized and naturalized as 'real.' Because geography is a form of power/knowledge, geographic renditions of the world can tell us much about those who have constructed the maps as the subjects and objects that are conditioned by the mapping process. But the fundamental difference, as Ferguson (1996) notes, is that 'those who do not take part in the mapping, whether through choice, distance, or exclusion, have their identities constituted for them' (1996, 179). Thus geography is an important site of political struggle, as 'it is also a conflict between competing images and imaginings, a contest of power and resistance that involves not only struggles to represent the materiality of physical geographic objects and boundaries but also the equally powerful and, in a different manner, the equally material force of discursive borders between an idealized Self and a demonized Other, between "us" and "them"' (Ó Tuathail 1996, 15).

Geography, then, can be seen as an ongoing contest between different ways of envisioning the world in which the positioning/prioritization of values establishes relationships between people, masked by an objective empiricism that claims to be describing (rather than constructing) these dynamics (ibid., 15; Ferguson 1996, 179).

Ó Tuathail (1996) argues that the construction of Otherness always involves 'exclusion which is inherently spatial' (1996, 179). The essential moment, then, of any geopolitical discourse is when 'the world is divided into "our" space and "their" space, the political function of which is to distinguish an "us" from a "them"' (Dalby, in ibid., 16). In trying to fix these representations as natural, 'geopolitical productions invariably appeal to and rely upon the rhetorical dimensions ... of objects, attributes, and patterns in order to persuade and make their arguments convincing ... the *visuality* of geopolitical productions ... is dependent upon an unrecognized and unacknowledged *textuality*' (ibid., 52).

Thus, a critical approach to geopolitics challenges the epistemological foundations of the contemporary geopolitical enterprise; though it makes claims to objectivity by adhering to an empiricist methodology that constructs 'a *disembodied* spectator of the subject who is above and beyond a *situated* space and time' and is therefore able to discern key characteristics through *his* sense of sight, the study of geography in fact *creates* relationships between subjects, objects, and texts ('sight, sites, and cite') that need to be problematized (ibid., 43, 71).[5] Moreover, it is important to note how *the* Western viewpoint and its corresponding narratives have been granted primary interpretive authority within contemporary geopolitical discourses (Ferguson 1996, 184).

Three of the most influential geopolitical treatises of the post–Cold War era that best demonstrate the chauvinism that plagues Western interpretative authority have been the works of Samuel Huntington (1996), Robert Kaplan (2000), and Francis Fukuyama (1992). In their respective geopolitical mappings of the new world (dis)order, Western culture and values are placed at the apex of human development; in this way they are granted the licence to ascertain the naturalized differences (and inferiorities) of Other political cultures while claiming to be scientifically objective. Each of these authors to varying degrees highlights the inevitable threats to Western civilization posed by global Others, whose barbarity can only be mitigated, if at all, by slow and painful processes of transformation in their own political cultures, until these more closely resemble Western modes of living.

The basic challenge for the new geopolitics, then, is how to quarantine the West from the physical and material flows that arise from conditions of fundamental – and within these discourses naturalized – inequalities such as poverty, underdevelopment, and political instability, which are said to derive from the practices of alternative cultural perspectives. For Huntington, the dangers engendered by hatred of the West rest on the civilization's material success relative to other modes of being. For Kaplan, material necessity in the developing world is threatening the economic standing of the core industrialized states. For Fukuyama, capitalist liberal democracies are located at the 'end of history,' on the neo-Hegelian assertion that Western socio-economic practices are the best that humankind can possibly produce. The disruptive effects of Western cultural imperialism and the imposition of specific practices (e.g., capital accumulation) are never implicated by these authors; the problems and their sources are localized outside the 'civilized' world. Moreover, Ferguson (1996) notes that these types of mappings of the world, which 'imbricate material and metaphorical space,' overcode cultural classifications in order to restrict them to specific spatial positionings. All ambiguity and plurality is removed from the description of culture, leaving a 'positivist descriptive category' that attempts to depoliticize and naturalize external relations among cultures (e.g., the clash of civilizations) while ignoring the diversity *within* cultures (1996, 170, 172).

There has been much discussion of the 'coming anarchy' and the 'West against the rest' based on traditional assessments of material conditions and power capabilities; there has been far less discussion of the dynamics of cultural flows in a globalizing world, and when there is, those flows are conceptualized as unidirectional transmissions whereby Western political civilization is exported to 'the rest' through democratization and marketization. Yet the implicit threat that arises in conjunction with the construction of material danger centres on the imperilment of the identity of the Self through the adoption of inferior modes of living associated with the Other. Thus, the new geopolitical discourse is a performative that defines the Western Self and its Others by providing nodal points for recognizing and concretizing difference; by imposing classification schemes whose objective assertions serve to naturalize and spatialize these differences; and by establishing a new global hierarchy that is both reflective of and constitutive of this politics of representation. Again, it must be noted that this is not a politically neutral process: its very coherence and effectiveness rest on power/relations defined by the ability to have one's representational claims listened to and accepted by target audiences, especially policy makers in Western states. Furthermore, power as a productive force is required to convincingly act out what has been written in these scripts of global politics. Also, productive power serves to justify those actions which transpire, by appealing to a commonsense understanding of how the world operates, which again, draws from these initial scripts. The reality of geopolitics thus rests on an inescapable tautology.

Geonarcotics

A corollary to geopolitics is the development of contemporary discourses of geonarcotics. Contemporary geonarcotics was primarily constituted within the practical discourses of the U.S. 'War on Drugs' in 1982, when the securitization of illicit drugs began to be reflected in American national security doctrine.[6] As an external threat with internal manifestations, illicit drug production needed to be located, analysed, and categorized to provide an intelligence foundation that could be utilized to stem the flow of drugs into the United States.[7] Performatives (and performances) of sovereignty could then be reasserted. Two processes worked in conjunction to produce this geographic imaginary. The first was the internalization of the external, expressed most starkly when President Ronald Reagan overrode the Posse Comitatus Act in 1983. U.S. military troops could now be deployed on American soil for the purposes of counternarcotics activities. From a sociology of knowledge perspective, it is interesting to note how traditional security analysts who were obsessed with external military threats almost totally ignored these developments. As a consequence, important implications for the theoretical and practical dimensions of national security strategies during the Cold War and for the blurring of the demarcation between domestic/foreign security policy were overlooked, and work remained fixated at the systemic level (e.g., in terms of balances of power).

The second process was that regions had to be coded as threatening the national security of the United States and stigmatized in order to legitimate a reinvigorated post-colonial political marginalization of these peripheral (yet essential) Cold War geopolitical spaces. These spaces were essential in that they provided an important nodal point for performatives and performances of American identity. As 'third world' countries, they made possible an American Self with the capacity to compartmentalize a range of social issues from poverty to the legitimacy of the national security state as being located outside the United States. This served as a comparison from which a strong and positive American identity could be drawn.

Once the threats posed by particular illicit drug–producing regions were naturalized, important processes of depoliticization were made possible that (re)produced certain states as incapable of agency and in need of intervention. The processes of determination were ad hoc during the early years of the 'war on drugs'; they became institutionalized with the creation of the International Narcotics Control Strategy Report, which identified all of the major drug producing and transit countries on a yearly basis. In combination with Section 490 of the Foreign Assistance Act, which requires that the president annually certify that each major country identified in the report had cooperated fully or had taken adequate steps on its own to meet the standards of the 1988 United Nations Drug Convention, we can see the constitutive interaction of geonarcotic's 'sight, site, and cites.' Governments that the president feels have not met the standard lose their eligibility for most forms of U.S. military and economic assistance. They also face an obligatory 'no vote' by the U.S. government for loans in six multilateral development banks.[8]

With the end of the Cold War and the growing prominence of practical discourses of democratization and marketization, geonarcotics took on a new urgency. In so doing, it broadened the scope of negative effects inextricably linked to illicit drug production/transit while strengthening a national security perspective that made the state the referent object of security strategy.[9] Reflecting the interplay of formal and practical discourses, Ivelaw Griffith (1993/4) provided a modified geonarcotics framework that expanded the objects of study to include the 'political, economic, military, health, environmental, and psychological consequences that offer actual and potential threats to the sovereignty, political stability, economic equilibrium, and social fabric of many societies' (1993/4, 2). Griffith saw his conceptualization of geonarcotics as a replacement for the policy certainties provided by Cold War geopolitical discourses; what remained a constant in his analysis was the assumption that all threats are implicit challenges to the geopolitical status quo and Western hegemony.

In portraying the international illicit drug distribution system as a vast 'Underground Empire,' both aggressive and violent and with its own armed forces, diplomats, intelligence agencies, banks, and transportation services, Griffith was remapping the world in a way that (re)territorialized threats to (inter)national security as emanating mainly from the global South (ibid., 5). He argued that 'drug operations present security problems not merely because of their international scope, in that very few of the nation-states in the United Nations system escape some kind of threat, but also because of their multidimensionality which means that they have an impact on the military, political, economic, and environmental areas' (ibid., 18).

From a military perspective, Griffith contended that the use of armed forces in developing countries for counternarcotics efforts, the increase in arms trafficking due to the demands of drug traffickers, and collaboration between drug operators and guerrillas should be viewed as escalating threats. In the political sphere, the combination of violence and corruption – constructed as inextricably linked to the drug trade – was infused with the power to undermine 'the institutional basis for the maintenance of good government and public safety in many places in Latin America, Asia, Africa, and Europe' (ibid., 19–24). Regarding the economic threat, Griffith contended that 'drug abuse decreases productivity through addiction, rehabilitation, and incarceration' while accelerating processes of hyperinflation and raising the "real" prices of goods and services in developing economies (ibid., 26). He also asserted, albeit implicitly, that the increased costs of health care and antidrug operations were diverting funds from areas where they might be more beneficial (ibid., 26–9). From the geonarcotics perspective, all of this was not making law enforcement activities and military operations less necessary; rather, it was creating a greater need to eliminate illicit drug use and production. Finally, Griffith proposed that the drug trade and drug production 'give rise not only to deforestation, but also to pollution, species destruction, soil erosion, and dangers to human health' (ibid., 29–31).

Griffith's conceptualization of geonarcotics was intended to replace the policy guidance offered by Cold War geopolitics. It is interesting to note, however, that Griffith's epistemological assumptions remained grounded in an empiricism that reifies the interpretations of experts as extensions of objective observations of naturalized phenomena. Seen in this light, Griffith was making the compelling declaration that whether or not academics and analysts went along with it, global events were redefining security. The traditional emphasis had been on the balance of power; now drugs and the international drug trade were an important part of any discussion on security (ibid., 17). Yet those phenomena represented as dangerous by the discourse of geonarcotics are made possible by the foundational assumptions about the legitimacy and righteousness of prohibition and the international politico-economic status quo that underpins the discussion. Moreover, geonarcotics fails to conduct a reflexive inventory of what could and should be considered an illicit drug and what could and should be considered dangerous patterns of consumption within a society.

Geonarcotics also dovetails with contemporary geopolitical discourses that give rise to panopticism by organizing around the identification and ranking of political cultures.[10] Under the formulation of Michel Foucault (1984c), a panopticon is a system of surveillance and observation, security and knowledge, individualization and totalization, isolation and transparency, that serves as a monitoring technology for disciplining abhorrent or deviant behaviour. The panopticon was originally conceived by Jeremy Bentham as the ideal architectural design for prisons. One guard tower was positioned facing a multilevel structure of cells so that any activity within any cell could be instantly monitored. The innovation with Bentham's panopticon was in the design of the guard tower, which was to be built with a high-powered illumination device fixed on the cells so that prisoners would never be able to discern whether they were being monitored at any given time (1984c, 217–18).

Reflecting its penal origins, by providing surveillance on a proscribed classification of *political* subjects positioned external to the viewer, panopticism allows for 'the operation on the underside of the law, a machinery that is both immense and minute, which supports, reinforces, and multiplies the asymmetry of power and undermines the limits that are traced around the law' (ibid., 212). By presenting a system of monitoring that is potentially omniscient and omnipresent yet leaves subjects open to uneven levels of surveillance, panopticons are capable of ensuring that behavioural norms are internalized by those subject to observation who wish to avoid further punishment. The absence of any definitive method to discern when one is being watched furthers the impetus to abide by the prescribed behavioural standard at all times, for the arbitrariness of the system and the unwavering commitment to punishment discourage feigned conformity to norms.

Within contemporary geopolitical discourses in general, panopticism has manifested itself in terms of the continuation of systems of surveillance based on assessments of political culture and economic development as measured by a legion of state, non-state, and interstate actors. For example, the 'Axis of Evil,' the Amnesty International Report on Human Rights, Democracy Watch, state and foreign department country assessments, democratic peace theory databases, International Monetary Fund reports, and UN rankings are all contributing to a body of knowledge that various institutional sites then draw from to classify actors and assign meanings to their activities and essences. Through the interpretative categorizations attributed to other actors within geopolitical discourses, existing power/relations privilege some interpretations over others. Thus, the political implications of being discursively constructed as threatening, marginal, or good can be tremendous. Moreover, the 'company a state keeps' has important effects on key performatives of the state's (inter)national identity. In this manner, the impetus to behave in particular ways extends beyond the deterrent of material punishment to a more fundamental concern about a loss of status and identity through the deployment of particular representational practices.

The mechanics of panopticism have been applied in two distinct ways where materiality intersects with textuality in contemporary geonarcotics. First, in a very crude form, intelligence is gathered in all states at the levels of cultivation, trafficking, corruption, political will, domestic illicit drug use, and the effectiveness of domestic law enforcement. Certain states are then classified as major drug producers and/or transit centres. The threat of (de)certification allow the United States to maintain its asymmetrical economic power/relations; at the same time, the deferential awareness articulated by these states of the intensive challenges posed by decertification reinforces the hegemonic position of the United States as *a* surveyor and *the* arbitrator of global geonarcotics knowledge.

The certification procedure has had implications even for countries whose economic position does *not* leave them vulnerable to the material penalties of certification. Well aware that they are probably being monitored (although they may not be) by the United States for drug-related activities, and that an extensive record is being kept of their transgressions, countries like Canada are steered into approaching the issues raised by illicit drugs from perspectives amenable to the American administration. It is widely recognized, as Hal Klepak (1993/4) has noted, that 'for the United States, the issue [i.e., drugs] has even become something of a touchstone for testing the loyalty of other countries in the post-Cold War era' (1993/4, 67). Under these conditions of surveillance, the asymmetry of the power/relations is not reflected in the public disciplining of those actors who do not obey; rather it is constituted by the extent to which potential transgressors internalize norms in ways that discipline their behaviour within parameters designated as acceptable.

In this conceptualization of power, discipline and punishment represent instances in which the hegemony of dominant actors has been challenged and exposed as weak, necessitating the public display of power to reinforce asymmetrical power/relations. When power/ relations are most potent and most productive, their mechanisms of control are most *hidden*. As such, the ultimate goal of American geopolitics in general, and geonarcotics more specifically, has been the production of docile states, defined as those who maximize their utility (politically, economically, and socially) for the United States through their political obedience (Foucault 1977a, 138). These processes, though, still create enough difference within the discourse of geonarcotics that naturalized divisions can be constructed between those states with intensive illicit drug problems and those which accept the international standard in terms of sanctioned behaviour and responses to deviations from the norm.

Perform(at)ing Canada in Geonarcotics

When we take a longer view of the dynamics of the global system, it is clear that the geopolitics of the post–Cold War, 9/11 era are not so new. Gerrit Gong (1984) has argued that to understand the social, legal, and institutional fabric of the contemporary society of states, we must pay attention to the global political dynamics of imperialism in the later part of the nineteenth and early twentieth centuries (1984, 4). Approaching European imperialism and resistance to it as 'fundamentally a confrontation of civilizations and their respective cultural systems,' Gong traces the development of the 'standard of civilization,' which as a representational practice placed certain human collectivities 'outside of the law's pale and protection' (ibid., 3 and 6). Gong defines a standard of civilization as the 'expression of the assumptions, tacit and explicit, used to distinguish those that belong to a particular society from those that do not' (ibid., 3). Thus he argues that many of the nineteenth century's military engagements, such as the Opium Wars, were extensions of conflicting standards of civilization by other means (ibid., 8).

In the construction of *the* 'law of "civilized" nations,' European imperial powers established several criteria to distinguish themselves from their civilizational Others. These included a respect for basic rights (particularly for foreign nationals), an institutionalized state structure and bureaucracy, the capacity to militarily defend territory, adherence to norms that were generally accepted as comprising international law at the time, upholding the principle of the rule of law domestically, maintaining diplomatic channels of communication, and conformity to the norms and practices of civilized international society, which required particular forms of biopolitical regulation against practices like slavery and polygamy. Thus Gong contends that what had previously been described as the 'law of Christian nations' had been altered and redefined as the 'law of "civilized" nations' (ibid., 5).

While the standard of civilization may have been recognized within European imperial powers as an objective gauge for determining the worth and legal status of competing political entities, Gong notes that the inherent subjectivity and intersubjective interpretation required for its enforcement made it difficult both to define and to put into practice. The problems were numerous. First, all the criteria were evaluative and descriptive, thereby requiring that key states identify and recognize a characteristic as conforming to the established norm. These key states might not always agree or be consistent in their agreement. As a consequence, indigenous systems not immediately recognizable or understandable to Europeans were discriminated against. Second, for reasons that are quite obvious, it was useful to leave particular regions of the world outside the community in order to justify engaging in behaviour that might otherwise have been subject to sanction, including genocide and institutionalized forced labour. Third, the standard was hypocritical, as most European imperial powers did not meet the criteria for it.

Even though it was not a universally accepted standard, the consequences to the non-European world of not making an effort to abide by its dictates became (painfully) obvious as 'European extraterritoriality became a badge of inferiority for many non-European countries, a sign of their "uncivilized" status' (ibid., 8). In this way, the standard of civilization orchestrated its own panoptic system, which frequently was able to internalize European norms in the non-European world. As a stimulus for 'reform' and as a 'guideline for the changes, adjustments, and adaptations needed to fulfil its requirements,' societal transformation became a way to argue that one qualified for 'civilized' legal status. Yet the impacts of this social engineering were devastating, for they undermined 'the traditional cultural and political foundations on which many non-European states were based' (ibid., 7). Gong argues that however direct the threats posed by the military component of European imperialism to political entities around the world, there was a recognition that 'confrontation with the European standard of civilization constituted the more fundamental threat to their existence' (ibid., 7).

From this perspective, Canada occupied an uncertain geopolitical position early in the twentieth century because of its legacy as a British colony. On the one hand, Canada could claim within geopolitical discourses of the time that it belonged to the higher echelons of the global community, based not only on cultural characteristics, which arguably conformed to the standard of civilization, but also on physiological similarities with Northern European races.[11] On the other hand, within the global system itself, Canada was usually unable to express its own voice as a sovereign nation-state; as a dominion and a member of the British Commonwealth, Canada deferred to Britain, which negotiated on its behalf in virtually all international forums, including key bilateral arrangements with the United States that settled territorial and commercial disputes. This arrangement continued until December 1931, when the British Parliament passed the Statute of Westminster, which granted all British dominions their full legal freedom, subject to voluntary restrictions.

While Canada initially was keen to remain politically attached to Britain in global affairs, it became increasingly clear – most prominently in an ongoing series of key negotiations with the United States – that Whitehall was paying little attention to Canadian wishes. Yet at the same time, Canadian distrust of the United States, and expressed fears of nationalists that Canada's distinct (and superior) way of life could be overwhelmed by its southern neighbour through cultural and/or military invasion were constructed by many policy makers as an overwhelming incentive to remain closely allied with Britain. As Jack Granatstein and Norman Hillmer (1991) have noted, '[the] belief that salvation and survival lay not simply in British values but in the potential for an application of British power' necessitated the perpetuation of a subordinate relationship with Britain (1991, 9).

Often, Canada utilized its close relationship with Britain in order to assert a global role as a loyal subject. Such as was the case with Canadian participation in the Boer War (1903). However, there was also a sense – which to a certain degree lingers to this day – that Canada was a political actor without a stage, a regional power without a region. While discourses of nationalism and Canadian identity were taking shape domestically, global political conditions limited the possibilities for Canada to articulate performatives and enact performances of its own unique (inter)national character. Thus, even before Confederation, within Canadian political discourses one can see the construction of Canada as a gendered body, a (potential) victim of external and more powerful Others (Mackey 2002, 12). Around the turn of the twentieth century, Canada did not constitute a political subject with (inter)nationally recognized agency. Instead, Canada was too often represented as an object of desire in the fulfilment of American and British geostrategic interests. Thus, Canada sought opportunities to raise its profile and project its own views outwardly to the global community.

The passage of the 1908 Opium Act, which established prohibitions on the importation, sale, and manufacture of opium for non-medical purposes, provided such an opportunity. As one of the few 'civilized' states with federal opium legislation, Canada was given a seat at the 1909 Shanghai Opium Conference as part of the British delegation. Canada's representative then was William Lyon Mackenzie King, who had drafted the act. Canadian participation in the Shanghai proceedings was presented as a significant achievement and as an international recognition of Canada's leading role in the advancement of morality and civilization.

In the *Toronto Globe*, an article on the Shanghai Conference ran under the headline, 'How Canada Has Pointed the Way in Regard to Reform Leading to the Abolition of the Opium Traffic,' and quoted Mackenzie King's observation that during the proceedings 'the American delegation generously admitted that their legislation for the suppression of the traffic in the United States had been copied from Canada' (Giffen, Endicott, and Lambert 1991, 75). By using his Shanghai experience to promote Canada as a pioneer (under his guidance) in the development of effective anti-opium legislation, Mackenzie King was establishing a performative of Canadian (inter)national identity by positioning the country as a leading international force for morality and virtue. However, as Giffen and colleagues note, Canada was not the first country to pass legislation dealing with opium traffic. From the available historical documents, it is clear that Mackenzie King was well aware that both New Zealand (1901) and Australia (1905) had passed statutes prohibiting the importation or manufacture of opium for smoking previous to the Opium Act (ibid., 76). Regardless of the originality of King's legislation, it bears noting that traditional accounts have emphasized that the Opium Act enhanced Mackenzie King's own reputation as a social reformer and opium expert, thereby furthering his own political career (he would later serve as prime minister for twenty-six years). The ways in which this legislation helped foster a nascent Canadian (inter)national identity are largely overlooked (Solomon and Green 1988, 92). Many of the leading works on the history of Canadian foreign policy make no reference to the 1909 Shanghai Opium Conference or to perceptions of Canadian inclusion in the process within Canada.

As discussed earlier, performatives of identity are often evoked to provide grounding (however illusory) to what is presented as a pre-existing foundation from which characteristics are said to naturally arise. Reflective of this conceptualization of the contingent foundations of identity claims, Robert Solomon and Melvyn Green argue that 'King's public posturing about Canadian moral leadership in the international anti-opium movement [was] ironic' (ibid., 110). They contend that 'as a member of the British delegation to the Shanghai Commission, King was hardly in the vanguard of this movement ... King, for his part, arrived late to the Commission because he had stopped in Britain and India to discuss methods of limiting Asiatic emigration to Canada. He apparently had little faith in the commission and was not particularly attentive, and misreported some of the proceedings' (ibid., 110).

Yet when discussions of drug law commenced once again in 1911, the Shanghai Commission was used as an argument for extending the range of regulatory mechanisms to place restrictions on morphine and cocaine, even though it made no such demands on national governments (Giffen, Endicott, and Lambert 1991, 553).

In this way, a performative/performance feedback loop was created between the national and global levels, whereby Canadian policy makers began to draw on the standards of international law/civilization with regard to illicit drug use in order to keep Canada positioned within the emerging discourses of (inter)national geonarcotics that contributed to particular political representations of Canada. So when Mackenzie King (as the Minister of Labour) introduced tougher legislation to curb opium use (The Opium and Drug Act of 1911), he was contributing to the propagation of this particular performative/performance (inter)national feedback loop: 'It may be of interest to the people of country to know that when the International Commission met in Shanghai, it was possible for the example of this country to be cited as one to be followed by other nations. It was pointed out that the example had been followed by the United States and the Commission hoped it would be followed by other countries (Mackenzie King, in ibid., 75).

The importance of this feedback loop in terms of Canadian (inter)national identity continues to this day, as can be seen with the Canadian Senate's exploration of the legal grounds and potential implications of decriminalizing marijuana in terms of international drug law and Canada's reputation as a good (and law-abiding) global citizen (Senate 2002d, 466–7).

Regarding the divisions established by geonarcotic representations, discourses, practices, and regulations during the 1920s, William McAllister (2000) has argued that Canada emerged globally as the most visible representative of the interests of 'consuming countries,' those that neither produced the necessary raw materials nor manufactured drugs (2000, 67). As a 'consuming country,' Canada required a steady and inexpensive supply of substances like opium for medicinal purposes, but from a moral standpoint it also wished for strong global controls on production and distribution to curb non-medical use (ibid.). To this end, Canada supported the construction of an extensive architecture of global regulatory mechanisms to control the cultivation, production, and distribution of drugs.

But besides using the development of a global drugs regulatory regime to establish itself as a good, upstanding, and moral global citizen, and utilizing that regime as performative of a nascent (inter)national identity at home, Canada also saw these proceedings as a means to secure opportunities to act independently of Britain. For example, Canadian authorities supported inviting all states to the second Geneva conference in 1924–5, as Ottawa wished to have its own, non-British voice in the proceedings (ibid.). Thus the international illicit drug regulatory system became a means for Canada to articulate a distinctive Canadian outlook on global affairs. While illicit drug issues may have been somewhat peripheral to broader developments at play in the League of Nations (on which Canada sat as a quasi-independent member), it is interesting to note the niche occupied by Canada within discussions of geonarcotics and attempts to add drug issues as an element of the standard of civilization.

Primarily, geonarcotic discourses at the time sought to deflect responsibility away from the great (and former great) powers that had encouraged their colonies to produce and in some cases consume drugs such as opium, cocaine, and heroin. It was often argued that these intra-empire drug trades were necessary in order to accomplish military and economic objectives. A drugs race gripped Europe, one with many similarities to the arms race of the same era, with states attempting to secure exclusive access to raw materials and to develop pharmaceutical production capacities. For example, before the First World War, it was generally acknowledged that the German synthetic drug industry was the world leader in research, development, and production. For decades, Britain had been using the opium trade to retain a positive trade balance with China – a circumstance noted by Karl Marx when he declared opium to be the lynchpin of the capitalist system. The Netherlands encouraged coca leaf cultivation in its Asian colonies, including Indonesia.

The United States and Canada were able to leverage the drugs issue into a potentially embarrassing situation for European colonial powers like Great Britain and the Netherlands, which had established lucrative drug production/distribution operations, by engaging in a politics of representation that constructed drug use as 'uncivilized' and morally deficient. In response, Britain in particular insisted that provisions for 'legitimate use' in the Shanghai Convention be expanded to include 'quasi-medical use' and that the International Opium Convention of 1911 include manufactured drugs such as morphine, heroin, and cocaine. Britain's goal in this was to deflect attention away from its own opium production in India (Senate 2002d, 443).

Thus, from the Shanghai Convention to the mid-1920s, Canada not only used its participation in drug negotiations to advance its case for global stature, but also exploited these early forums as a means to concretize an (inter)national identity that positioned Canada (and the United States) as above the dirty realpolitik that shaped European political dynamics and the questionable practices that underpinned them. Unlike Europeans, not only would Canadians and Americans not go to war with each other, but they would also refuse to defend the illicit drug trade for self-interested gain.

After the passage of the International Opium Convention in 1925, the Canadian government helped perpetuate this distinction by ratifying the agreement quickly and urging other states to follow suit. Having already prohibited marijuana since 1923, Canada was able to claim that it was at the forefront of illicit drug control even before the League of Nations pressed for the control of Indian hemp at the urging of South Africa in 1925 (Giffen, Endicott, and Lambert 1991, 182). Furthermore, the Canadian delegation took credit for quietly brokering the most widely acceptable agreement that circumstances permitted and used this example of its diplomatic utility to press for a seat on the Opium Advisory Committee (OAC) within the League of Nations. This diplomatic manoeuvring, and Canada's role as an intermediary between Britain and the United States with regard to the renewal of the Anglo-Japanese Alliance in 1920–1, made it possible to construct (inter)national performatives of Canada as the 'helpful fixer.' McAllister (2000) argues that by the time membership in the OAC was extended to Canada in 1934, the country within the international imagination 'had emerged as the *primus inter pares* of consuming states' (2000, 80).

The close relationship between Canada and the United States on international drug control issues continued throughout the 1920s into the post–Second World War era. Colonel H.L. Sharman, head of the Canadian Narcotics Service, the domestic agency tasked with coordinating Canadian law enforcement efforts, has been described as the 'soulmate' of Harry Anslinger, the head of the American Federal Bureau of Narcotics: 'the two thought and behaved very much alike' (2000, 94).[12] In particular, both desired strong global regulatory mechanisms to control the supply side of the illicit drugs equation, in combination with harsh punitive domestic measures to prevent consumption and distribution. Their shared belief in the merits of a law enforcement (rather than public health) approach to illicit drug use was unfailing.

In 1936, when the Permanent Central Opium Board (PCOB) in the League of Nations contended in a report that strict control measures that had been implemented internationally had entirely failed to stem the illegitimate drug trade, Canada and the United States – both vocal advocates of these measures – demanded that the passage be removed (ibid., 125). After the PCOB amended this assessment, it became clear to both countries that in partnership they could wield a dominant influence over the global drug control regime. Furthermore, each country could claim within discourses of geonarcotics and nationalism that they were part of the regime's elite driving force.

Colonel Sharman, along with Anslinger and other American diplomats, formed an inner circle that exerted tremendous influence over international drug negotiations, regulations, and prohibitions even during the Second World War (ibid., 152). McAllister notes that through a series of diplomatic moves in response to the circumstances of the war, they were able to establish the United States as the supplier of most of the industrialized world's medicinal pharmaceuticals (excluding the Axis powers) in return for pledges by formerly recalcitrant states such as Britain that they would comply in full with the global control regime. When European states (re)acquired territories in Asia and Africa after the war, great care was taken to ensure that local control structures were resurrected in liberated and occupied areas and that any existing colonial opium monopolies were eliminated (ibid., 154–5; Walker 1991, 165). The supply-side strategy pursued by Canada and the United States aimed to ensure that global drug production would be just enough to meet what were defined as legitimate medical needs. The success of these two countries in entrenching this regime in a world ravaged by war bolstered the bureaucratic positions of Sharman and Anslinger in their respective countries (McAllister 2000, 154–5). More important, key performatives of (inter)national identity and the associated relations of power were reproduced as a result of their activities.

Canadian efforts were also rewarded internationally when Sharman was appointed first chairman of the UN Commission on Narcotic Drugs (CND). From that position of authority, Sharman made sure that a radical, supply-side agenda continued to be pursued on the global stage (ibid., 157). But by the early 1950s, he was becoming increasingly critical of the regime. Soon after, during a series of negotiations to establish the International Opium Monopoly, he claimed that Canadian interests as a consumer dependent on foreign supply sources were being ignored. Given the prestige that Canada had been able to garner from its active role in international drug negotiations, the Canadian government began to worry that his attitude would anger the Americans and the British.

Canadian officials were concerned that Canada was no longer perceived as a leader in global drug regulation and that it had in fact assumed the role of a 'spoiler,' that is, an impediment to progress. So, in 1953, Sharman was removed as head of the Canadian delegation to the Opium Protocol negotiations. However, the Canadian position in these negotiations would remain very similar to the one he had been pursuing (ibid., 177–81): any agreement should allow as many countries as possible to produce opium for licit sale. Furthermore, in an effort to ensure access to a plentiful and inexpensive supply, Canada supported the producing states in their efforts to weaken inspection and embargo provisions. Despite these efforts, the final protocol included only seven countries with official export status (ibid., 181).

In bilateral terms, Sharman's early retirement from domestic responsibilities in 1946 effectively ended the special relationship between Canada and the United States with regard to illicit drugs. Specifically, a deep rift developed between Kenneth Hossick (Sharman's replacement) and Anslinger over growing Canadian discussions around drug abuse treatment and American fears that Canada was moving to adopt a medicalized approach to drug use.[13] Communications soon stopped between Ottawa and Washington on the drug front (ibid., 191).

Around this time, Canada began to adopt more moderate positions on global drug control that de-emphasized the imposition of draconian supply control measures, especially if prices for materials might rise as a result. Canada's role had shifted: no longer was it an ardent supporter of tight restrictions; now it was a leading consumer state intent on promoting international harmony rather than radical schemes. To this end, Canada supported the Single Convention, which would be passed in 1961. However, neither the United States nor Canada was able to dictate the global drug control agenda to the extent that the two countries had previously enjoyed in concert (ibid., 193–5).

While a Canadian internal commission was examining illicit drug use in Canada, the Canadian delegation at the negotiations for the Psychotropic Convention (1971) pressed successfully for changes that would make the agreement far less rigid, thereby establishing opportunities for Canada to move away from hard-line policies if it so desired. At the time, many involved in the Le Dain Commission, which was perceived to be strongly supportive of a liberalization of Canadian illicit drug policy, worried that the Canadian government would use the commitments outlined in the Psychotropic Convention to ignore the commission's findings (Hartley 1971a, 1971b). The eventual weakening of this convention contributed to a reformulation of the performatives of Canada in Canadian geonarcotic discourses, with newspaper reports at the time (mis)representing the move as 'the

Country's first successful attempt to exert major influence on international drug policy' (Hartley 1971a, 35). Canada's key role in founding the global drug control regime had been forgotten.

Prior to the Second World War, geonarcotics had been defined primarily along an axis that separated the Great Powers and their producer colonies from other states that primarily consumed these substances. After the war, divisions were framed by discursively distinguishing the industrialized states of the North (manufacturers) from the post-colonial non-industrialized states of the South (raw material providers). In addition, the Soviet Union and other 'socialist' states aligned themselves with the South's organic producers and largely supported their efforts to counteract the demands of the North's manufacturing states. The growth in illicit drug use in the North was perceived by the Soviet Union as proof of the inherent social corruption in capitalist states.

These divisions crystallized during negotiations over the Single Convention in 1961. Key players in the manufacturing camp included the United States, Britain, Canada, Switzerland, the Netherlands, West Germany, and Japan. Performatively constituting themselves as states with 'no cultural affinity for organic drug use,' while concurrently representing drug use in their respective societies as a severe social problem, they pursued strict controls over the production of illicit raw materials such as opium and over trafficking in illicit drugs – activities that they claimed were external in origin. As a group, they tended to favour strong regulatory global bodies 'as long as they continued to exercise de facto control over such bodies' (Senate 2002d, 452).

The deployment of particular discursive representations of drugs and drug use within dominant understandings of these issues made it possible at the global level to essentially 'shift as much of the regulatory burden as possible to the raw material-producing states such as India, Turkey, Pakistan, Burma, and Indonesia while retaining as much of their own freedom as possible' (ibid., 452). Moreover, as the primary producers of synthetic psychotropics such as amphetamines and tranquillizers, they opposed any restrictions that they considered undue with respect to research or the production and/or distribution of manufactured drugs. Within the terms of discourse employed, they constructed these substances as medically legitimate.

For the most part, the raw material states argued that synthetic psychotropics also needed to be subject to strict regulations and that controls on substances like coca, opium, and cannabis should be loosened.

They also desired to weaken the authority of global control mechanisms, reduce reporting requirements, eliminate on-site inspections, and expunge any provisions they viewed as a threat to national sovereignty (McAllister 2000, 206). Cognizant of the asymmetries that defined the international political hierarchy at the time and the impossibility of mounting a serious challenge to notions of prohibition that had become ingrained in international drugs discourses, these states worked together to weaken the Single Convention's provisions and to demand compensation for the income losses that would result from it. To both these ends, the Soviet Bloc offered support, arguing that 'developing countries should not be barred from exploiting their resources as they see fit' (ibid., 207).

The power/relations among post-colonial and industrialized states made it possible for the discourses of geonarcotics to engage in a (geo)politics of representation that developed particular sets of classificatory schemes to categorize substances based on specific performatives embodied in the dynamics of a reproduced standard of civilization. As the Canadian Senate Committee reported, 'in the 1961 Single Convention negotiations, when the placement of a drug in a particular schedule was disputed, the drug almost always ended up in a schedule not favoured by the organic group – for example, the placement of cannabis in Schedule IV' (Senate 2002d, 457). The manufacturing group argued that this method of classification was justified based on the notion that *these* organic drugs should be considered hazardous until scientifically proven otherwise.

Furthermore, a representational tautology developed within geonarcotic discourses which declared that known drugs not currently in use by Western medicine were by definition hazardous. Thus, it became increasingly difficult to make the case at the (inter)national level that substances like marijuana could be used medicinally and were no more hazardous than synthetic drugs that were widely prescribed. With the Psychotropic Convention of 1971, this tautology was further entrenched in geonarcotic discourses when the American delegation argued successfully in numerous circumstances that raw materials should be classified in the most strict schedules whereas their manufactured derivatives should be placed under far less onerous restrictions (ibid.).

Traditionally, these moves have been viewed by observers as reflecting the desire of the manufacturing states (especially the United States) to ensure that their pharmaceutical industries were not harmed.

However, when an evolving standard of civilization is used as an interpretative guide, performatives of (inter)national identity can be read through the classification schemes. Rather than being a causal relationship between discourse and effect, the performatives at play here mark and reproduce a standard of civilization that writes countries such as Canada and the United States in very different ways from Mexico and Burma. It is these narratives of civilized manufacturing states and uncivilized organic states that have made it possible to authorize a variety of actions at the global and national policy levels.

Drugs that were considered to require a degree of scientific and technical expertise to create and produce were given a privileged status that allowed them to be subject to far less onerous controls because of what they were constructed as representing, both as a substance and as a reflection of the superior status of those who *could* produce them. Moreover, substances of considerable importance to Northern cultures such as tobacco and alcohol were totally ignored. Through these schedules, new dynamics constitutive of the 'civilized/uncivilized' split can be detected based on cultural preferences, the possession of certain types of pharmaceutical technology, and the invocation of an ethnocentric medical model that is predisposed to seeing all organic substances as either totally harmful or an inferior method of delivery in comparison to a synthetic equivalent.

These representational practices continue to be dominant even after Mexico's demand, during the negotiations for the 1988 United Nations Convention, that *all* synthetic drugs also be banned. Yet the tighter restrictions eventually placed on synthetic drugs not only reinforced a global regime based on prohibition, but also left unchallenged (by failing to recognize) the cultural assumptions underpinning the regime regarding what must be considered a drug whose dangers (both direct and associated) require the imposition of global controls.

Canada and the United States

As previously mentioned, during the 1980s long-standing American representations of the dangers posed by illicit drugs underwent a series of securitizations that made possible for militarized responses both at home and abroad. Domestically, Canada embarked on its own search for a national drug strategy in response to the prioritization of the issue in the United States; however, beyond its territorial boundaries, Canada did not construct illicit drugs as a pressing international issue to the same degree. Yet as Hal Klepak (1993/4) has noted, 'American perceptions of the drug trade condition[ed] to a considerable extent Canada's ability to act independently on the issue in ways which might [have] differ[ed] widely from its southern neighbour' (1993/4, 73). Thus, once again Canada and the United States became very similar in their approaches to furthering global legislative controls, and the 1988 United Nations Illicit Trafficking Convention came into force in less than two years thanks to their efforts within a coalition of like-minded states, which included India and Mexico (McAllister 2000, 243).

Yet at home, as the excesses of the 'war on drugs' became more apparent, the Canadian state felt compelled to create some distance between itself and the United States in terms of the approaches to illicit drugs. The Canadian government looked with some concern on the tendency of the United States to militarize responses to the drug trade in the Western Hemisphere and the effects of this on the expansion of democracy and human rights (Klepak 1993/4, 89). Given the Cold War context, American interventions in Latin America for the purposes of illicit narcotics control allowed for the anticommunist and antidrug agendas to become conflated, thereby making it possible for the imperatives of both discourses to be deployed in the justification of military action – or sometimes inaction, where avowed anticommunists were generating income from the illicit drugs trade.

Canada's own National Drug Strategy staked its ground by claiming to have adopted an approach to 'reduce the harm' rather than prohibit and punish illicit drug use, and Canadian actions abroad with regard to illicit drugs fell squarely within multilateral and developmental agendas which contributed to performatives that constituted differences between Canada and the highly interventionist policies of the United States (Health Canada 1998, 4). For example, instead of engaging (or funding) crop eradication programs, Canada donated resources towards crop substitution programs.

While domestic drug discourses within Canada continue to position it away from the American approach, Canadian actions have played a supporting role in the reproduction of dominant geonarcotic scripts and the power/relations that underpin them. For example, Canada offers financial support for the International Drug Control Program (an organization whose outlook has been dominated by the United States) and the Inter-American Drug Abuse Control Commission (CICAD) of the Organization of American States (again, an organization in which the United States wields almost omnipotent influence), and it has been active on the Chemical Action Task Force, which has been organized to foster consensus on international agreements to reinforce the UN convention dealing with the control of precursor chemicals (Klepak 1993/4, 76).

All of these organizations support the foundations of the American geonarcotic problematique – primarily, that prohibition is the only legitimate response to illicit drugs because illicit drug use is inherently threatening to the values and materialities of developed societies. While there is opposition to the ways in which responses to illicit drugs have been framed within many of these hemispheric organizations, Klepak has argued that 'both the Latin Americans and the Americans frequently look to Ottawa as a potential honest broker' (1993/4, 79). Thus, contemporary Canadian actions have contributed to the representational practices of geonarcotics, and furthermore, these same actions have aided in the reproduction of performatives of Canada as the 'helpful fixer.'

Bilaterally, since the 1980s, there has been extensive border security and law enforcement collaboration between Canada and the United States. These processes have only been accelerated by threat perceptions in the aftermath of 9/11. Most notable has been the American construction of illegal immigration, illicit drugs, and terrorism into an external threat nexus that has created policy imperatives to territorialize the identity of the United States by placing increasing restrictions on the flow of people into its sovereign space. This new threat nexus reflects past American security discourses that linked illicit drugs to immigration and, quite separately, illicit drugs to revolutionary terrorism (Marez 2004). What is new about the contemporary configuration is that all of these issues have been collapsed into an indistinguishable threat to American sovereignty and security. Moreover, within both geonarcotic and broader geopolitical discourses, the issues of illicit drugs, migration, and terrorism have been deployed to reproduce a geopolitical calculus (centred on notions of evil) whose representational practices continue to leave particular states vulnerable to the 'corrective' (i.e., militarized) actions of the United States.

Within North America, a vast array of initiatives involving Canada and the United States have been developed, implemented, and/or redesigned to augment border security, thereby impeding the flow of illicit drugs, illegal immigration, and terrorism. These have included the redeployment of NORAD towards interdiction efforts;[14] the drafting of numerous memoranda of understanding on key border issues; the development of the Customs Mutual Assistance Agreement (CMAA); the establishment of reciprocal access to databases and police technology, including criminal record databases and intelligence; information sharing via automated border-monitoring technologies; joint enforcement operations involving the Royal Canadian Mounted Police (RCMP) and the Drug Enforment Administration (DEA) such as Operations Pipeline, Convoy, and Jetaway; the establishment of the Canada–U.S. Cross Border Crime Forum (1997) to improve cooperation and information sharing (cochaired by the U.S. Attorney General and the Canadian Solicitor General); the deployment of the Integrated Border Enforcement Team to track and impede criminal activities across the British Columbia–Washington state border; and the Project North Star initiative to further enhance existing partnerships and operations between Canadian and American law enforcement in addition to promoting cross-border training and the effective use of resources and intelligence (U.S. Department of Justice and Solicitor General Canada 2001, 22–3). Furthermore, many ad hoc operations have taken place at the local and provincial/state levels in terms of interdiction efforts relating to illicit drugs.

This high level of cooperation has been formally acknowledged by the United States in several policy documents. For example, the U.S.–Canada Border Drug Threat Assessment notes that 'numerous federal, state, provincial, and local law enforcement and intelligence community agencies are working bilaterally to suppress drug smuggling and use' (ibid., vii). Yet the high levels of interagency cooperation have not been enough to relieve American pressure on Canada to adopt a more punitive approach to illicit drug issues. Sticking points have included Canada's refusal to prohibit the sale of less expensive prescription medications from Canadian pharmacies to American consumers over the Internet; refusal to place stricter controls on substances that can be used in illicit drug production such as pseudoephedrine and precursor chemicals; and Canada's federal medical marijuana exemptions and proposed decriminalization of marijuana possession for personal use.

The prescription medication issue has arisen because the exact same medicines made by the exact same producers are noticeably less expensive in Canada than in the United States owing to government price controls. Anecdotally, there have been stories for decades of seniors taking bus trips to Canada to buy their medications. With the growth of the Internet, purchasing meds from Canadian distributors has been made far easier, and a growing number of Americans are engaging in the practice to realize savings between 33 and 80 per cent for the most popular drugs (Canadian Press 2003n). New Hampshire, Wisconsin, Vermont, Minnesota, Washington, North Dakota, and Illinois are encouraging their residents to buy Canadian and in some cases are considering (or have begun) purchasing prescription medications from Canada for their state health insurance plans. The U.S. federal government has been discouraging this practice, claiming that Canadian prescription medications and the pharmacies that distribute them are unsafe (Canadian Press 2004). Food and Drug Administration (FDA) Commissioner Mark McClellan has urged Canadian officials to take more aggressive actions to halt the cross-border trade in pharmaceuticals. In Canada, this situation has further entrenched notions of Canadian superiority with respect to the United States based on the provision of health care; however, concerns that Canada's prescription medication supply may become depleted as a result have been growing (Porter 2002, F3). FDA officials themselves have been central in disseminating knowledge of this 'threat' (Baillie 2003; Harper and Lawton 2003, A3).

Furthermore, the United States has been demanding tighter security measures at points of entry into Canada, as well as a more aggressive counterterrorism strategy. Dissatisfaction has reached the point where Canada has been identified as one of the 'nations hospitable to organized crime and terrorism' (Federal Research Division, Library of Congress 2003). Perceptions of Canadian reticence on these issues are being explained in a number of interrelated ways by Washington.

First, Canada is discursively represented as incapable of securing itself due to its 'long borders and coastlines [that] offer many points and methods of entry that facilitate movement to and from various countries, particularly the United States. These factors combine to make Canada a favoured destination for terrorists and international organized crime groups' (ibid., 145). In this manner, geography (in terms of both topography and location) and an implicit reference to demographic limitations (i.e., Canada does not possess the required pool from which to draw personnel) present Canada within the imagination of American policy makers as vulnerable and as requiring additional protection not only to ensure Canadian security, but also, more importantly (because of proximity), to ensure the national security of the United States.

Second, it is argued that the Canadian political, economic, and social conditions encourage penetration by criminal organizations and terrorist groups. For example, it has been asserted that

> as a modern liberal democracy Canada possesses a number of features that make it hospitable to terrorists and international criminals. The Canadian Constitution guarantees rights such as the right to life, liberty, freedom of movement, freedom of speech, protection against unreasonable search and seizure, and protection against arbitrary detention or imprisonment that make it easier for terrorists and international criminals to operate. In addition, a technologically advanced economy and infrastructure facilitate operations and activities as well as providing a myriad of opportunities for abuse. (ibid., 145)

Within this formulation of threat, it is precisely the characteristics that define membership in the grouping of 'civilized' states in dominant Western geopolitical discourses that are being used to construct Canada as a security vulnerability. Ironically, given Canadian performatives of (inter)national identity, it is the American identification of Canada as being *too* 'civilized' that is contributing to the dynamics of the bilateral security problematique. Even with recent moves to harmonize Canadian security policy with American initiatives and to ape the American homeland security organizational infrastructure, the U.S. policy community remains unconvinced that Canada is going far enough to be considered onside.

For example, the analysis of Canada in the report on Nations Hospitable to Organized Crime and Terrorism concludes: 'Canada's new legislative initiatives have the potential to reduce the country's appeal to terrorist organization [*sic*], international organized crime groups and alien smugglers, as well as their ability to operate. However, the economic necessity of expedient movement of persons and goods across the US–Canada border and Canada's *liberal democratic identity* may continue to *limit* the adoption of security measures *necessary* to completely halt the operations of these groups' (ibid., 154; italics added).

The explicit reference to Canadian identity is extremely important here as it is employed to initiate processes of securitization based on an assessment of difference defined by dominant American constructions of threat. Yet this representation is completely contradictory to those in official American geopolitical discourses, which assert that the expansion of liberal democracy is the panacea for all global ills. But instead of interpreting these statements as moves towards the construction of a clearly demarcated 'Otherness' with regard to Canada, from a performative perspective on identity and security, we should make links to broader discourses of the body (politic).

Butler's conceptualization of performativity and the politics of theorizing the gendered and sexed body can be transposed onto states. When binary understandings of male/female and masculine/feminine are infused in dominant conceptualizations of the individual body, these influence representations, meanings, and political possibility in the construction of foreign policy/Foreign Policy in very problematic ways that often exclude particular actors from the exercise of political agency. Thus, from a gender perspective, current representations of Canada in American security discourses can be seen as a resurgence of prior notions of the sexed body (previous to the Industrial Revolution), which constructed a male–female continuum in which females were considered a weaker and less robust version of males (but still faintly male) rather than as an entirely different biological designation based on a clear binary classification system.

The conditions of possibility realized in this discourse mark the 'special relationship' between Canada and the United States. Moreover, the gendered construction of Canada is unique in American geopolitical and geonarcotic discursive practices in the hemisphere. For most Latin American countries, characteristics constructed as difference are mobilized into an Otherness that feminizes these states by way of a binary (rather than a continuum), creating clear boundaries of political inclusion/exclusion that legitimize, in the United States, highly intrusive counternarcotics measures.

Pushing the reproduction of gender further into the American understanding of Canada via queer theory–inspired analyses undertaken by Cynthia Weber, there is also a perceptible unease with which the panoptic mechanisms gaze at the Canadian body politic (Weber 1998; 1999, 1–9, 127–38). On the one hand, the keen cooperation, pro–U.S. policy positions, and desire for further integration among the Canadian security community (including law enforcement, the military, and the intelligence sector) are perceived as exhibiting the same kind of masculine characteristics ingrained in performatives and performances of the American Self in the confrontation with global 'evils.' On the Other hand, the values that have been accepted by American officials as held by the Canadian body politic through a long series of performatives, such as multiculturalism, human rights, secularism, and respect for international law, are seen as too soft, too forgiving, and too feminine. Thus, in the American imagination, Canada appears as transgendered, simultaneously male and female, as extremely masculine in some respects but ultimately too feminine for the new global security environment.

This ambiguity or 'queerness' in its northern neighbour makes the American body politic, which draws from performatives of its own hypermasculinity, extremely uncomfortable. For example, will the proximity to queerness make the United States turn queer? Does having a queer friend eventually make one queer? Will being associated with something queer lead to everyone else thinking you are queer? It also creates a policy conundrum: How can Canada best be disciplined? Here, Canada is too masculine to be (violently) penetrated to the extent that Other countries have been in the name of national security, but too feminine not to be berated and controlled. Given my interpretation, I find Bennett's (2003) portrayal of Canada as a gay man in her column extremely fascinating.

Thus, within American geopolitical and geonarcotic discourses, Canada occupies a unique position, with its performative constitution being located both inside and outside the American Self. Because of the representations of Canada as a naive, weak, and incapable of securing itself from looming dangers, Washington has constructed a relationship in which it feels it has to protect Canada from external threats like criminal organizations and terrorist cells, as well as from Canada's own inability to recognize its own seductive charms, in order to effectively defend itself. This has made it possible for calls from American policy makers (even prior to 9/11) that a North American border system (a Fortress North America) be established, with American officials present at all entry points into Canada, a joint customs union, and a shared visa program, to gather resonance within American homeland security discourses. Recently, these ideas have gained popularity among Canadian elites.

Within Canada an interesting politics shaped by Canadian geopolitical and geonarcotic discourses has developed around this, with discernible splits between the Canadian body politic and the state and business communities. Traditionally, perceived differences vis-à-vis the United States have always been popular with the Canadian body politic. While difference was initially constructed around the nodal point of race, in the contemporary moment it is perceptions of contrasting social policies and security policy outlooks that are used to distinguish Canada from the United States in nationalist discourses. More important, these markers of difference are used performatively to place Canada in a superior moral position. Thus any talk of further integration in the post-NAFTA era is portrayed not just as an assault on Canadian sovereignty but as threatening to erase a distinguishable Canadian identity based on notions of Canada's moral purity. Yet, as Eva Mackey (2002) has noted, this has made it possible at the domestic level for the unrecognized 'feminization of Canada through popular discourse which constructs Canada as a natural, pure, fertile, yet vulnerable woman, constantly defending herself from the more masculine and aggressive hulk of the United States' (2002, 10). As such, maintaining programs like the Marihuana Medical Access Regulations and retaining full control over points of entry into Canada become means by which to spurn unwanted American (sexual) advances.

Canada's own security apparatus, including the military establishment, has strongly advocated even deeper security integration with the United States, while the law enforcement community has consistently sided with American opposition to proposed changes in Canadian drug laws. Signs of solidarity range from the Department of National Defence's lobbying for Canadian participation in the National Missile Defence program to a growing number of reports that the Canadian Security and Intelligence Service (CSIS) and the RCMP have extrajuridically handed over Canadian residents suspected of terrorist activity to American authorities, who in turn have deported them back to their countries of birth, where they have been subject to months of interrogation and torture. J. Marshall Beier (2001) has interpreted the support for this among the Canadian military establishment as embedded in the social dynamics of 'belonging, privileged access [i.e., to technology Canada cannot afford; to information Canada cannot obtain independently; to American decision making], and empowerment'·– dynamics made possible through cooperation with U.S. initiatives and membership in the inner circle of *the* global hegemon, rather than through the dangers posed by credible threats (2001, 48).

Similar work on the culture of law enforcement has not been undertaken in Canada. These concerns, though, along with envy of American colleagues who have more resources (from both state funding and forfeiture seizures), more discretionary power, and a far more aggressive and punitive legal system (in terms of laws and sentencing), appear to strongly influence attitudes towards the United States, as can be inferred from the ways in which members of the law enforcement community talk publicly about criminal activity in Canada.

Specifically, Canadian police forces are constantly publicizing how, unlike their American colleagues, they are hamstrung by a lack of funding and by a legal system that is too lax. This construction of the underempowered police officer has struck a chord with the Canadian public even though crime rates in general have been in decline across the country. For example, Toronto's former police chief, Julian Fantino, has claimed that Canada's justice system promotes a 'life of crime' and that in response, 'we [Canadian police] need a criminal justice system that works more efficiently and effectively to deter people intent on engaging in a life of crime ... In today's reality, in the minds of far too many criminals, gangsters ... crime pays ... Going to court every couple of days is the price of doing business, legal aid is provided, they get bail forever, (and) sentences are discounted like bargain-basement kinds of sales' (Habib 2004). Fantino also argued that a weak criminal justice system was working at cross-purposes to efforts to rebuild Toronto's international reputation as a safe and secure city in the aftermath of SARS.

Previously, Fantino had argued that unlike in the United States, where marijuana grow operators face heavy sentences if convicted, in Canada, 'the sentences that these people [the growers] are receiving in the courts are totally and absolutely inadequate and in no way reflect the seriousness of this particular very serious and difficult crime' (Ljunggren 2003, A18).[15] Yet the legislation initially drafted to decriminalize possession of marijuana also would have increased the maximum sentence for growing marijuana from seven to fourteen years, and the maximum penalty for drug trafficking would have remained a life sentence (Canadian Press 2003e). Also, it had been argued that undercover police officers should be granted the power to break the law while conducting investigations (in what are sometimes referred to as 'reverse stings'). Eventually, the law was changed to grant them this power ('Police Chiefs Push ...' 2001, A7).

Increased security integration and acquiescence to American demands have also been strongly supported by business and political elites, who fear that the failure to stay on side with the United States will have dire economic consequences resulting from tighter Canada–U.S. border controls and a less favourable disposition towards Canadian interests in Washington. For example, Perrin Beatty, a former federal Tory cabinet minister and president of the Canadian Manufacturers and Exporters Association has argued that failure 'to invest the political capital needed' to rectify American anger over Canada's lack of direct participation in the invasion of Iraq had the potential to damage the Canadian economy as upwards of 90 per cent of Canadian exports go to the United States (Whittington 2003b, F4). Hershell Ezrin, chair of GPC International Communications, has argued that 'any change in American buying habits or plans [would hurt Canada]' and that this would occur whether or not the change was brought on 'because of a view of Canada, or because the war is making Americans less likely to make certain purchases, or because security trumps trade as Mr. Cellucci [the American Ambassador] says' (in ibid.). To minimize potential fall-out from differences in opinion, in January 2003 the Canadian Council of Chief Executives proposed a jointly managed North American perimeter in order to appease U.S. security concerns (Canadian Press 2003g). At least publicly Prime Minister Paul Martin was later less than enthusiastic about the proposal.

These warnings and proposals demonstrate that from *the* Canadian perspective, since the start of the Bush administration the rules of the game in the Canada–U.S. relationship have changed. More broadly, the history of the bilateral relationship in the Canadian imagination has been constructed based on an understanding that past disagreements in an issue area will not be transferred to other issue areas (Hilmer and Granatstein 1994). In all fairness, looking at the history of Canadian–American relations, this is not an unreasonable interpretation of the relationship over the course of the twentieth century. A great number of problems between Canada and the United States have been managed without resorting to linkage. However, the current dominant understanding of Canadian elites is that issues are being linked and that failure to stay on side with the Americans in one issue area will be punished in another.[16]

Publicly released documents from government departments (such as Presidential Determination 2003–14) and statements made by American officials – including a series of public lashings by the American ambassador Paul Cellucci regarding Canada's unwillingness to join the Coalition of the Willing – are presented as compelling examples of the national imperative not to stray too far from the Americans' position on security issues.[17] For example, with specific regard to the proposed decriminalization of marijuana possession for amounts under 15 grams, American officials have publicly responded in the following ways:

- John Walters, director of the White House Office of National Drug Control Policy (ONDCP), stated in December 2002 that Canada is 'a dangerous staging area for some of the most potent and dangerous marijuana' and that because people are unaware of how powerful it is, they 'seem to be living with the view of the "reefer madness" of the 1970s' (Moore 2003).
- In May 2003, Walters lambasted the decriminalization of possession, saying it threatened Americans by unleashing a large flow of pot into the United States and by providing funds for terrorists. He also argued that 'you expect your friends to stop the movement of poison into your neighbourhood' and threatened to take dramatic steps to keep Canadian marijuana from entering the United States (Gorrie 2003, H3). He warned that as a result, there would likely be slower traffic at the border and trade losses for Canadian companies ('How Far ...' 2003, A14).
- In May of 2003, U.S. Ambassador to Canada Paul Cellucci warned that if Canada decriminalized marijuana possession there could be delays at the border: 'If the perception is it might be more easy to get marijuana here, then it could lead to some pressure on the border because U.S. Customs immigration officers ... would have their antennae up' (Canadian Press 2003i).
- Jennifer de Vallance, a spokesperson for the ONDCP, contended in July of 2003 that 'clearly any threat to the United States or any potential for an increased amount of marijuana trafficking into the United States will force U.S. officials to take a look at the protective measures they have on the border and if and how they have to increase those measures' (Moore 2003).
- In an interview given at a Detroit drug treatment centre in August 2003, Walters declared that 'the kind of marijuana coming from Canada is essentially the crack of marijuana ... It is dangerous. It is destructive.' He continued that a multibillion-dollar marijuana industry had developed in Canada to distribute drugs to the United States and that 'the problem is the political leadership in Canada has been utterly unable to come to grips with this ... They're talking about legalization while Rome burns' (Canadian Press 2003e).
- In September 2003, Luis Arreaga, the U.S. Consul General for British Columbia, argued that 'two to three billion dollars in marijuana goes south every year' and that firearms and hard drugs flow back into Canada in exchange for the marijuana (Canadian Press 2003m).

• Walters once again voiced Washington's opinion on the inadequacies of Canadian drug law in September 2003 when he claimed 'what Canadian officials tell us is that they have laws on the books that could be used here, but that the Canadian system has developed the practice of not sentencing people to anything approaching serious time unless they committed a violent crime ... So you can set up grows, you can ship drugs, you can be caught, and very little happens to you' (Gillespie 2003).

In light of the heavy American pressure on the Canadian government and the popular perception that this should be perceived as bullying, a small scandal erupted in the early fall of 2003 after details emerged about a closed-door meeting between several Liberal backbench MPs, including Roger Gallaway, Brenda Chamberlain, and Dan McTeague, and U.S. Deputy drug czar Barry Crane regarding Canada's plan to decriminalize marijuana. The MPs claimed that they asked for the meeting so that they could confirm what the consequences of the bill would be in terms of trade and border issues; but reports later surfaced that the real purpose of the discussion had been to ask for more vocal opposition from Washington regarding proposed changes to Canadian drug laws.

An official from the Department of Foreign Affairs and International Trade (DFAIT), who was required to sit in on the exchange, became concerned about the content open for discussion, and detailed in a memo that Chamberlain and others had tried to encourage U.S. officials to apply heavy pressure on the Chrétien government. McTeague's actions in particular seemed to indicate mens rea: he had asked one DFAIT official to leave the room before the discussion began. Thus, he seemed unaware that another DFAIT official was still in the room and taking notes (Laghi 2003c).

The MPs expressed hope that if the public learned that there would be negative consequences to cross-border trade, the government would be forced to abandon the plan for decriminalization. According to the DFAIT official, not only did McTeague convey the impression that only U.S. influence could stop the bill, but he also provided American officials with an internal memo that outlined the weaknesses in the proposed legislation (ibid.).

In response to these revelations, Jack Layton, leader of the New Democratic Party, accused the MPs of gross misconduct and argued that MPs should be going to Canadians for advice, not to Americans

(Layton 2003). Even other members of the Liberal Party tried to distance themselves from these actions, with MP John Godfrey arguing that 'whether it's fair ball to try and use the United States' system to put pressure on the Canadian system seems debatable' (Laghi 2003d). The MPs in question rejected the charges as overblown, as not reflecting the actual events of the meeting, and as an attempt by Chrétien loyalists within the Liberal party to discredit them.

Whatever happened during this discussion, or did not, the controversy and its wider implications both reflect and help constitute what many analysts identify as the overriding question in contemporary Canadian governance: How can Canada appear onside with the United States in Washington while also pursuing independent objectives (domestically, regionally, and globally) in the eyes of the Canadian body politic, which detests any indications of American encroachment on Canadian security policy? For example, Denis Stairs and his colleagues (2003) have argued emphatically that 'it is ... of vital importance for Canadians to understand that the only *real* imperative in Canadian foreign policy is Canada's relationship with the U.S. *All* other Canadian international interests are far behind the importance of maintaining friendly and workable relations with the Americans ... Canada should be more selective in openly expressing differences of opinion with the United States ... and it should restrict those differences to issues that directly threaten Canadian interests' (2003, viii, 18; emphases in original).[18]

If this does indeed become the dominant understanding of the environment within which political choices must be made, the proceeding analysis in this chapter leads to key questions about how this will interplay with hegemonic and counterhegemonic performatives and performances of Canadian national identity.[19] What, then, are the political and ethical implications when Canadian nationalist discourses assume that Canada is inherently different from the United States and shift discussion to whether difference is in the interests of the Canadian state?

Conclusions and Beginnings

In constructing a genealogy of Canada's participation in global drug discourses, this chapter has highlighted the Canadian collective amnesia regarding the key role this country has played in the construction of the global geonarcotics panopticon and the discursive representations that constitute it, as well as how Canadian (inter)national identity has been performatively configured by drawing particular meanings from the dominant practices of geonarcotics. Performatives of Canadian national identity that attempt to mark difference between Canada and the United States in terms of illicit drugs policy obfuscate the mutually constitutive practices that have allowed difference to be identified, categorized, and acted on as indicators of real vulnerabilities that arise from these supposedly different security perspectives. While certainly not the *only* force or the *driving* force, geonarcotics has been a convenient means through which both Canada and the United States have been able to demarcate clear boundaries of territoriality and, more important, identity between each other in the contemporary political context.

In Canada itself, drawing from other discourses of security/identity has made possible 'the construction of Canada as a gendered body, victimized by external and more powerful others, [which] creates a fiction of a homogenous and unified body, an image that elides the way the Canadian nation can victimize internal 'Others' on the basis of race, culture, gender, or class ... [It] creates a national innocence whereby oppressors can be located outside of the body politic of the nation' (Mackey 2002, 12).

This notion of national innocence is remarkable not just in its pervasiveness in Canadian society but also in terms of how it has contributed to international performatives that, as Bennett (2003) and the Federal Research Division, Library of Congress (2003) illustrate, have been accepted as accurate portrayals beyond the territoriality of Canada. As this chapter has shown, the entrenchment of the image of Canada 'the good' and/or 'the cool' partner in terms of the supposed necessities of the Canada–U.S. relationship has been a focus of discussion for some time in Canada. What has received considerably less attention are the power/relations constitutive of these performatives, particularly in terms of cultural diversity, individual liberty, and security *within* the constructed territoriality of Canada. To this end, the following chapters examine the implications of this construction of the Canadian Self with regard to their performances in illicit drugs policy.

4 Race and Illicit Drugs in Canada: From the Opium Den to New Drug Khatastrophes

Introduction: A New Drug Khatastrophe

In October 1999, Abdulkadir Mohamoud, a Somali Canadian, filed a formal complaint over injuries he received during an April 1999 raid by the Toronto police. Suspected of distributing khat, a mild natural amphetamine grown in the horn of Africa, he alleged that after a police tactical unit broke down his door to place him under arrest, he was kicked in the head twice, rendering him unconscious. He was then left on the ground for an hour, hogtied, and had his elbow broken by a police officer who stepped on his restrained arms. The police officers involved never denied that they had caused the injuries, which also included a broken nose; but, according to police officials, Mohamoud had been violent and attempted to escape – a charge later refuted by several civilian eyewitnesses. The drug charges were eventually dropped after several of the officers involved in the arrest were charged under the Police Services Act in unrelated cases of corruption (Rankin 2000, B1).

Mirroring the violence committed by members of the Airborne Regiment serving in Somalia in 1993 that resulted in the murder of a teenage boy named Shidane Arone, Mr Mohamoud's ordeal was a shocking precursor to an escalation in Canadian law enforcement's preoccupation with stemming the distribution and use of khat. In May 1999 the Toronto Police Service initiated sweeping tactical operations targeting suspected khat dealers with raids on private dwellings and physical altercations that drew the ire of the Somali-Canadian community. In a meeting with police, concerns were raised that officers were not identifying themselves during raids, that items other than khat were being seized and not returned, and that search warrants were being signed by justices of the peace from outside of the appropriate jurisdictions. There were also reports of police harassment, intimidation, and abuse.

In July 2001, tempers boiled over during the arrest of a khat dealer in a west-end Toronto shopping plaza. An angry crowd surrounded the police officers and damaged a police cruiser. Witnesses said that the police punched and kicked a man to the ground after he asked if they had a search warrant. Community leaders alleged that the police were consistently harassing Somali Canadians who frequented the plaza and that they were being unfairly profiled. Staff Sergeant Norman Rowntree denied that members of 12 Division were targeting Somali Canadians and stated that 'Black, brown, green, or white, a drug dealer, is a drug dealer, is a drug dealer. I make no apologies' (quoted in Yelaja 2001).[1]

A letter to the editor published the next day in the *Toronto Star* illustrated the ways in which the issues surrounding khat were being constructed by many 'Canadian-Canadians': 'I am outraged that in a *civilized* country such as Canada, anyone would treat officers of the law in such a manner. To assault police officers and throw garbage cans at the very people who protect your rights as a citizen? ... I am also quite amused that someone has allowed this story to be *twisted* from a simple drug bust into some kind of racial targeting by the police ... The Somali community is outraged that the police arrested criminal suspects? Maybe there is some *confusion* as to how the law applies' (Xavier 2001, A23; emphases added).

The representational politics of identity, shaped by a racialized logic of difference, come to the fore in discursive moments like this. Canadians are 'civilized' people who understand how laws are applied and who do not try to manipulate their way around them. Somalis are largely an 'uncivilized' people who lack knowledge of how laws are applied in Canadian society and who try to avoid legal sanctions by playing the race card; it follows that the crux of the problem is that *they* are incapable of recognizing their own criminality. With these representations, it is possible to view the khat issue as an instance where foreign elements in Canadian society were attempting to hold on to a dangerous practice that threatened to undermine *the* Canadian way of life and *the* Canadian identity by defying Canadian norms. Chewing khat became a political challenge that had to be confronted. Yet at the same time, the focus on an illicit drug deflected attention from other issues facing the Somali-Canadian community, including poverty, poor housing, immigration problems, and unemployment, that the state apparatus seemed less interested in addressing.

Somali Canadians are among the most maligned of the new immigrant communities in Canada today. The majority of them arrived fleeing the civil war and political chaos that led to the collapse of the Somali state in the early 1990s. A rather small subpopulation of the Canadian body politic (approximately 80,000), Somali immigrants to Canada tended to concentrate in large urban centres, especially Greater Toronto. As a result, popular perceptions grew that Canada was experiencing a Somali invasion that threatened to undermine the cultural core of Canadian identity.

Traditional critical analyses might be content to highlight the social status of the Somali-Canadian community as the essential condition that has constructed khat as a pressing social problem requiring state intervention; my central contention, however, is that the conditions of possibility for both the marginalization of Somali Canadians and the khat prohibition can be found in the discourses of nationalism, race, culture, religion, and illicit drugs that became dominant in Canada during the early twentieth century.

Critical Multiculturalism and Canadian Identity

Eva Mackey (2002) has argued that formal, practical, and popular efforts to define a Canadian national identity are symptomatic of the belief that a strong nation 'must have a bounded and definable national "culture" and identity, a culture that is distinct and different from all other national cultures' (2002, 11). Thus, while *a* national identity is seen as both desirable and necessary in Canada, the project to construct one is usually perceived by Canadians as an absolute failure given the ongoing 'hyphenation' of Canada linguistically, regionally, and ethnically into sub-groups such as Francophone-Canadians, Western-Canadians, and Pakistani-Canadians. However, echoing David Campbell's (1998) assertion that threats and insecurity are necessary for the maintenance of the nation-state as a political unit, Mackey interprets the reproduction of crisis in dominant narratives of Canada as a strategy to regulate the politics of identity (ibid., 9, 13).

Multiculturalism has been institutionalized in the cultural politics of Canadian identity. As a result, the concept of *the* Canadian nation is structured around white, Anglophone culture, with Others positioned as exotic objects that are the recipients of pluralist and tolerant benevolence (ibid., xix; 2; 5). The term *dominant culture* does not mean that only one particular culture is infused within a specific social environment. Here it refers to 'a selective worldview that is continually being challenged by alternative systems of meaning and belief' (Williams 1980, quoted in ibid., xvii). Dominant cultures are omnipresent and are able to modify themselves in order to absorb counterhegemonic challenges to their position.

Canadian cultural politics does not aim to eliminate Others; it *requires* the presence of Others in order to reaffirm the Canadian self-image of tolerance and plurality, manage relations with Quebec, and differentiate Canada from the United States (ibid., 2, 16). In countries like Australia and Great Britain, multiculturalism is recognized as a break with an overtly racist past and as a means to reflect social transformations initiated by changing demographics; in Canada in sharp contrast, it is seen as reflecting a heritage of tolerance, beginning with the benevolent treatment of indigenous people and special exemptions for French Quebecers. If Canada can be said to have a heritage of tolerance, 'it is a heritage of contradictions, ambiguity, and flexible interpretations [of tolerance]' (ibid., 24). Tolerance is the key word here as it does not imply acceptance of difference but rather that the object in question is somehow deficient and in need of being reformed at some future time (ibid., 162). By historically being able to assume the position of the unmarked core of Canadian identity from which all other identities are classified and coded, white anglophone Canada has become the fulcrum that balances the social space of legitimate political expression and the limits of tolerance.

As a cultural anthropologist, Mackey self-consciously situates her work in the area of 'Whiteness Studies,' a field that examines the subjectivities of people who view themselves as mainstream or normal.[2] In the case of Canada, this refers to people who would describe themselves as 'Canadian-Canadians' (ibid., 3). Given that 'white anglophone' is discursively considered to be ordinary/normal/uncoded, 'it is both constitutive of, and an effect of structural advantage and power, and the cultural authority that culture brings because it is implicitly invoked as the standard by which all the cultural contributions of Others *must* be evaluated' (ibid., 21).

Thus, cultural pluralism is legitimate so long as it is congruent with the project of nation building and does not attempt to disrupt the implicitly established Canadian cultural hierarchy by challenging or appearing to threaten established cultural mores and norms. Changes to the dominant culture must be respectfully requested, not demanded. Permanent tolerance of specific cultural differences, rather than cultures writ large, is entertained, but only in terms of exceptions to the already performatively constituted rules of what is considered to be Canadian (ibid., 66). Other cultures are expected to subordinate themselves to Canadian cultural norms; in instances of incompatibility, the onus is on Other cultures to defer and change their practices.

In the proliferation of New Right discourses in Canada during the 1990s, '"the people" [i.e., white, anglophone, heterosexual Canadians] [were] constructed as a natural and non-political category of authentic citizens who resist the political correctness of radicalized minorities and police the limits of pluralism by employing their common sense' (ibid., 108). Thus the idea of a normalized and uncoded people was deployed to naturalize the exclusion of Others from projects to define the limits of tolerable behaviour, on the basis that these Others had disruptive political agendas and thus were not 'real Canadians' (ibid., 140). In common parlance, 'They do not know how good they have it here; why must they take advantage of our generosity and not respect our culture?' Or 'They have to be Canadian now that they live here.' All of this reflects some of the more dangerous threats (or dragons) from which the Canadian body politic feels it must defend itself.

The power of categories of identity such as white, Western, and liberal is that people who insert themselves into their confines do not think of themselves as ethnic; rather, they see their customs, beliefs, practices, morals, and values as normative and universal (ibid., 157). Other practices and beliefs are thus considered a priori to be inferior, if not deviant; moreover, the degree to which they are inferior/deviant should be measured in terms of how far they stray from Canadian values and culture. Thus, the discursive space that allows for the inclusion or exclusion of particular characteristics as Canadian constitutes one of the performatives of Canadian identity and should be seen as an exercise of foreign policy. The specific policies that address these issues are the performances and can be considered Foreign Policy practices even though they extend beyond the traditional boundaries formed by interstate diplomatic activity.

So instead of treating all cultures on equal ground, Canadian multiculturalism 'promotes the idea of minority cultures as fragments of cultures, constructed from folkloric and culinary remnants ... [which] become conceptually divorced from politics and economics, and become commodified cultural possessions' (ibid., 66). This sort of multiculturalism focuses on 'saris, samosas, and steel bands' in order to diffuse potential 'resistence, rebellion, and rejection' of the dominant white anglophone culture, its values and norms, and its corresponding national identity (ibid., 67). It follows that the scope of tolerable practices of Other cultures must be limited, lest they subvert the ways in which the Canadian Self perceives its own culture and identity. It is specific cultural traits like language, dance, food, and art that mark the traits of Others (i.e., the signifiers), who can still be seen as part of the larger Canadian community of Self (i.e., the signified). The existence of quaint differences in food or dress is what embodies diversity, not the acceptance of Other people as political actors. These minority groups must remain invisible as political communities and individuals; there seems to be an unspoken fear that their interests, beliefs, and identities may not reflect the dominant Canadian culture or identity as it is performatively constituted.

When dominant cultures fear potential challenges to their notions of identity – challenges embodied in alternative forms of life – 'cultural differences when mobilized politically by minorities are seen to threaten and fragment ... the progress of the nation' (ibid., 153). Thus Canadian multiculturalism limits difference to symbolic characteristics; it does not extend to political forms of difference that might challenge the Canadian view of the Self (ibid., 70). In this construction of multiculturalism, 'we have a core Canadian national culture as a "whole way of life" and the multicultures exist as fragments of culture, only valued for the ways in which they contribute to this "whole way of life" of the national culture' (ibid., 67). Difference is recognized as legitimate, but only as an object that allows for the (re)production of the Canadian national identity as civilized, unified, progressive, and tolerant (ibid., 86). When this version of multiculturalism is celebrated, questions about how far Canada needs to go in order to begin accepting diversity and fostering intersubjective understanding are not asked. As a consequence, historical and present day violence undertaken to manage Otherness is erased and forgotten in dominant Canadian discourses of the Self and performatives of Canadian identity.

Early Canadian Nationalism and Race:
The Canada First Movement

Mackey argues that Canada was the product of a political alliance and that therefore the emergence of *a* national identity was not guaranteed. In the aftermath of Confederation, the federal government attempted to create *a* national identity by promoting national cultural, educational, and sports institutions. Even with deliberate federal management, an economic depression, the Riel Rebellion, French-Canadian resistance, and the growing popularity of continentalism all threatened the possibility of ingraining a national identity (ibid., 29). In this turbulent environment the Canada First movement developed as the first manifestation of a fledging Canadian nationalism. Its members included high-ranking politicians, business leaders, academics, and medical practitioners, whose views were often presented in forums and publications organized by the Royal Society of Canada, the Imperial Federation League, and the Empire Club. In sum, the Canada First movement arose within institutions already invested with interpretative authority in Canadian society.

The discourse and politics of representation put forward by the Canada First movement were constitutive of *and* a response to a perceived identity crisis whose resolution was seen to rest in the assertion of Canadian distinctiveness from and superiority to the United States. This discourse was also imbricated within the nascent discipline of geopolitics, which had begun to biologicize global space by combining elements of Darwinism and biomedical discourse in the study of geography (Ó Tuathail 1996, 36–8; 54).

Environmental relativism was the node around which the Canada First movement interpreted the Canadian Self, classified its Others, and established a logic of difference that fixed these identities as stable and self-evident.[3] The main argument of environmental relativism was that national character (i.e., identity) was directly related to climatic conditions – an idea that can be traced back to Montesquieu's travel literature. It was argued that Canadians, as a northern people (like the British) facing a cold and harsh climate, by definition possessed the virtues of energy, strength, self-reliance, health, and purity that made freedom and liberty possible. One doctor at the time commented that the climate was favourable to the development of a highly intelligent people who 'will be taller, straighter, leaner people – hair darker and drier and coarser; muscles more tendinous and prominent and less cushioned' (Berger 1970, 129). The hyperbole of a superior Canadian race was almost limitless; Governor General Dufferin remarked that 'a constitution nursed upon the oxygen of our bright winter atmosphere makes its owner feel as though he could toss about the pine trees in his glee' (in ibid., 129).

Canada as *a* northern race was deemed to be homogeneous because the racial lineage of English and French Canadians could be traced back to the same Scandinavian roots prior to the Norman Conquest of 1066. Thus the Canada First movement attributed all of these same characteristics to French Canadians and ignored existing cultural conflicts. Moreover, as a hedge, it was predicted that Canada's French population would decline and eventually be completely subsumed. Note that indigenous people, who had lived in the Canadian climate for thousands of years, were left out of discussions of *a* northern race.

In contrast, the character of southern countries – including the United States – was associated with decay, effeminacy, sexual deviancy, and disease, all of which predisposed these social entities to tyranny. Moreover, the United States was viewed as a heterogenous collection of southern races (e.g., Americans proper, African Americans, Southern European immigrants), providing further evidence of its inferiority. Sir Andrew Macphail, editor of the *Canadian Medical Journal* and a member of the Canada First movement, argued that 'whenever races are mixed the lower always prevails' (in ibid., 151).

The Canada First movement also believed that Canada's northern climate would ensure that Darwinian processes of natural selection would keep undesirable races from being able to flourish here, which would help Canada avoid the problems of racial pluralism that confronted the United States. Yet as Canada the geographic entity began to extend westward, and as the country's material needs accelerated, the popular perception became that large increases in immigration were necessary to sustain growth. At the same time, it was becoming clear that immigration flows from the United Kingdom would not be sufficient to meet these needs. The health of Canadian society, then, rested on what were constructed as two contradictory needs: growth and homogeneity.

Thus the dilemma was how to meet the increased need for immigrants without upsetting the demographic balance that contributed to the Canadian imagined community as envisioned by the Canada First movement. Given that the United States was presented in popular Canadian nationalist discourses as an example of the degenerative impacts of a mixture of southern races, controversy arose over whether to admit southern Europeans into Canada. Canadian immigration policy to a certain extent was guided by pragmatism, and it initiated an influx of southern Europeans into the country. However, between 1910 and 1953 the immigration law was also used to exclude nonwhites on the basis that the climate would not suit them.[4] Furthermore, a 1919 amendment to the immigration law situated cultural unsuitability, defined as 'peculiar customs, habits, modes of life and methods of holding property ... and probable inability to become readily assimilated' as a legitimate reason to prevent entry (in Mackey 2002, 33).

The Canada First movement was symbolic of *and* constitutive of a social and political environment in Canada which held that a national identity must be carved out using a logic of difference grounded in racial classifications. Race was a nodal point around which *any* and *all* differences between Self and Other could be mapped. The invocation of *the* Canadian identity today utilizes performatives that together construct a history of tolerance; yet forms of racism have served as the foundations for formal, practical, and popular Canadian nationalist discourses. At the turn of the twentieth century it was perfectly acceptable for media commentators to express bald hatred towards racial minorities. For example, in 1907 the *Edmonton Journal* printed an exposé on Vancouver's Chinatown that began as follows: 'Let not the sympathy of the tenderhearted be aroused by these poor Chinks. They do not live like rats from the force of circumstances. They prefer the stench and filth of their vile surroundings. They prefer the squalor because it is cheaper to live in filth than in cleanliness' (in Gray 1972, 44).

Race and the Limits of Diversity

During the nineteenth century, the knowledge and ability to successfully treat the underlying causes of many ailments had not yet been discovered. Thus, physicians themselves regularly prescribed drugs like morphine, heroin, and cocaine for a wide variety of ills in order to alleviate their painful manifestations. The potential for addiction to these substances was recognized but seems to have been outweighed by the potential benefits. Thus addiction was seen as an unfortunate consequence of prolonged exposure to these substances, something that one would not wish on anyone, but at the same time, not a threat to people or to society at large. Martin Booth (1996) notes that medical textbooks did not even refer to drug addiction until 1900, and not as a medical concern until 1910, fifty years after morphine injections had become a standard practice (1996, 76). For most of the Victorian era in Canada, consuming drugs was neither uncommon nor socially stigmatizing, inside and outside of medical supervision.

However, in contrast to the mainstream use of morphine, heroin, and cocaine, opium smoking was closely identified with Chinese labourers and immigrants, who began immigrating to Canada during the 1850s, a time of severe labour shortages in the West. Public disapproval of opium arose not from the effects of the drug itself, but rather from its association with a group perceived as biologically and culturally inferior. In 1885, despite the need for labour, public pressure to fix the 'Chinese Problem' led the government to impose a $50 head tax on all Chinese migrant workers entering Canada. The tax was raised several times over the years, until by 1904 it stood at $500 (Boyd 1984, 106–10).

In 1885 the Royal Commission to Inquire into the Subject of Chinese Immigration into the Province of British Columbia contended that opium smoking was a pagan practice incompatible with the lifestyle of a Christian nation (Senate 2002c, 252). Ironically while opium had been known and used in China since at least the seventh century, the practice of smoking it had been introduced there by Westerners (1996, 105–6). The same inquiry also heard that crime was very common among the Chinese but that efforts to arrest Chinese offenders were stymied by the fact that 'they are so much alike' that perpetrators could easily disappear into the crowd in Chinatown and avoid detection (Giffen, Endicott, and Lambert 1991, 64). During the 1902 Royal Commission to Inquire into the Subject of Chinese and Japanese Immigration into the Province of British Columbia, one public health physician testified that opium smoking made the Chinese potential carriers of infectious disease (ibid., 60). However, as long as opium use was largely confined to the Chinese community, it was not considered a problem requiring state intervention.

After the September 1907 race riot in Vancouver organized by the Asiatic Exclusion League and municipal politicians, the federal government stepped in and offered to compensate some victims for the destruction of their property. It undertook an investigation to assess how much compensation it should offer. Initially only people of Japanese descent were to receive any compensation for damages because the Japanese were considered to be somewhat civilized; the perception was that they appreciated high Western culture such as classical music and art.[5] Eventually, because the damage to Asian neighbourhoods had been so devastating, the compensation mandate was extended to the Chinese.

During on-site investigations led by William Lyon Mackenzie King, reports began to circulate that whites – particularly white women – were being enticed into using opium, thereby contributing to an 'unnatural mixing of races.' Given the social mores of the time, sexual activity had to be hinted at rather than explicitly stated. For example, a newspaper article that has been identified as one of the catalysts for the opium prohibition was printed under the headline 'What Opium Does: Young British Columbia Girl Found among Chinese.' It reported that a teenage girl of 'respectable parentage' had been found in a Chinese house with 'Chinamen' and with an 'opium smoking outfit' beside her. Vancouver's police chief was quoted in the article as saying, 'To think that Chinese and Hindus can debase and degrade our women like that ... Every time I think of it, my blood boils' (Giffen, Endicott, and Lambert 1991, 62).[6]

Curtis Marez (2004) has argued that the constellation of meaning created by the tying together of Otherness and sexuality in the real and metaphorical space of the opium den fit into a broader global narrative on race that sought to hide the dynamics of Euro-Asian relations. For example, 'white expressions of racial disgust deny ... intimacy with imperial interests in Asia by constructing the Chinese as absolutely foreign ... [and the] fascination with the absolute difference between whites and non-whites diverted attention away from the unequal economic and political relationships that bound them together' (2004, 64). Marez argues that 'by making whites – especially women – the people who ultimately pay for the opium trade, this set of narratives imaginatively inverts the ruthlessly hierarchical relations that defined [the domination of Asia]. Whereas historically Britain had used military force to promote the opium traffic into China, these stories depict the Chinese as a source of a contagious vice that threatens English or "Anglo-Saxon" racial integrity ... The imaginary Chinese threat to white women helped to partly eclipse criticism of ... imperialism' (ibid., 66).

Opium was being discursively constructed as a catalyst for the corruption of Canadian women by Chinese men. Hence, by representational definition, its use had to be stopped. Even the Anti-Opium League, comprised of the community's leading Chinese business owners, pressured the government for action to curb opium use among all Canadians – a point noted by Mackenzie King who would later employ their views to justify prohibiting the opium trade. It remains unclear why the Chinese merchants formed an Anti-Opium League. Nor is it clear why they called for a prohibition of opium. Did they believe it was dangerous? Or was this position a political move to demonstrate their willingness to be integrated into Canadian society?

Regardless, Mackenzie King quickly drafted the Report on the Need for the Suppression of Opium Traffic in Canada. Within a month of its release, Canada had passed federal legislation prohibiting the importation, sale, and manufacture of opium for non-medical purposes, becoming one of the first Western countries to enact anti-opium legislation. Opium use and possession were criminalized in 1911 with the passage of the Opium and Drug Act. Subsequent amendments reduced the legitimate scope of medical opium, increased penalties, increased police powers of search and seizure, and added drugs like cocaine and marijuana to the list of prohibited substances.[7]

It is important to remember that the publicly stated rationale for the Opium Act (1908), the legislation that made further acts possible, did not have to do with the potentially harmful effects of opium. Rather, it was based on reports of the narcotic's 'dire influence' – specifically, on reports that young white women had been found in an opium den (Boyd 1984, 115). The irony is that the compensation process – a process that could be interpreted as intended to strengthen social relations between the Canadian Self and Other – ended up initiating legislation that specifically targeted the groups to which the federal government was supposedly making amends. For example, in 1921, out of 1,864 drug offences in Canada, 1,211 implicated Chinese Canadians (Chapman 1979, 103; Solomon and Green 1988, 99).

Canadian identity at the time rested on ideas of racial superiority. Since opium smoking was the activity of Chinese inferiors, it became an easy target in that it represented practices (i.e., opium smoking and the repression of opium smoking) that easily differentiated the Self from the Other (Boyd 1984, 115–16). Furthermore, the prohibition process facilitated the categorization of two types of Chinese Canadians: those, like the members of the Anti-Opium League, who had the potential to become partially Canadian by adopting Canadian practices and values, and those who were incapable of abandoning vile and dangerous habits.[8] In this way, it was possible to blame the failure of members of the Chinese community to integrate into Canadian society on the Chinese themselves; after all, it was *they* who were unwilling to follow *Canadian* practices. For a time, this left unproblematized the level of drug use in 'proper' Canadian society. For example, during the First World War, Canadian soldiers had a reputation as drug users; according to English newspaper reports, they introduced cocaine to their British counterparts (Chapman 1979, 100). Between 1912 and 1919, legal imports of cocaine to Canada jumped from 35 ounces to 13,333. Morphine imports increased from 1,523 ounces to 30,087 between 1907 and 1919 (ibid., 99). This, though, may also be a reflection of the strict drug laws newly enacted in the United States and the use of Canada as a staging point for smuggling.

The use of drugs by Canadian Canadians became a growing concern after the First World War. Alcohol prohibition at the provincial level became commonplace, though not universal, and illicit drug use was presented as a potential plague in sensationalist newspaper accounts. This coverage may have reflected an increase in drug use in Canada; however, the numbers are less important than the growing prevalence of the *interpretation* of drugs as a threat and the growing awareness of the prominent role that drugs played in late-Victorian society.

In the 1920s, with the publication of her *Maclean's Magazine* articles and her book *The Black Candle*, judge Emily Murphy contributed strongly to the racial discourse around drugs. In discussing the supposedly racial dynamics of the drug industry, Murphy argued that

> it is hardly credible that the average Chinese peddler has any definite idea in his mind of bringing about the downfall of the white race, his swaying motive probably being that of greed, but in the hands of his superiors, he may become a powerful instrument to this very end. In discussing this subject, Major Crehan of British Columbia has pointed out that whatever their motive, the traffic always comes with the Oriental, and that one would therefore be justified in assuming that it was their desire to injure the bright-browed races of the world.' (Murphy 1922, 188)

Moreover, Murphy believed that

> some of the Negroes coming into Canada, and they are no fiddle-faddle fellows either, have similar ideas (the overthrow of the white race), and one of their greatest writers has boasted how ultimately they will control white men. Many of these Negroes are law-abiding and altogether estimable, but contrariwise, many are obstinately wicked persons, earning their livelihood as free-ranging peddlers of poisonous drugs. (Murphy 1922, 189)

She saw the drug trade as a conspiracy to lower the health of the Canadian body politic, a body politic that physically, mentally, and morally was demonstrably superior to these southern races. In the context of Canadian identity at the time, illicit drug use was a threat in that it constituted political acts of defiance against the progress and modernization of *the* Canadian people. Murphy did not differentiate the effects of various drugs; for her, they all led to moral degeneration, crime, physical and mental deterioration, disease, intellectual and spiritual voids, and material loss (Boyd 1984, 129–30). In sum, she represented drugs as the path to becoming uncivilized.

Another key concern for Murphy was the fate of Canadian women and girls (i.e., white, Anglo-Saxon, Christian females) who were being reduced to drug addiction and consequently, prostitution through the efforts of Chinese and 'Negro' peddlers. She contended that as prostitutes, these women and girls would infect Canada's male population with social diseases. For shock value (one can assume), the *Black Candle* provides several photographs of bedroom poses of Canadian women with their 'foreign' partners. According to Chapman, this concern with female drug use can also be linked to fears about the downgrading of what was known at the time as 'domestic virtue,' a key aspect of the highly gendered Canadian way of life. Formal and popular discourses of the time 'expounded the maternal nature of women ... piously elevat[ing] the service which women tendered to home and family to a wholesome social virtue' (Chapman 1979, 98). As part of efforts to protect women from the temptations of drugs, which were represented by Murphy and others as the first step towards prostitution, social regulation went as far as to prevent Canadian women from living in or close to Vancouver's Chinatown (ibid., 98).

Clearly, the discursive relations of race and identity created a nexus of meaning that constructed drug use as an activity partaken mainly by inferior racial Others, who were represented as contagions within the Canadian body politic. Drug use was something that no self-respecting proper Canadian would engage in unless completely degenerate or unwittingly duped. Work and sobriety were natural traits of the Canadian race; they ensured productivity and the continuing superiority of white Anglo-Saxons (Senate 2002c, 249).

Despite the increase in police powers, the circumscribing of traditional medical privilege, and the broadening of the range of prohibited substances, the number of drug convictions had fallen by the end of the 1920s to about two hundred a year, after peaking in the early 1920s. According to Solomon and Green (1988), 'probably the most important factor in this decline was the dying out of the older generations of Chinese opium smokers who had provided the bulk of the offenders' (1988, 99; see also Chapman 1979, 103). They also point to the 1923 prohibition against Chinese immigration, the deportation of five hundred convicted Chinese offenders during the 1920s, and reduced public interest as decisive factors (Solomon and Green 1988, 99). Yet the fear that Canadian virtue could be undermined by Others continued even as the number of arrests for drug offences dropped over the course of the 1920s. Thus, the construction of drug use as both foreign and imminently threatening lingered.

The Social Gospel and the Regulation of the Canadian Body Politic

In understanding how racial discourses made it possible for opium and other drugs to be represented as threats to the identity and health of the Canadian Self, and for state power to be used to define and enforce the limits of tolerable behaviour, it is also important to examine the discourses of the social gospel movement in Canada at the time. The haste with which legislation was enacted and the expanding scope of successive acts were made possible by a constellation of racial and evangelical discourses that imbued drug use with a series of meanings that constructed prohibition as a technology for upholding the sanctity and sacredness of Canadian society.

The social gospel movement emerged as a response to challenges posed to Christianity by Darwin's theory of evolution, long-standing debates over the meanings of redemption and reform, and deep transformations in Canadian society resulting from industrialization, urbanization, and the social disjunctures of capitalism. According to Ramsey Cook (1985), it marked the 'union of the sacred and the secular, of Christianity and "progressive civilization," sanctified by theological liberalism' (1985, 195). In its most fully developed version, the social gospel insisted that

the principal, perhaps the only, goal of Christianity was the reform of society, the building of the Kingdom of God on earth. It is important to emphasize that the social gospel was more radical in its religious implications than merely a social reform movement inspired by religious ideals. Social action had always been seen as a religious duty but it had always been insisted that individual salvation would have to precede social regeneration. However, the social gospel reversed the order of regeneration: society rather than the individual became the object of salvation. (ibid., 176)

Discursively, the social gospel movement connected proposed social reforms with the religious heritage of the nation, 'endowing reform with an authority it could not otherwise command' (Allen 1975, 45). The policies it advocated to achieve moral and social improvement included woman suffrage, alcohol prohibition, the regulation of working conditions, and keeping Sunday as a mandatory day of rest. All of these would require state action (Cook 1985, 137). In this social context, the role of the church was transformed: 'The social gospel tended to justify or even compel a church's interference in politics. If society were capable of regeneration along Christian lines, a heavy responsibility rested with the churches to employ every means in bringing this about. To those firmly imbued with the reforming vision, traditional methods of teaching and preaching appeared too slow. Legislation and government activity represented the obvious method of implementing large scale reform' (Forbes 1975, 65).

The social gospel movement discursively represented alcohol as a social ill responsible for crime, disease, poverty, physical injury, and the breakdown of the Canadian family. The use of other drugs was a secondary part of the social gospel platform. Even so, the social gospel could mobilize public opinion over drugs and harness moral outrage in order to reform Canadian society. For example, during the Montreal cocaine scare of 1910–11, launched by a probation officer who claimed to have met fifty to sixty children in one day who were cocaine habitués, the Children's Aid Society of Montreal released this statement: 'The cocaine habit must be stamped out of Canada. It is undermining our boyhood and cutting away the moral fibre of our girls. It is turning our people into criminals and imbeciles ... Will YOU help the Children's Aid Society fight cocaine? You can do so by asking your clergyman to preach about it, by writing to your member of parliament, or by many other methods' (quoted in Murray 1987, 35).

The social gospel should be seen as an important element of the discursive relations of early Canadian responses to drug use. Four important aspects of the social gospel intertwined with other discourses and enabled drug use and drug users to be inscribed with undesirable meanings. First, the social gospel provided a moral basis for attacking drug use: core values within the discourse were a strong work ethic, domestic virtue, and a deep suspicion of anything that brought corporeal pleasure, all of which dovetailed with notions of Canadians as *the* superior northern race. Thus, the industriousness and health of the individual body became subject to a moral code that, because of its importance to the larger body politic, should be a matter of individual obedience based not on choice but rather on the state imposition of proscribed limits to individual behaviour. For example, Mackenzie King himself proclaimed in 1908 that 'in enacting legislation to this end [i.e., the Opium Act], the Parliament of Canada will not only effect one of the most necessary moral reforms so far as the Dominion is concerned, but will assist in a world movement which has for its object the freeing of a people from a bondage worse than slavery' (in Green 1979, 46).

Second, while it emphasized societal transformation, the social gospel made it possible to conceptualize and implement proactive and overt controls on individuals in order to achieve social goals. Third, in doing so, the social gospel provided an impetus for linking moral deficiencies to dangerous criminal activity in order to implicate the state in the regeneration of Canadian society and the achievement of 'heaven on Earth.' Fourth, the social gospel linked individual and social regeneration with Protestantism and early social science. This relationship transformed the character of morality from one based solely on religious authority to one based on religious authority *and* backed by 'scientific' evidence of the deleterious effects of immorality on the health of the nation.[9]

Biopolitics and Governmentality in the Early Securitization of Drugs

Drugs were reinterpreted at the beginning of the last century in terms of a discourse of Canadian nationalism that was anchored in a particular conception of race and the discourse of the social gospel movement. This created new spaces for the state to impose control on the individual body. Both the production of drugs as threat and the instability of this construction are apparent. These discourses produced what *had* to be secured: *the* Canadian national identity, which drew from a classificatory scheme to position white–anglophone–protestant Canadians at the top of the racial hierarchy. In essence, the characteristics said to be inherent in this identity – energy, strength, self-reliance, health, purity – were prerequisites for the freedom and liberty of the Canadian body politic. Yet even though these attributes had been naturalized among Canadian Canadians, they were perceived as fragile and capable of being corrupted and depleted. Thus, the Canadian body politic had to be protected vigorously from what were represented as the insidious practices of southern races. At this juncture, a racialized view of the Self, insecurity over the strength of Canada's national character, and a fear of moral, physical, and spiritual contagions embodied in and practised by racially inferior Others provided the discursive space to code particular drugs as a threat.

Yet the rapidly expanding scope of government involvement in securing the Canadian body politic from illicit drugs and illicit drug use was not inevitable. The ethos of social regulation that constituted the backbone of the social gospel discourse made a state response possible by linking individual morality to the exercise of state power, and by doing so in ways that drew from roles the state was already playing. This is why it was imperative that drug use be linked to the security of the Canadian nation. Again, the discourses of the social gospel movement did not declare that the Canadian state must act this way, but they made it possible for such a response to be understood as necessary.

For example, alcohol prohibition was not adopted federally until March 1918, and even then only as a temporary order-in-council based on powers contained within the War Measures Act. (Some provinces, though, had local prohibition legislation in place before the order-in-council was made.) The order-in-council was replaced in November 1919 by the Canada Temperance Act, which did not prohibit alcohol consumption but made it illegal to ship alcohol into provinces that were dry. However, as part of the act, all dry provinces were required to resubmit prohibition to provincial plebiscite (Gray 1972, 104–8).

In Foucauldian terms, these responses to drug use in Canada exhibited a concern with biopolitics exercised through practices of governmentality. Governmentality arose in the eighteenth century in western Europe as the ultimate objective of government shifted: no longer was the purpose of government to aggrandize the state; the view now was that the population was an instrument that must be mastered through knowledge of political economy and apparatuses of security if the people were to be governed effectively (Foucault 2003b, 244). Governmentality required that a novel series of apparatuses and complexes of knowledge be developed in order to improve the welfare, living conditions, health, wealth, and longevity of the population. In this context of shifting priorities of governance, biopolitics refers to those endeavours which attempt to rationalize the problems presented to governmental practice by the phenomena characteristics of living human beings constituted as a population (Rabinow and Rose 2003, xxix).

Thus biopolitics provided an answer to the question of 'why must one govern' that was being raised at a time when economic and political liberalism was being entrenched in Western societies (Foucault 2003a, 204). According to Foucault, within this reconfigurement of the ethos of government, one can see 'in the rationality of biopolitics, [that] the new object is life and its regulation of its mechanisms' (Rabinow and Rose 2003, xxix). This rationality was clear in the introductory statement to the Opium and Drug Act that Mackenzie King made before Parliament: 'The first of all resources to be conserved are the health and life, moral as well as physical of *our* people, and it is to keep these intact, and to help to build up in Canada a strong happy, and a moral people, that the government brings forward this legislation, and does so in the belief that it will pass the House without any opposition' (in Chapman 1979, 97; italics added).

The imperative, then, is to gain knowledge of mechanisms and to forge technologies and institutions to achieve the regulation of everyday life in order to promote efficiency and rationalization, thereby maximizing gains and minimizing costs. Early in the twentieth century in Canada, much of the emphasis from a public policy standpoint was on (a) public sanitation to stem the spread of disease and (b) the institutionalization of the insane (see Cassel 1994, 132–64). Very rapidly, though, the imperative expanded to include the normalization of all individual conduct. Fostering (moral) life through the social regulation of *all* activity, no matter how seemingly minor, became the agenda of governments (Foucault 2003a, 2003b).

It is under the rubric of biopolitics that one can locate the discursive relations constituted by the Canada First movement (as a discourse anchored by race) and the social gospel movement (as a discourse of social regeneration through state action). Both were central to the securitization of drugs at the beginning of the twentieth century in Canada. The biopolitical apparatus pertinent to this historical accident continues to resonate in present-day responses to illicit drug use.[10]

The New Right, New Racism, and Contemporary Canadian Biopolitics

With the emergence of communicable diseases like AIDS and SARS, the identification of syndromes like ADHD, and a new concern with obesity in children, it is not very difficult to demonstrate that biopolitics continues to play a central role in the regulation of Canadian society. Despite the contingent construction of the illicit drug threat early last century, these interpretations have both persisted and hardened to the point where the supposed dangers of illicit drugs and the characteristics of those who produce and/or consume them are taken to be self-apparent and commonsensical.

Many of the same meanings and representations have coalesced within contemporary discursive relations around illicit drugs, but the discourses themselves that constitute these relations have changed. The regime of truth about illicit drugs and drug users that has been created has been concretized, allowing for the ongoing securitization of illicit drugs. The regime of truth has become so ingrained that despite the appearance of new discourses on race and governance, it has managed to sustain itself with little difficulty. Yet solid foundations for the dominant representations and meanings attached to illicit drugs and drug users remain elusive and must continually be invoked in order to provide the illusion that they are indisputable. This contradictory coexistence of entrenchment and contingency can be seen in the reaction to the use of khat by the Somali-Canadian community in the 1990s.

The Canada First movement made use of a discourse that centred on a conception of race in the biological sense. Contemporary nationalist discourses draw from the superiority of Canadian political culture, especially the notion that Canada is among the most tolerant societies in the world (if not *the* most tolerant), with a long tradition of accepting Otherness. Thus, Mackey (2002) has argued that 'new racism' – or what might be better labelled cultural racism – has 'shifted from crude notions of biological inferiority and superiority to a language that excludes by using concepts of national culture and identity' (2002, 8).

This new racism can be found in formal, practical, and popular discourses. It is present in contemporary geopolitical writings that unabashedly and unreflexively tout the virtues of Western political, economic, and social systems. It is also present in practical American post-9/11 geopolitical discourses, which divide the world into allies and enemies, as well as in discourses of sovereignty and of development (Dauphineé 2003). New racism is able to avoid being recognized as racism because the terms of its discourse are nationhood, patriotism, and nationalism rather than physiological characteristics (Mackey 2002, 8). Eugenics and notions of racial stock have been dropped; instead, the objects that the discourse of new racism describes, classifies, and performatively creates (i.e., various human collectivities) are constituted based on a hierarchy of culture whereby Western European traditions are represented as the acme of civilization and all other cultures are evaluated based on how closely their practices resemble Western ones. Who occupies which rungs on the ladder has remained essentially the same. Thus, within Canada, where the previous biopolitical concern was on how to prevent the intermixing races through practices like immigration barriers or segregation, the emphasis is now on facilitating processes of acculturation in order to ensure that foreigners become significantly Canadian. Tolerated are differences that are interpreted as not threatening the core of Canadian identity, such as those relating to food or dance; practices that are perceived as political and thus insubordinate are viewed as threats to Canada's social fabric.

Related to new racism has been the rise of New Right political ideology in countries like Canada, the United States, Great Britain, and Australia. The New Right political outlook combines classical economic liberalism, social conservatism, and in many cases fundamentalist Christian doctrine, to argue for the promotion of free markets and a return to 'family values.' New Right discourses offer a commonsense notion of 'who we are' – a move that defines the limits of pluralism by restricting what can be embodied within this notion of the 'we.'

The neoclassical liberalism embedded in the New Right political discourse has provided justification for the contraction of state redistributive practices and of budgets for programs like welfare, health care, and education spending. At the same time, there has been a double movement towards a more interventionist state in terms of law enforcement. As Mark Heeler (2003) has argued, within the discourses of the New Right crime has been constructed as a phenomena that is 'remorselessly rising' (2003, 17). The New Right law-and-order discourse is not seen as a socially constructed concept; rather, it draws from scientific realism to argue that certain acts are criminal by their very nature. Interestingly, this discourse also draws from notions of common sense in defining particular acts as deviant and in arguing that the only way to deal with deviant behaviour is to punish it. As Heeler notes, for leading proponents of this position such as J.Q. Wilson, 'crime is simply seen as an "evil" requiring a vigorous and concentrated response,' thereby necessitating the use of 'social control models and a clear distinction between criminals and non-criminals' (ibid., 20). Rehabilitative models that construct offenders as products of other social ills who require treatment have been abandoned in New

Right discourses; the emphasis now is on 'the individualistic nature of offending' and its protective and deterrent effects of harsh punishment (ibid., 20).

Returning to the New Drug Khatastrophe

Like most newcomers before them, Somali Canadians have faced ongoing suspicions about the character of their community as well as the various forms of discrimination that arise from this type of distrust. Many of the accusations levelled at the Somali-Canadian community are the inevitable cultural products of the circumstance that they have come to Canada from an anarchical society devoid of law and order. This was how their country was often described during Canada's military involvement there in the early 1990s.

The Somali-Canadian community has also been accused of containing a large number of welfare cheats and false refugee claimants. In part, these accusations were spurred by reports that the wife of a Somali warlord was collecting multiple welfare cheques in Toronto. Thus, Somali Canadians have been tainted with a reputation for ongoing criminality. They have also been blamed for depressing property values in the neighbourhoods where they have settled because of what have been represented as specific cultural practices, including congregating around storefronts and living in large, extended families. The community has also been denounced for bringing the political problems of their homeland to Canada and for supporting warlordism. Many Somali Canadians are Muslim, and this has also contributed to their alienation.

The Canada First movement found particular groups to be unsuitable based on climate. Contemporary discourses of Canadian nationalism and identity focus on cultural suitability. The dilemma for the Canadian state has become how to manage differences (both real and perceived) between the Somali-Canadian community and Canadian society writ large. Canada's identity as a tolerant, pluralist, and multicultural nation makes overt forms of discrimination or assimilation unviable. These moves are now possible as a result of recent antiterrorism legislation, yet it is still difficult to deport individuals without reason, overtly segregate them, or deny Somali Canadians their constitutional rights and privileges on a whim. However, the continuing preoccupation with biopolitics made possible by the discourses of new racism and the New Right have presented an imperative to acculturate

Somali Canadians while protecting the boundaries of the identity of the Canadian Self. In this context, we can see the prohibition of khat as a response to the perceived threat posed by the (deviant) Somali Other.

Khat (properly pronounced *gut*) refers to the leaves and young shoots of *Catha edulis*, an evergreen shrub grown in Yemen, Kenya, and Ethiopia. It has been chewed by people in East Africa and the Arabian Peninsula for centuries, both for its medicinal properties and for pleasure. The active ingredient in khat leaves is cathinone, an unstable chemical stimulant that begins to lose its potency within forty-eight hours of being picked. Thus, freshly harvested leaves are highly valued. Khat also contains cathine, another stimulant that does not lose its potency after harvesting (DEA 2002).

The effects of chewing khat are very similar to those of stimulants like coffee or amphetamines: energy, clarity, suppressed appetite, pleasure, euphoria, and alertness. Advocates of khat use contend that it provides relief from symptoms of diabetes, asthma, and gastrointestinal disorders. More important, khat chewing is considered a facilitator of communication and social interaction. During chewing sessions, community members come together to discuss matters of interest, catalysing community building and social integration. This has led to parallels being drawn with the (ideal) use of alcohol in Western societies. In many East African communities, chewing khat is an important ritual for building friendships and mutual trust.

In Somalia, khat chewing was historically an activity reserved for Sufi mystics. Then, in the late 1940s, it began to gain popularity with urban and secular groups. British colonial authorities in Somalia tried to eliminate the practice, which they saw as backward and counterproductive. In response, khat chewing became a means of protest and a symbol of Somalis' refusal to accept British colonial authority. The anti-imperialist symbolism may have faded; even so, it is estimated that 80 to 85 per cent of Somali men chew khat more than once a week and 50 to 60 per cent of Somali women do the same. Khat chewing is interpreted by many within the community as an important aspect of Somali culture (Bali 1997).

Khat gained attention in Canada after an article first published in the *Washington Post* appeared in the *Toronto Star* in 1990. It described a visit to Yemen by then Secretary of State James Baker. The article reported how Baker, an occasional tobacco chewer, refused an offer to chew some khat because the substance was illegal in the United States (cathine had been added to the prohibited drug schedule in 1988).[11] It went on to describe khat as a 'mildly narcotic leaf' that 'functions as a basic forum for social intercourse where business deals are consummated, marriages are brokered, and political bonds are sealed.' The article concluded by stating that in Yemen, some households spend over half of their monthly income on khat ('A Day of Chewing Khat' 1990).

In 1992, khat was mentioned again in the *Toronto Star*, under the headline 'Yemen Makes a Habit of High Living.' The article went on to describe how khat chewing had become part of daily life for most Yemenis. The focus of the article, though, was the cost of khat chewing to Yemen's economy, estimated at $5 billion per year plus 'the staggering amount of person-hours' arising from the fact that 'it often seems that the entire day in Yemen revolves around qat,' with five or six hours a day dedicated to chewing (Hundley 1992).

With the UN's 1992 intervention into the civil war in Somalia and with the deployment of Canadian and American troops there, khat was propelled into the global spotlight. It was reported that Pentagon planners were unprepared for the 'khat factor' and that 'it is hard to determine what US soldiers ought to do when confronted with an armed man who has just consumed the equivalent of six cups of espresso' (US News and World Report 1992). More importantly, furthering representations of khat as dangerous, the drug was routinely referenced in chilling descriptions of Somali militia members and devastated cityscapes:

> Baidoba now plays hellish host to uncounted thousands of starving Somalis who have fled a countryside barren of food after three consecutive years of drought, and who await death in its gutted buildings or in tiny makeshift huts of brambles and pieces of tin. Small fires lit from twigs or garbage burn for evening warmth, casting an acrid-smelling haze down desolate alleys once thriving with cafes, shops, and market stalls. And through that eerie scene saunter boys and young men, dazed by an amphetamine-like drug called khat, shouldering weapons with which they wage battles for control of stolen food and aid supplies. (Wallace 1992, 21)

Echoing the post-apocalyptic tone of most media representations of the Somali civil war, *The Economist* described the scene as being 'ruled by roving gunman in their aviator sunglasses, high on the intoxication weed khat.' *US News & World Report* provided the following portrait:

Heavily armed fighters wander through Mogadishu's desolate streets, striking elaborate Rambo or Chuck Norris poses and firing their Kalashnikovs or G-3 rifles from behind shattered walls and doorways. One or two blocks away, their opponents do exactly the same thing. Most of these warriors have been chewing khat ... a leaf containing a mild amphetamine that is smuggled in daily by plane from Kenya. From time to time, a 'Mad Max' vehicle mounted with a heavy machine gun or rocket launcher prowls by, pausing to lob a few projectiles before roaring off. (Giradet 1992, 39)

In these reports, khat was being categorized as a threat, not because of its chemical properties but rather because of what it could be said to represent and the ways it was deployed as a contributor to the civil war in Somalia. This, of course, glossed over a complex series of geopolitical factors that made the conflict possible.

These early articles portrayed khat mainly as an exotic curiosity, but they also helped foster perception that khat use is backward, counterproductive, hedonistic, uncivilized, and dangerous. In this way, discursive space was created to represent khat chewing as an inferior cultural practice – an argument bolstered by the position of Yemen and Somalia in the new geopolitical hierarchy. At the time, neither khat nor khat chewing was illegal in Canada. However, it was illegal to import it into Canada, though enforcement was sporadic and dependent on the volumes intercepted at points of entry. Over the following four years, infrequent reports of arrests appeared in Canadian newspapers.[12]

Cathinone (along with its derivates or salts) was among the more than 150 new substances added to the Canadian drug regulatory regime when the Controlled Drugs and Substances Act (Bill C-8) was drafted in 1995. Many of these drugs were included to ensure that Canada met its commitment to abide by international best practices, which, however, were not codified. Once Bill C-8 was pass in June 1996, cathinone (the most potent active ingredient in khat) was categorized as a Schedule III prohibited substance, with maximum sentences of three years for possession and ten years for trafficking. Khat was now a prohibited substance.

The same year, khat became demonized in popular Canadian discourses with the publication of an opinion piece in the *Toronto Star* by Hassan Hirave, a member of Toronto's Somali community. Titled 'New Drug Finds Home in Metro,' the piece argued that khat was medically dangerous and not much different from cocaine or heroin in its social consequences. The negative health effects of khat (explicit and implicit) were listed as liver damage, malnutrition, impotence, birth defects, and increased susceptibility to infectious diseases like tuberculosis. Khat chewing was also claimed to cause users to become belligerent, aggressive, paranoid, lazy, irritable, and violent and to engage in manic behaviour.

Little known to readers at the time, these claims were highly contentious among those few in the medical community who had any familiarity with khat. In 1980 the World Health Organization (WHO) had classified khat (still little known outside of the region in which it had been traditionally consumed) as a drug of abuse that produces mild to moderate psychic dependence. Then in 1986 a report commissioned by WHO stated that psychotic behaviour from khat chewing was exceptional because of the physical limits involved in reaching the consumption of a dose that might cause such actions. The report also found that while there was a certain degree of danger associated with cathinone consumption, immediate and severe medical problems were infrequent with khat chewing (Kalix 1986).

But more damning than any potential physical affects were Hirave's allegations that khat was a major revenue source for 'tribal warlords and their street thugs' back in Somalia and that khat-related violence in Toronto bore a striking resemblance to drug violence in American cities. Yet he provided no evidence for this claim. The piece ended with a personal anecdote. While working as a translator for the Children's Aid Society, Hirave walked into an apartment

> unfit for human habitation inside with cockroaches everywhere. What was even more depressing was that the seven children who surrounded the lady of the house seemed as though they had not eaten for days ... In the family fridge, the investigating team found two large black garbage bags full of khat. It was estimated each contained at least 50 kilos ... with a street value ... [of] $50,000–$60,000. Clearly the woman and her husband ... were not merely khat chewers, but also dealers. They were prepared to sacrifice the lives of their own children just to get rich quickly, or help one of the warlords back in Somalia to buy more guns.

By building on previous representations provided in accounts of the Somali civil war, Hirave's exposé constituted khat and khat chewers as not just foreign but dangerous, violent, and immoral – this, just before the impending criminalization of khat. The very tone of his description of the khat house constructed users as deviant. Moreover, as in the case of the Chinese Anti-Opium League, his membership in the Somali community provided expert credentials that allowed his report to be taken as factual and objective rather than as one possible interpretation among many.

In the spring of 1996, before the Controlled Drugs and Substances Act became law, Rick Chase, a drug squad detective with the Toronto Police Service, called for a ban on khat. What was surprising, though, were his reasons why: 'We hope the government criminalizes [khat]. If people get involved in this type of thing, we are going to end up with a lot more people on welfare. They are going to become no good to go to work. Then we are going to have to support them socially' (Sharif 1996).

Thus, within a few months khat had gone from an obscure cultural ritual practised by a small minority in Canada, to a social catastrophe in the making. Not only did khat lead to violence, but the (foreign) pockets of users in Canada also threatened to drain the economy through the loss of worker productivity and – even more despicably in the New Right era – by lengthening welfare lists. But these negative representations were backed merely by assertions; little evidence, except the authority of experts, was ever provided for these accusations. Furthermore, the Somali-Canadian community was not consulted about criminalization, even though reports indicated that between 20 and 50 per cent of the community in Toronto chewed khat occasionally.

Given the dearth of reliable information about the effects of khat at the time, Perry Kendall, the president of the Addiction Research Foundation in 1996, argued that it was bad policy to criminalize a product that very little was known about: 'I don't know that the framers of this bill gave much thought to the Somali community when they included khat in [the Controlled Drugs and Substances Act]. If one had the time and the resources, one would probably go to the community and find some health professionals within that community, to find out what are the problems caused by the use of khat' (in ibid.).

While well intentioned, these concerns missed a crucial aspect and consequence of the legislation. In part, khat and khat chewing were being criminalized to protect *all* of the communities in Canadian society from falling prey to a drug of choice that was flourishing in a supposedly uncivilized and undeveloped society. The medical effects were secondary to the potential political effects of accepting what had been constructed as an illegitimate social activity. Thus, when questioned about the reasons for banning a substance that was a cultural practice of a minority group, the Justice Department's senior counsel Paul St Denis reportedly responded: 'It doesn't really matter what the hell they do in Ethiopia [sic], the fact is that this is Canada and these are *our* laws' (Larsen 1999; italics added). If Somali Canadians were to be full Canadians, they would have to abandon the practice.

In 1998 the City of Toronto established the Khat Habit Awareness in Toronto (KHAT) project to review the social, economic, and health effects of khat use in the city. Based on a survey of just thirty-eight people in the East African community, it was reported that 76 per cent believed khat had no benefits at all; that the main khat-associated behaviour was aggression and violence (32 per cent); and that khat led to social and financial problems (47 per cent). Also, 92 per cent believed that khat led to family problems. A majority of respondents (68 per cent) had not read or were unaware of any information about khat, and 98 per cent believed the community would benefit from such information. Finally, 39 per cent of respondents stated that there was a lack of awareness in the community that khat was a prohibited substance (KHAT Project 1998).

The stated aim of the report was to gather information on khat. But it also served as a useful tool for the Canadian state as an indicator of community approval for the law and as evidence that khat was indeed harmful. With its ambiguous wording, its highlighting of negative attitudes (even when they were in the minority), its extremely small sample size, and its failure to provide a copy of the questionnaire used to generate the data the report seems mainly an attempt to justify the prohibition after the fact.

In light of the confrontational situation with many members of the Somali-Canadian community, the report opened the discursive space to construct two types of individuals: Somali Canadians who were trying to assimilate themselves into Canadian society by abandoning old practices and respecting the law, and Somalis living in Canada who wilfully disobeyed the law by continuing to engage in cultural practices that even members of their own community believed to be harmful. These were deviants from which the Canadian Self had to be protected and who were challenging *the* Canadian identity by refusing to adopt Canadian customs and abandon a destructive and backward cultural practice. Moreover, notions of threat were amplified by a long-standing societal biomedical imperative to prevent this behaviour from spreading throughout the Canadian body politic.

Conclusions

In the Canadian context, the securitization of specific drugs has been made possible through biopolitical discourses of race. In adopting a Foucauldian approach that highlights the contingent character of the discursive relations that made it possible for opium and khat to be represented and accepted as threatening to the Canadian Self, I have made it clear that these threat constructions had very little to do with the chemical properties of these substances. Opium and khat were constructed as threats because of the political challenges they presented to Canadian identity and culture within their contexts of securitization.

At a time when discourses of the Canada First movement were creating the notion of *a* northern race, opium was perceived as a threat to the purity of Canadian racial stock because it encouraged an 'unnatural' mixing of the races and impeded the development of dominant racial characteristics. Khat was framed as a threat to Canadian culture in that it encouraged a disregard for Canadian law and promoted laziness and other characteristics of uncivilized societies inhabited by Others. In popular discourses, khat chewing was represented as a backward cultural practice that could not be tolerated in an advanced and progressive society such as Canada. To tolerate khat would not just be to risk acquiring these characteristics through cross-cultural transmission; it would be to risk the dominant position of Canadian culture by making concessions to a culturally inferior Other. Thus the biopolitical discourses employed in the securitization of these substances constitute an important component of Canadian foreign policy.

This suggests the extent to which perceptions of the Canadian Self have been products of a national collective amnesia regarding the ways in which difference has been managed and continues to be managed. The dominant representation of Canadian identity rests on the ongoing reproduction of Canada as a tolerant, pluralist, multicultural mosaic; yet disapproval has accompanied efforts by cultural minorities to engage in what can be perceived as political practices. Early Canadian drug laws and the more recent khat prohibition can be interpreted as arbitrarily constructed limits to behaviour and as responses to what these substances are claimed to represent. Yet the *medical* dangers supposedly arising from the chemical properties of these substances are at best debatable. For example, Health Canada has claimed that '[khat] is illegal because it creates a sense of euphoria in the user, it elevates the mood and sometimes causes hallucination ... Khat has *potentially* harmful effects' (in Jones 2001). To this, the Canadian Substance Abuse Centre has responded that the effects of khat are 'mild' in comparison to other illicit drugs like cocaine, heroin, and marijuana; 'on a scale of addictive substances in this country, khat's impact doesn't even make a bleep on the radar screen' (in ibid.).

In the case of minority populations in Canada who have often been targets in the reproduction of *a* national identity, drug prohibitions have provided the discursive space to construct 'safe' minorities (those who try and acculturate themselves to Canadian society) and 'risky' minorities (those who retain dangerous cultural practices). Instances where members of communities subject to these representations speak out against proscribed cultural activities help reinforce the distinctions made between Self and Other by transforming Otherness into deviance. Within the discourses pertinent to the construction of an illicit drug threat, the ability to define and categorize people and practices is one of the most important sites in which power/relations are operating.

5 A Genealogy of the Body of the Canadian Drug User, Part I: From Criminal Addiction to Medicalization

The Body Politics of Illicit Drug Regulation

In 1998, James Wakeford, an AIDS patient suffering from nausea and loss of appetite, launched a legal case that sought a constitutional exemption from marijuana prohibitions contained in the 1996 Controlled Drug and Substance Act (Senate 2002c, 299). He hoped that the judicious use of marijuana could help him settle his stomach, regain his appetite, and maintain a healthy weight that could prolong his life. On hearing his case, the Ontario Court ruled that the CDSA infringed on his constitutional rights to liberty and security of the person by denying him the autonomy to choose how to treat his illness; however, at the same time the court found that the marijuana prohibition was not an arbitrary law, given that there was some risk of harm in using it (ibid., 299).

On the basis of these conflicting foundations, the ruling stated that the law was generally consistent with the principles of fundamental justice codified in Section 7 of the Charter of Rights and Freedoms (1982) but that in the case of use where it could be shown that marijuana would have significant medical benefits for the treatment of debilitating and deadly disease, there needed to be a process for obtaining an exemption from prosecution. Initially, the court found that Section 56 of the CDSA which states that 'the Minister may, on such terms and conditions as the Minister deems necessary, exempt any person or class of persons or any controlled substance or precursor or any class thereof from the application of all or any of the provisions of this Act or the regulations if, in the opinion of the Minister, the exemption is necessary for a medical or scientific purpose or is otherwise in the public interest,' provided such a process. Later, after some consideration, the court ruled that the exemption was 'illusory' and gave Mr Wakeford an exemption (Senate 2002c, 299–300). This case is cited by Canadian legal authorities as creating a precedent for medical marijuana in Canada (ibid., 300).

Yet in the years since this landmark decision, access to medical marijuana for Canadians who are terminally ill or in chronic pain, or who suffer from diseases that can be treated with the substance, has been sporadic and inconsistent, hampered by a nightmarish application process that has pitted physicians against their patients and that has combined with the ongoing reluctance of the federal government to guarantee a supply of medical-grade marijuana. The Senate Special Committee on Illegal Drugs reported in 2002 that only 255 people in Canada had been authorized to possess marijuana for therapeutic purposes under the Marihuana Medical Access Regulations (MMAR) initiated in 2001; moreover, only 498 patients had been able to apply. In July 2003, Health Canada reported that only 16 of 582 licensed medical marijuana users had submitted applications to buy from the federal government – a low response that medical marijuana users attributed to an application process that required coordination with a doctor willing to receive and dispense the product, a sworn oath by the patient witnessed by a lawyer, and forms requiring the expertise of lawyers for both the patient and the doctor.

By thwarting attempts at research and quashing its own clinical trials, Health Canada had created a situation in which it was asking doctors to state that treatment with marijuana would benefit a patient in the absence of accepted standard medical evidence. As a result, fearing lawsuits in the event of harmful consequences from marijuana treatments, the Canadian Medical Association advised physicians not to sign medical marijuana exemption forms, even for the terminally ill. Moreover, the absence of a supply of legally grown medical marijuana until the summer of 2003 meant that even those with exemptions had to obtain their supplies illegally.

As further evidence that barriers were being raised to Canadians seeking medical marijuana, law enforcement authorities began targeting compassion clubs, which distributed marijuana to ill people, many of whom were unable to get official exemptions at a time when no legal avenues for purchase existed. For example, one law enforcement operation in Toronto in August 2002 resulted in 1,200 medical marijuana patients losing their supply of medicine. The Toronto Compassion Centre was raided by the Toronto Police Service, which seized several pounds of marijuana and 448 grams of hashish and charged the founders with four counts of possession and two counts of trafficking and proceeds of crime (Damuzi 2002a). Thus despite formal legislative and legal acceptance of medical marijuana, official procedures remained 'illusory' in that they created extraordinarily difficult requirements. And those who attempted to operate outside the byzantine institutionalized channels found themselves victimized by law enforcement and subject to the full weight of the law.

The Canadian government granted a contract to grow medical-grade marijuana as part of the MMAR program. Early in 2002, however, it tried to renege on its pledge to supply marijuana to those who were ill. Consequently, nine users sued the federal government for access to the crop (Canadian Press 2002e).[1] In essence, then, medical marijuana in Canada exists as a performative of a liberal Canadian identity; with regard to performance, it has been largely ineffectual.

Problems determining the boundaries of law enforcement, medical judgment, and individual freedom in the area of medical marijuana reflect long-standing contestations over the control of the body of drug users in Canada. In 1948 a Quebec man named Belleau sued the Minister of National Health and Welfare as well as the Chief of the Narcotics Division for enforcing a de facto prohibition on the provision of maintenance doses to drug users trying to manage their addiction.[2] As a First World War veteran who had returned from Europe with tuberculosis, he had been placed in various state-run sanatoria and prescribed morphine to treat his condition. Though his tuberculosis was arrested, Belleau developed an addiction to morphine from his treatment.

Belleau claimed that these offices, by initiating an extralegal prohibition that had no legal basis, were interfering with his physician's right to provide him with morphine to treat his addiction. From 1920 to 1938 he had been granted a medical permit that allowed him to purchase morphine from his doctor, and during this time he had been able to hold a job and support himself and his wife. In 1939, Colonel C.H.L. Sharman, head of the Narcotics Division, demanded that Dr G.H. Courchese, Belleau's physician, confine the man for treatment. The doctor refused and was threatened with legal proceedings. In 1942, Dr Courchese was able to get the Minister of Justice to conduct his own investigation in addition to one undertaken by the Division of Narcotic Control. In both reports, which were based on the opinions of leading physicians in Canada at the time, hospitalization was deemed to be totally unnecessary and potentially counterproductive from a medical standpoint. Even Sharman's own investigators refused to recommend the cessation of morphine, finding that Belleau's age and length of addiction (twenty-seven years) made success doubtful. Moreover, they pointed out that Belleau had weaned his consumption of morphine to a level that allowed him to work. Forced confinement would cause him to lose his job and therefore the means to provide for himself.

Instead of risking legal proceedings during which the rights and responsibilities of all parties could be determined, Sharman revoked Dr Courchese's licence to purchase morphine and blacklisted Belleau with all physicians in the region by threatening repercussions against anyone who treated him with maintenance doses. Belleau was forcibly confined in an institution, where he lost his job and was denied necessary amounts of morphine. His health quickly deteriorated. Over the next five years until the trial began, Belleau found himself in and out of hospitals, weak and ill from withdrawal.

The minister and Sharman claimed that because Belleau was no longer suffering from a diseased condition that did not originate with his own addiction, he could not legally be given morphine. The judge presiding over the case found that the minister through his agent Sharman 'was not exercising an administrative function but performing a quasi-judicial act which is, or at least should be, outside the sphere of his jurisdiction. It seemed inconceivable ... that a Minister could take the place of a physician and prescribe the treatment to be given to the latter's patients and the drugs they ought to receive' (in Giffen, Endicott, and Lambert 1991, 335).

Yet charges against the minister and Sharman were dropped on a legal technicality: under the Exchequer Court Act, the defendants were not considered to be officers of the Crown and thus fell outside of the court's jurisdiction. The fate of Belleau after this decision is unknown.

By juxtaposing the case of Belleau with the current situation regarding medical marijuana, we can interpret not only how the past is reflected in the present but also how the present is reflected in the past of the representational practices of the Canadian drugs discourse, as well as the policies those practices make possible. Imperatives of governmentality, biopolitics, discipline, and power/knowledge are essential to understanding the policies pursued in contemporary and historical contexts in Canada. Notwithstanding claims that the drugs discourse has become increasing progressive in its representations of drug use and drug users, a genealogy of the body of the drug user in Canada reveals that this is a highly contentious interpretation. Yet it is a popular interpretation because it ties into performatives of national identity that distinguish Canada from the United States on the basis of more just and humane social programs that have been able to avoid typical American moments of overreaction.

In revisiting the Canadian drugs discourse, instead of perceiving a fundamental shift in discursive parameters that stress individual autonomy over the body in lieu of state-sanctioned control, one finds that its constitutive power/relations have been reconfigured to better mask its technologies of management. In this regard, John Helmer (1975) has pointed out that 'expert evidence on narcotics may have changed ... but the role of science and the expert is little different from [the beginning of the twentieth century]. Not ignorance but selectivity has determined narcotics policy and will continue to determine it' (1975, 4, in ibid., 533). The mutually constitutive nature of the practices of *neo-parrhesia*, power/knowledge, and the Canadian drugs discourse that create this selectivity can be read through a genealogy of the body of drug users in Canada.

From Victim to Criminal Addict

As discussed in the previous chapter, early Canadian responses to drug use were representative of a growing awareness of biopolitics and the implementation of practices of governmentality. Logic suggests that the institutional sites most interested in drug use and drug users would be medical; however, because of the application of legal sanctions to try to curb use, law enforcement was viewed as a necessary mechanism of control, albeit under the supervision of the Department of Health.[3]

The institutional arrangements of drug control in Canada made it possible to reproduce drug use as a threat; furthermore, having the office of the Chief of the Narcotics Division serve as the hub for information, policy planning, and international negotiation greatly shaped what were considered reasonable propositions in Canadian drug discourses at the time.[4] Giffen and his colleagues contend that this concentration of power/knowledge was not planned by the government, nor was it the result of bureaucratic manipulation (1991, 126). Rather, it was made possible by the rapid implementation of a Narcotics Division in 1919, under the auspices of the Department of National Health, which required the establishment of an enforcement network that could gather and disseminate information on drug use and drug users, conduct criminal investigations, and prosecute criminal offences in response to what was discursively represented as a pressing social problem.

The Office of the Division Chief was given an all-encompassing mandate that positioned it in the organization as the sole conduit through which information on drug use and drug users was collected. This information was then passed on to professional groups like the Canadian Medical Association (CMA), the Minister and Deputy Minister of Health, and the general public. In this way, the Office of the Division Chief became *the* warehouse of truth with regard to the power/relations that constituted the Canadian drugs discourse, the subjects/objects of which it could speak, and who could speak of them. Giffen and his colleagues note that the Division Chief's 'superiors, others in the enforcement network, the mass media, and even medical journals tended to accept [the Division Chief's] word as being authoritative and incontestable' (1991, 139–40). As a consequence, the formal and popular articulations of the Canadian drugs discourse came to be constitutive of practical law enforcement discourses. Moreover, the Division Chief held considerable influence in concretizing criminal representations of drug use through policy design and implementation.

The power/knowledge of the Office of the Division Chief was augmented by the police work of the RCMP, whose mandate at the time was primarily drug related. In its early years, the RCMP (then called the NWMP) had patrolled the Canadian West undertaking traditional law and public peace duties. Once law and order had been established in that region, for the sake of organizational survival, the Mounties expanded their mandate, including undertaking counternarcotics operations and wresting jurisdiction from local police agencies to investigate these activities (ibid., 127–30).

RCMP counternarcotics activities were publicized through annual reports that did much to strengthen popular perceptions that drug use was shredding Canada's social fabric. For example, in 1921 the Mounties released this assessment of the Canadian drug scene:

Indeed our investigations have convinced ... that the evil is greater than appears on the surface, and that a serious national menace has arisen ... Our investigations have uncovered a volume of addiction which seriously *threatens our national life*, and numerous most distressing and lamentable cases have come to our notice. The dreadful suffering endured by those addicted to the drugs, and the ruin of lives which should be useful, do not constitute the whole evil, for *the evil spreads* to their families. Children rob their parents, husbands plunge their families into misery, wives ruin their husbands. (In ibid., 130; italics added.)

While drug use was represented in practical discourses as evil, during the first two decades of the twentieth century in Canada a dichotomy existed regarding the classification of those who used drugs such as opium and cocaine. On the one hand, as discussed in the previous chapter, drug use was coded primarily as a foreign practice of disrepute that threatened the health of the Canadian body politic and *the* national life. On the other hand, once it became evident that 'Canadian Canadians' were also using these drugs, it was necessary to reformulate how these users were portrayed in order to preserve the distinctive characteristics of Canadian identity. To sustain the notion of the biological superiority of *the* 'northern race,' a way had to be found to delineate, within the boundaries of deviance, a lost or fallen Self from an Other.

The preoccupation with Canadian users was in part a consequence of the success that early Canadian drug laws and concurrent immigration laws had in terms of targeting Chinese Canadians and Chinese-Canadian opium users. Arrests, deportations of users, head taxes, other immigration controls, and a dramatic fall in Chinese-Canadian users brought on by the deaths of elderly opium smokers changed the demographic pool within which drug use could be located. The interests of the law enforcement community required that ways be found to sustain perceptions that a drug threat continued (see below). By the 1920s, for the sake of its own credibility, that community had to look within proper Canadian society for evidence that this was the case, given that narcotic convictions had been dropping steadily from a high of 1,864 in 1921 to a low of 136 by 1942 (ibid., 593).

What emerged here was a portrait of drug users that painted these individuals as victims of a terrible affliction that had been deceitfully thrust upon them by foreign drug traffickers and/or unscrupulous manufacturers of patent medicines (and later just the traffickers), if they were considered to be 'Canadian-Canadians.' It is likely that most drug users in Canada at the beginning of the twentieth century were individuals who consumed patent medicines containing high levels of alcohol and often opium and/or cocaine. Legislation, including the Proprietary and Patent Medicine Act (1908), and the Opium and Narcotic Drug Act (1911), and amendments to the Opium and Narcotic Drug Act during the 1920s, placed increasingly tighter regulations on patent medicines and prohibited the use of opium and cocaine in their preparation. Some individuals who had become addicted through patent medicines turned to the black market as restrictions began to be placed on the right of doctors to prescribe these substances in order to manage addiction (Murray 1988; Carstairs 2006).

This discursive construction of the Canadian drug user as a victim was only possible within discourses that represented drug use as causing irreversible physical damage and moral degeneracy, all of which were attributed to the direct influence of drugs on moral character. These negative effects could be read from the popular representations of foreigners, particularly the Chinese, who as a 'southern race' were seen as biologically inferior and of questionable moral fibre. Given the entrenchment of notions of superiority and the values of the social gospel, within the iterative boundaries of the day it would have been counterintuitive to believe that any 'Canadian Canadians' would willingly engage in behaviour that jeopardized their natural superiority and thrust them into the degenerative world of addiction. Moreover, within the acceptable terms of discourse, there was no space for benignly defining a person as a drug user; anyone who used drugs was necessarily an addict whether or not he or she was dependent on these substances.

Yet paradoxically, the drug user as the victim of foreign traffickers cohabited with representations of drug use as existentially dangerous because of the types of behaviour that drugs encouraged, both through their direct pharmacological effects and as offshoots of addiction. Even infant medications that contained narcotic substances were not exempt from condemnation. The Baby Welfare Committee of Montreal argued that 'many of these subjects fit for our asylums or even our jails, were the early victims of these soothing syrups' (in Giffen, Endicott, and Lambert, 1991, 296).

The most damaging development for drug users was that a discursive relationship developed that linked drug use with violent crime and sexual misconduct. The popular media took full advantage of this to present shocking stories of the activities of drug fiends. For example, Emily Murphy (1922) reported that 'When a man is criminally inclined, cocaine and heroin produce delusions which actually make him "insane and dangerous to be at large." These drugs also give him courage without reason; make his vision more accurate, and steady his hand so that he may commit murder with ease ... The taking of drugs is undoubtedly the cause of a great deal of crime because people under its influence have no more idea of responsibility of what is right or wrong than an animal' (1922, 57, 59).

Tales from the United States of 'cocaine Negroes,' who were said to be orchestrating devastating waves of robbery, rape, and murder in the Old South, would have further contributed to these representations. For example, reports of the incredible strength of African Americans under the influence of cocaine, and of their ability to resist the pain from gunshot wounds, led many American police departments to upgrade their standard firearm from a .32 to a .38 calibre (Williams 1914).

Evidence of a less extreme variety was often provided by police officers who offered estimates of what percentage of the criminal element engaged in drug consumption. In November 1908 the *Canadian Pharmaceutical Journal* reported Montreal's police chief as stating that '2/3 of pickpockets and similar criminals were cocaine habitués' (in Murray 1987, 34). These sorts of testimonials were directly referred to by William Lyon Mackenzie King when he outlined the need for stricter legislation, which was provided by the 1911 Opium and Narcotic Act. For example, he referred to a parole officer who claimed that 12 to 15 per cent of young prisoners he came into contact with attributed their downfall to drugs, and to a Montreal probation officer who spoke of 'little girls taken out of cocaine dens and of young boys whose futures had been ruined' (in Mosher 1999, 7).

As mentioned previously, sexual misconduct attributed to drug use was almost always framed in terms of liaisons in which white Anglo-Saxon females may have come into contact with ethnic males. In the Canadian context, illicit drugs were seen as a means by which virtuous Canadian women were transformed into prostitutes or 'white slaves.' In contrast to American drug scare stories, which tended to focus on particular drugs leading African-American males to assault and rape white women, Canadian tales emphasized how drugs were being used to deceive Canadian women into engaging in sexual relations with ethnic partners. For example, Murphy (1922) contended that with opium smoking 'the seduction of women addicts becomes easy ... Under the influence of the drug, the woman loses control of herself; her moral senses are blunted, and she becomes a "victim" in more senses than one' (1922, 17–18). Drugs thus served a means for inferior races to circumvent the naturally chaste character of Canadian women.

The confluence of drug use, criminality, violence, and sexuality was strengthened even more by the widespread acceptance of the contagion theory, which posited that all users and traffickers try to convert others into using drugs. This theory, which was originally put forward by the American Medical Association, was endorsed by the leadership of the CMA, which published the views of a Montreal doctor who claimed that 'the drug addict is not content with destroying himself, but has a fiendish desire to promote this addiction to his friends and associates' (in Giffen, Endicott, and Lambert 1991, 157). Obviously, this theory drew heavily from representations of evil that had been a part of the Judeo-Christian tradition for centuries. The conversion of the godly to evil, initially the work of devil, was now constructed as being performed (in part) by illicit drug users. The biological roots of the desire to convert were never fully made clear in subsequent articulations of the contagion theory by physicians, law enforcement agents, and politicians. Even so, this theory did make it possible to establish increasingly strict controls over illicit drug use and illicit drug users.

First, the contagion theory made the acceptance of any degree of illicit drug use untenable within the terms of the drug discourse at the time. Accepting drug use would have been akin to sanctioning the growth of addiction: drug use could never be fully isolated and contained, as one drug user would quickly spread his or her addiction like a cancer through the Canadian body politic. Second, the use of the word contagion served as a logical bridge between illness as injury to the self, and crime as injury to others, at a time and in a country where the outbreak of communicable diseases often had devastating consequences (Szasz 1970, 20, in ibid., 157). In particular, people would still have drawn upon visceral images from the global influenza outbreak of 1919 when presented with a problem that was being framed as contagious by credible authorities.

The problem having been defined in the terms of socio-medical biology as a contagion, a logical response was to remove the carrier by enforcing isolation through a state-imposed term of confinement. Drug addiction was often talked about as a disease and users as victims; even so, measures were always punitive rather than rehabilitative. Most often, drug use was represented as a such a serious threat to the individual body and to the Canadian body politic that incarceration was the only reasonable way to prevent further injury. As Murphy (1922) succinctly argued, 'we have no option but to send [drug addicts] to jail, there being no other place of detention where they may be kept away from the drug' (1922, 153).

Over time, the paradox of the drug user as a victim/criminal was replaced with the representation of drug users as psychologically deranged. This discursive transformation is first visible in the differences between the 1922 and 1923 Department of Health annual reports. In 1922 addicts were portrayed as 'young men and women ... in the clutches of unscrupulous individuals [i.e., traffickers] who prey on the vices of humanity' (in Giffen, Endicott, and Lambert 1991, 140). By 1923 drug users were no longer the victims of traffickers but were themselves responsible for the spread of addiction (the contagion theory). Given the move away from victimization, two possible ways of classifying the causes of drug use were drawn from by the medical and law enforcement communities.

The first was to view drug users as mentally ill. Alberta, for example, amended its Insanity Act in 1924 to include drug addiction, and drug users in that province became eligible for forced sterilization in 1928 with the passage of the Act Respecting Sexual Sterilization (Chapman 1979, 106). The second was put forward at the federal level, where law enforcement officials began to argue that most users were criminals except for a small number of people suffering from medical problems or professionals, such as nurses and doctors, who had succumbed to addiction owing to life pressures and easy access to the substances. This classification scheme was slowly transformed until by the 1950s the dominant assertion was that rather than being an outgrowth of drug use, criminality *preceded* drug use: drug users were first and foremost criminally inclined. The first public articulation of this classification came in 1947 with the release of the 'Criminal Addict' as a supplement to the RCMP's annual report. Written by H.F. Price, a constable with the Vancouver RCMP, it argued that since most addicts were criminals prior to addiction, their addiction was an offshoot of their criminal behaviour. It followed that established addicts, who by definition were incurable, needed to be permanently incarcerated to prevent them 'from spreading the virus of infection to others' (in Giffen, Endicott, and Lambert 1991, 364). However, since permanently incarcerating all known addicts was impossible, Price outlined the need to legislate progressively longer sentences for repeat offenders, culminating in life imprisonment after a set number of offences.

Between the mid and the late 1920s, medical discourses and law enforcement discourses disagreed over the proper representation of drug users: some provincial jurisdictions classified drug users as mentally ill, while the federal government defined them as criminals who needed to be punished according to the law. These representational differences would become more pronounced several decades later; at the time, though, they were often negligible in practice for drug users who found themselves brought into state systems of control. Neither the mental health model nor the law enforcement model was based on what today would be considered treatment. Each employed confinement for a period of time (made possible by viewing drug use as contagious) and then released people without providing any means to manage a substance dependence problem. No treatment programs for drug abuse existed in Canada at this time.

It is interesting that none of the assertions made about the nature and character of drug use or drug users presented data that would have met the standard scientific rules of evidence at the time in question. The large majority of the evidence that was presented was anecdotal, and its authenticity was provided by the social position of those who were allowed to speak and be listened to: credible Canadian medical, law enforcement, and political authorities, who were almost never publicly challenged. Giffen and his colleagues (1991) note that the first Annual Report of the Narcotics Division (1921) mainly published statistics on convictions and on declines in the importation of narcotic drugs brought about by the establishment of a licensing system. In 1922 the format of this report was changed to a narrative that espoused alarmist views about the extent of addiction in Canada, but with little systematic empirical evidence provided (1991, 140). As was pointed out in the previous chapter, many claims made by authorities were self-evident propositions derived from constructions of the day's dominant discourses of Canadian identity. In particular, the discourses of the social gospel and the Canada First movement combined to create a filter, heavily influenced by notions of biological vulnerability and Protestant morality, that could distil the truth about drug use and its effects on Canadian society.

In this respect, the Canadian Self constructed a social problem that only required the unsubstantiated statements of accepted experts to generate a fear and loathing of endogenous elements perceived as potentially undermining a nascent Canadian identity. Even though by 1929 the number of convictions for drug offences was in severe decline and the number of known 'addicts' was decreasing, the threat was reproduced by the Office of the Division Chief, which warned that the danger of reversal was always imminent (ibid., 143).

The Sick Addict? Treatment of Drug Addiction and the Medical Community

Drug addiction and the substances alleged to contribute to the degenerative state of criminal addiction – including opium, heroin, and cocaine – were not represented as problems in medical discourses until long after they had been introduced to the practices of medicine. This coincided with the medical community's realization that the popularity of patent medicines – concoctions that often contained copious amounts of alcohol and/or other drugs like opium or cocaine – was undermining their medical authority. Glenn F. Murray (1987) has shown that 'editorials in Canadian medical journals suggest that the medical profession in Canada seemed to be more concerned about curtailing the trade in patent medicines than about the potential dangers of the drugs contained in these preparations' (1987, 32). It has also been observed that patent medicine manufacturers 'mimicked, distorted, derided, and undercut the authority of the profession ... The contrasts they [patent medicine manufacturers] drew were vivid. Doctors wanted to cut people up or give prolonged treatment, while their "sure cure" would instantly provide relief. Physicians charged high fees; their remedies were cheap' (Starr 1982, 127–8, in ibid., 32).

The anxieties of pharmacists over dispensing patent medicines in terms of their effects on consumers – but more important, in terms of growing scrutiny from other members of the medical community – is often cited as a key factor in the founding of the Canadian Pharmaceutical Association (CPA) in 1907. At that time the 'competence and integrity' of pharmacists was being publicly questioned and the profession was being depicted as an 'assassin' engaged in 'diabolical and evil' conduct such as dispensing patent medicines (ibid., 33). Yet because the trade was so lucrative, pharmacists were divided over whether to stop selling patent medicines.

The Proprietary and Patent Medicine Act (1908) was the federal response to concerns raised about the safety of popular medications. All manufacturers had to be registered with the government, cocaine and excessive amounts of alcohol were prohibited as ingredients, and the use of opium and cannabis as ingredients had to be noted on the label (Green 1979, 48). Concurrently, the non-medical use of opium was prohibited with the Anti-Opium Act of 1908. It seems that by encouraging legislation in order to protect its professional authority, the medical profession was preparing itself to ride the wave of panic generated by law enforcement, moral crusaders, and the media in the early part of the twentieth century.

Paradoxically, the medical community's embrace of this representational nexus of criminality, insanity, sexual deviancy, and drug use in order to prohibit sales of patent medicines did significant damage to the profession's autonomy. The 1923 amendments to the 1911 act restricted the ability of doctors to administer and prescribe drugs, thereby potentially criminalizing medically sound judgment. Those amendments also set the foundations for further regulation and infringement on medical prerogative. Law enforcement was thus positioned as the highest authority with regard to the legitimate and illegitimate uses of drugs, their effects, and what constituted sound medical practice in the area of drug use/addiction.

Colonel Sharman, Chief of Division of Narcotic Control from 1927 to 1946, went so far as to lecture to medical students at McGill University, Queen's University, the University of Toronto, and the University of Western Ontario. He also wrote articles for several professional journals and forwarded information to the *Canadian Medical Association Journal*, which often utilized this material in its editorials on illicit drugs (Giffen, Endicott, and Lambert 1991, 143). With criminological discourses shaping understandings of drug use in the medical community, the debate over the nature of the addict (tragic mental illness vs criminal) – a debate that had been conducted in some jurisdictions – began to fade. However, by incorporating elements of other discourses in an effort to maintain a societal monopoly on the control of medicine and an exalted position as *the* authority on medical knowledge, the medical profession essentially undermined what it had desperately been trying to protect.

Examples abound of instances in which the Office of the Division Chief either ignored attempts by physicians to medicalize responses to drug use or subverted calls for the extension of treatment beyond confinement. For example, no mention was made in the annual reports of the 1920s of doctors who wrote to the Department of Health articulating the difficulties they were having trying to treat addicts and the need for provincial treatment facilities (ibid., 141).[5] The 1929 annual report outlined a tripartite classification of drug users that included those who consumed drugs because of painful disease, professionals (mainly doctors and nurses) whose stressful working environment led them to drugs, and the vast majority of users, who were defined as criminal addicts living in an underworld environment. This classification scheme made it possible to delegitimize calls to establish medical treatment centres, as the vast majority of users were criminal addicts who, as antisocial types with little to gain or lose, would not respond to treatment (ibid., 159).

Despite the dominance of law enforcement in the discursive power/relations that constructed the body of the drug user and the consequences of drug use in a manner that favoured the expansion of criminal sanctions and the contraction of medical autonomy, the CMA never voiced any strong opposition to the representational practices of the Narcotics Control Office (ibid., 321). Differences of opinion did arise, though, with regard to the practicalities of enforcing amendments to the 1911 legislation. The result was the Opium and Narcotic Drug Act of 1929, which was implemented to end the practices of 'script doctors', that is, physicians who sold narcotic drug prescriptions for commercial gain, by limiting professional discretion. Measures to combat these practices included requiring physicians to keep detailed records of their patients' prescriptions for scheduled substances, which were collected by the RCMP; eliminating automatic prescription renewal for patients; limiting the volume or size of prescriptions to prevent future acts of self-medication by patients; eliminating over-the-phone prescription orders to pharmacies (prescriptions had to be in writing and signed); and limiting the ailments for which particular substances could be prescribed (Solomon and Green 1988; Murray 1988).

Some resentment arose within the medical community over the RCMP's use of entrapment to tempt doctors into violating the law. Most important, the ambiguity of provisions regarding what constituted proper medical treatment in terms of prescribing scheduled substances, adopted in 1923, created a great deal of confusion over whether maintenance doses of drugs could be given to addicts in order to alleviate suffering or as a treatment for overcoming addiction. The

Minister of Health assured physicians that under the legislation, physicians retained their ability to provide scheduled drugs for medical use so long as they did not give addicts drugs to take away. But by 1927 this interpretation had changed, and the Department of Health, at the urging of law enforcement officials, had placed a de facto prohibition on maintenance doses for addicts.

Despite this infringement on professional autonomy, there was no organized protest over the banning of maintenance doses for addicts even though a number of doctors spoke publicly against the policy, including a number of MPs who were also physicians. Giffen and his colleagues (1991) contend that the lack of protest was likely made possible by the small number of doctors who would have had any contact with addicts, given the small number of illicit drug users in Canada at the time; and that since the ban was administrative rather than legislative, forms of punishment other than criminal sanctions were used in enforcement, including warning letters and (in extreme cases) the revoking of licences (1991, 323).

What remained apparent even with the de facto ban on maintenance doses was that some kind of treatment needed to be available for addicts, especially medical and professional addicts who – to use the terminology of the time – did not want to slip into the irredeemable condition of 'criminal addiction.' In 1927 the Deputy Minister of Health pleaded in the *Canadian Medical Association Journal* for physicians to demand that the provinces establish special treatment facilities – albeit no more than holding cells overseen by doctors – 'for the difficulty in hospitals is that very thing; [addicts] cannot be held' (in ibid., 362). By the early 1930s the Department of Health had stopped appealing for treatment facilities. Law enforcement authorities had entrenched their hegemonic position in the power/relations of the Canadian drug discourse. The criminal approach to drug use had become *the* one legitimate approach for policy formulation.

During the 1930s and 1940s, challenges to the dominance of the law enforcement perspective were few and far between. Even when the portrayal of drug users as criminals was dismissed, the suggested policy alternatives that derived from competing understandings were no better – and sometimes even worse – than the dominant punitive approach. For example, in 'Our Medieval Attitude to Addiction,' a *Saturday Night Magazine* article published in 1947, drug users were constructed as blameless sick people. The remedy, eerily reminiscent of

Aldous Huxley's *Brave New World* combined with a neomedieval sensibility, was to create an addict colony 'where government doctors under the supervision of the Mounted Police would administer enough drugs to keep the addict comfortable and able to work' (in ibid., 364).

Challenging Criminal Addiction: The Return of Medicalization

A series of bureaucratic reorganizations in the 1950s disrupted the network used by the Office of the Division Chief to control the flow and dissemination of information on drug use and drug users, as well as the parameters of the Canadian drugs discourse (ibid., 355). In the new environment, the discursive responses of the law enforcement community were less easily coordinated and often less uniform; that community also lacked a well-positioned champion holding a monopoly over the flow of information to policy makers. Thus it became possible for the medical treatment movement in Canada to challenge status quo representations of drug users as criminals requiring punishment, and to try to revive the notion of drug users as sick individuals requiring medical attention.

The revival of the treatment paradigm began in Vancouver, given impetus by the discourse of a city drug scare involving teenage users that was being enabled by the popular media and abetted by the local law enforcement community. An independent committee to examine the city's drug problem was appointed by the Community Chest and Council of Greater Vancouver (a forerunner to the United Way). The findings of this committee were released in 1952 as the Ranta Report, so named after the committee chair, Dr Lawrence Ranta. The report made only two recommendations, yet both fundamentally challenged Canadian approaches to illicit drug use at the time. The first called for a pilot medical treatment and rehabilitation centre for drug users. The second advocated provincial narcotics clinics where registered narcotics users could receive maintenance doses of drugs. However radical the proposals looked, the report's discursive matrix was ensconced in the same narrative archetype as material released by the law enforcement community. The report did not compile and analyse data that was well documented; rather, it relied on anecdotal stories, some of which were later found to be completely inaccurate (ibid., 368).

The same year, a permanent medical lobby for treatment, the Standing Committee on the Prevention of Narcotic Addiction, was organized by the Community Chest and Council of Greater Vancouver. In a policy brief, the committee produced a new tripartite classification scheme of drug offenders: the addict who possesses drugs for his or her own use and who should be treated as a medical problem; the addict who traffics small amounts of drugs and who should be subject to light criminal penalties with room for discretion; and persons who traffic only for commercial gain and who therefore should be subject to severe punishment. The committee also recommended that provinces enact legislation that would allow 'habitual users' to be detained for compulsory treatment and that the de facto prohibition on maintenance doses be removed (ibid., 368). Clearly, the medical community was beginning to publicly challenge law enforcement's guardianship of the regime of truth that had for so long shaped Canadian drugs discourse:

> In response to his committee's proposals, Dr. Ranta noted that:
> There was immediate (and intense) reaction in Ottawa to the report – mainly consternation that somehow the silence barrier had been broken. Narcotic control people, law enforcement people, and mental health consultants descended on Vancouver with what appeared to be an effort to determine if the study had been done by a bunch of cranks and to downplay the treatment aspects of the report and anything else that went beyond confinement of addicts and traffickers ...The most important feature in the whole affair was the hyper reaction that came from the Ottawa 'Mandarins' who somehow felt that they were being attacked by the report. (In ibid., 369)

The Ranta Report and the policy brief of the Standing Committee on the Prevention of Narcotic Addiction amounted to a partial shift in the Canadian drugs discourse and a reconfiguration of its power/ relations. The law enforcement community found itself on the defensive, with its claims to 'truth' being publicly questioned by the medical community. A member of the Technical Advisory Committee on Narcotic Drug Addiction and a former RCMP superintendent published a critical article just two weeks after the Ranta Report was released, in which he argued that maintenance doses would never satiate addicts, and would in fact encourage crime and a continuation of the illicit drug trade. However, the author did agree that drug use was a mental disease that could be cured – which was a break with previous law enforcement representations of treatment as futile and of drug users as irredeemable (ibid., 370–1).

Subtle changes in attitude became apparent. Even Paul Martin, Sr, the Minister of National Health and Welfare, publicly stated that the Division of Narcotics Control was reassessing its current position and was beginning to explore the possibility of treatment models. In British Columbia, the provincial government agreed at the end of 1954 to fund a pilot treatment centre, the first of its kind in Canada. At the same time, though, treatment advocates were applying the existing terms of discourse to represent drug use as a threat, their purpose being to highlight the seriousness of Canada's drug problem. This actually undermined their position, however, by reinforcing dominant representations of drug use and drug users that made maintenance programs 'hard to sell' (ibid., 366).

In the wake of the reassertion of the power/knowledge of the medical community, a Special Senate Committee on the Traffic in Narcotic Drugs was established in 1955 to determine how to eliminate both the supply of and the demand for illicit drugs. As the first witness to give testimony, Paul Martin set the tone for the entire proceedings by delivering a set of assertions, which were then repeated by law enforcement witnesses who followed. The minister approved of plans for the treatment of drug users, but this was conditional on the treatment model being used. He rejected claims that Canada should adopt a system of treatment based on maintenance doses (dubbed the British System). To circumvent any arguments that might support this position, he gathered testimony from British officials, who stated that their system was actually no different from the current Canadian approach. The minister argued that maintenance programs were 'not proper treatment' and that isolating drug users from the general population through confinement was the most effective way to treat addiction (ibid., 375). Dismissing the view that drug addicts were victims, he stressed the criminal nature of drug users, which necessitated harsh corrective measures. Moreover, to quash any further attempts at a medical approach to drug use at the federal level, he argued that any treatment program was a provincial responsibility because of how powers were divided in the Canadian political system (ibid., 375).

As calls grew louder for some type of treatment response, the discursive representation of drug users as criminal addicts became central to law enforcement's efforts to maintain a privileged position within the power/relations that constituted the regime of truth regarding drug use. This made it possible for drug use to be perceived as a criminal threat rather than as merely a medical problem. Thus, during the course of the Senate Special Committee, law enforcement testimony stressed the criminality of drug users. One RCMP witness argued that 'essentially, it would appear that too much emphasis is placed on the addiction factor, with insufficient reference to the primary factor of criminality. In essence, a criminal addict is as the adjective implies a criminal first and an addict second' (in ibid., 376).

Another RCMP witness framed the problem as follows: 'Habitual criminals are psychopaths, and psychopaths are abnormal individuals who, because of their abnormality, are especially liable to become addicts' (in ibid., 381). The RCMP Commissioner presented statistical evidence from the records of convicted drug users which showed that 1,668 out of 2,009 had initial arrests for crimes other than drug violations. Moreover, a medical study from British Columbia that was submitted to the Senate Special Committee reported that of all the drug users held in Oakalla Prison Farm, 75 per cent had been delinquent before starting to consume drugs (in ibid., 376).

Perhaps the most interesting move in the law enforcement community was the abandonment of claims that drug users were engaging in violent crime. According to one RCMP sergeant, 'under reasonable circumstances, the addict goes undetected in any crowd, and he is by no means the hollow-eyed, hopped-up dope fiend the public is led to believe' (in ibid., 378). This can be interpreted as demonstrating that the politics of the drug discourse at the time made law enforcement's previous representations of drug users as manically violent difficult to accept and thus capable of derailing the reaffirmation of securitization by discrediting the fundamental claims that were central to the law enforcement position. Portraying drug users as naturally criminally inclined, though not necessarily violent, allowed law enforcement to defend its position within the Canadian drugs discourse as a *neo-parrhesiastes* while making the continued securitization of drugs possible.

The construction of the drug user as criminal addict was also central to law enforcement attempts to undermine the idea put forward by the pro-treatment community that maintenance doses would reduce crime as well as weaken any sympathy for drug users that might arise if drug use was portrayed as an illness (ibid., 377).

While the criminal addict proposition was contested by several witnesses who favoured treatment-centred approaches, these concerns were unable to unseat what had become conventional wisdom for the senators on the Special Committee.

The portrayal of drug users as criminal addicts allowed questions to be raised as to whether drug addiction was even curable, but the answers possible within the existing terms of discourse had the potential to undermine the positions of those who employed them. The medical community conceded that there was still no known totally effective cure for drug addiction, in part because of the limited opportunity for research. This was echoed in law enforcement's representation of the criminal addict as incurable. However, portraying addicts as incurable also lent impetus for maintenance programs, an approach that all elements of law enforcement found unacceptable. Many law enforcement witnesses favoured prolonged psychological treatment to deal with underlying psychopathic conditions as a way of promoting the long-term confinement of those drug users who had thus far avoided the criminal control system (ibid., 379–80).

Once again, as in the 1920s, the medical treatment/rehabilitation paradigms and the law enforcement criminal/punishment paradigms were at loggerheads. However, they found common ground in the contagion theory. Almost all of the witnesses before the Senate Special Committee agreed that contact with users served as the definitive exogenous catalyst for initial use by others, though medical witnesses sometimes included psychological vulnerability as another crucial prerequisite. This was interpreted in the final report of the committee as follows: 'The evidence of medical authorities was to the effect that drug addiction is not a disease in itself. It is a symptom or manifestation of character weaknesses or personality defects in the individual. The addict is usually an emotionally insecure and unstable person who derives support from narcotic drugs' (in ibid., 387).

The entrenchment of the contagion theory was best illustrated by the following exchange among members of the Senate Special Committee, recorded by transcript:

Senator Hodges: As I understand it, one of the main objects of isolating or segregating addicts is that ... you might do something for them ... and ... if addicts create addicts, you take out of society a festering wound, or a cancer, and thus prevent the infliction of the disease on more people.

The Chairman: Yes, you cut the parts of the cancer away at least.
Senator Hodges: Well, I mean you take them away. After all if a person has diphtheria or scarlet fever, you isolate them.
Senator Baird: For life?
Senator Howden: Yes, if necessary.
Senator Hodges: Until you find they are amenable to society.
Senator Woodrow: Your idea would be to treat them as one would treat leprosy – confine such persons to a lazaretto and immure them for life, if necessary.
Senator Hodges: Yes. (In ibid., 384)

A Vancouver Chief Constable suggested that a suitable island large enough for a colony farm would be a perfect location to house addicts needing treatment, and several senators voiced their approval of this idea (ibid., 386). Most important, the deployment of the contagion theory within the Canadian drugs discourse made the consequences of drug use so dire that it was possible to legitimately advocate the compulsory committal of *all* drug users to treatment facilities.

Despite ostensibly being created for the purposes of offering proposals for a new approach to treatment in response to challenges raised by the medical community's pro-treatment lobby, the Senate Special Committee's Final Report, strongly influenced by the discourse of the law enforcement community, interpreted the need for treatment in a very limited manner, viewing it as an additional means of confining drug users rather than as an alternative to securitization. Furthermore, the report saddled the provincial governments with the full responsibility of promoting or establishing treatment clinics by arguing that the British North America Act (1867) limited the segregation and rehabilitation powers of the federal government to within the penitentiary system. In this way, it divested federal authorities of any necessary involvement.

In 1957, after receiving a policy brief from the Vancouver treatment lobby, the new minister of justice agreed to remove the minimum six-month sentence for possession of illicit drugs. In 1958 the Department of Justice formed a Correctional Planning Committee to design methods that might cure and rehabilitate 'persons addicted to narcotic drugs' who had been convicted of criminal offences. Despite suggestions from the minister of health that an experimental maintenance program might be worth exploring, the final report produced by the committee did little more than rehash the representations of drug use employed by law enforcement, stressing the prior criminality of the addict and the need for federal and provincial laws to make drug users 'liable to detention and treatment for an indefinite period,' with the possibility of being committed to custody indefinitely in the case of relapse (ibid., 393).

This last proposal, and the power to prosecute the preventative detention of convicted drug traffickers, were incorporated into the Part II of the Narcotic Control Act (1961), though the section was never proclaimed into law. More positively for those interested in evening the power/relations defined by the Canadian drugs discourse, the Narcotic Control Act eliminated the de facto ban on physicians prescribing scheduled drugs in cases where patients required these substances for their medical treatment; however, the burden of proof remained on the physician to demonstrate that the patient required the drug for a medical condition. This provision opened the door for voluntary experimental and permanent treatment facilities over the following decades, including methadone clinics, therapeutic communities, and treatment programs in federal penitentiaries.

Yet the development of treatment facilities and the growing number of medical professionals engaged in treatment research and practice was matched by a sharp increase in the number of convictions for narcotic offences in Canada: from 495 in 1961 to more than 12,811 by 1972 (ibid., 593). There was a growing reliance on the medical community's input for the creation of new policy, yet law enforcement continued to act as an agency of control and as an architect of the body of the drug user. This was made possible by the increasing popularity of marijuana among Canadian baby boomers.

In 1967, in response to these developments, the Standing Committee on Justice and Legal Affairs was tasked to review Bill C-292 (later C-96), a private member's bill respecting the observation and treatment of drug addicts that was intended to remove the stigma of criminal conviction for drug users. The committee called seven witnesses, none of whom were from law enforcement (ibid., 512). While the bill did not pass, it did push the parameters of discourse so that a comprehensive review of illicit drug use and policy became possible in Canada.

Criminal Addiction Reconsidered? Marijuana and the Discourse of Drugs in Canada

Previously almost unknown in Canada, marijuana (or cannabis) was first brought to the attention of the Canadian public and law enforcement in the writings of Emily Murphy. In one particularly robust section of *The Black Candle*, she quoted the Los Angeles police chief on the consequences of using marijuana:

> Persons using this narcotic smoke the dried leaves of the plant, which has the effect of driving them completely insane. The addict loses all sense of moral responsibility. Addicts to this drug, while under its influence, are immune to pain, and could be severely injured without having any realization of their condition. While in this condition they become raving maniacs and are liable to kill or indulge in any form of violence to other persons, using the most savage methods of cruelty without as said before, any sense of moral responsibility. When coming from under the influence of this narcotic, these victims present the most horrible condition imaginable. They are dispossessed of their natural and normal will power and their mentality is that of idiots. If this drug is indulged in to any great extent, it ends in the untimely death of its addict. (Murphy 1922, 332–3)

Clayton Mosher (1999) has argued that in light of the absence of any alternative discursive representation of marijuana use/users, Murphy played a pivotal role in the securitization of cannabis when it was capriciously added to the schedule of prohibited narcotics in 1923.[6] Moreover, Mosher contends that Murphy ignored existing literature that presented evidence that marijuana was *not* dangerous – for example, the Indian Hemp Commission Report (1894) (1999, 20).

Although this substance was prohibited, most Canadians were totally unaware of its status. For example, in trying to align existing legislation with the Geneva Convention on Narcotic Drugs (1931), even the Minister of National Health and Pensions was confused. He declared that cannabis had to be added to schedule; yet marijuana, which he thought was legal, was already prohibited (ibid., 22). This lack of familiarity was made possible by the absence of marijuana use in Canada at the time, in contrast to the United States, where marijuana use, while not common, was familiar to law enforcement officials and subject to legal sanction in several states. Yet even though there with little or no use in Canada, the first seizure in 1933 led to the release of the following statement in the Annual Report of the Office of the Division Chief, which drew from the American experience to contribute to the securitization of the substance: 'The use of these cigarettes, which are closely related to the oriental drug of addiction known as hashish, has, in the comparatively recent past, increased to a considerable extent in the United States ... They are particularly dangerous to young people, to whom their use is almost exclusively confined, as all indications point to the fact that their illicit sale takes place in cabarets and dance halls, where young people, not previously addicted to any form of narcotic congregate' (in Giffen, Endicott, and Lambert 1991, 183).

The following year the *Canadian Medical Association Journal* published two articles about marijuana in the same issue. The first reported that the substance was being sold in Walkerville, Ontario, and that thirty addicts were living in Windsor. The second indicated that marijuana was responsible for most of the crime in the U.S. Southwest and that 'marijuana when mixed with hay, causes death to the horses that eat it' (in Mosher 1999, 22).

The annual RCMP reports made infrequent references to small seizures of marijuana in the early 1930s. The first conviction for possession of marijuana did not occur until 1937. In rendering his decision, the judge cited an article written by the commissioner of the U.S. Federal Bureau of Narcotics regarding the horrible effects of marijuana: 'It deals in a graphic and arresting way with the ever growing menace attending the use of this deadly drug to which so many young men and girls of high school age in the United States are becoming rapidly addicted. The Commissioner states that murders, suicides, robberies, criminal sexual assaults, holdups, burglaries, and deeds of maniacal insanity are yearly being caused by the use of this deadly narcotic drug' (*R. v. Forbes* 1937, in ibid., 24).

News of the American domestic crusade for federal marijuana legislation came to public attention in Canada through the popular media and likely made it possible for marijuana to become a focal point in the drugs discourse. Interest may have been generated as well by a new law prohibiting the cultivation of hemp. Again, in the run-up to that legislation, the American commissioner was quoted to lend credence to the dangers of marijuana use (ibid., 25). In 1938 the *Toronto Daily Star* reported on the trade in the drug at the Detroit/Windsor border crossing – a trade that was supposedly targeting school-age children. In the same article a Canadian district narcotics supervisor was quoted on the dangers of marijuana: 'Hideous crimes have been committed by smokers of these cigarettes, and we have had reports and investigations that show even school children have been smoking them. Our files also show that many victims are confined to institutions for the insane after smoking these cigarettes for a period of time' (in Giffen, Endicott, and Lambert 1991, 184).

A *Maclean's* article published later that year strengthened the 'reefer madness' representation of users, hypothesizing that 'plants growing right here in Canada could produce enough of this drug which maddens, to send a large proportion of the Dominion's population to the insane asylum' (in ibid., 186). In the global context, marijuana was also becoming closely associated with post-colonial rebellions and resistance, especially in light of Hollywood depictions of the Mexican Revolution, which highlighted the lawless violence, sexual deviancy, and communist radicalism of regular marijuana users (Marez 2004, 105–222).

These representations, which made it possible for law enforcement officials to maintain that marijuana needed to be securitized, went unquestioned for nearly three decades. Yet from 1930 to 1946, there were only twenty-five convictions for marijuana offences in Canada (Mosher 1999, 21). However (as discussed earlier), the employment of the contagion theory by law enforcement in the drugs discourse, in combination with the resulting popular understanding that any illicit drug use placed Canada on the verge of a socially devastating epidemic, allowed for ongoing securitization in the absence of more tangible indications of a threat.

Not until the number of people convicted of marijuana offences began to rise dramatically, from 42 persons in 1965 to 10,695 in 1972, did law enforcement's nightmare scenario appear to be coming to pass (Giffen, Endicott, and Lambert 1991, 600). But unlike past drug scares, this new wave of drug use could not easily be interpreted as the outcome of the inferior cultural practices of a racial minority group, or of marginalized 'criminal addicts' at the fringes of decent society.[7] Rather, Canada was being confronted with discovering that marijuana users were predominantly Canadian youth from middle- and upper-middle-class families; marijuana was in fact being used primarily by elements of the Self and was not limited to the confines of the foreign and/or deviant Other (ibid., 491).[8] This interpretation might have made possible a thorough reassessment of the drugs discourse and Canadian drug law by seriously undermining dominant understandings of drug use and drug users. But as it turned out, the identification of marijuana with countercultures reproduced the necessary representational practices that made it possible for law enforcement and other conservative institutions to code marijuana use as an indication of the ongoing threat posed to *real* Canadians by the drug use of a fallen Self (if not an Other).

Yet at the same time, the use of marijuana by 'Canadian Canadians' marked a significant transformation in the dynamics of the power/relations that defined illicit drug use and the identity of illicit drug users. The drugs discourse was no longer the contested purview of law enforcement and the medical community over the control of the bodies of individual drug users. Many marijuana users felt themselves to be politically conscious and empowered, a consequence of ideological as well as socioeconomic circumstances; thus a situation developed whereby law enforcement, the medical community, *and* marijuana users contributed to the Canadian drugs discourse, with marijuana users most often aligning with and appealing to the medical community (ibid., 499). The point is not to condemn the original targets of Canadian drug law for not speaking out publicly against prohibition; rather, it is to draw attention to how in general, marijuana users beginning in the 1960s occupied far more advantageous positions in Canadian social power/relations than illicit drug users of the previous three generations.

Proponents of prohibition continued to represent illicit drug use – even if predominantly undertaken by Canadians proper – as foreign, deviant, diseased, lazy, and capable of undermining the established societal order. For example, in a brief to the Le Dain Commission on the Non-Medical Use of Drugs (1969–73), the RCMP reported that

> there are in Canada a large number of young and able-bodied people, preoccupied with Cannabis, leading a life of indolence. Not only are these people not contributing to the economy of Canada, but we believe they are a charge against the public purse through welfare assistance. The wastage in human resources is real and should be considered in any study of this problem. We are currently experiencing a perversion of the social mores, with illegitimate births and disease a consequence, to say nothing of the virtual destruction of the family unit. (in ibid., 507)

Echoing this fear of social disintegration, former Prime Minister John Diefenbaker, a supporter of harsher sentences for marijuana possession, believed that illicit drug use combined with an increase in sex and violence was part of a permissiveness that threatened '*the* Christian society of Canada' (in ibid., 507; italics added).

Claims made by members of the medical community and marijuana users regarding the relative safeness of the substance were derided by law enforcement officials as completely false. In a 1968 *Globe and Mail* article, one RCMP officer retorted: 'There are high flying theories about it [marijuana] not being habit-forming. All the theorists have to do is look at the kids who are hooked. We had a case this week of eight living in one room in Yorkville. They had scabs all over their bodies, scales of dirt – they are diseased, useless members of society. Excuse me for telling you but there was a bathroom down the hall which they did not bother to use – they defecated in the corner of the room. That's what marijuana can do to some people' (in ibid., 498).[9]

These kinds of representational practices built on previous characterizations of illicit drug users while amplifying what were identified as indicative negative qualities. Marijuana users were no longer merely foreign and/or deviant and/or diseased. They were now being portrayed by Canadian law enforcement as less than human, with animal-like habits that spread communicable diseases in addition to addiction.

The Le Dain Commission

In 1969, amid the new hubris over the effects and affects of illicit drug use on Canadian society, the federal government established another Royal Commission to gather information on the 'factors underlying or relating to the non-medical use of drugs' (Le Dain Commission 1973, 4). Central to the investigations of the Le Dain Commission, so named after its chair, was an assumption regarding the role of the state in controlling the individual body – a role that justified Canadian governmentality: 'The state has a right in principle to prohibit the production and distribution of dangerous substances, and ... whether it is justified in doing so in a particular case depends on the facts – and in particular, on a weighing of the deprivation it is causing against the harm it is preventing' (ibid., 51).

After four years of research, 120 projects, and the release of three separate public reports, the Le Dain Commission had a significant impact on the shape of the Canadian drugs discourse in that it both catalysed discussion and served as an institutional site through which the Canadian drugs discourse could operate. For example, the commission abandoned the term 'addict' and replaced it with 'user.' What emerged was a fundamental shift within the power/relations made possible by the drugs discourse – a shift that occurred once medical authority began to eclipse law enforcement's claim to *neo-parrhesia* over drug use and the body of drug users.

In its interim report (1970), the Le Dain Commission noted that its information gathering had been frustrated by a lack of reliable data. With respect to marijuana, the commission lamented that

> although the current world literature on cannabis numbers some 2000 publications, few of these papers meet modern standards of scientific investigation. They are often ill-documented and ambiguous, emotion-laden and incredibly biassed, and can, in general, be relied upon for very little valid information. Scientific expertise in the area of cannabis is limited by the simple fact that there is little clearly-established scientific information available, and preconceived notions often dominate the interpretation of ambiguous data. (1970, 161–2)

The commission lauded the Indian Hemp Drugs Commission Report as the most thorough investigation of cannabis available, even though it was nearly seventy-five years old and based on information from colonial India. That Report, undertaken by the British Colonial Authority, had concluded that moderate use of hemp (i.e., marijuana) may be beneficial; while excessive use might cause some health problems, including bronchitis and mental illness in persons predisposed to psychiatric episodes, these effects were extremely rare (1970, 218–20).

What is most significant here is not so much the lack of scientific information, but the fact that for the Le Dain Commission, knowledge claims had to be cloaked in the scientific method. This disrupted the anecdotal foundations of law enforcement's power/knowledge, which constructed a particular view of drug use, and drug users, that necessitated a punitive approach to what was predefined as a social problem.

In asserting the privileged position of science as the arbitrator of truth in the Canadian drugs discourse, the Le Dain Commission was challenging the long-standing representation of drug users as naturally predisposed to criminal activity – that is, the very idea of the 'criminal addict.' The commissioners argued that 'although possession of cannabis is a crime, and in obtaining it an individual must normally come into contact with other individuals committing drug

offences, there is no scientific evidence that cannabis itself is responsible for the commission of other forms of criminal behaviour. [One
study] suggest[s] that cannabis use may, in fact actually reduce the
occurrence of crime and aggression by decreasing general activity'
(1970, 181).

Furthermore, the RCMP's attempts to re-establish the discursive
validity of the criminal addict proposition through statistical evidence
were rejected by the commission: 'It was reported [by the RCMP] that
85% (3450 of a sample of 3804) of persons convicted of drug offences,
who were addicted to hard drugs had "criminal antecedents" ... We
feel it would be dangerous to draw general conclusions from the
records of prison inmates insofar as they cannot be considered to be a
representative sample of the present population of drug users' (1970,
469). With increasing scepticism being held towards past representations of drug users, the terms of intelligibility within which the (constructed) Canadian drugs reality could be known, and acted upon,
had shifted.

Yet the Le Dain Commission did not mark a clear break with the representational practices of the past. Though willing to challenge other
presuppositions, it was also willing to classify drug users (even marijuana users) as outside Canadian social norms, on the basis of their
value system. For example, it noted a close association between marijuana users and what it dubbed the 'hang loose' ethic:

> Central to this notion is the questioning of such traditional patterns of
> behaviour and belief as conventional religion, marriage, pre-martial
> chastity and the accumulation of wealth. Subscribers to this ethic appar-
> ently do not necessarily reject the *mores* of the established order, but are
> strongly critical of them. In [the Suchman] study, the stronger the student
> embraced this ethic, the more favourable he was towards marijuana use.
> Smoking marijuana was highly associated with 'non-conformist' behav-
> iour such as participating in mass protests ... the 'hang-loose' ethic, while
> it may represent antagonism to the conventional world, does not appear
> to create apathy and withdrawal. (1970, 178)

Differences that extended beyond the use of illicit drugs continued
to be noted between marijuana users and 'normal' Canadians.

Still, the Le Dain Commission opened up enough discursive space
that many of its recommendations, which would have been almost
impossible to articulate coherently within the Canadian drugs dis-

course a decade earlier, became possible to advocate, though most met resistance from the law enforcement community. While the Le Dain Commission is most often remembered for advocating the decriminalization of marijuana possession, its recommendations were more extensive than that. They included

- maintaining maximum sentences for drug offences;
- establishing an automated control system for monitoring prescription drugs;
- the orderly withdrawal of criminal sanctions for the possession of illicit drugs;
- replacing incarceration with probation and medical treatment;
- no compulsory medical treatment for those who only occasionally use drugs that do not have a significant dependence-producing potential;
- the continuation of methadone maintenance programs;
- more research on illicit drugs, and easier access to illicit drugs for research projects;
- improving government statistical data gathering and data sharing; and
- placing strict controls on alcohol and tobacco advertising.

Given the extent of these recommendations, Canadian state responses to drug use were still steeped in biopolitical concerns over the health of the Canadian body politic. The major change was that drug use and public health were being discursively placed under the purview of the medical community, with a corresponding de-emphasis on law enforcement.

Responding to Le Dain

In response to the trend towards a privileging of medical authority over control of the body of the drug users – a trend that reached discursive culmination with the Le Dain Commission – law enforcement reframed the dangers of marijuana use by deploying quasi-scientific terminology and newly discovered evidence to reproduce marijuana as a threat (Giffen, Endicott, and Lambert 1991, 533). Claims that marijuana was addictive and that it caused violent behaviour were now less likely to be accepted by the public or by policy makers. Even so, the law enforcement community developed and publicized the following two assertions about marijuana use. The first was known as the gateway, stepping stone, or escalation theory. It posited that marijuana use inevitably led to heroin use and was backed by research findings that most heroin users had tried marijuana first. The second was that marijuana altered the behaviour of individuals by making them apathetic and unambitious. Lending credence to this proposition was a scientific-sounding term to describe the condition: 'a-motivational syndrome.' Moreover, law enforcement in Canada began a concentrated campaign to publicize any medical findings that marijuana, or any other drug, caused harm (while ignoring those that showed limited or non-existent harms).

One of the most often referenced studies by law enforcement in Canada during the 1970s was an article in the *Journal of the American Medical Association*. These findings were based on observations of twenty male and thirteen female marijuana users who smoked two or more times weekly. Negative effects highlighted by the researchers included 'poor social judgement, poor concentration, confusion, anxiety, depression, apathy, passivity, indifference, and often slowed and slurred speech.' More damning though were claims made in the article that one male research subject turned homosexual after smoking marijuana and that females turned sexually promiscuous, 'which ranged from sexual relations with individuals of the opposite sex, individuals of both sexes, and sometimes individuals of both sexes at the same time' (Kolansky and Moore 1971, 486–8, in Mosher 1999, 28).

Further reports surfaced in the media that claimed to be based on scientific data. Some of these played against the conventional representational type by equating marijuana use not with sexual virility, but passivity. For example, it was reported that marijuana led to male sterility and impotence, birth defects and cancer, chromosome damage, and the development of enlarged breasts in males. Harking back to earlier representational practices that placed both drug use and alternative sexual practices in the realm of deviancy, the Marijuana Education Society of British Columbia went as far as to argue that 'the growing gay population is largely due to ... the female estrogen in cannabis ... Unless the data we have is soon transmitted to the public we will probably witness the decline of Western civilization as we have known it' (*Vancouver Sun* 1979, 3, in ibid., 31).

Thus the increasing medicalization of the Canadian drugs discourse did not desecuritize drug use. Rather, law enforcement was able to adopt medicalized aspects of the Canadian drugs discourse and adapt its own representations of drug use and drug users to reproduce the perception of threat. Medicalized aspects of the drugs discourse, the medical community, and new research projects undertaken were all imbricated within these dominant law enforcement representations, which still constituted commonsense knowledge of drug use and drug users. Many drug treatment and research initiatives found themselves located in institutional sites of social control within the criminal justice system. For example, treatment programs were often inside prisons, while drug research facilities were used to garner information for antidrug materials (Giffen and Erickson 1988, 361). Thus, instead of leading to radical change, the adoption of a medical model made it possible for the drug menace to be portrayed as a multidimensional problem that combined criminal and medical threats to the individual body and the Canadian body politic, necessitating the ongoing securitization of the issue.

Several legal changes were proposed and tabled during the 1970s and early 1980s. Two significant reforms did occur in 1969 and 1972. The first was the establishment of fines as an option in cases of conviction for possession of marijuana (i.e., instead of incarceration). This was done in order to reduce the severity of punishments for 'young persons who were not ordinarily of the criminal class' (ibid., 355). The second was allowing for findings of guilt without conviction in cases of marijuana possession. However, major reforms, including decriminalization by moving cannabis out of the Narcotics Control Act and into the Food and Drugs Act (proposed in 1968, 1970, 1974, and 1980), were not approved (Erickson 1992, 246). However, the Charter of Rights and Freedoms (1982) rendered unconstitutional some of the procedural disadvantages that had applied to suspected or accused drug users/traffickers but not other categories of potential criminals (ibid., 246). Still, convictions climbed dramatically in the 1970s, to nearly 44,000 per year by 1981 (ibid.). Erickson estimates that 90 per cent of these were for simple possession (ibid.). Moreover, between 1980 and 1985, Canada's rate of drug offences (based on charges laid by the police) reached nearly 300 per 100,000 – according to the UN, the highest rate in the world during that time period (ibid., 241). Thus medicalization and increasing securitization were able to operate hand in hand.

6 A Genealogy of the Body of the Canadian Drug User, Part II: From A National Drug Strategy to Medical Marijuana

The Politics of the Possible in the 'War on Drugs' Era

In 1986, U.S. President Ronald Reagan declared that 'drugs are menacing our society ... there is no moral middle ground.' Within two days, Prime Minister Brian Mulroney aped his American counterpart by announcing that 'drug abuse has become an epidemic that undermines our economic as well as our social fabric' (in Erickson 1992, 248).[1] The use of the word 'epidemic,' borrowed from medical discourse, created an image of drug use as rampant and as spreading uncontrollably like a highly infectious disease, an image reminiscent of the contagion theory of earlier generations. As one high-ranking official in Health and Welfare Canada explained, 'when he [the PM] made that statement, *we* had to make it a *problem*' (in ibid., 248). Illicit drug use was still being reproduced as a threat to the Canadian body politic.

Given the perceived severity of the situation, the goal of the Canadian government was to develop a comprehensive and coordinated plan to reduce both the demand for and the supply of illicit drugs in Canada. Perhaps both a reflection of the ongoing medicalization of the drugs discourse and an attempt to differentiate Canadian drug policy from the disturbingly punitive approach adopted by the United States, the central focus of the National Drug Strategy (NDS) was on reducing demand through education and treatment programs; heavy reliance on law enforcement initiatives to reduce supply was viewed as inadequate to the task at hand (ibid., 248). The overall objective was 'to reduce the harm to individuals, family, and communities from the abuse of alcohol and other drugs through a balanced approach that is acceptable to Canadians' (Canada 1988, 5). Beginning in 1987, the strategy was granted a five-year budget of $210 million, with a planned allocation of 70 per cent for prevention and treatment and the remaining 30 per cent for enforcement and control. Because of the terms of discourse deployed and the fiscal commitment to prevention, many interested parties at the time argued that the strategy was a tentative step towards a medical harm reduction model of drug control for Canada.

Yet harm reduction did not imply a loosening of control over individual bodies. For example, the CEO of the Canadian Centre on Substance Abuse (formed as part of the strategy), a proponent of harm reduction approaches, argued that 'a successful attack on the harm associated with drug use will require comprehensive social policy ... Every aspect of how human beings organize and govern themselves becomes an issue, because drug use is associated with nothing less than who we are as individuals, how we see our world and our place in it, and how we exercise our individual skills and abilities to live life as we wish' (in Erickson 1992, 256).

Clearly, the practices of governmentality in Canada made it possible for responses to drug use and illicit drug use, be they medicalized or criminalized, to be framed in a manner that made technologies of social control necessary. What remained contested was which institutional site (health or law enforcement) could respond most effectively to drug use and reduce, if not eliminate, the threat. Continued securitization and moves towards harm reduction could both lead to a societal panopticon that disciplined individuals by imposing mechanisms intended to contribute to the strict regulation of their behaviour.

For law enforcement, the influx of resources from the strategy made it possible to pay increased attention to drug offences. Thus, the overall drug crime rate in Canada (measured by the number of drug charges laid by the police) rose from 221.9 per 100,000 in 1986 to 258.9 in 1989, even while drug use itself was declining sharply. Moreover, a significant amount of funding for preventative approaches to drug use was being channelled to police-controlled educational programs involving a thousand local officers from 128 units, who were trained to deliver these programs by the RCMP's special unit, PACE (Police Assisting Community Programs) (ibid., 252).

By 1990 it was increasingly unclear whether the focus of the strategy should be on demand reduction or supply reduction. Perrin Beatty, the Minister of Health and Welfare, contended that 'the first course of action in *combatting* drug abuse is to *help* the drug user or *potential* drug user. While the *major priority* is demand reduction, curbing supply is *equally important*, especially as a *complement* to demand reduction efforts' (in ibid., 255). Rising drug offence rates, falling prices, increased purity, and easier availability were exposed to myriad interpretations, including the failure of the demand reduction approach, the failure of the supply reduction approach, and 'ambivalence regarding both priorities and objectives' (ibid.). In response to these allegations, Solicitor General Pierre Cadieux, drawing from the metaphor most favoured by the United States, remarked that 'what we're saying is that the *war* has not been *won* yet but that we are making steady progress' (in ibid.).

Despite not having any discernible successes, the NDS was renewed in 1992 and renamed Canada's Drug Strategy (CDS). Funding also increased to $270 million over five years, with 60 per cent earmarked for prevention and treatment programs, around 30 per cent for law enforcement, and the remaining 10 per cent for advertising, information, and research (Senate 2002c, 238).[2] The CDS had been a limited-term program subject to renewal; in 1998 it was renewed in principle, but without any specified funding allocations being made or a term limit being imposed.

The goals of the CDS were listed as follows:

1 Reduce the demand for drugs;
2 Reduce drug-related mortality and morbidity;
3 Improve the effectiveness of accessibility to substance abuse information and interventions;
4 Restrict the supply of illicit drugs and reduce the profitability of illicit drug trafficking;
5 Reduce the costs of substance abuse to Canadian society. (Health Canada 1998, 4–5)

Within the dynamics of these targets, drug users occupied a nebulous and uncertain position, caught as they were between the representations of the medical community (harm reduction) and those of the law enforcement community (criminality). In practice, however, prevention and treatment were completely eclipsed by a concentration of effort on responses coordinated by law enforcement. In 2001, an Auditor General's report documented that of the nearly $440 million spent annually by eleven departments and agencies at the federal level to address illicit drug use in Canada, roughly 95 per cent had been spent on supply reduction. This figure was an estimate, though, as 'the federal government could not provide complete information on resources spent to address illicit drugs' (Auditor General 2001, 14). The report also noted that in 1999 roughly 50,000 people were charged with offences under the CDSA, that two-thirds of those charges were cannabis related, and that half of all charges had been laid for possession. Reflecting this trend more broadly, over 50 per cent of all drug charges (for all substances) were for possession (ibid., 4). Thus supply-reduction strategies did not seem to target supply reduction, but rather made it possible, through an increase in resources for the law enforcement community, to actively pursue minor possession charges.

Decriminalization and Medical Use

Concurrent with the ongoing tweaking of the CDS was the design, passage, and implementation of Bill C-8 in 1996. This piece of legislation continued to code marijuana use as deviant and as best responded to through criminal sanctions. Bill C-8 was portrayed as an attempt to meet Canada's international obligations under the Single Convention on Narcotic Drugs (1961), the Convention on Psychotropic Substances (1971), and the United Nations Convention Against Illicit Traffic in Narcotic Drugs and Psycotropic Substances (1988). Titled the Controlled Drug and Substance Act (CDSA) once it was passed, Bill C-8 was greeted with widespread opposition by most of the witnesses who had been called to testify on its merits before it was passed. It was argued that the CDSA took an American organizational approach with the legal intent of perpetuating the criminalization of drug use. Proponents of the bill pointed to various of its provisions – reduced sentences for cannabis possession, the removal of the possibility of a traceable criminal record for possession offences, and treatment and rehabilitation as declared goals of sentencing – when making claims that it was progressive legislation. Other interpretations, however, highlighted the disingenuous intent of these provisions. For example, the Canadian Bar Association noted that the reduction in possession sentences (from seven years to five) left defendants unable to request trial by jury; that summary convictions for possession still gave those convicted a criminal record; and that continuing harsh sentencing guidelines would encourage disrespect for the law, as marijuana was a relatively 'harmless substance' (Canadian Bar Association 1996).

These contending interpretations were possible in part because the CDSA reflected competing representations of drug users in medical and law enforcement discourses. While drug use and drug users remained criminalized, Section 56 entitled the Minister of Health to grant exemptions from the provisions of the act 'for medical or scientific purpose or "the public interest."' In this way, the CDSA retained a backdoor for the further medicalization of representations of Canadian drug users. However, there had been similar clauses in earlier Canadian drug laws, and health ministers had rarely resorted to them, as seen in the Belleau case outlined in the previous chapter.

The Charter of Rights and Freedoms (1982) opened up space for aspects of Canadian drug law to be challenged on a constitutional basis. For example, penalties for importing/exporting were reduced because of the decision in R. v. Smith that a minimum prison term of seven years for the offence was unconstitutional under Section 12 of the Charter, which defines cruel and unusual punishment. In an environment in which dominant representations of drug users fluctuated between potential patient and criminal suspect, the Canadian government engaged in performatives of a medicalized harm reduction approach, while law enforcement accelerated the criminalization of drug use, marijuana users themselves would increasingly challenge Canadian drug law as set out in the CDSA. Overzealous investigations by police and prosecutions by the Canadian state provided opportunities for medicinal users to launch Charter cases that would push not only towards safe access to medical marijuana, but also towards the decriminalization of marijuana possession.

In 1997 an Ontario Court accepted in R. v. Clay that marijuana was a relatively harmless substance. Though he was found guilty of cultivating and trafficking marijuana, Clay was variously described by observers as 'white,' 'middle-class,' 'articulate,' and 'respectable' (Erickson and Oscapella 1999, 314). In the same year in Ontario, another landmark case was heard. In R. v. Parker a man who suffered from epileptic episodes was charged with the possession and trafficking of marijuana. In reaching a decision, the judge conceded that marijuana helped his medical condition by controlling his seizures and that to deprive him of it would deny his primary Charter right to health and protection of life. His right to grow marijuana for himself was recognized; however, he was found guilty of trafficking because he had given marijuana to others who suffered from various illnesses. The decision and conviction were appealed (ibid.).

In 1998 an Alberta man with multiple sclerosis was charged with possession of marijuana for the purposes of trafficking after he made it known that he was going to supply a fellow sufferer, who was on trial for possession of marijuana, on the steps of the courthouse. In *R. v. Krieger*, the judge found that this case should be considered an exception to the rule that all traffickers must receive jail time. The judge cited the defendant's motive (to alleviate suffering) and the healing abilities of marijuana in levying a fine instead of a jail sentence (ibid.).

In 2000, Parker's appeal was heard. The Ontario Court of Appeal found that the blanket prohibition on possession did not accord with the principles of fundamental justice as the ongoing criminal prohibition for bona fide medical users infringed on their Charter right (Section 7) to liberty because of the possibility of imprisonment (Senate 2002c, 300). Because no doctor at the time would write a prescription for marijuana, no pharmacist would fill it, and no legal supply existed, the court argued that the medical exemption established in *Wakeford* was illusory, with too much power vested with the minister to grant exemptions on an ad hoc basis (under Section 56 of the CDSA).[3] The court declared the prohibition on the possession of marijuana to be unconstitutional and of no force and effect, though it gave the government one year to amend the law to include adequate exemptions for medical use (ibid., 301). Forced by the courts, the federal government introduced the Marihuana Medical Access Regulations (MMAR) on 30 July 2001, one day before the deadline.

In this context of legal and legislative modification, it is instructive to think beyond traditional cause/effect explanations and move towards an understanding of how these changes became possible. In his assertion of the causal properties of legal norms, Melvyn Green (1979) has argued that 'Canadian narcotics control, then, is not the product of conflicting interests. Nor does it represent a translation of public morality into legal norms. It is rather those legal norms that created the public morality that were responsible for the moral transformation of a private indulgence into a public crime ... The law is as likely to be a vehicle for social change as social change is to precipitate legislative revision' (1979, 78).

Green's approach, though, both reifies and mystifies law by alienating it from its social context (Boyd 1984, 105). Law as a technology of power, both reflective of and constitutive of other social relations of power, does not arise in a social vacuum. Therefore, two interrelated questions come to the fore at moments of change: How was it possible? And why was it deemed necessary to modify legal norms at this particular time?

The argument is not that changes to the law or interpretations of the law that have occurred since 1998 should be dismissed outright as instances of law establishing new boundaries of morality and practices of representation. Rather, a slightly different but extremely consequential point needs be to made: these instances illustrate the mutually constitutive relationship between law (policy) and dominant representations of drug users (theory). As is outlined above, with everything else being equal, it seems unlikely that appeals for medical marijuana or decriminalization of possession would have succeeded sixty years earlier because of the dominant representation of illicit drug use/users. At the same time, one has to recognize how contemporary legal decisions have provided space for alternative representations of illicit drug use/users to be brought forward into the common iterative of the drugs discourse.

In this context of legal uncertainty and ongoing tensions in the representations of illicit drug users in the Canadian drugs discourse, the government began to seek the best means for controlling the bodies of individual drug users and the body politic. Furthermore, growing public interest in the issue made it politically viable to devote considerable attention to Canadian policy on illicit drugs. Concomitant calls for the maintenance and the reform of drug legislation could not be authoritatively arbitrated as it became clear to most interested parties that contemporary knowledge of the issues was limited, and this gave impetus to the creation of both a Senate Special Committee on Illegal Drugs (March 2001) and a Parliamentary Special Committee on the Non-Medical Use of Drugs (May 2001) to map the terrain of illicit drug use and users in Canada.

The Senate Special Committee on Illegal Drugs: Mandate and Framing

The Senate Special Committee was tasked with examining the approach taken to cannabis by Canada, the effectiveness of the approach, other policy options practised in other countries, Canada's obligations under previously signed international agreements, the social and health consequences of cannabis, and with exploring the possible policy consequences (Senate 2002a, 8). In pursuit of these aims, this inquiry was discursively framed around the notion of individual autonomy: 'In a free and democratic society, which recognizes fundamentally but not exclusively the rule of law as the source of normative rules and in which government must promote autonomy as far as possible and therefore make only sparing use of the instruments of constraint, public policy on psychoactive substances must be structured around the guiding principles respecting the life, health, security, and rights and freedoms of individuals, who naturally and legitimately seek their own well-being and development and can recognize the presence, difference, and equality of others' (ibid., 7).

In contrast to the introduction to the Le Dain Commission almost thirty years earlier, the Senate Committee had shifted the burden of proof for the legitimacy of regulation and social discipline onto the state. The *state* would have to prove that marijuana was harmful in order to justify prohibition; moreover, it would have to prove that even *with* harm, the current system of control did not unduly infringe on individual rights and freedoms. Thus, directly citing the liberal communicative theory of Jurgen Habermas, the committee argued that 'ethical public policy on illegal drugs, and on cannabis in particular, must *promote reciprocal autonomy built through a constant exchange of dialogue within the community*' (ibid., 11). In the eyes of the committee, as a facilitator of human action, 'particularly ... processes allowing for the building of arrangements between government of the citizenry and governance of the self,' the state could impose criminal sanctions only where actions cause significant direct dangers to others (ibid., 11). Steeped in the discourse of contemporary liberal theory, the committee demonstrated a naivety to the scope and methods of contemporary power/relations. First, communication between the state and individuals is rarely if ever on equal terms. Second, as has been illustrated by this genealogy of drug users in Canada, there are a variety of disciplinary technologies besides criminal sanction that can regulate social behaviour, the most important being the representational practices constituted within discourse itself.

In negotiating the borders of individual autonomy and state intervention, one of the key roles assumed by the Senate Committee was of a truth producer. The process of truth telling placed science in the privileged position of the adjudicator of competing truth claims. Though it was argued that 'scientific knowledge cannot replace either personal reflection or the political decision-making process,' science was presented as a methodology that 'supports the public policy process' (ibid., 12). Furthermore, committee members asserted that Karl Popper's principle of falsifiability was the most appropriate method for assessing competing truth claims (Senate 2002b, 131). In adopting a scientific approach to the study of drug use and drug users in Canada, the committee members believed that they had a duty to 'educate,' not just to disseminate information that would 'convince' the general public (Senate 2002a, 10). As such, the Senate Committee saw itself as probing the limits of contemporary knowledge and exposing the myths which 'clouded' it (ibid.).

During their deliberations and the expert testimony, but prior to speaking truth through the release of their report, committee members stated that their desire to overcome the 'cloud of myth' required them to treat the testimony of various experts differently. In the report, they stated that

> it can be said that we did not handle the testimony of researchers and those of practising experts in the same way. That is true in part. To the extent that researchers presented data lending itself to critical review, containing verifiable data, which does not mean proof, on specific subjects, making it gradually possible to answer our empirical questions, we attached a certain degree of importance to them ... The information from practitioners more often tended to express opinions than to present study data. They also did not have the same concern to give precise answers to the questions put to them. Those opinions are important, as are those of the Canadians we heard and who wrote to us, but they are nevertheless opinions, not cold hard data. (Senate 2002b, 20)

The deference to the quality of the information provided by academics and physicians was matched by the quantity of witnesses from these professions who appeared before the committee in contrast to the number of law enforcement presenters. Approximately eighteen medical doctors, sixteen treatment professionals, twenty-eight academic researchers, and thirty law enforcement officers appeared over the course of testimony (Senate 2002e). This marked a further shift in the power/relations that help constitute the Canadian drugs discourse and representations of the bodies of drug users in that it privileged systematic investigations of academic and medical researchers over the claims of practitioners, particularly law enforcement.

Representation of Drug Use/Users

In attempting to discredit drug mythology, one of the first discursive representations to be challenged was the notion that illicit drug use is harmful by definition; it was argued that claiming 'use is abuse' not only was inaccurate but also undermined the kinds of distinctions that were necessary for establishing successful prevention programs (Senate 2002a, 25–6). The committee also abandoned terminology that it considered inflammatory and ultimately counterproductive in constructing an accurate mapping of the individual drug user. For example, 'drug addiction should no longer be used and we should talk instead of substance abuse and dependency,' and 'regular use does not necessarily mean problem use' (Senate 2002b, 124). Furthermore, 'in our view it is clear that the term addiction, severely criticized for its medical and moral overtones, is inadequate to properly describe the different forms of at-risk and problem uses. It is even less useful when it comes to cannabis, whose addictive potential is low' (2002b, 164).

Thus, committee members implicitly argued that for a truly effective harm reduction approach to be implemented, new language, though not a new discursive framework, needed to be adopted.

Marijuana as a substance was also discursively separated from other illicit drugs. In the report, the following distinction was made by committee members: 'It has been maintained that drugs including cannabis, are not dangerous because they are illegal but rather are illegal because they are dangerous. This is perhaps true of other types of drugs, but not of cannabis' (Senate 2002a, 38). Marijuana users themselves were represented as largely being upstanding members of society who did not deserve or require criminal sanctions. Alan Young, a high-profile defence lawyer for medical marijuana cases, stated during his testimony that

> I get two to three calls a week from otherwise law-abiding citizens who are pot smokers who have been fired from their jobs or have been denied entry into the United States or access to their children or government employment. These people have been treated like common criminals. This is the biggest problem with the marijuana prohibition: If you treat someone who is otherwise law-abiding as a common criminal, they will start to disrespect people like Chief Fantino [Chief of Toronto Police Ser-

vices] and the other people who really do try to serve and protect our interests. (Senate 2002c, 380)

The distinction made between marijuana users and common criminals permeated the report. Most important, enough discursive space had been opened in the illicit drugs discourse that it was no longer a matter of debating whether lengthy stints of incarceration were inappropriate, but whether the stigma and associated social consequences of a criminal record were appropriate. The authors were able to conclude that 'cannabis, the criminal organizations that control part of the production and distribution chain aside, neither leads to crime nor compromises safety. Even its social and health costs are relatively small compared to those of alcohol and tobacco. In fact, more than for any other illegal drug, we can safely state that *its criminalization is the principal source of social and economic costs*' (Senate 2002d, 582).

Essentially, we see the dichotomous construction of a new typology of persons involved in illicit drugs, one that blends with some traditional representations: consumers, who are relatively harmless (the new), and producers/sellers, who are a threat (the old). In establishing a regulatory system for cannabis that would remove the prohibition against possession, the Senate Committee was advocating a simultaneous effort to target organized crime and illegal trafficking (ibid., 604).

In reaching conclusions that amounted to a call to legalize and thus potentially desecuritize marijuana use, the Senate Special Committee was vehemently opposed by Canadian law enforcement. It is interesting that law enforcement framed the marijuana threat mainly in terms of its alleged medical consequences, instead of merely attempting to reassert traditional representations that focused on links to criminality. This highlighted the fundamental shift that had occurred over the previous five decades in the terms used for framing the illicit drug discourse. For example, Michael J. Boyd, Deputy Chief of the Toronto Police Service and Chair of the Drug Abuse Committee for the Canadian Association of Chiefs of Police, distinguished himself as one of the most aggressive proponents of the prohibition cause with the following statement to the committee:

Message number one is that drugs, including cannabis, are harmful ... There is considerable misinformation about the physiological consequences of cannabis use. There is no doubt that heavy use has negative health consequences. The most important are in the following areas: respiratory damage, physical coordination, pregnancy and postnatal development, memory and cognition, and psychiatric effects ... Generally, marijuana (cannabis) and its derivative products are described in this context to distance the drug from the recognized harm associated with other illegal drugs. This has been a successful yet dangerous approach and contributes to the misinformation, misunderstanding and increasing tolerance associated with marijuana use. Marijuana is a powerful drug with a variety of effects. Marijuana users are subject to a variety of adverse health consequences that include respiratory damage, impaired physical coordination, problem pregnancy and postnatal deficits, impaired memory and cognition, and psychiatric effects. Marijuana use is associated with poor work and school performance and learning problems for younger users. Marijuana is internationally recognized as a gateway drug for other drug use. Risk factors for marijuana dependence are similar to those of other forms of drug abuse. (in Senate 2002b, 80–2)

Boyd did not offer or provide the names of reports or studies that had reached these conclusions; rather, he presented them as commonsensical facts. Later in his testimony he reverted back to more traditional representational practices in law enforcement discourses by reasserting that 'increased drug availability and drug use will worsen our crime problems. Increased drug use has terrible consequences for our citizens' (in Senate 2000c, 398).

One of the most striking aspects of the Senate Report was that unlike previous state investigations of drug use in Canada, it questioned the credibility of law enforcement and challenged and undermined that credibility at every opportunity. Over the report's four volumes, the testimony of law enforcement was often presented as illustrative of misinformed and untenable positions that must be extinguished in order to engage in rational public policy choices with regard to marijuana. For example, the authors of the report felt compelled to quote one member of the law enforcement community in order to point out the factual errors in his statement (Senate 2002b, 134). Moreover, in what can be interpreted as an attempt to further circumscribe the discursive authority of law enforcement, committee members urged that education and prevention programs, which had long been controlled by police services and taught by police officers, be reconsidered. Police were represented as lacking both expertise and credibility in the provision of drug education and as possessing a clear conflict of interest that promoted an unrealistic focus on abstinence in lieu of effective education that could reduce the potential harms of illicit drug use. Yet at the same time, the frequent references to the opinions of the law enforcement community demonstrated its continuing privileged position within the power/relations that constitute the drugs discourse, even if that position was no longer hegemonic.

Representations of the Medical Community

When medical marijuana became possible in Canada, the CMA and the Canadian Medical Protective Association (CPMA) opposed the program and recommended that their members not prescribe any type of medical marijuana treatment, even in cases of terminal illness. In his testimony before the Senate Committee, Dr Henry Haddad, the CMA's president, described the situation as follows:

> While our understanding of all the possible long-term health effects that prolong Canada's use is still evolving, what we do know is troubling. The health risks range from acute effects such as anxiety, dysphoria, or the feeling of being ill; cognitive impairment to the chronic effects such as bronchitis, emphysema, and cancer. Canada's youth have also been subject to pulmonary damage comparable to that produced by tobacco use but the effects are much more acute and rapid. Evidence suggests that smoking two or three cannabis cigarettes a day has the same health effect as smoking 20 cigarettes a day. Therefore, the potential long-term health effects of cannabis use could be quite severe. The CMA's concerns regarding the impact of cannabis are in part why we are opposed to the federal government's current medical marijuana access regulations. In our May 7, 2001, letter to the Minister of Health, the CMA noted 'lack of credible information on the risks and benefits of medical marijuana.' During discussions on the government's medical marijuana regulations, we highlighted the health concerns and research that indicates that 'marijuana is an addictive substance that is known to have psychoactive effects and in its smoke form is particularly harmful to health.' We have concluded that while benefits of medical marijuana are unknown, the health risks are real. Therefore, it would be inappropriate for physicians to prescribe marijuana to their patients, a position that was supported by the Canadian Medical Association. (In Senate 2002b, 194)[4]

In assuming the roles of a *neo-parrhesiastes* over the effects of marijuana, the CMA was unwilling to accept counterevidence, both clinical and anecdotal, that showed that the substance helped relive pain, alleviate muscle spasms, reduce nausea, stimulate appetite, retard glaucoma, and control epilepsy and other nervous disorders. In this manner, one possible interpretation of the CMA's position was that in denying the efficacy of marijuana treatments, physicians were exerting their traditional professional privilege to determine what constitutes safe and effective treatment, rather than having standards imposed on them by government. The irony is that several decades earlier, physicians had been fighting to retain the right to prescribe scheduled drugs. Now, when presented with the opportunity to legally to do so, they were largely unwilling.

Yet, even though it opposed the medical marijuana regime established by Health Canada, the CMA had been in favour of the decriminalization of possession. In calling for decriminalization, the CMA argued that 'the minimal negative health effects of moderate use would be attested to by the estimated 1.5 million Canadians who smoke marijuana for recreational purposes. The real harm is the legal and social fallout' (CMA 2001c).[5]

However, as much as their opposition may have been about upholding professional principles and the requirements of scientific proof, a memorandum issued by the CMPA to all Canadian doctors constructed the issue as one primarily concerned with avoiding lawsuits by patients and professional sanctions by fellow physicians. In that memorandum, the legal advice given by CMPA was that 'Given the consequences that may befall physicians with respect to their licensing body, or potential medico-legal liability, physicians will want to be very careful when determining whether to assist a patient in making an application under these regulations ... Any physician who does not feel qualified to make any of the declarations required by [medical marijuana] regulations should not feel compelled to do so' (CMPA 2001).

Thus, the message given to physicians by their own professional governing bodies was two pronged: the CMPA instructed its members not to prescribe marijuana unless they had detailed medical knowledge, while the CMA contended that no one could possibly have detailed knowledge because sufficient clinical trials had not been undertaken to determine whether marijuana had any health benefits. However, knowledge of its negative effects, often based on dubious research methods, could be considered to hold the status of medical knowledge.

In trying to counteract the medical community's reticence towards medical marijuana, the Senate Special Committee in its report, drawing from the self-representation of physicians as read through the Hippocratic Oath, initially argued that 'the question, and the only question for physicians as professionals, is whether, to what extent, and in what circumstances, marijuana serves a therapeutic purpose' (Senate 2002a, 18). This discursive deployment was perhaps intended to nudge Canadian physicians into participating in the provision of medical marijuana. At the same time, it was congruent with the CMA's own refusal to give approval based on the absence of scientific knowledge of therapeutic applications. Thus, later in the report the committee pushed further, maintaining that

> the proper role of the physician should be to make a diagnosis of the patient's medical conditions or symptoms. If the condition or symptom is one where cannabis has potential therapeutic applications, the patient would be authorized to use the therapeutic product of his or her choice, including cannabis. This would also mean eliminating the current requirement [in the Marihuana Medical Access Regulations] that all other 'conventional treatments' have been tried or considered before the use of cannabis is authorized. There is no justification for making cannabis an option of 'last resort.' (Senate 2002c, 311)

The authors of the report realized that 'requiring medical practitioners to act as "gatekeepers" in the use of marijuana for therapeutic purposes' would continue to create significant impediments to access, particularly as medical marijuana was represented as 'challenging us on the very concept of modern medicine' because it was a natural product rather than a chemically synthesized one (ibid., 309; Senate 2002b, 190).

Faced with the conundrum of how to further medicalize the drugs discourse while also medicalizing the representational practices that constituted marijuana use/users – and this without the cooperation of the medical community – the Senate Committee stated the following in its report in an attempt to undermine medical authority in this area:

> The true harm, the worst of all, the most intolerable, the only one that must absolutely be repressed is wanting to make people happy by deepening their fear of disease and death, without asking each individual to make personal choices and realize his or her preferences. The true, the

[*sic*] only harm stems from health ideology, from the *furor sanandi*, which sketches out our happiness without us being able to enjoy it. Does this mean that everything should be permitted without distinction? Of course not. But the test is still to discover step by step through our trials and errors, and it cannot be imposed on us by experts – doctors or economists – in the name of a prior and death causing order. The joy of fertile disorder is better for life than the boredom of a type of planning, the arbitrary nature of which equals nothing but sterility. (J.F. Malherbe, in Senate 2002c, 409)

By challenging the authority of the medical *and* law enforcement communities, the committee was attempting to unsettle the contemporary power/relations constituted by the drugs discourse.

Recommendations

In making their recommendations, the authors of the report felt it necessary to distinguish decriminalization from a harm reduction approach to illicit drugs:

Decriminalization of use is a weak variation of prohibition, in the long run entailing more disadvantages than advantages. In addition to failing to affect the production chain and retaining the illegal aspect, it leaves no room for dispensing information to and promoting responsible behaviour by users, or for strong preventative measures. Conversely, the harm reduction approach is a strong variation of a prohibition system. While this approach recognizes the impossibility of eliminating the damage done by market criminalization, it seeks nonetheless to reduce the negative effects of prohibition on users, who are the focus of its main thrust, by introducing education on drug content. (Senate 2002d, 600–1)

In light of this contention, the committee's primary conclusion was that marijuana possession should be legalized and its production and distribution regulated by an appropriate government agency. Moreover, it argued for a loosening of medical marijuana access regulations and for a licensing system for compassion clubs. It asserted that these policy choices should not be interpreted as 'abandoning ship and giving up on promoting well-being for Canadians,' or as 'fly[ing] in the face of the fundamental values of our society' (Senate 2002a, 45).

Rather, the senators proposed this transformation in drug policy based on the belief that 'the continued prohibition of cannabis jeopardizes the health and well-being of Canadians ... [and] that the continued criminalization of cannabis undermines the fundamental values set out in the *Canadian Charter of Rights and Freedoms* and confirmed in the history of a country *based on diversity and tolerance*' (ibid.; italics in original). By framing the transformation of drug law in this manner, the report was making a conscious attempt to engage with established performatives of Canadian identity in order to provide legitimacy for its recommendations.

In positioning itself as significantly different from the status quo, the Special Committee was prescribing what it asserted was a reformulation of the role of the State and criminal law in Canada. Those roles should be defined by '*developing and promoting but not controlling human action* and as *stipulating only necessary prohibitions* relating to the fundamental principle of respect for life, other persons, and a harmonious community, and as *supporting and assisting others, not judging or condemning difference* (Senate 2002d, 45; italics in original).

Thus the committee's justification for ending the marijuana prohibition was based on its assessment that current research into the effects of marijuana could not provide a definitive justification for its prohibited status in terms of its probable medical and social effects. In addition, the committee argued that only behaviour causing demonstrable harm to others should be prohibited: illegal trafficking, selling to minors, and impaired driving under the influence of marijuana (ibid., 39).

At the same time, the committee found that despite being a public policy issue for more than ninety years, there was a dearth of reliable, systematic, and accessible information on all facets of illicit drug use in Canada. It maintained that further research was necessary on medical marijuana, the effects of driving under the influence of marijuana, and the long-term effects of marijuana use. Furthermore, the committee called for up-to-date national survey data on drug use and consumption patterns, as well as improvements in police and treatment statistics that would provide more details on drug use and drug users. It noted that knowledge continued to be lacking in part because Canada had not given itself the proper means by which to gather it (Senate 2002c, 242).

The authors of the report considered it imperative that public policy on illicit drugs draw from available knowledge and scientific research.

It did not, however, expect science to provide the answers to political issues: science was to serve as a support mechanism in decision making at the individual and governmental levels (Senate 2002a, 12; 2002b, 45–9). Thus it was argued that Canada needed both an illicit drug and dependency monitoring agency and a nationally coordinated research program to help future decision makers. To these ends, the committee called for Canada to create the position of National Advisor on Psychoactive Substances and Dependency. This advisor, who preferably would have a medical background, would be responsible for advising Cabinet, coordinating departments, overseeing the creation and satisfaction of objectives in Canada's drug strategy, and serving as an international spokesperson. Finally, the committee demanded that comprehensive education programs and information campaigns be established to prevent abuse, dependency, and other at-risk behaviours.

Parliamentary Special Committee on Non-Medical Use of Drugs

In May 2001, concurrent with the investigations of the Senate Special Committee, the House of Commons established the Special Committee on Non-Medical Use of Drugs. This committee was given a broad mandate to study 'the factors underlying or relating to the non-medical use of drugs in Canada' and to bring forward recommendations that in the opinion of the committee would reduce 'the dimensions of the problem involved in such use' (House of Commons 2002, 1). In contrast to the Senate Special Committee on Illegal Drugs, which had been granted a narrow mandate to study marijuana, the House of Commons Committee was being asked to take an expansive view of the illicit drug problem and to examine 'all aspects of Canadian drug policy, including Canada's Drug Strategy, the effectiveness of existing prevention efforts, and what is being done to address linkages with organized crime' (ibid.). According to its final report, 'members agreed that the non-medical use of drugs in Canada is a *pervasive and growing problem* that must be answered with sustained, broad based, adequately funded policy initiatives that can be applied to all substances of abuse, regardless of their source or legal status' (ibid., 2). Given this representation of non-medical drug use, 'we cannot ignore the impact of the pervasive use of substances on Canadian society. This is not someone else's problem. All orders of government and the private sector must work harder to reduce the use of substances and ensure Canadians enjoy healthy, safe lives' (ibid., 21).

The low level of public awareness about the extent of the issues was explained as a result of the 'marginalization and stigmatization of drug users [that] has created a "conspiracy of silence" around the incidence of substance abuse and its negative impact on individuals, families, and communities in Canada' (ibid., 68).

Regarding the non-medical use of drugs, the committee stated that the issues raised were primarily 'public health issues that must be addressed within a public health framework' (ibid., 5). Abstinence was presented as the 'best way of preventing all types of dependence' and as a catalyst for the adoption of safe and healthy behaviours (ibid., 66). For those who were already using drugs, the committee declared that 'everything possible must be done to improve the health of substance users and keep them healthy enough to be able to seek treatment when they are ready' (ibid., 87).

Clearly, the House of Commons Special Committee and the Senate Committee differed vastly in their perceptions of issues surrounding drug use. The Senate Special Committee framed the overarching issue as one about the legitimate scope of control over the behaviour of individuals; the House Committee simply assumed that controls were required. The primary issue, then, became what types of controls would be most effective in the promotion of the health of the individual body and the Canadian body politic. Moreover, the House Committee also began from the premise that non-medical drug use in Canada was a pervasive and growing problem; this shaped what kinds of policy options could be considered acceptable. A reduction in the overall levels of state control over individual behaviour became a less likely possibility, though this did not preclude a change in the technologies of control and discipline.

On a more superficial level, there was also a marked difference in writing style between the two sets of reports. The Senate Committee report reads very much like a research paper, with extensive citations and references to legal/academic/medical sources. By contrast, the House Report is stylistically modelled on a policy document, with less attention devoted to alternative viewpoints.

Representations of Drug Use/Drug Users

According to the committee's final report, 'harmful use of substances (mostly of psychoactive substances including alcohol) has been related to a wide variety of social and health issues, including HIV/AIDS, Hepatitis C, homelessness, family violence, prostitution, sexual exploitation, delinquency, crime, and child abuse and neglect' (ibid., 5). For example, the authors of the report noted that in 1993 less than 3 per cent of new HIV/AIDS cases were linked to injection drug use. By 2001, 24.6 per cent of all new cases were linked to injection drug use (ibid., 74).

Canadians who demonstrated 'a pattern of harmful use of substances' were described as often having a 'history of victimization, sexual and physical abuse, family violence, mental health issues, learning disabilities, school failure, and criminality' (ibid., 69). By associating 'harmful' drug use with social problems, health issues, and other forms of deviant behaviour, the committee managed to retain the core of traditional representations of drug users in Canada while utilizing softer language that made these representations more convincing. As in traditional representations, drug users were being portrayed above all else as abnormal. Some were portrayed as victims of broader social problems, others are simply deviant. Perhaps most interesting is how these representations of drug use and drug users are able to continue to imply the notion of the contagion theory. When harmful drug use is associated with a host of social problems, and then it is argued that these in turn encourage harmful drug use, drug use becomes *the* catalyst for the spread of social problems, and by definition further drug use.

A majority of committee members expressed the need for reforms in cannabis legislation; but given the interpretation of drug use and drug users, the range of policy choices to be adjudicated was necessarily constricted. Committee members argued that 'removing prohibitions would send the wrong message by normalizing use, especially for young people' (ibid., 128). It was argued that smoking marijuana in any amount was unhealthy because of the high concentration of tar and benzopyrene in the substance.

Furthermore, credence was given to the old notion that 'cannabis serves as a gateway to the use of other more harmful drugs, if not directly through dependency, then indirectly through the social milieu and risk taking aspects of the behaviour' (in ibid., 129). Echoing the opinion of law enforcement witnesses that 'Canada's existing laws have been successful in limiting the harm caused by illicit drug use' and that 'we need to reinforce a balanced approach that instills meaningful and proportionate consequences for serious crime, combined with measures to reinforce desired behaviour in our young people,' some committee members argued that the legislative status quo should be maintained and that the deterrent effect of prohibition could be 'more effective with increased enforcement efforts' (ibid., 113–14).

The medicinal benefits of marijuana were described as only being *potential* until Health Canada's five-year research plan (begun in 2001) could provide a better understanding of the use of cannabinoids for medical purposes (ibid., 19). However, not all members of the committee had confidence in the federal government's ability to provide medical marijuana. The minority report acknowledged that medical use of marijuana extended beyond the mandate of the committee; the New Democratic Party (NDP) committee member wished to 'draw attention to the serious problems and flaws in the federal government's medical marijuana program,' including restrictive and overly bureaucratic regulations that were limiting access to legitimate users (ibid., 182).

Representations of Law Enforcement

In stark contrast to the members of the Senate Special Committee, the members of the House Committee generally took a positive attitude towards the opinions of law enforcement and allowed them to assume the role of a *neo-parrhesiastes* by raising few objections to their interpretation of the current situation in Canada and the best way to respond. This deference to law enforcement testimony made it possible to reaffirm the links between organized crime and illicit drugs, with an added emphasis on the new presence of terrorist organizations in the global drug trade. The Deputy Solicitor General stated that sales of illicit drugs are a major source of funding for organized crime and terrorism and estimated that 80 per cent of funding for organized crime comes from illicit drug sales (ibid., 5, 109). Based on the testimony of Julian Fantino, the Toronto police chief, the committee reported that 'it is believed funds derived from ... [hydroponic marijuana growing] operations are used to fund other drug importation, such as that of heroin, MDA, and ecstasy, and other criminal enterprises' (ibid., 9).

It is interesting, though, that even when some witnesses countered that prohibition itself encouraged the participation of criminal syndicates because of the risks and rewards involved, the association between organized crime and the illicit drug trade remained firmly entrenched within the drugs discourse, with no reference to the legal context that made the rewards possible. The only clear break with the law enforcement community occurred with regard to financial resources. While many law enforcement members demanded more resources and improved legislation during their testimony and in their submissions, the committee recommended that the government stick with the fiscal and legislative status quo (ibid., 109–10).

Besides utilizing a discursive framework that reflected its understanding of the issues at play, one that maintained the securitization of illicit drugs, and despite its own role as 'crime fighter,' law enforcement attempted to protect its privileged position in the dissemination of information to young people. It argued, for example, that the DARE (Drug Abuse Resistance Education) program in Canadian schools was 'an important service to the community as well as a valuable opportunity to establish a relationship with youngsters at an early and impressionable age' (ibid., 66). No mention was made in the report about this being inappropriate, despite criticisms raised that the 'just say no' message discourages honest discussion of risks (ibid., 66). These omissions made it possible to improve the position of law enforcement within the power/relations constituted by the drugs discourse.

The only dissension to the deference shown to law enforcement was from the NDP member of the committee, who concluded in her minority report that law enforcement was totally ineffective in its approach. She argued that 'law enforcement efforts have almost completely failed to stop the flow of illicit drugs into Canada' despite having an 'overwhelming share of the federal funds.' Moreover, she commented that if drug misuse is a public health issue, why do the police deliver drug education programs? (ibid., 180).

Representations of the Medical Community

One of the biggest surprises of the House of Commons Report was the disproportionate amount of space devoted to the interpretations of law enforcement in comparison to those of the medical profession. The medical community was barely even referred to in the report other than being described as dedicated professionals in a difficult job facing difficult situations created by a lack of resources, lack of training, and lack of information; however, potential medical consequences of illicit drug use that reinforced the interpretations of law enforcement were present throughout the report (ibid., 76). This politics of exclusion illustrates the power/relations constitutive of this process in terms of the entrenchment of law enforcement as a *neo-parrhesiastes* within Canadian drug discourses at the policy level, as well as the committee's own predisposition towards a primarily enforcement-based solution to the issues, in order to combat organized crime and terrorism, which had been linked as constitutive threats.

Yet an inherent contradiction needed to be settled; by their own initial admission, the committee felt that a medical approach was the most effective manner in which to address illicit drug use. Thus, law enforcement practices with regard to illicit drugs that for legitimation were already drawing on preventing adverse medical effects, themselves became perversely medicalized. In the opinion of the majority of committee members, those practices offered what they considered were viable solutions to the problems that were being identified. In this way, the need for the expertise of physicians was diminished.

Issues and Recommendations

As with the Senate Special Committee's conclusions, one of the most prominent issues raised in the House of Commons Report was the lack of information resources that could be drawn from to gauge the level of non-medical drug use in Canada in order to develop comprehensive and effective responses. They lamented that the United States was spending six times as much on research into Canadian illicit drug issues as Canada itself and that the total budget of the U.S. National Institute on Drug Abuse ($1 billion) accounted for 80 per cent of funding for illicit drug research worldwide. The committee members were able to note that 'in Canada there is an alarming lack of information on the prevalence of use and harmful use of substances, trends, and overdoses which impedes the development of sound drug policymaking' as well as a lack of police statistics on specific charges laid, convictions, sentencing, and drugs seized in Canada (ibid., 20, 45).

Moreover, strongly influenced by the previous Auditor General's Report (2001), the committee raised troubling concerns about the lack of information on the achievements and shortcomings of the CDS. The authors of the House Report expressed that they had received anec-dotal evidence from a small number of witnesses about the good things being orchestrated under the CDS; however, the lack of infor-mation, coordination, accountability, evaluation, and cohesion was deeply worrisome (ibid., 36, 43). The CDS was presented as a potential failure of Canadian drug policy unless key changes were made to its structure and organization.

The key solution offered for this problem was exactly the same as the one put forward by the Senate Committee: the creation of a National Drug Commissioner, 'preferably with a background in health issues,' for a five-year term appointment with an annual budget of $1.5 million (ibid., 42). The role of the Drug Commissioner would be to 'assist in the overseeing and implementation of a renewed CDS and provide *objective, independent analysis*, and policy making recommen-dations' (ibid., 42; italics added). What remained undiscussed were the drawbacks to handing one institutional site a potential monopoly on illicit drugs knowledge (or, less dramatically, the distribution of this knowledge), especially given the historical record of previous depart-ments tasked with these responsibilities, such as the Office of the Divi-sion Chief.

While the issues of the compilation of knowledge and institutional coordination were significant, the committee will be best remembered for its recommendation that the possession of small amounts of cannabis be decriminalized, a recommendation that was heeded in principle by the federal government. What is interesting here, though, is that the committee argued that it was necessary to maintain all other existing prohibitions and to continue to prosecute all possession charges for other illicit substances as well as all production/trafficking charges for all illegal substances. The committee also urged that safe-injection facilities be implemented for intravenous drug users as a pilot program in order to determine whether these sites might help reduce the spread of HIV/AIDS and hepatitis. The authors of the report also recommended that special drug courts, which at the time were operating in Toronto, be established in various jurisdictions in order to force dependent drug users to undergo treatment. Instead of giving out prison sentences for crimes committed by drug-dependent individuals, drug courts require that the defendant undergo drug rehabilitation. The defendant avoids jail time if he or she successfully completes a treatment program and does not reoffend.

These policy recommendations were considered quite radical and were disputed even by some members of the House Committee itself. Furthermore, they should be seen as reflecting the long-standing tensions between law enforcement and the medical community for control of the individual body of the illicit drug user. In one sense, decriminalization can be interpreted as the culmination of the process begun during the late 1960s to desecuritize and medicalize the use of marijuana. At the same time, the use, production, and distribution of other illicit drugs remained securitized, thus maintaining a continuing role for law enforcement. Canadian Alliance members of the committee argued that 'harm reduction approaches' would encourage 'addicted Americans and others to relocate to Canada,' bringing a whole host of social problems and placing a drain on Canadian resources. Thus, we see the discursive construction of a new impending threat to Canada: the drug refugee (ibid., 171).

Safe-injection facilities became a contested site, one where medical prudence might well clash with the imperatives of policing. Generally, though, the House Committee blurred the divisions between the disciplines of control utilized by law enforcement and the medical community over drug users. For example, the notion of drug courts brought a medicalized response under the purview of an overall approach to illicit drug issues that was still securitized and punitive.

Findings and New Starting Points

In their respective examinations of Canadian responses to illicit drugs, the Senate Committee and the House Committee approached the issues from very different starting points. For the Senate, marijuana was not initially defined by the *problematique* of (ab)use; rather, the starting point was that individual behaviour should not be circumscribed except where it could be shown that demonstrable harm was being inflicted on others. In this way, the burden of proof that prohibition works was placed squarely on the state's shoulders. All evidence was ideally to be subject to careful scrutiny, and with direct reference to Karl Popper, no proposition was to be considered true; at best, it would be possible to say that any evidence had not yet been proven false (Senate 2002b, 132). The Special Senate Committee demonstrated at times a reflexive understanding of the social construction of knowledge and the relationship between knowledge claims and power in Canadian society.

For the House Committee, the starting point was that Canada was facing a widespread and dangerous problem with non-medical drug use. Its inquiry was framed as operating in a crisis environment in which quick and decisive action was required; as a consequence, key questions about the appropriateness of this construction were largely avoided. Moreover, the terms of discourse were favourably predisposed towards those who could present evidence that mirrored this assessment and who could buttress the parameters that had already been set. The concern of the majority of committee members became what *must* be done, given the commonsense construction of an illicit drug threat to Canadian society, rather than an assessment of whether placing the non-medical drug issue within a threat classification scheme was the most useful way to proceed. The committee cast illicit drugs as a health issue, yet its report almost exclusively quoted the testimony of law enforcement witnesses – an indication of the ongoing importance of law enforcement to the reproduction of illicit drugs as a security threat. What makes this particularly remarkable is that the House Committee heard testimony from at least eighty-five witnesses who were either physicians or from the treatment community, compared to only fifty from law enforcement. By contrast, the Senate Committee heard from approximately thirty-four medical and treatment witnesses and thirty law enforcement witnesses.

These vastly different starting points are what made possible many of the divergent recommendations of the two committees, particularly the split over the legalization and decriminalization of marijuana possession. There may also be a case for considering the politics made (im)possible by electoral exigencies. In the Canadian parliamentary system, senators are not elected; they are appointed for indefinite terms by the prime minister. So it is conceivable that less radical schemes were considered by the House Committee in order not to hinder re-election chances both for individual MPs and for the governing Liberal Party that convened the committee. However, if this was a factor, it clearly demonstrates the hardened positions of dominant representations of illicit drug use/users and what those representations consider legitimate responses. More importantly, it points to the disciplinary power of these conceptual norms.

At the same time, the two reports were remarkable for their key areas of convergence. For example, both delineated the use of illicit drugs as primarily a health issue, called for the creation of a National Drug Advisor, pointed to the need to increase the quantity and quality of illicit drug information, and recommended that organized crime be targeted. The popular representation was that both committees and their recommendations reflected a liberalizing of Canadian values suggestive of an increasd tolerance of behaviour outside of previously established norms. However, the changes proposed should be interpreted as reflecting *reconfigurations* in the power/relations of social control rather than their abandonment. Moreover, each report explicitly and implicitly conveyed and represented a politics of identity about who and what could be considered Canadian.

(Re)Reading Canadian Identity through the Canadian Drugs Discourse

Questions of national identity and of control over the individual body, in response to the perception of a security threat, are inextricably intertwined and mutually constitutive. At its heart, this relationship is fundamental to practices of contemporary Canadian society to an extent beyond Foucault's contention that liberalized forms of governance have gone hand in hand with increasing amounts of state dedication to biopolitics, discipline, panopticism, and corporeal regulation. What is to be considered threatening and the limits and rationales on the controls over individual bodies performatively underscore the collective sense of Self that is required to make a claim to *a* national identity. *The* national identity is performatively constituted by who/what *must* be feared, who/what *must* be controlled, and how they/these *must* be controlled. In the process of creating the realm of possible responses to a threat via the power/relations manifested in the representational practices of related discourses and those *neo-parrhesiastes* who at certain moments are able to shape them, an etching of *the* national identity is formed. Thus, national identities reflect both a collective sense of threat and what is considered to be *the* legitimate range of responses to that threat. The bodies of illicit drug users and illicit drugs themselves have played a central role in these dynamics.

Co-constitutive of the bandwidth of legitimate responses to illicit drugs have been decisions rendered within the Canadian legal system that have made decriminalization possible and medical marijuana necessary. As·mentioned earlier, the decision in *R. v. Parker* by the Ontario Court of Appeal in July 2000 found that the CDSA sections on marijuana had the potential to force those suffering from illness to have to choose between effective treatment and arrest (Senate Report 2002c, 300). The court gave Ottawa a year to change its laws to allow for the medical use of cannabis. The court also threatened to strike down all marijuana possession laws if the federal government failed to comply. In January 2003, in *R. v. Hitzig*, the case against the operators of the Toronto compassion club that had been raided in November 2002, the presiding judge ruled that the existing medical marijuana regulations were unconstitutional because they failed to give sick individuals real access to the drug. The federal government was again given time to respond and make changes (six months); if it did not, the possession law for everyone would be struck down.

In May 2003 the Ontario Court of Appeal upheld a lower court decision to acquit a Windsor teenager caught smoking marijuana in a park (*R. v. JP*). The judge found the laws prohibiting less than 30 grams of cannabis to be null and void because the MMAR had not responded adequately to the appeal court's decision in *Parker* based on a legal technicality. Almost immediately, federal Justice Minister Martin Cauchon adopted the advice of the House Committee and introduced legislation to decriminalize possession for up to 15 grams of marijuana. Persons found with less than 15 grams would be subject to a fine of up to $150 but would not receive a criminal record.[6] In July 2003, in response to the January ruling, Health Canada began to supply patients with medical marijuana.

Despite the increased attention devoted to Canadian drug law by the legal system, marijuana users remained in legal limbo for most of 2003. Decriminalization legislation still was not passed by Parliament, and existing legal rulings – particularly the May 2003 decision – and several ongoing court cases and constitutional challenges contributed to the confusion. Police in Ontario, Nova Scotia, and British Columbia stopped laying charges for possession of less than 30 grams of marijuana, as justices of the peace and judges interpreted the sections of the CDSA pertaining to the possession of small amounts of marijuana to be inoperable. Concurrently, federal prosecutors began to withdraw, adjourn, or stay proceedings for possession until legal clarity could be obtained.

All of this changed in October 2003 when the Ontario Court of Appeal ruled that the MMAR did not provide adequate access to medical marijuana for those with serious medical conditions, forcing them to turn to the illicit market for their supplies. However, instead of striking down the entire scheme, the court opted to tinker with the MMAR provisions in order to make them 'comply with the constitutional right to life, liberty, and security of the person' (Makin 2003). To this end, the ruling removed the following regulations:

- The need for a second physician to endorse a patient's request for inclusion in the program.
- A restriction which prevented designated, licensed growers from being financially compensated for supplying medical marijuana to persons eligible to receive it.
- Regulations that prevented growers from supplying more than one medical marijuana patient.
- A provision that prohibited licensed growers from producing crops in conjunction with more than two other growers.

The court contended that by making these revisions, it had removed barriers to access for patients under the MMAR, thus making the entire scheme constitutional. Critics, though, noted that in not altering (or removing) sections of the MMAR that imperil medical licences – the key factor leading colleges of physicians across the country to advise their members against signing marijuana exemption forms – the ruling had failed to address the most significant barrier to access (Damuzi 2003).

While the October ruling attempted to address some of the most glaring problems identified with the MMAR, the decision also upheld the constitutional legality of the prohibition against the possession of small amounts of marijuana – a prohibition that had been in legal limbo since *R. v. Hitzig* in January. The judges themselves argued that 'the interests of justice are best served by removing any uncertainty as to the constitutionality of the possession prohibition while at the same time providing for a constitutionally acceptable medical exemption' (Canadian Press 2003h). In other words, given the initial ruling in *Hitzig*, the Ontario Court of Appeal was able to ensure that the criminal prohibition was constitutional by addressing the concerns over access to medical marijuana. With the medical exemption now constitutional, the laws against possession once again became legally enforceable. In assessing the situation with regard to prospects for decriminalization legislation, Alan Young (on behalf of the decriminalization movement) remarked that 'politically, we lost big-time' (Makin 2003).

Yet even in the aftermath of a ruling that was strongly favourable to the federal government with regard to the MMAR and the reinstatement of laws against marijuana possession, Health Canada chose to defy aspects of the Ontario Court of Appeal ruling with respect to allowing licensed growers to provide marijuana to multiple patients with MMAR exemptions, in order to reduce the risk that production might go to non-medical use. In an unapologetic display, Health Canada's own press release stated that 'the limitations of production of marihuana by designated growers have been maintained: Designated-person Production License holders can grow for only one holder of an Authorization to Possess; and not more than three holders of licenses to produce can cultivate together. It was necessary to maintain these limitations to minimize the risk of diversion and to allow Canada to continue to meet its international obligations' (Health Canada 2003a).

Brian McAllister, lawyer for the teen in *R. v. JP*, argued that this reverted the legal context back to the pre-7 October situation in that possession laws were no longer constitutional. Young stated publicly that he planned to take Health Canada to court for contempt (Van Wageningen 2003).

Further justification of the marijuana prohibition came in December 2003, when the Supreme Court of Canada ruled 6–3 in favour of continuing with the prohibition against marijuana possession. In this case, *R. v. Malmo-Levine, Caine, and Clay*, the defendants had challenged the constitutionality of the law. In reaching the ruling, the justices attempted to distance the Canadian courts from the politics of decriminalization by divesting them of the responsibility to change Canadian marijuana laws; moreover, they would not have to take into account Health Canada's reticence in adopting the revisions to the MMAR demanded by the Ontario Court of Appeal. The decision concluded: 'It is within Parliament's legislative jurisdiction to criminalize the possession of marijuana should it choose to do so. Equally it is open to Parliament to decriminalize or otherwise modify any aspect of the marijuana laws that it no longer considers to be good public policy' (NORML 2003). While the decision in many respects was seen as a setback, it at least opened the possibility that changes could be made to domestic drug law notwithstanding Canada's participation in numerous global legal regimes. During the same month, in a separate ruling, the court upheld by a 9–0 decision all federal laws prohibiting marijuana possession for the purposes of trafficking.

In interpreting the political dynamics of these legal reforms in Canada, it is important to note that all activity took place in a context in which the prohibition against possession of marijuana remained legally contentious. Successive federal government proposals for decriminalization should not be seen as a relaxation of Canadian drug laws. Rather, these proposals represent their reassertion in a legal climate whose status quo at decisive moments was congruent with the legalization of possession of under 30 grams by upholding the opinion rendered by the Ontario Court of Appeal in R. v. JP. Moreover, access problems for persons exempted under the MMAR and legal prohibitions on possession remained. Additionally, as part of proposed decriminalization legislation, penalties for possession for the purposes of trafficking, trafficking proper, and the cultivation of marijuana were set to be substantially increased.

Most recent changes and proposed changes to Canadian drug law – and, by proxy, law enforcement practices – have not been substantiated by corresponding legislation. Yet, they still have been portrayed within popular Canadian discourses as evidence of a liberalization of social mores that clearly distinguishes Canada from the United States. Where Canada was once considered the conservative member of the dyad, the proposed reforms to marijuana law have allowed Canada to present itself as socially progressive and even 'cool.' More important, within popular discourses, Canada can be discursively represented as prudential and as divorced from the irrational fear production of American illicit drug policy.

For example, in her testimony to the Senate Committee, Patricia Erickson remarked that

it is evident in US drug policy that, the people for whom drug use is a moral issue, the cost is unimportant. The costs are irrelevant to them. What is relevant is making sure that the use of drugs is seen as wrong. In Canada, however, we have always been more balanced and more evidence based. That is a good distinction from the US. Canadians are at least able to measure and discuss the costs of policy and consider alternatives. We are not willing to pay any price. (In Senate 2002c, 380)

Moreover, the Senate Committee itself argued that

Canada can and indeed should provide leadership on drug policy ... Canada must also play a leading role in the Americas. We believe that Canada enjoys a favourable international reputation and that it can promote the development of fairer and more rational drug, [*sic*] in particular cannabis policies. (Senate 2002a, 49)

Such observations continued Canada's tradition of asserting its superiority over the United States. However, two points are noteworthy here. First, these same observations demonstrate that the essence of difference identified within nationalist discourse has changed from a racialized locus (i.e., the conception of the northern race) to one centred on notions of intellectual and cultural superiority as reflected in social policy. Second, in that these views are articulated in official government documents, they indicate that Canadians believe that the superiority component of the discursive performative of Canadian identity can be accepted by other parts of the global Self, such as Western Europe.

The decriminalization of marijuana possession (under 15 grams) and the establishment of a medical marijuana program were touted as ground-breaking innovations that placed Canada at the leading edge of responsible social policy. The initiatives served as a marker of distinction from the United States; that said, representational practices and identity politics are also extremely important in the construction of *the* Canadian Self. Of utmost importance here was that these recent policy changes served as a mechanism to recode the use of marijuana from a deviant non-Canadian activity to one that is now closely associated with the very idea of *the* distinctive Canadian identity.

Concurrent with the decriminalization of possession were moves to increase penalties for unlicensed marijuana production and distribution. Furthermore, all other illicit drug prohibitions were to be retained. In 2002, for example, police forces across the country coordinated two large-scale multicity operations targeting indoor marijuana-growing operations (grow-ops). The first, GREENSWEEP I, as reported by the Criminal Intelligence Service Canada (CISC), occurred on 30 January, when police 'executed 189 search warrants, arrested 162 people on 367 charges and seized 56,201 marijuana plants worth an approximate $56.2 million and growing equipment worth about $3.8 million' (CISC 2002, 3). In the second operation (GREENSWEEP II), carried out in April, 'police executed 208 search warrants, arrested 255 people on 510 charges and seized 60,128 marijuana plants worth an approximate $60 million and growing equipment worth $4.8 million from operations across the country' (ibid.). More than seven hundred police officers took part in these raids.

It is noteworthy that law enforcement's construction of the threat posed to average Canadians by marijuana grow-ops has nothing to do with the properties of marijuana itself. Rather, it has to do with safety issues raised by the practice of hydro bypassing to avoid paying for electricity, overloading of residential power supplies, high levels of mould and pollen caused by plants and humidity, carbon monoxide poisoning from extensive plant cultivation without proper ventilation, and unsafe storage of chemicals (ibid., 6). The threat posed by indoor marijuana grow-ops is considered so serious that an information package has been prepared for the general public: 'Signs a Marihuana Growing Operation May Be in Your Neighbourhood.' These signs include the following:

> Residents appear rarely to be home; residents are home only for a few hours, then leave again; windows are boarded or covered up; a strange odour emanates from the residence; little outside maintenance: unshovelled snow, uncut grass; sounds of electrical humming, fans; unusual visitor behaviour; beware of dog signs or guard dogs; bright lights; localized power surges/decreases; flyers left in the mailbox; television or radio left on all night; signs of digging or disturbance around the hydro box; layer of condensation on the windows; air conditioner never runs, windows are always closed. (ibid., 7)

Furthermore, echoing the gateway theory of drug consumption, law enforcement has constructed the gateway theory of drug *production*, arguing that 'proceeds from marihuana operations are frequently funnelled into other criminal activities, such as the importation and trafficking of cocaine, ecstasy and heroin, or are laundered to be reinvested in legitimate businesses' (ibid., 4–5).

Not surprisingly, these activities are represented within law enforcement discourses as the preoccupations of non-Canadians or people who should not be considered Canadian. The 2002 Criminal Intelligence Report produced by the CISC made such explicit reference to the ethnicity of individuals and organizations involved in the drug trade that the following warning appeared on the cover: 'References to organized criminal activity associated to particular ethnic organizations in the report are not meant to suggest that all members of that specific ethnic group are involved in organized crime or that the government of the country of origin or its lawful agencies permits or participates in any illegal activities. These references allude to the illegal activities or particular criminal organizations, the majority of whose members share ethnic similarities' (ibid., front cover).

Priorities identified in the report included the following groups, which were being associated by law enforcement with the illicit drug trade: 'Asian Based Organized Crime,' 'Eastern European Organized Crime,' 'Traditional Organized Crime,' and 'Outlaw Motorcycle Gangs' (ibid.). In the report all of these groups were identified as either largely composed of 'non-Canadians' or individuals who, like outlaw motorcycle gang members, do not see themselves as members of Canadian society. This linking of identifiable groups did not hold for the final priority of the report, the 'Sexual Exploitation of Children,' where, for example, a compelling link could be made to the activities (and inactivities) of the Roman Catholic Church. In sharp contrast, much attention was paid to the number of children found in residences housing marijuana grow-ops, with the issue classified as 'a serious concern' (ibid., 3).

This reaffirming of the foreign and deviant characteristics of aspects of activities associated with illicit drugs is reproductive of the centrality of state-sanctioned control over the individual bodies of people found within the borders of Canada, both those considered non-Canadian and Canadians proper. Changes to Canadian drug laws reflect the imposition of new technologies of control and discipline that have been made possible by the power/relations constitutive of the illicit drugs discourse. From a Foucauldian perspective, then, 'power is everywhere not because it embraces everything, but because it comes from everywhere' (Foucault 1990, 93). Power is being exercised from innumerable points in the construction of the Canadian illicit drug discourse; it is not necessarily defined by a strict case of ruler and ruled, and it depends on points of resistance (ibid., 94–5).

This is certainly true of the drugs discourse and the representational practices it sponsors, which themselves are exercises of power and control. The interpretive genealogy of the body of the illicit drug user in Canada has demonstrated clearly that the Canadian drugs discourse has been a series of dialogues/debates/divisions over who (i.e., the medical and law enforcement communities) controls what, and who should be considered the legitimate source of truth. The ongoing discursive (re)construction the body of drug users through a health perspective at the current juncture is not a power-neutral exercise: science can be used as a means to shape and control individual behaviour. The contemporary configuration of power/relations shaped by a public health approach to drug use is one in which law enforcement has been granted control over individuals who are involved in the production and distribution of illicit substances, while the medical profession has been granted greater authority over the body of the individual illicit drug user as a threat to public health.

Most important, power is tolerable only on the condition that it be able to mask a substantial part of itself; this creates an imperative for the exercise of power to try to remain invisible in contemporary society (ibid., 86). Thus, the current Canadian drugs discourse and the associated performatives of Canadian identity as progressive and liberal deflect, and even conceal, the continuing exercise of power by law enforcement and the medical profession over the Canadian population in the performances that follow. For example, Robert Solomon (1988) has noted that even as the scope of police powers has diminished, including the elimination of controversial writs of assistance, 'police [continue to] have far broader enforcement powers in even a minor drug case than they have in a murder, arson, rape, or other serious criminal investigation' (1988, 263, in Alexander 1990, 34). In the case of the medical profession, physicians are exercising their power in order to derail the medical marijuana program by refusing to prescribe the substance.

Furthermore, three recommendations raised by the Senate and House Committees have far-reaching implications for societal power/relations. First, the shared recommendation that Canada improve its data on illicit drug use, illicit drug arrests, and the effects of illicit drugs appears at first glance to be *common sense*, given the lack of systematic and accurate information. From the perspective of contemporary biopolitics, an understanding of risks that are casually related or correlated to illicit drugs can only be generated through comprehensive data-sets that allow for the precise calculation of probabilities. The knowledge of probabilities is therefore necessary in order to garner the ability to control or adequately insure against risks linked to illicit drugs. Yet it needs to be remembered that knowledge in this area will be used to monitor, control, and discipline both targeted segments of the population such as illicit drug users, and the population at large. While control over individual actions is not necessarily a bad thing, the reasons and justifications given to legitimate the imposition of technologies of control must be evaluated. In particular, it must be asked, 'Who/what is being controlled by who/what?' and 'What power dynamics are made possible from this, and which are actually produced?'

In light of these important questions, concerns need to be raised about the mixing of legal and medical control in the second recommendation (made by the House Committee), for drug courts that would be able to impose mandatory drug treatment for drug users convicted of crimes. Is the potential criminalization of what is discursively constructed as a public health issue, one that is acknowledged as having no cure, a useful precedent? Will this encourage the placing of other social health problems that may respond to medical treatment within the legal system? For example, would Canadian society be comfortable with court-ordered diets for the obese or pharmaceutical regimes for those with attention deficit disorder?

Wariness should also be exercised with regard to the joint recommendation for a Drug Commissioner to evaluate information, disseminate information, and coordinate the Canadian response to issues raised by illicit drugs. While the commonsense proposition as demonstrated by the Auditor General's assessment of the CDS is that drug policy making needs to be centralized to be responsive and effective, there did not appear to be any awareness of the incredible amount of power such an office would wield, as illustrated by the dangerous historical precedent of the Division Chief from the early 1920s to the 1950s. Moreover, the fact that no plan was offered for regular oversight of such a commissioner, apart from the standard Auditor General Assessment, is troublesome.

Conclusions

The preceding exploration of the genealogy of the body of drug users illustrates how they have been represented over the past decades in Canada; it also shows the limits of the possible in terms of what are considered at any given time to be legitimate responses to them as defined by the borders of acceptable control. The central argument has been that responding to illicit drugs upon their securitization has been primarily about disciplining and controlling the Canadian body politic as a part of the Canadian biopolitical agenda. In particular, in pointing to recent changes in marijuana law brought about by a 'public health' or 'harm reduction' approach within the performatives of Canadian identity as progressive and liberal, it must not be forgotten that dynamics of power and control of individual behaviour are still crucially important to illicit, and now semi-illicit, drug issues; they have not disappeared but rather have been reconfigured, with a substantial portion of the power being exercised having scrutiny and attention deflected away from its activities. Thus, the preceding analysis also suggests that contemporary Canadian biopolitics is not singularly focused on controlling illicit drugs in order to mitigate the physical risks to individual bodies and the body politic that are said to be associated with their use. Rather, biopolitical control is being exercised in tandem to ensure against any risks that might threaten the performatives that constitute Canadian identity.

In a practical sense, it is important to try to assess what can be learned from the long process that has led to moves towards the desecuritization of marijuana use. In some respects, this process can be seen as marking a substantial victory for individual freedom. Yet if a victory, it is one that has been pyrrhic in that the performative has been far more substantial than the performance. Specifically, the problems with access to medical marijuana have been bogged in a bureaucratic quagmire that was initially compounded by internal politics within the governing Liberal Party based on the split between supporters of Prime Minister Jean Chrétien and those of former Finance Minister Paul Martin. At this time, it is unclear whether Canadians are aware that quality medical marijuana is not getting to the patients who need it – a fiasco made possible by the refusal of many physicians to give prescriptions, by the initial unavailability of legal medical marijuana, and by government profiteering on its sale, which has established financial access barriers for users.[7]

In August 2003 the Canadian government released its first batch of medical marijuana, grown under its auspices by a company in Flin Flon, Manitoba. Located in an underground mineshaft, the growing operation was plagued with problems from the beginning, causing many advocates to wonder why such a vital element of the medical marijuana program had been assigned to rank amateurs rather than professional growers. Furthermore, after one failed crop, the batch distributed to medical marijuana users who had applied for government supply was condemned for being expensive, weak, hard to smoke, awful tasting, and laced with carcinogens from the growing environment. In a stunning display of hypocrisy, Health Canada had been consistently condemning medical marijuana on the basis that 'delivery systems' did not eliminate carcinogenic trace elements; yet it was presenting medical marijuana users with a product that contained unnecessary amounts of these very substances. Moreover, ongoing demands that government-sanctioned marijuana contain 10 per cent or less THC (the medicinal and intoxicating chemical) in contrast to regular, illegally grown medical marijuana (15 to 25 per cent THC) required medical marijuana users to smoke more of the government product to gain therapeutic effects.[8]

Whether the mismanagement of the medical marijuana program will become a larger political issue as a result remains to be seen. Moreover, other illicit drugs with probable therapeutic applications, including heroin, remain securitized; it is still a commonsense proposition that they threaten the fabric of Canadian society and must be prohibited. With all of the recent attention given to marijuana, the creation of two governmental special committees, and the election of a Conservative federal government in 2006, reconsidering the securitization of other illicit drugs may be something of a dead issue in Canada, particularly if dominant interpretations of current policy postures maintain the performative of a tolerant Canadian society in sharp distinction from the United States.

Moreover, a (re)turn to a punitive model of drug control may be closer than Canadians think, given the views of members of the governing Conservative Party and their eagerness to follow American policy leads. For example, prior to forming the new Conservative Party, Canadian Alliance members of the Special Parliamentary Committee warned in their minority report section that 'the Liberal government has already adopted the 'harm reduction' model of Europe which is proving to be a failure (because it maintains drug addicts on drugs) while at the same time ignoring the United States and Mexico who are moving in significant directions of intervention, education, rehabilitation and treatment based upon abstinence. Canada does this at its own social peril' (House of Commons 2002, 172).

Now in office, it is possible for Canada's neocons to act on these dispositions. Concerned with the levels of use in Canada, federal health minister Tony Clement has outlined the intention to launch 'a massive anti-drug campaign to provide young people with the "plain truth" about illicit drugs' (Picard 2007). This does not promise to be a good turn of events for the security of Canadians, regardless of whether they are directly involved in illicit drugs. As the preceding analysis has indicated, the reinvigoration of a securitized drugs discourse will further accelerate the ways in which forms of power impose themselves on individual and collective bodies. What will be interesting to see are the performatives and performances of identity that will be a central part of this 'new' antidrug campaign.

7 The (Geo)Politics of Dancing: Illicit Drugs and Canadian Rave Culture

Early in the morning of 11 October 1999, at a rave located in an underground parking lot in Toronto's west end, Allen Ho, a twenty-year-old Ryerson University student, collapsed on the dance floor. Several hours later he died in a Toronto hospital from causes determined by an autopsy to be MDMA (ecstasy) related. A post-mortem drug test revealed that Ho's MDMA level was 0.13 milligrams per 100 millilitres of blood. One leading toxicologist at the time noted that MDMA-related deaths had occurred previously with as little as one-third of that amount present in the bloodstream (Keung 2000).

According to eyewitness reports, the venue itself was poorly ventilated, dusty, overcrowded, and without running water, a combination of environmental factors that experts agreed would have exacerbated the dehydrating and metabolic side effects of MDMA that contributed to his death. As the ninth MDMA-related fatality in Canada in 1999, Allen Ho's passing was perceived as a preventable tragedy by Toronto's rave community as well as by public authorities; however, interpretations differed greatly as to who and/or what could and should be blamed. As a (para)site through which popular and practical discursive representations of youth, illicit drugs, illicit drug use, culture, and identity interplayed, the death of Allen Ho has interesting similarities (and differences) with the disappearance of a Toronto high school student more than a decade earlier.[1]

Eleven years previous, on 13 May 1988, Benji Hayward attended a Pink Floyd concert at Exhibition Stadium on the grounds of the Canadian National Exhibition (CNE) in Toronto and never returned home. Police, friends, family, and other concerned community members participated in a search for the fourteen-year-old, a search that was given heightened impetus by his parents' publicly expressed worry that he might have taken drugs at the concert and become disoriented. Five days later his body was recovered in Lake Ontario, off the shore of Coronation Park, southeast of Exhibition Stadium. An autopsy revealed that he had drowned and that no foul play had been involved. However, with the revelation made by authorities that his best friend, who accompanied him to the concert, had been picked up by police in a nearby neighbourhood 'stoned on LSD,' suspicions grew that he, too, had been under the influence of the substance at the time of his death (Morris 1988i). Thus the popular interpretation of the circumstances surrounding Benji Hayward's death was one that argued that illicit drugs were *the* direct cause and that borrowed from existing discursive representations of the particular dangers posed by drug use to young people. While the initial suspicion of drug use was later confirmed by the results of a post-mortem toxicology report, it is important to remember that LSD was blamed prior to any concrete evidence of its involvement in this tragedy.

Even though all the available data at the time clearly showed that youth drug use had fallen dramatically since the 1970s, the Benji Hayward case contributed to a renewed reaffirmation of the securitization of illicit drugs in Canada. In one media report it was contended that illicit drugs were becoming more socially acceptable to teens, that 'LSD, cocaine, and crack' were passed around openly at the Pink Floyd concert attended by Benji, and that 'everybody is doing needles now' ('Fewer Are Doing Drugs,' 1988). Police at the time claimed that 'children can buy any type of illegal drug in [Toronto] if they do a bit of searching' and that 'we have a hell of a serious problem ... It's frightening' (Orwen 1988; Millar 1988). These representations of illicit drugs as a menace made it possible to shape the terms of the drug discourse in such a way that illicit drug use was given greater impetus to be framed as a threat to Canadian youth. This representation proscribed a particular set of responses as reasonable; it also eliminated the discursive space for articulating alternative approaches that would not have necessitated the utilization of increased societal controls and punitive measures.

In this climate of fear and fervour, a coroner's inquest was convened, primarily to ascertain exactly how Benji Hayward died, what factors contributed to his death, and what measures could be put in place to reduce illicit drug use and prevent other children from meeting the same fate. At the time of the inquest the dangers associ-

ated with youth illicit drug use had been localized within popular discourses as originating within the lifestyle promoted by rock'n'roll
musicians. It was argued that 'the world of rock ... is a world without
standards, the world of our ugliest thoughts, a world to which the
entry key is frequently drugs' (Jones 1988). An American expert
invited to Toronto to give a public talk on the subject argued that
heavy metal rock music was 'a potent negative force ... It gives them
[teens] inspiration for evil and violence and hatred' (Canadian Press
1988, C2). What was lost on most observers at the time was that Pink
Floyd was not by any stretch of the imagination a heavy metal rock
band.

Thus the ultimate problematic raised by Benji Hayward's death was
the proliferation of the 'rock'n'roll lifestyle' – most dramatically symbolized by illicit drug use – into the confines of the (future) Canadian
Self: its youth. In this climate constructed by the discursive invocation
of tragedy, outrage, and fear, efforts were made to securitize rock
music and the venues in which bands gave live performances. Peti-
tions circulated demanding that tough new measures be taken by the
provincial and federal governments to combat what one Toronto councillor called 'the rampant drug problem that is infesting our children's
lives both in the schools and in the streets' (James 1988). For several
months afterwards, arrest statistics were published after every major
rock concert, becoming the representational equivalent of a Vietnam
post-battle body count.

The notion that illicit drugs pervaded youth lifestyles was given
further credence by testimony given at the inquest that Hayward had
previously been questioned by police on Yonge Street for suspected
participation in a drug deal. Outraged by the lack of police disclosure
at the time of the incident, Susan Hayward (Benji's mother) demanded
that a way be found to stop the 'blatant exchange' of drugs in Toronto.
She argued that 'it would appear that we have a law [against drugs]
but we suspend that law on Yonge Street and at concerts' (Morris
1988c). The linking of drug use with rock concerts – particularly heavy
metal events – and other geographical locales in the city such as
Yonge Street, contributed to an already existent geopolitical binary in
Canada. This representational understanding was utilized to demark
and even create clear boundaries to separate spaces that hosted illicit
drug activities from those that did not, in order to prevent transmissions between the two positions. This is similar to the geopolitical
reasoning that prohibited 'Canadian Canadian' women in Vancouver

from living close to the city's Chinatown during the early decades of the twentieth century, and that advocated isolated island colonies for drug users during the 1940s and 1950s.

The representational and discursive groundwork established by the revelations provided during the inquest drew from pre-existing geopolitical sensibilities that made it possible for the coroner's jury, in reaching its conclusion, to call drugs 'the curse of the century' and to urge that 'governments at all levels should declare a war on drugs' (Morris 1988f). To these ends, the jury recommended the following measures to eliminate youth drug use:

- More funding must be given to police drug squads across Ontario.
- Children should receive an increased amount of drug education in school (up to half an hour a week for children in grades three to ten).
- All churches and community groups must fight drugs from the 'pulpit and the podium.'
- Stricter drug sentences should be given to anyone found guilty of trafficking illicit drugs, including life in prison for those who sell to children.
- More police foot patrols must be established in the downtown core of Toronto.
- The Canadian National Exhibition (the venue of the Pink Floyd concert) should take a more active role in providing security for its events.
- Concert promoters should advertise a drug-free environment, and security staff should be screened, trained, and licensed (ibid.).

Given that a looming drug threat was being constructed within popular discourse, various government departments initiated their own investigations following the conclusion of the coroner's inquest. For example, Toronto Mayor Art Eggleton established his own task force on reducing youth drug use, in which children participated. Youth who participated complained at the time that their opinions (which were reported to be strongly antidrug) were not valued and that their objections to the soft tone of drug education techniques were ignored (Morris 1989a).

Ontario Premier David Peterson formed his own special Premier's Task Force, which echoed the recommendations of the coroner's inquest:

- The establishment of government-regulated training for private security guards who work rock concerts.
- Mandatory drug education for all students in Ontario schools.
- Resources to double the size of the Ontario Provincial Police (OPP) drug enforcement squad.[2]
- Specific offences for those who provide youth with drugs (Maychak 1988).

The head of the Premier's Task Force argued that Canada was facing a drug threat. However, he drew from representational understandings that discursively separated Canada from the United States by asserting that 'we're still not the United States. Toronto is still not New York, Detroit or Los Angeles, but the problem is serious' (ibid.). In this way, youth drug use was discursively represented as worrisome and threatening but not as extreme as concurrent drug use in the United States.

In retrospectives on the Benji Hayward inquest, two other important recommendations made by the jury are often forgotten. The first was that a major overhaul was required in standard operating procedures used by police in missing persons cases, particularly with respect to teenagers. Over the course of testimony, it was revealed that the police had not taken the disappearance very seriously; they had not devoted any officers to the search until the Hayward family contacted media outlets asking for help from the public two days after he went missing. Moreover, even with growing public attention, it was the family's efforts to organize searches around the CNE that led to the discovery of Benji's body, not work undertaken by the police. Yet criticism of police conduct in popular discourses remained focused on the police officers who did not arrest Benji Hayward on Yonge Street rather than on the lackadaisical efforts of the missing persons squad.

Second, it was recommended that the City of Toronto improve lakefront safety, including providing ladders and chain links along waterfront breakwalls to make it possible for people who fell in the water to remove themselves. The location where Benji Hayward entered the water had no devices in place to allow people to climb out. However, these important recommendations received little media attention in comparison with the calls to fight against illicit drugs because the issue had already been framed by the terms of discourse to be exclusively one of illicit drugs. That issue was *the* problem that needed to be addressed, not police professionalism or public safety around Lake Ontario. Moreover, reflecting the specificity of the threat matrix at play, very little attention was given to the deaths of more than ninety young people in the province of Ontario in the six months following the Benji Hayward inquest from car accidents directly linked to alcohol consumption (Solomon 1995).

The deaths of Allen Ho and Benji Hayward are inherently tragic, in part because both were very likely preventable. The senselessness of their passings galvanized particular types of threat construction that targeted specific classifications of people, substances, and spaces as inherently dangerous to Canadian society. While important differences in the circumstances and contexts exist between the two cases, the discursive and practical responses to Allen Ho can be seen as having precursors in the responses to the Benji Hayward situation that restricted the discursive bandwidth of policy possibility. How, then, did Allen Ho's passing contribute to the securitization of Canadian rave subculture? The answer can be found by analysing the politics of representation that argued that raves posed a growing threat to young Canadians and Canadian society at large.

Of particular importance are the spatial dimensions of this process in terms of the production of geographically defined areas within the territorial confines of Canada as outliers in need of readmission through the (forced) elimination of their identifiable differences. These (contingent) spaces that are claimed to be 'the outside' within 'the inside' of Canadian society can metaphorically be considered 'dragon's lairs.' How does it become possible to represent spaces said to be inhabited by 'dragons' (i.e., foreign and/or deviant Others)? And what forces shape responses to them? The answer is that the 'geographing' of social space in Canada is intimately linked with governmentality, biopolitics, and the regulation of personal conduct (Ó Tuathail 1996, 2, 6–10).

Performatives of personal and national identity take particular elements found in the Self and reconstruct them as the objectively verifiable 'defiling,' 'deviant,' and 'disturbed' characteristics of the Other; similar discursive tactics give meanings to the spaces we occupy, traverse, and avoid (Campbell 1998, 9). While these meanings are often naturalized as objectively defined truths reflected by the real world, actually they are subjective constructions based on value-laden judgments about the characteristics that could/should be attributed to a particular spatial area or to the very boundaries of the spatial area itself. For example, Canadians who live in geographic locales defined as high-crime areas may feel safer in them than inside the walls of a police station. The dominant discursive representations of particular spatial entities are inherently political and reflect asymmetrical relations of power/knowledge operating in a context that defines the possibilities of categorization. Even context itself 'is not a pure original point, an objective space/time coordinate, or a final resting place. Context is an open structure, the limits of which are never absolutely determinable or saturated' (Ó Tuathail 1996, 72–3). Raves have been constructed as dangerous spaces based on an interpretation of threat that perceives them as containing deviant practices that are capable of spilling over into the sanctified space of Canadian territoriality. Saddled with an outlier status by public authorities, Canadian rave subculture found itself embroiled in a geopolitics of dancing as all levels of policing attempted to securitize the practices and spaces popularly represented as being indicative of this culture. Ravers themselves mobilized in response and waged what appeared at the time to be a successful defence of their cultural practices; however, the victory would be short-lived, culminating in the implosion of the Canadian rave scene and the growing prominence of a new set of drug dealers in the community: tobacco and alcohol companies.

Genealogy of Rave

For a social practice that has attracted a large amount of (unwanted) attention in Canada and beyond over the past two decades, rave itself remains a difficult experience to define.[3] But defining rave has been essential in mapping its contours and boundaries as an illicit space within the confines of the Self as a territorialized identity. Definitions have given sanction to a type of biopolitics and social regulation that seeks to impose various disciplines on the recalcitrant bodies that participate in these practices. To borrow Giorgio Agamben's term, rave in Canada has constituted a 'state of exception' in which technologies of biopolitical regulation that would otherwise be considered excessive have been justified as 'de facto necessary according to circumstances' (Agamben 1999, 37).

Given the possible implications for events considered raves, a definition is not merely an academic exercise; it is also a political event, a contestation that involves the delimiting of normal/abnormal behaviour, licit/illicit activities, and safe/dangerous spaces. Defining rave is a means to determine the 'outside' inherent within the 'inside' by identifying people, places, and practices as threatening; yet definitions are always generalizations, and they necessarily mask the richness of diversity. Simon Dalby has suggested that 'the essential moment of geopolitical discourse is the division of space into "our" place and "their" place' (quoted by Ó Tuathail 1996, 16). The following discussion does not attempt to define rave or establish its uncontested foundations. Instead, for those unfamiliar with the practice, it seeks to provide an introduction to the spectrum of definitions as well as a genealogy to establish a context for the geopolitics of dancing.

Tara McCall has noted that the word *rave* has its origins in the Bible, where to rave is to prophesy. More recently, raving as a word has its roots in Jamaica, when it alludes to letting loose on the weekend. At its most basic level, to rave is to have fun. As Juan Atkins, a Detroit DJ and co-originator of the techno sound, succinctly puts it: 'Well, rave, what it means to me is just a big party' (in McCall 2001, 15). Yet the discourses of rave, from both inside and outside rave subculture, are heavily influenced by dominant cultural understandings and practices that make possible particular approaches to comprehending rave. For example, several aspects of dominant culture can be seen in the subculture of rave. First, raves are usually (though not always) commercial ventures that involve customers exchanging money for goods and services. Second, rave culture often experiences many of the same social tensions exhibited in the dominant culture based on class and/or race. In Canada, for example, a set of ethnically specific derogatory terms exist for ravers who are not perceived as Canadian Canadian. Third, the gender imbalances of society are reflected in rave culture, in that the vast majority of people occupying privileged positions (as DJs, promoters, music producers, and record label owners) are male.

The inherent embeddedness of dominant-in-sub and sub-in-dominant culture, as well as the performatives of difference that make it possible to speak of distinctions between them, contribute to how rave is understood, classified, and (re)acted to by participants and/or observers. These intersubjective tensions are brought forward with McCall's argument that the word 'rave' instantly conjures a multitude of images, attitudes, and reactions. It's a scene ripe with dichotomies: beautiful, utopian moments that exist in tandem with accusations of underworld criminal activity. For some veterans, the word is devoid of meaning, describing a scene that has become cliché. They no longer embrace the scene or simply deny the classification of rave because for them it has become mainstream. For newcomers and those less jaded, the word invokes an inviting community where peace, love, unity, and respect – PLUR – flows as freely as it did in the beginning. (2001, 14)

Thus, competing definitions and opinions of raves do not represent a series of dualisms with vastly different discourses operating in total isolation from one another; they are mutually constitutive dichotomies (if not dialectics) in that they are parasitic to one another in a way that creates an ongoing politics of definition, objection, repression, and resistance. This not to say that these contending interpretations of rave are given equal discursive weight. A hierarchy based on pre-existing social power/relations automatically privileges the interpretation of public authorities like the police within popular discourses.

If rave can even be considered to exist – many contend *the* spirit of rave died long ago – the point of contention is always centred on the role of illicit drugs in rave culture and the meanings attached to specific practices that are identified, often commonly, as central to raving. The following definitions from public authorities and members of the rave community highlight the discursive interplay:

ROYAL CANADIAN MOUNTED POLICE Rave parties can be described as many different things. Most notably, they are all night dance parties with loud techno or industrial music ... Rave events typically begin at 10:00pm and continue into the next morning, until about 8:00am. Visual aids such as laser and light shows, and glow sticks along with steady pounding music (0 to 400 beats per minute [with an] average of around 130BPM) aid in an experience known as 'synesthesia,' a blending of the senses that causes users to hear colour and see music while under the influence of drugs. The main hours of a rave are conducive for stimulatory hallucinogenics such as MDMA (known as ecstasy, the most desired rave drug) and MDA. This is because of their mind altering effects and endless energy supply, and the way they create feelings of *peace, love, unity, and respect*; these later four ideas are collectively known as PLUR which is an underlying theme of most raves ... Raves are associated with 'techno' music. (RCMP 2001, 5, 7)

CANADIAN MEDICAL ASSOCIATION JOURNAL   Raves which are nocturnal dance parties, have become increasingly common since the late 1980s. They are usually alcohol free and are characterized by vigorous non-stop dancing to computer-generated music. Attendees are generally middle-class 15 to 25 year olds who typically spend 2 years in the rave scene. Recreational drugs used include marijuana, cocaine, and methamphetamine, as well as 3,4-methylenedioxymethamphetamine (MDMA also known as ecstasy), ketamine, and gamma-hydroxybutyrate. (Rieder 2000, 1829)

CITY OF CALGARY   Gatherings lasting more than five hours with the primary purpose of listening and dancing to music. (In RCMP 2001, 43)

ONTARIO BILL 73 (RAVE ACT 2000)   Rave is defined as a dance event occurring between 2:00am and 6:00am for which admission is charged. (Bill 73 2000)

TORONTO DANCE SAFE COMMITTEE   A rave is a public, all ages, commercial electronic music event held in a special event venue attended by ticket or pass holders generally extending into hours when entertainment venues are usually closed. (Basrur 2000, Appendix 2)

US AIR FORCE   A rave = ecstasy party ... They are usually 'all ages' (often appealing to those too young to legally purchase alcohol); charge high entrance fees; overnight parties with hours of operation beginning in the late evening and continuing until the early morning hours; disc jockeys play house or techno style dance music with a fast, pounding beat and choreograph light or laser shows; 'chill rooms' where people can go to cool off; large overcrowded dance floors with no air conditioning; attendees frequently take mind-altering drugs, dance holding glow sticks, wear glow bracelets, necklaces, or pins with flashing lights, wear candy necklaces, suck pacifiers or lollipops, wear surgical masks and utilize otherwise legal substances like Vick's Vapour Rub to enhance the effects of illegal drugs. (Looney 2002)[4]

DRUG ENFORCEMENT ADMINISTRATION   (The) rave experience ... is characterized by loud, rapid-tempo 'techno' music (140 to 200 BPM), light shows, smoke or fog, and pyrotechnics. Users of drugs such as MDMA report that the effects of the drugs heighten the user's perceptions, especially the visual stimulation. Quite often, users of MDMA at clubs will dance with light sticks to increase their visual stimulation. Legal substances such as Vick's nasal inhalers and Vick's Vapo-rub are often used to enhance the effects of the drugs. (DEA 2001)

In contrast to these attempts at providing a precise definition of rave, McCall (2001) argues that

> the definition of rave should be as lucid and amorphous as the event itself. It can exist for a few hours, a whole night, or an entire weekend. A rave can be an indoor party with 50 people or an outdoor happening with 15,000 people. Participants can be 15 years old or even 45; gay or straight, and any ethnic background. There may be two DJs or more than 20; spinning banging techno music, uplifting trance, or happy hardcore. Some ravers may take ecstasy, LSD, marijuana; some take nothing at all. Other than DJs, electronic dance music, willing participants, and a venue, what can be called a rave defies parameters. Rave has begun to signify a culture that is in continual flux. (2001, 16)

This (non)definition can be interpreted as one way of undermining current representational practices (seen above) that discursively construct raves as drug fuelled, hedonistic, and dangerous wastelands that threaten the principles and mores of normal society. In contrast to this representation, Robert Bartholomew (2000) has drawn parallels with the dancing practices of medieval societies and from a functionalist perspective has suggested that 'modern day raves resemble [medieval] dancing manias within a different historical and cultural context, fulfilling similar social and psychological needs' (2000, 1132).

There is an awareness within the global rave community itself that ongoing attempts to classify and fix an exact definition of rave for the purposes of social regulation can ultimately be linked to concurrent processes for defining security and security threats. However, a transitory definition is not a guaranteed panacea. For some thing/person/event/place/activity to be threatening as well as useful for the purposes of biopolitical regulation, it needs to be both settled and unsettled in its discursive construction: settled so that what is being identified is coherent and understood by others as encapsulating particular dangers; and unsettled so that a growing range of phenomena can be linked under its auspices and reproduced as threats requiring securitization. Thus, a politics of resistance to procedures of definition from the rave community faces a paradox: accept a narrow definition that ultimately obfuscates and marginalizes the diversity of a securitized subculture, or promote a rich definition that, in trying to initiate processes of desecuritization, potentially exposes a wider range of activities to the disciplinary technologies of the state.

Ecstasy

Ecstasy (or MDMA) and electronic music were essential in the development of rave culture (McCall 2001; Reynolds 1999). What remains contentious is the ongoing relationship between ecstasy and rave. While the rave community continues to assert that ecstasy consumption is marginal to rave and practised by a minority of participants, law enforcement around the globe has succeeded in perpetuating a politics of representation that constructs rave not only as inextricably tied to ecstasy (i.e., there cannot be rave without the drug) but also as a site that facilitates the proliferation of illicit drug use within regular society. This goes beyond the use of ecstasy to include other substances such as methamphetamine, GHB, and ketamine. Given that the truths about the effects of illicit drug consumption have been amenable to the dictates of power, it is not surprising that the securitization of rave and ecstasy has arisen in the absence of definitive evidence of harm when used safely.

For example, in September 2003, researchers from the Johns Hopkins University School of Medicine retracted a paper they had published in the academic journal *Science* the previous year. The original research finding was that a typical dose of ecstasy could cause permanent brain damage in humans, leading to Parkinson's disease. The retraction resulted from the discovery that the monkeys and baboons used in the study had not been injected with MDMA but with another methamphetamine at overdose levels (two of the subjects died). Further investigation revealed that the head of the research team, Dr George A. Ricaurte, had received more than $10 million in funding for his research on amphetamines from the National Institute on Drug Abuse, a department of the U.S. government. All of his previous research had claimed that amphetamine use led to Parkinson's disease. Questions about Ricaurte's credibility and political motives became more pointed when the connection was made that the results of the MDMA study had first been released at a time when the anti-rave act was being debated in Congress (McNeil 2003a, 2003b; Morris 2003).

Unadulterated ecstasy is pure MDMA (3,4 Methylene-dioxymethamphetamine), an amphetamine that facilitates feelings of euphoria. MDMA was originally synthesized in 1912 by Merck, a German pharmaceutical corporation, and was intended for use as a blood coagulant (Reynolds 1999, 81). In 1965, MDMA was rediscovered by Dr Alexander Shulgin, an American biochemist working for Dow Chemical, who took a profound interest in exploring the boundaries of human consciousness by harnessing abandoned compounds with psychoactive properties. After several experiments on himself, Shulgin referred to MDMA as 'penicillin for the soul' (Jenkins 1999, 87). Because of the feelings of empathy generated by MDMA consumption, during the 1970s the drug came to be used increasingly by therapists, who found that it helped create a psychologically safe environment in which patients could openly discuss their feelings and/or traumas. Under the nickname ADAM, MDMA became a widely prescribed drug by therapists and gained a popular following among New Agers and people seeking spiritual experiences outside of traditional religion (ibid., 87–8).

Concurrent to its therapeutic use, MDMA began to be distributed within the straight and gay club scenes in Dallas and Austin, where it was openly sold in clubs from the bar as a substitute for alcohol after legal serving hours. Given that MDMA was not prohibited under U.S. drug laws, it began to spread to New York and Chicago, and acquired the nickname ecstasy or XTC to highlight its pleasurable effects (ibid., 88). Jenkins argues that the name change discredited the therapeutic effects of MDMA that saw it providing 'most of the positive features and few of the drawbacks of other commonly used drugs (both licit and illicit) during the 1970s and 1980s' (ibid.). Outside North America, ecstasy became popular in European resort regions like Ibiza, off the Spanish mainland.

After disturbing reports of its growing use in the United States, MDMA came under scrutiny from the Drug Enforcement Administration (DEA) based on researchers' claims that it caused brain damage. MDMA was considered so dangerous that in 1985 the DEA circumvented standard procedures and undertook an emergency reclassification, placing it as a Schedule One substance – the most restrictive drug scheduling, one reserved for drugs with no medical application. Attempts to reclassify it as Schedule Three, which would have allowed MDMA to be prescribed by therapists, were unsuccessful (ibid., 89). This decision was upheld in 1989, and Dr Ricaurte has claimed that his research had been essential in maintaining the ban (Reynolds 1999, 82; McNeil 2003b).

Two points are of interest here. The first is that the United States lagged behind both the UK (the late 1960s) and Canada (1977) in making MDMA illegal. The second is that the classification of MDMA in the UK and Canada was not in response to its use or effects; rather, it was the result of MDMA being considered a chemical derivative of other amphetamine substances that had already been classified as illicit.

Physiologically, MDMA increases the amount of serotonin and dopamine available for neurotransmitters in the brain. Excess dopamine stimulates locomotion, increases metabolism, and creates feelings of euphoria. Serotonin typically regulates mood and general feelings, but in abnormal amounts it intensifies sensory stimuli and makes perceptions more vivid (Reynolds 1999, 83). Given these general effects, the relationship between ecstasy and rave centred around three major synergies.

The first was that as an amphetamine, MDMA provided the required energy boost for all-night dancing. The second was that latent feelings of empathy, openness, and well-being were amplified by consuming ecstasy. Users became friendlier, more sociable, and less guarded, which made it possible for early ravers to coalesce around a feeling of community spirit very easily because of the levels of interaction occurring among participants (ibid., 83). For example, unlike other social venues, it was not uncommon for total strangers to turn into lasting friends over the course of an event. Moreover, MDMA helped rave cut through the sexual politics and tensions commonly found in youth social scenes. In contrast to the highly sexualized media representation of MDMA, for anyone who has gone to a rave, it becomes very clear that people are generally there for the music, not to find sexual partners.

The third synergy has been described as follows: 'All music sounds better on E – crisper and more distinct, but also engulfing in its immediacy. House and techno sound especially fabulous. The music's emphasis on texture and timbre enhances the drug's mildly synesthetic effects' (ibid., 84).

However, as Simon Reynolds has noted, 'beyond its musical implications, ecstasy is above all a *social* drug,' and the ways in which it facilitates meaningful social interactions with friends and peers are an often overlooked aspect of the drug's appeal to youth (ibid., 85).

Most physical side effects of MDMA consumption are minor: dry mouth, nervousness, slight nausea, jaw tension, and teeth grinding. Furthermore, unlike drugs such as alcohol, MDMA does not cause a hangover the following day. However, two or three days later a user can become somewhat irritable and emotionally fatigued from the initial disruption to sleeping patterns and the rebalancing of the brain's neurochemistry. With regard to these effects and the impact on one's mental state, taking ecstasy has been described as like 'going on an emotional spree, spending several days of happiness in advance' (ibid., 86). Thus prolonged and regular use of MDMA reduces the experience of a serotonin high, but leaves the amphetamine effects; the diminishing returns of regular ecstasy use are one of the primary reasons why the drug is not considered physically addictive (ibid., 86–7).

What, then, has been the problem with MDMA use? What has made it possible for this substance to be securitized? Based on observations of the rave scene in the UK, Reynolds has argued that

> most problems associated with ecstasy seem to be caused by the way it is used. The psychological costs stem from reckless excessive long-term intake; the physical dangers are almost all related to its usage in the rave context, where overexertion and dehydration can lead to heatstroke. (Ibid., 87)

He continues:

> Although there have been a few cases of people dying after taking just one pill because of a statistically remote allergic reaction, most ecstasy related fatalities have involved binging, overexertion, and mixing of drugs ... In the first 10 years of British rave, ecstasy has been implicated in approximately 70 deaths ... Given the vast number of people taking the drug during those 10 years (conservative estimates put it at half a million a weekend in Britain) ecstasy appears to be relatively safe – at least compared to other socially sanctioned leisure activities. (Ibid., 88)

Reynolds's point is pertinent to the biopolitics of raving and demonstrates the contradictions within the initial securitized responses of state actors and public authorities.

If, as Reynolds suggests, the potential dangers of raving cannot be reduced solely to the consumption of MDMA, a far more effective strategy for reducing levels of harm would be to concentrate on providing safe venues for these events along with education on the ways to reduce the risks of MDMA use. However, the representational practices that have coded rave as a dangerous geopolitical space, because of claims that drug use is inherent to the event/culture, make it possible for arguments to be made that these spaces should be outside the realm of *normal* social regulation. Rejection of rave makes it possible to fixate on disciplinary mechanisms to eliminate these spaces within the bounded territory of the state. In essence, to provide for safe venues would be to admit rave culture into the Self – an unacceptable move if national identity has been tied to particular patterns of drug consumption. Thus, on the basis of calculations to define a specific threat matrix, Canadian responses to rave have embodied a series of paradoxical dichotomies between Self/Other, inside/outside, and safe/dangerous in attempting to confront issues raised by the Allen Ho tragedy.

Rave in Toronto

After 1989, rave spread all over Europe and North America from its starting points in the UK. In the UK, where rave first became popular in the late 1980s, the media and the police were initially quite positive, with the no-alcohol policy of raves gaining praise. However, as reports began to surface of ecstasy consumption and as outdoor parties became increasingly unruly, the police responded with raids and crackdowns while politicians enacted new laws to abolish rave (McCall 2001, 40; Reynolds 1999, 56–79).

What is interesting is that rave in the UK was increasingly represented within the popular conservative political discourse as emblematic of the growing disorder in English society. Thus, the 1992 Criminal Justice and Public Order Act targeted a range of people and events that symbolized the growing perception of internal anarchy: squatters, travellers, raves, and free festivals (Reynolds 1999, 173–8). To deal with these communities, police powers were extended. For example, the right to remain silent was removed, and the police were granted the authority to stop and search those they suspected might be planning to attend a rave (ibid., 173).

Although rave was defined as at least one hundred people playing amplified music 'characterized by the emission of a succession of repetitive beats,' police forces were now able to harass gatherings as small as ten people; they could also stop individuals within a one-mile radius of a suspected rave venue and order them to leave (ibid.). Ironically, the end result of the legislation was that raves moved into the mainstream club environment, where they attracted an even larger patron base (McCall 2001, 36–40).

The first raves began to be held in Toronto in the early 1990s, partially made possible by Toronto's status as one of the earliest cities for house music in North America (Silcott 1999, 79). Reasons for this are unclear. Some point to the geographical proximity to New York and Detroit, but this would seem to only present an easier opportunity for transmission. Others highlight Toronto's ethnic and sexual diversity as well as specific radio DJs at the time, like Chris Sheppard (CFNY), who pushed the sound to the audiences of their programs. Exhibiting a similar genesis to the rise of rave in the UK, the community developed in Toronto with small after-hours clubs, which were often run by British expatriates who had experienced the scene in London.

Toronto's first rave was held in August 1991. The events soon began to flourish, with several production companies competing among one another. Initially, the police assumed a 'non-reactionary' stance, seeing the parties as a way to keep kids off the streets and away from alcohol. According to Mireille Silcott, Sergeant Guy Coirvoisier, tasked with investigating Toronto's growing rave scene at the time, noted that 'it's going to be a long hot summer. Unemployment is high. People need something to do. Raves don't need to be a problem. They can be a solution' (in ibid., 83). Yet by April 1992 the Toronto police had compiled a full dossier on rave promoters and had brought several in for interrogations (ibid., 84).

Despite heavy monitoring, the police continued to take the attitude that the primary goal for law enforcement was to ensure that events and venues were safe. The rationale was that 'they would rather have two thousand young people in a safe controlled environment on weekends than running loose on the streets causing mischief' (ibid.). As a result, according to many observers, the Toronto rave scene during the first half of the 1990s encompassed one of North America's biggest rave populations (ibid., 75). In 1995, for example, Toronto was declared by one British magazine to have the largest jungle scene in North America (ibid., 76).[5] By the end of the 1990s, events were attracting upwards of 15,000 people and Toronto remained one of the continent's most vibrant rave centres (ibid., 75).

Allen Ho's death occurred at a time when rave was reaching its apex in Toronto. Large events were occurring on a weekly basis with world-class talent. At the same time, an ever growing number of nightclubs in Toronto were hiring DJs and playing varieties of music (including house, jungle, trance, breaks, and techno) to attract a mature crowd who could legally consume alcohol. Venues included System Sound-bar, Industry, The Guvernment, Kool Haus, Element, Space, X-it, Meow, Bassmint, Area 51, Turbo, Audiowerks, and the Comfort Zone. The Toronto police made no distinction among these clubs (most of which had liquor licences) and raves (which were usually alcohol-free events).

In early November 1999, Ontario's Consumer and Commercial Relations Minister, at the request of the Toronto police, called for a summit of public authorities to develop a plan for controlling raves (McCarten 1999). With the announcement of a coroner's inquest scheduled for the spring, Toronto's rave community pre-emptively sought ways to regulate events in a manner that would not lead to the demonization of the subculture. To promote responsible raving, members of the rave community, rave promoters, lawyers, Toronto City Council members, security operators, and city officials formed the Toronto Dance Safe Committee (TDSC) to establish a protocol for rave venues.

Despite its diverse membership, the committee reached a consensus on what needed to be done. Raves were to be licensed on the following criteria: assessment of the venue density, the provision of free water, operational toilet facilities, adequate ventilation, no smoking as per existing legislation, one Ontario Provincial Police (OPP)–bonded security officer for every hundred patrons, two paid duty officers for the first five hundred patrons and one for every additional block of five hundred, ambulance services for events of more than one thousand people, space within the venue for community-based drug/health education, and communication with city officials within one week of the event of the confirmed location and maximum attendance (TDSC 1999). Failure to register events with the city and to comply with the protocol were to result in the rave being immediately shut down by the police and the potential laying of criminal charges.

The rave community felt that by adopting the Protocol for the Operation of Safe Dance Events, it had shown itself able to work with public authorities to address legitimate safety issues and thereby avoid the securitization of raving. Yet even with this licensing system, raves drew an increasing amount of attention from the police, who as *neo-parrhesiastes* made the strategic move to use the upcoming inquest (and the accompanying media attention) as a means to secure their privileged social status as *the* monopolizer of truth. Early in the spring of 2000, the Toronto Police Service (TPS) began to make its presence felt at events by initiating forty-seven arrests at two raves held on the city-owned CNE grounds. Police laid ninety-five drug charges and reportedly seized quantities of ecstasy, ketamine, cocaine, crack, hashish, and marijuana (Ruryk and Artuso 2000).

The police began to argue that these figures provided irrefutable evidence of a growing illicit drug problem among Canadian youth. The rave community responded that these arrests were made at events that had a combined attendance of over 25,000 people – an indication of how marginal drugs were to the scene. Even Toronto's mayor, Mel Lastman, was initially unperturbed by these arrest figures and defended the practice of holding raves on city-owned property:

> The kids – good kids – are going to these places [raves] because they're looking for a place to go ... This is what we should be doing [holding raves on city property] and we should be having people there to supervise them, look after them ... We know there will be police there – whether they're undercover or whatever – but they will be there and they will be there to watch and they will be there to make sure that the kids don't get into trouble ... I endorse that wholeheartedly. (Wanagas 2000c)

Lastman continued:

> I don't want to see kids get into trouble. I don't want to see kids get killed. I don't want to see kids get hurt. I don't want to see them get hit over the head with a bottle. I want to see some adults there. I want to see some protection there and that's what this does. So let's endorse it wholeheartedly – not partially. I know this is the right way to go. (Ibid.)

Thus it was possible at this time for biopolitical regulation to cohabit within the confines of rave instead of seeking to eliminate the practices of raving.

Given that there was little awareness in Canada at the time, the TPS began to classify any after-hours event as a rave, regardless of the purpose or characteristics of the gathering. This made it possible for the TPS to link rave with the violence associated with many after-hours clubs in the Greater Toronto area. After the shooting deaths of two bouncers in the downtown core in the winter of 2000 at venues described as 'rave clubs,' the TPS created 'Operation Strike Force,' a special unit that targeted twenty-two after-hours clubs that had a history of violence.[6] Over the first six weeks of operation, fifty-three arrests were made and weapons were seized, including twelve handguns and two sawed-off shotguns (Shephard and Huffman 2000). These weapons were often presented during press conferences as items seized from raves. By conflating rave with other types of events/environments (specifically after-hours nightclubs), the TPS shaped the ways in which rave was represented in popular discourse, thus making it more amenable to securitization. The linking of rave with violence was also made possible by the high-profile murder case in the United States of a drug dealer by Michael Alig, the self-proclaimed and flamboyant leader of New York City's 'club kids.'[7]

Outside Toronto, rave subculture had begun to receive national attention in Canada shortly after Allen Ho's passing with a provocatively worded cover story in *Maclean's*: 'Rave Fever: Raves Are All the Rage but Drugs are Casting a Pall over Their Sunny Peace-and-Love Ethos' (Oh 2000, 38).[8] Besides offering *a* primer on rave culture for the uninitiated, the article incited public opinion by portraying raving and ecstasy as inseparable and then reporting that 'ecstasy has been implicated in at least 14 Canadian deaths in the last two years ... Many more kids have become sick from rave drugs ... Trafficking in ecstasy and other rave drugs, meanwhile, has become a virtual epidemic' (ibid., 39–40).

Within a month, in popular discourses, the richness of rave subculture had been reduced even further to solely encompassing illicit drug use after Toronto mayor Mel Lastman did an about-face and began pushing for a citywide ban on raves. He argued that 'what it [a rave] turns out to be is a place for drug pushers ... That's where they get known ... That's where they sell their drugs' (Ruryk and Artuso 2000). Sandra Pupatello, a Liberal member of the provincial legislature, claimed that while on a fact-finding mission at a Windsor rave, she was offered ecstasy. She asserted that 'I did find many, many ... very young people out in the middle of the night and most of them stoned ... It took about 20 minutes from my arrival to be offered the Ecstasy for $35' (ibid.). The price quoted by Ms Pupatello was approximately $15 over market value for a single ecstasy pill at that time in Southern Ontario.

Newly appointed Toronto police chief Julian Fantino spearheaded the antirave bandwagon in Toronto by publicly inviting Prime Minister Jean Chrétien to a rave for the sake of demonstrating to him that the events were 'threatening the very fabric of Canadian life' (Kingstone 2000). In an open letter to Chrétien, Fantino described raves as 'bringing together thousands of young people under one roof – with 80% of them using drugs – raves have become a source of huge profits for drug dealers who have an open-field of impressionable minds.' He presented rave participants as 'kids, most of them under 16, high on drugs, [and] dancing' (ibid.). He asserted that ecstasy use was placing 'Canadian youths at risk and creating a health and safety emergency that could easily become an epidemic' (ibid.). Fantino asserted that ecstasy was easy to produce from 'recipes on the Internet for pennies a pill, and sold for up to $45. And the partiers will often buy two Ecstasy tablets to make it through the twelve-hour marathon of dancing' (ibid.). He concluded that 'there is a national ignorance on the subject of raves' and that 'the government of Canada needs to address the problem and rectify this frightening situation' (ibid.). Reports also surfaced around the same time that 'night club and rave cultures are mixing Viagra with illicit drugs despite warnings that users could be setting themselves up for heart attacks' ('Viagra Finds Favour with Ravers' 2000, A6).

Strongly influenced by Fantino's stance, Mayor Lastman abruptly declared that raves *must* be banned from city property: 'We can't control them ... You can't control the drugs, you can't control what [people] do and you can't control how crazy people get once they take the drugs' (Rusk 2000). Yet many city councillors opposed both the representations of rave and the imposition of a citywide ban because such moves would place rave outside the scope of effective regulatory mechanisms. Olivia Chow, a city councillor and former Board of Edu-

cation trustee, served as a crucial liaison between ravers and city officials as the former responded to the accusations levelled by Fantino;
she also lent ravers her expertise as their community mobilized itself
politically. Joe Pantalone, another left-wing councillor, argued that
banning raves on city property 'is not really a solution ... If we lose the
good operators and the outcome is ... simply to drive it underground
in an unsafe situation, then I think we're all the losers for it' (in ibid.).
He added that though more than 100,000 young people had attended
raves at the CNE over the previous two years, there had not been a
single serious injury, an act of serious vandalism, or any reports of violence (ibid.).

Councillor David Miller, who would later become Toronto's mayor,
argued that the city-owned CNE grounds were an excellent venue for
raves because the location was far enough removed from residential
areas that no one would be disturbed (Wanagas 2000a). He believed
that Julian Fantino was 'over-dramatizing' the drug problem at city-
sanctioned raves, where on average ten to fifteen persons were being
charged for drug offences per thousand people (in ibid.). Interestingly,
though, in challenging the police discourse that made it possible to
position rave as a dangerous space because it embodied illicit drug
use, Miller was both undermining and reinforcing the representational
practices that were making it possible to portray rave in this particular
manner.

First, in undermining dominant spatial representations, Miller was
offering his own geopolitics of drug use in Toronto by asserting that 'if
you go into Rosedale [an affluent Toronto neighbourhood] right now
with 20 or 30 police officers and stop every single young person until
you get up to 1000, you're going to find way more than 20 kids with
drugs' (in ibid.). However, Miller also distinguished between city-
sanctioned raves with police and 'good security' and 'what raves were
in the beginning [when not under city control]: huge unsupervised,
wild crazy parties with tons of drugs' (in ibid.). Thus, pardoxically the
issue of whether or not to permit raves on city property was constructed across an axis of governmentality that differed on the best
means to control and discipline the practices of rave. In essence, the
dilemma centred on what kinds of activities could be brought within
the spatial confines of the Self without losing the proclaimed characteristics (e.g., order, non-use of illicit drugs, stoicism) that constituted
this identity and that demarcated a border between the 'inside' and
'outside' of legitimate Canadian society.

Banning Rave and the Allen Ho Inquiry

While exhibiting a degree of naivety towards the biopolitical implications of how rave had been constructed as a social problem, one reporter's comment that the Allen Ho inquest was set to begin in May 2000 as 'anti-rave and anti-drug rhetoric [were] hitting a fever pitch' is telling of the political context in which the broader issues raised by his death were to be examined (Powell 2000). Members of the Canadian rave community worried that instead of addressing the dangers relating to drug use in the rave environment, the inquest would focus on representing raves as the source of youth drug (ab)use (ibid.). The Toronto Police Service (TPS) saw the inquest as a means of drawing attention to the 'root of the evil' – evil that it defined as the use of illicit drugs – but worried that the inquest was merely a publicity manoeuvre, a way for the authorities to look like they were doing something (Powell 2000).

However, two days into the inquest, before either concern could bear itself out, Toronto City Council at the urging of Mayor Lastman approved a motion to suspend all raves on city property indefinitely by a margin of 32 to 18 (DeMara and Moloney 2000). Key to this policy reversal were statements made by Chief Fantino to Council, at the invitation of Mayor Lastman, about three raves held on city property earlier that year. His statements included the assertion that 'there were a number of episodes where we witnessed young people rolling around on the floor, basically squirming around in their own vomit' (ibid.). Fantino claimed to be 'informing' Council about a critical public safety issue. Yet Will Chang, a lawyer and member of the TDSC, contended that 'the police chief has no idea what the rave scene is all about in Toronto,' given that Fantino had never attended one (Levy 2000).

After the decision, some councillors complained that instead of answering direct questions as had been agreed to earlier, Fantino had taken it upon himself to deliver a sermon that drew from Benji Hayward's death twelve years earlier 'in an attempt to equate that tragedy with what's happening at raves on the CNE grounds today' (Wanagas 2000d). He even declared 'drugs and drug abuse are the curse of this century,' quoting directly from the the Hayward inquest's final report (ibid.).

The decision was derided by Toronto's rave community. It was interpreted as reneging on previous agreements embodied in the

Rave Protocol; it was also perceived as making it possible for raves to become the very thing that was already being presented in popular discourses: dangerous, drug-filled events. Kim Stanford, a community health nurse, founder of the Toronto Rave Information Project (TRIP), and member of the TDSC, argued that the ban would be a total disaster: 'Venues owned by the City of Toronto are ideal. They have ample ventilation and running water. These are essential to prevent overheating, dehydration, and other health complications associated with dancing all night at raves' (TDSC 2000).

A few weeks later, in the opening editorial of the *Canadian Medical Association Journal*, Dr Michael J. Rieder (2000) argued that 'risk-reduction is much more likely to succeed in reducing the serious adverse effects associated with rave parties than is prohibition' (2000, 1830). Responding to critics of the move, Lastman argued: 'This is not the Toronto I want, this is not the Toronto I want to be a part of and these are not the things we want to see happen ... When people take this ecstasy ... they go nuts and you cannot control them, and the cops cannot control them ... I don't want to be known as the rave capital of Canada' (DeMara and Moloney 2000; Levy 2000). Lastman's rationale can be interpreted as one made possible by his particular representation of the Toronto Self, which he read as being threatened by the practices of rave.

Concurrently at the provincial level, Sandra Pupatello, on the basis of her fact-finding mission, introduced Private Member's Bill 73 (Raves Act 2000) in the provincial legislature, which initially received bipartisan support. Pupatello framed the Raves Act as merely a means to regulate safe raves in Ontario; the explanatory note stated that it would prevent anyone from holding a rave (a dance event occurring between two a.m. and six a.m. for which admission is charged) without having a permit issued by the municipality in which the event would be taking place. It would also prevent any property from hosting a rave unless a permit had been issued. Although this seems innocuous, the intent of the legislation was to discourage raves by instituting a Byzantine and costly permit process while saddling ravers and rave organizers with a prohibitive spectrum of legal liabilities and responsibilities.

The Raves Act placed a legal burden on organizers to remove anyone from an event who '*may* be engaged in unlawful activity.' Under the act, police were to be given the powers to enter, without a warrant, any place where they reasonably believed a rave was being held in violation of the act or a bylaw. The range of infractions that could legitimate a police inspection spanned from the obvious (like overcrowding) to the nebulous suspicion that organizers had not removed people who *might* be engaging in unlawful activity. During inspections, police were to have the authority to make reasonable inquiries of any person and require the production for inspection of any document or thing that was relevant to the investigation. In sum, the Raves Act was designed to legalize the harassment of a subculture of which the police were already deeply suspicious. The police would be invested with the authority to enter a rave on just about any pretense and conduct a fishing expedition for potential criminal activity, holding organizers and other patrons directly responsible for the activities of others. The police were also to be granted the power to order everyone to vacate a premises suspected of hosting a rave, subject to a $5,000 fine for non-compliance. Thus, even with formal regulation, rave was to become a space that was legally recognized as so distinct from normal Canadian society that it was necessary, and politically possible, for individuals within that space to be subject to a range of disciplinary impositions beyond what would normally be acceptable. For example, if law enforcement agents were given similar powers to police corporate crime, could we expect agents to consistently enter brokerage houses demanding to see records and licences and to hold corporations criminally responsible for the behaviour of employees and/or their clients outside their business relationships?

With the City of Toronto banning raves from its property and the first reading of a bill in the provincial legislature that seemed poised to impose a range of legal liabilities on ravers themselves that would discourage such events from being held, things looked grim for the rave community. Thus, on 1 June 2000, when the coroner's inquest into Allen Ho's death released its verdict and recommendations, that community's members were shocked and overjoyed to read that the jury's primary conclusion was that city-owned properties should be made available as rave venues because they offered a level of safety unlikely to be surpassed by privately owned properties. With regards to venues and rave promotion, the jury also recommended that the following should be established as standard operating procedures:

- There must be access to unlimited drinking water for rave patrons.
- No admission to be granted to persons under sixteen.

- Rave advertising must not depict drugs or drug use.
- Rave locations must be printed on each ticket.
- All raves must advertise as being drug free and state the minimum age for admission.
- Search areas must be established at all venues.
- People found in possession of drugs should not be admitted.
- Paid duty police officers must be hired to supplement security.
- Increased drug education and harm reduction.
- $0.50 surtax on tickets to go to harm reduction projects.
- Increased government funding for harm reduction strategies and education (Coroner's Inquest into the Death of Allen Ho 2000).

These measures received the bulk of the media coverage and were represented as a victory for the rave community. But there were other recommendations that not only mirrored those made by the Benji Hayward inquest, but also would place increased power in the hands of public authorities:

- Having the final decision on the number of paid duty police officers required for an event left up to the police, with no means by which to appeal.
- Agreeing with the powers granted to police under the Raves Act 2000.
- Making illicit drug use a reportable disease for physicians so that patterns of use could be tracked.
- The development of drug recognition experts (DREs) in police forces who would establish whether someone was under the influence, the type of drug they were on, and whether they needed medical attention.
- Meaningful sentences for those who traffic drugs to young people.
- The expansion of the schedule of prohibited precursor chemicals in order to make it more difficult to produce drugs like ecstasy (ibid.).

Yet even with the jury's recommendation that city-owned properties be opened to rave, Mayor Lastman refused to permit raves in Toronto until the provincial government gave 'municipalities stricter powers of control' over the events (Freed 2001). This can be interpreted as Lastman's request that the Raves Act be passed; however, that act was a private member's bill initiated by a member of the Opposition, and it disappeared from the docket after the summer of 2000, with the provincial government deciding to leave the issue to the discretion of municipalities.

In response to the intransigence on the part of public authorities with regard to raves on city property, Toronto's rave community began to organize a public protest, to be held in Nathan Phillips Square on 1 August during City Council's next scheduled meeting. Yet the rave community was almost apologetic about having to mobilize politically. Will Chang, an organizer of the rally, stated that 'we want to show the powers that be that even though people involved in the rave scene really don't want to get political ... if our culture is being threatened by a lot of misinformation, we can and we will be a strong political force' (DeMara 2000). The issue as framed by the rave community was the safety of rave attendees and the unwillingness of public authorities to ensure this safety by providing venues. Alex D., publisher of *Tribe Magazine*, Toronto's rave community magazine, argued persuasively that 'there are 50,000 people going out every weekend looking for places to dance in Toronto after midnight. And if legal, safe spaces aren't available, they're going to go to unsafe spaces. It's that simple' (ibid.).[9]

Thus, an interesting geopolitics of dancing arose in Toronto at that time. The publicly owned spaces of the Canadian Self were represented in the discourse of rave as offering unrivalled safety and protection, even by those whose practices had placed them outside of the boundaries of the dominant construction of Self, both spatially and in terms of a shared (cultural) identity. However, the strategy chosen by the Canadian Self, represented by the City of Toronto and its public authorities, was to resist this proposed incorporation and leave rave firmly on the outside looking in.

One of the possibilities open to rave at that time was to reshape the terms of public discourse so that it no longer immediately conjured up images of rampant illicit drug use. Over the summer of 2000, the rave community did not defend illicit drug use, and as much as possible, it created distance between the act of dancing and illicit drug taking within the space of rave. For example, Kim Standford presented figures from the Centre for Addiction and Mental Health that showed while 25 per cent of Ontario high school students had attended a rave, only 4 per cent had tried ecstasy (Moloney 2000). This was a dramatic difference from Chief Fantino's earlier claim that 80 per cent of all rave patrons were on drugs.

This decoupling of rave (as dance space) and illicit drug use gained momentum within public discourse. Slowly, illicit drug use began to be seen as an aberration within the practices of rave; this made it possible to link rave with performatives of the Canadian Self. Thus the problem was transformed from the rave as *the* site that encourages the use of illicit drugs by young people, to one constructed around the provision of safe venues for raving that would discourage lingering illicit drug use. Even the *Toronto Star* bought into this problematic, as can be seen in the following passage from an editorial: 'It's far preferable to have these dances in a safe location where emergency personnel are on standby for medical problems and where a bolstered police presence can keep an eye out for drug use. City councillors can't vote raves out of existence. But they can vote to make them safer' ('Council Should ...' 2000). Clearly, Toronto's rave community had begun to gain the sympathy of the general public by affirming its adherence to performatives of *the* Canadian Self. More important, an increasing number of city councillors were publicly affirming that they were willing to reconsider the ban.

Sensing that the ban was set to be lifted, and still deeply suspicious of the rave community, the TPS pre-emptively designed a protocol on raves, which was passed by the Police Services Board on 27 July, five days before the scheduled rally at Nathan Phillips Square (Quinn 2000). The police asked Toronto City Council to approve the new protocol on 1 August, after it lifted the ban on raves, so that an effective legal mechanism would be in place to ensure proper regulation and public safety. The protocol itself was largely based on the original Protocol for the Operation of Safe Dance Events designed by the TDSC and previously adopted by Toronto rave promoters. It also incorporated recommendations from the Allen Ho inquest.

Provisions for a legal rave included undertaking a risk assessment of the event and a physical inspection of the site, meeting requirements for licensed security staff, conducting extensive background checks for promoters and others involved, and making arrangements for emergency medical services and hired paid-duty police officers (ibid.). But unlike the previous protocol, the ultimate authority regarding whether a planned rave met these requirements and the number of paid-duty police officers deemed necessary was left to the discretion of the unit commander of the police division in which the event was to take place (ibid.). Thus, the TPS had designed a protocol that not only positioned it as the overseer of rave in Toronto but also granted it an inordinate amount of authority, without any independent oversight of its decisions or any means by which to appeal them. Despite this imbalance in enforcement power, the protocol remained attractive for politicians because it addressed the concerns being raised about the safety issues surrounding rave venues. Ironically, the popular discourse of rave in Toronto is what made the revised rave protocol possible. The ability to discipline the practices of rave remained firmly in the hands of the police.

On 1 August 2000 the iDance rally was held in Nathan Phillips Square. An estimated ten to fifteen thousand protesters participated in the outdoor rave/political protest. The event was legal as it took place between five p.m. and ten p.m. As ravers/protesters danced to music played by several world-renowned DJs who had offered their services free of charge, Toronto City Council reversed its earlier decision banning raves on city property by a 50 to 4 margin (Stanleigh 2000). The council also approved the revised rave protocol drafted by the TPS without any revisions. Once again, raves were to be allowed within the territorial confines of the Canadian Self.

Popular representations of the iDance rally portrayed the event as an overwhelming success: kids had fought City Hall and won. Organizers had privately hoped that as many as five thousand protesters might show up over the five hours of the event; in most estimations triple that number attended. Some commentators, overwhelmed by 1960s nostalgia, believed the rally might serve as a link between the current rave generation and their baby boomer parents by drawing from a people power ethos that had been absent from Canadian politics for many decades (Rayner 2000a, 2000b; Klein 2000). Some hoped that iDance would become an annual event in Toronto, much like the Detroit Electronic Music Festival or Berlin's Love Parade, bringing in tourists and positioning Toronto as a premier rave city. Even the police were pleased at the behaviour of the protesters; there had been only one reported ecstasy overdose and nine arrests over the course of the event. The police admitted that this 'was a small number of incidents given that nearly 11,000 people attended' (Harding 2000a).

While the feeling was celebratory, the rave community realized very quickly that it had not secured a clear political victory because of the regulations imposed by the new protocol. The community agreed that there needed to be rules to protect ravers from unsafe venues, but many worried that 'police discretion over the number of paid-duty officers required could kill events by making them too costly' (ibid.).

As Will Chang bluntly put it, 'ravers don't trust the police' (ibid.). He continued: 'How do you think we'll trust them not to abuse the paid-duty procedure in the protocol?' (ibid.).

Now that the original protocol's stipulation of one officer per five hundred ravers had been abandoned, many in the community worried that in order to discourage events, the police would inflate the number of paid-duty officers considered necessary. The TPS as an institution was still inherently biased against raves. The same fears were echoed by organizers of other subcultural events in Toronto, including Caribana and (Gay) Pride, whose festivals would also fall under the rave protocol guidelines because of the time periods in which certain activities took place. Thus, the rave protocol had the capacity to potentially discipline a broad spectrum of non-hegemonic cultural practices in Toronto.

Chief Fantino dismissed the idea of any bias with his own discursive performative of the role of the TPS: 'I'd like to think we are honourable people ... We would not engage in that kind of discriminatory conduct. Our primary focus, attention and mandate is to public safety' (ibid). Yet when asked about his personal view of raves on city property, he claimed that 'I've approached this strictly from my mandate as police chief ... If I was to moralize on a personal basis, I'd probably be saying a lot more' (Harding 2000b).

The rave community's fears about increases in the number of paid-duty officers required for events quickly found cause. 'Freakin',' the first major rave to be held on city property under the new rave protocol, on Halloween 2000, was expected to draw seven thousand participants. Police demanded that forty-five paid-duty officers be retained at a cost of more than $20,000. In comparison, in 1998 only ten paid-duty officers had been deemed necessary for a Halloween rave at the CNE Automotive Building attended by more than 13,000 ravers. Police at the time declared that this earlier event had been held 'without incident,' noting that the total cost to the promoter had been less than $5000. By New Year's Eve of 2000, a rave at the CNE's Better Living Centre that expected a crowd of five thousand was required to have thirty to forty paid-duty officers at a cost of $22,000. The police also demanded that undercover paid-duty officers be allowed to patrol the crowd and arrest those suspected of trafficking, possessing, or using illicit drugs. Will Chang lamented: 'Whether this is an attempt to price them [rave promoters] out of business, or some other purpose, I don't know. But the police gave their word to city council and to us that they would be reasonable and rely on past historical practices in determining how many paid duty officers would be required. They have not been doing that' (Raphael 2000b).

The TPS ignored the accusations of institutional bias. Meanwhile, the protocol was being used as a template by numerous other municipal police forces across Canada (including Calgary, Edmonton, Richmond, and Vancouver) to control – and ultimately prevent – raves within their respective jurisdictions.

In response to police actions, a second instalment of iDance was planned for the Labour Day weekend of 2001. Organizers hoped to bring attention to the issue of paid-duty police serving as a barrier to a vibrant rave scene in Toronto. A comparable crowd attended, but unlike the first rally, it was a party rather than protest atmosphere.[10] The issue of covert police harassment failed to generate the same level of public outrage as the overt securitization of raves. The issue now was far more complex and subtle than prohibition, and the popular terms of discourse, of which the rave community was a major contributor, had made a police presence necessary for perceptions that an event was safe. Thus, organizers found it difficult to convey their message about the arbitrariness of police practices and ultimately failed to generate the political pressure necessary for Toronto's public authorities to consider revising the rave protocol. However, the appearance of corporate sponsorship from the *Toronto Star*, *Eye Magazine*, Microsoft, and MuchMusic for the event did symbolize that rave was entering the Canadian mainstream (Rayner 2001; Rayner 2002a).

The normalization of rave was also visible in the rather muted public outcry (in comparison with Benji Hayward or Allen Ho) over the death of a sixteen-year-old boy and a twenty-one-year-old mother from ecstasy overdoses at two Toronto nightclubs in the summer of 2001. Compared to other issues raised by rave, very little media attention focused on the $10,000 fine for fire code violations given to the promotion company that organized the rave at which Allen Ho died. Furthermore, the stabbing death of a university student at another event promoted by the same company in 2001 did not have the staying power of the Allen Ho overdose (Canadian Press 2001).

Unfortunately, iDance was to be the last hurrah for the rave community as large, all-ages events became increasingly infrequent. The spiralling costs of organizing events that resulted from the Rave Protocol were compounded by the financial reverberations of 11 Septem-

ber 2001, including increased insurance costs for events, less sponsorship money, and general decreases in the amounts of disposable
income directed towards personal entertainment because of the economic downturn. Even in these circumstances, the pace at which a formerly vibrant subcultural practice appeared to retreat seemed extraordinary, even with its covert securitization and resulting financial
pressures.[11] As Alex D. noted in 2002 after iDance organizers cancelled
the third instalment of the event: 'The rave scene is dead, it's finished,
it's over. It's gone ... For the last few months, everyone I meet – friends,
DJs, promoters – I ask: "What do you think happened?" And nobody
knows. Nobody knows where everybody went and nobody knows
what's going to become of the scene' (Rayner 2002b).

Ironically, at a time when raving had imploded, the RCMP publicized the findings of its own intelligence probe of 'the Rave scene and
chemical drugs.' Heavy surveillance of rave by the RCMP had begun
in 1997. An initial report was released early in 2000; however 'due to
high demand for that booklet and the rapidly changing drug scene,' an
updated report was released in 2001. While the report can be easily
dismissed as an instance of the RCMP kicking rave when it was down,
it can also be interpreted more ominously as an attempt by the authorities to reshape public discourse surrounding rave in Canada to ensure
that it could never come back.

Designer Drugs and Raves

Designer Drugs and Raves, a report produced by the Drug Enforcement
Branch's 'E' Division, provided extensive information on rave, the
typology of ravers, their organization, clandestine laboratories, designer drugs, drug analyses, and Canadian legislation. In particular,
the section titled 'The Raver' provided a typology of 'stereotypical
ravers' that was filled with misinformation. This gross unfamiliarity
with the discourse of Canadian rave scene was surprising, given that
the report was the culmination of five years of extensive intelligence
by the RCMP (RCMP 2001, 6).

The RCMP claimed to be offering a 'non-biassed, fact based perspective,' in order to counteract the message that 'there is a possibility
for "safe use"' of drugs like MDMA by securitizing practices represented as being indicative of rave. The approach the report followed
was two-pronged and deployed its own constructed spatialization of
illicit drug use. The title of the report itself provided a geopolitical nar-

rative that attempted to ground the use of particular illicit drugs within the spaces provided by rave. Moreover, the illicit drugs themselves were described as generating a spectrum of threats beyond their immediate effects on the (human) body. Thus, in *Designer Drugs and Raves*, one can see the fabrication of links between 'club and rave drugs' and other deviant forms of behaviour, wherever their location. Even the term 'club drug' points to the continuing conflation of 'nightclub' and 'rave' for the purposes of securitizing both sets of spaces.

The report's overriding metaphor was that of proliferation in three distinct senses. The first was in terms of the spaces in which 'club and rave drugs' were supposedly being consumed. The report warned the reader that 'chemical drug use is not isolated within ... [the rave] scene. These drugs are used anywhere from house parties to nightclubs to high schools and college and university campuses' (ibid., 4). Yet, given that the report focused exclusively on rave and implicitly framed it as the epicentre, rave could be blamed as the source of behaviour that was occurring elsewhere.

The second was that more and more ravers were no longer limiting their illicit drug intake to MDMA and were becoming poly-drug users. This observation can be interpreted as an attempt to erase representational differences that may have existed in popular discourses about ecstasy users being benign and non-threatening while under the influence of MDMA (the love drug) in comparison to other hard-drug users, by erasing the distinction between them.[12] Ecstasy users were, then, just as threatening and erratic as the stigmatized users of other illicit drugs, because according to the RCMP, they had likely also consumed those other substances.

The third way in which the metaphor of proliferation was interwoven into the text was with regard to the production of MDMA, methamphetamine, and GHB.[13] According to the RCMP, it was not the number of clandestine labs that were being discovered by police that was worrisome, so much as where these labs were being found – specifically, in suburban neighbourhoods (ibid., 4, 17–19). Supposedly to maintain the sanctity of suburban living, the report included a checklist of indicators that a clandestine drug laboratory might be operating near one's home:

- Blacked-out windows or curtains always drawn.
- Chemical odours coming from the house or apartment, garbage, or a detached building.

- Garbage that often includes numerous bottles and containers such as for acetone, toulene, muriatic acid, red phosphorous, ephedrine, methanol, sodium, hydroxide, and ammonia.
- Metal drums and boxes with labels removed or spraypainted over.
- The setting out of garbage in another neighbour's collection area.
- Unfriendly or secretive neighbours.
- Paranoid or odd behaviour, such as watching cars suspiciously when they pass the residence.
- Coming outside to smoke cigarettes.
- Expensive security.
- Frequent visitors, often in expensive vehicles.
- Frequent late-night activity.
- Unemployed, yet drive expensive cars, seem to have plenty of money, and pay bills in cash (ibid., 19).

These of course were similar to the warning signs that a marijuana grow-op might be operating in one's neighbourhood (see the previous chapter).

Through the geographing of illicit drug use, there was a blurring of club into rave as the locus of these practices. But to make a strong case, rave's illicit practices needed to be shown to be escaping beyond these boundaries. In employing the metaphor of proliferation, the RCMP was raising the possibility that *your* children and *your* neighbourhood might be the sites where these were occurring. The report's geographing of illicit drug use could also be read through the discussion of particular substances identified by the report as 'club and rave' drugs. These included MDMA, drugs of deception being sold as MDMA (MDA, 2C-B, MMDA, PMA, MDE), date rape drugs (GHB and Ketamine), methamphetamine, LSD, Quaaludes, Psilocybin, DXM (an over-the-counter cough suppressant), PCP, fentanyl (synthetic heroin), nitrous oxide, and legal highs (caffeine, ephedrine, and ephedra). According to the RCMP, the 'real danger of designer drugs is the fact that users feel they are in control. Even with the occasional or weekend use, users become *addicted to the lifestyle*' (ibid., 6; italics added).

While the choice and categorization of these drugs was presented as self-evident based on factual evidence, three important sites of representational politics emerged within this discussion of 'club and rave' drugs. The first important site centred on the RCMP's attempt to link raving to the use of heroin even though the drug had never been associated with the rave scene. Heroin makes people sleepy and is more expensive than MDMA – not exactly qualities that would make the drug attractive to young people who want to dance all night. Two tactics were employed. The first was to point out that capsules sold as MDMA could contain heroin – this, even though the RCMP's own laboratory analyses (both in the report and others released subsequent to the report) had not shown the presence of heroin in any substance being sold as MDMA in Canada. The second move was to classify fentanyl or synthetic heroin as a 'club and rave' drug, even though the RCMP in its report admitted that no amount of the substance had been seized from raves over the course of its intelligence investigations (ibid., 36). Despite the virtual absence of heroin from the Canadian rave scene, the RCMP geographed the substance within the space bounded by rave; this served to harness the strong negative representations of opiate use in general, and heroin more specifically, in Canada. This move had the potential to transform the discursive representation of raves by equating them with opium dens and 'shooting galleries' and ravers with heroin junkies – arguably the least positively represented group of illicit drug users. At the same time, the addition of heroin might scare the public into applying political pressure for even tougher antirave regulations.

The second strategy was to link the use of particular 'club and rave' drugs with sexual assault (ibid., 5). Specifically, the RCMP classified GHB (gammahydroxybutyric acid) and ketamine as 'date rape' drugs. GHB is a liquid that was developed as an anaesthetic but became popular with bodybuilders during the 1970s because its consumption prevented muscles from tightening up, allowing for more training sessions over the course of a day. GHB is a central nervous system depressant, and its effects are similar to those of imbibing large quantities of alcohol without a hangover effect. However, it is very easy to overdose (or what is called 'G-ing out') because GHB is very powerful and its effects are amplified when it is used in conjunction with other commonly consumed substances like alcohol (Rosenberg 1997; Cudmore 1999). Ketamine is an anaesthetic used for veterinary surgery. Sold as a powder, it produces feelings of euphoria, dissociation, hallucinations, and in larger doses often an inability to move (referred to by users as 'the k-hole'). Because of GHB's strong, salty taste and ketamine's powdery composition/bad taste, both drugs are more difficult (though still possible) to slip to someone without them being aware of it. In comparison, Rohypnol, another sedative, until recently was both colourless and tasteless.

With respect to GHB, the RCMP argued that it relaxes inhibitions and increases libido, which could 'facilitate sexual assault.' With ketamine, the RCMP argued that it 'can be used as a date rape drug. In September 2000, a local university had an incident where a female student was found unconscious on campus; her unconscious state was found to be the result of ingesting ketamine. No assault occured [sic], however due to her unconscious state, one could have easily happened' (RCMP 2001, 35).

One cannot fault the RCMP for linking these two drugs with the possibility of sexual assault (despite the lack of evidence they have ever been deployed for that purpose), given their potential to be used in this fashion. However, if the RCMP was trying to raise awareness of chemically aided sexual assault or date rape among young people, alcohol, given the preponderance of its use and its availability, should have been presented in the same manner. Yet this legal drug was neither identified as a threat or even mentioned in passing. Rave, then, was being linked to deviant sexual practices through the stigmatization of specific drugs as aids to sexual assault.

The third site was in terms of the legal drugs that were absent from the discussion of 'club and rave' drugs: alcohol and tobacco. Both substances have extensive medical evidence of their harmful effects, yet the use of either drug was not classified as problematic by the RCMP in this probe. Moreover, both are among the most widely consumed drugs in clubs and, to a lesser extent, in rave environments. Thus, in claiming to present a 'fact-based approach' to raves, the RCMP subjectively attached particular meanings of threat to illicit drugs while completely ignoring the harmful effects of licit drugs – a move rich in ethical content. Given changes within the Canadian and (more specifically) Toronto rave scenes, this absence was not merely academic.

Smokes, Booze, and Rave

By 2004, very few Toronto-based promotion companies remained with the capacity to host a rave of more than a thousand patrons. Events of this size occurred approximately quarterly, whereas five years earlier, Toronto had several large promotion companies, and raves were being attended by thousands of people on a weekly basis. Although the large all-ages parties that had helped define rave in the city had been largely abandoned, club nights that catered to the former rave crowd in licensed venues that served alcohol, and smaller underground events, continued (Rayner 2002b).

Marketers had been waiting for several years for an opening into the rave scene, and the ongoing financial hardships facing rave promoters provided opportunities.[14] In an effort to build brand recognition and target a key demographic, tobacco and alcohol companies increasingly began to sponsor club-night events in Toronto, Montreal, Edmonton, Calgary, and Vancouver, mirroring tactics that were being employed in the UK, Brazil, South Africa, the United States, Australia, and China. Companies involved in the sponsorship of club events included Rothmans (Benson and Hedges Gold Club Series), Camel Cigarettes (The Hump), Imperial Tobacco (DuMaurier Red Seat Series and Club Rogue in Quebec), Smirnoff (The Smirnoff Experience), Baccardi (Rev DJ Tour), and Heineken (Heineken Thirst DJ Competition and Tour). Sometimes the companies formed subsidiaries to organize the parties; other times they contracted them out to independent marketing firms.

Usually, sponsorship has been dependent on making the sponsor's products the exclusive brand available at the venue for the event (and sometimes longer). For example, during Smirnoff Experience events, the only alcohol available is Smirnoff vodka. Anecdotally, the popularity of Benson and Hedges cigarettes has increased amongst club goers, in part because the company has negotiated exclusive concessions at several Toronto dance clubs that host its events. As tobacco advertising in Canada cannot legally target new smokers, companies have asserted that the goal of their marketing efforts is to encourage smokers to switch their choice of cigarette based on competing brand images.

Some within the rave scene welcomed sponsorships because they ensured that popular international DJs would continue to come to Toronto at a relatively low admission charge for attendees. Others saw the move to clubs as evidence of the maturing of the Canadian rave scene and as similar to processes that had occurred a decade earlier in the UK. Critics charged that tobacco and alcohol sponsorship was unethical, and that although previous popular representations that linked rave to health dangers based on substance (ab)use were wrong, the culture was finally living up to these representations by allowing itself to be pimped to sell dangerous drugs. It was also argued that a 'Wal-Mart effect' was taking place in the Toronto rave scene, in that tobacco and alcohol sponsorships were helping drive the remaining cadre of small promoters out of business by overpaying international talent and not passing the costs on to consumers.

Given that sponsorship of these events was considered an advertising expense, these companies did not have to show an immediate profit from revenues generated by admission charges. Most important, though, from a cultural perspective, these events sponsored by tobacco and alcohol companies took place in licensed venues that restricted admission to those nineteen or older. As the original no-alcohol aspect of rave grew increasingly rare, the ability to attract and maintain a youth audience slowly diminished.

As news of tobacco sponsorship became widely reported, tobacco companies found themselves being investigated by Health Canada under suspicion of violating Canada's strict tobacco advertising laws. While no formal charges were laid, once the final phase of the Tobacco Act came into effect on 1 October 2003, effectively banning all public advertising of tobacco products, overt sponsorship of events could no longer take place without prohibitive legal liabilities. Undeterred, Imperial Tobacco found a way to circumvent the spirit, if not the letter, of these regulations by forming a subsidiary company named Definiti Events, which then contracted out event organization to third parties (Tuck 2003; E. Thompson 2003). The events themselves feature no obvious advertising except for scantily clad women and men selling du Maurier cigarettes. While many marketing executives have been impressed with the switch to guerrilla marketing by tobacco companies, critics contend that the intent is to corner tobacco sales within a subculture that is perceived as trend setting, in order to promote sales throughout the general population (Vasil 2003).

Conclusions

In examining the geopolitics of dancing, what becomes apparent is that governmental responses to rave have drawn from pre-existing discursive representations of the spatialization of drug use and the dangers posed by its proliferation beyond these spaces. The securitization of rave in the aftermath of Allen Ho's death was made possible by particular aspects of the dominant Canadian illicit drugs discourse that incorporated geopolitical visions that initially desired the maintenance of a border to give the appearance of keeping sites of illicit drug use outside the confines of the Canadian Self. Furthermore, popular discourses made it possible for the Allen Ho tragedy (much like the Benji Hayward incident) to be framed as one centred solely on the use of illicit drugs.

In opposing the securitization of rave, the rave community played into these very same discourses, which did not see any legitimate use for illicit drugs, by engaging in performatives that excluded drug use from rave culture. Paradoxically, while the transformation of popular representations of rave was able to generate enough political pressure to lift the ban in Toronto, it ultimately made it possible for covert processes of securitization to occur as the police became firmly entrenched as the managers of rave safety. The practices of rave were in this way displaced into the nightclub environment, and the rave community was exposed to the potentially harmful effects of being targeted by tobacco and alcohol companies. From a biopolitical perspective, the great irony is that the incorporation of rave into Canadian society – symbolized by allowing events on publicly owned property to promote safety and prevent illicit drug use – has led to an ongoing exposure to substances known to cause serious health effects.

One of the most fascinating aspects of this story is that the responses of public authorities, which have geographed rave as a site requiring biopolitical management, have been able to sustain themselves despite the dramatic changes in the dominant representations and understandings of the practices and spaces associated with rave. Even the mainstreaming of rave has not been able to avoid the calculations of governmentality that have sought to control individual bodies for the purposes of orchestrating a particular performative of the Canadian body politic. Thus the examination of rave in Toronto draws attention to the discourses and representations of sites associated with illicit drugs, how these exhibit the effects of governmentality, and the type of politics that becomes (im)possible. Conversely, rave has also served as a site that has exhibited varying degrees of biopolitical resistance over the course of its brief history. Perhaps, then, it is not surprising that tobacco companies chose the new spaces occupied by rave, rather than other cultural phenomena such as sporting events or rock concerts, to test the limits of the Tobacco Act restrictions on advertising.

The current feeling among many Canadian ravers is that rave as a particular set of subcultural practices is now dead. This may be an exaggerated interpretation; even so, the current context can be seen as one in which rave culture appears to be on life support.[15] Yet as bad as things may be for rave culture in Canada, Canadian ravers are also quick to point out that government policies with regard to rave are not as extreme as those that have been pursued in the United States, which has seen the passage of the Rave Act 2003 as well as proposals to amend sections of the CLEAN-UP Act.[16] Thus, even Canada's rave subculture is engaged in a performative that differentiates Canada from the United States based on constructed notions of moderation and extremity.

Conclusion

During Caribana celebrations in 2000, Jason Burke, an African Canadian in his mid-twenties, was approached by two white police officers who accused him of selling drugs to one of his companions (Rankin et al. 2002b). Claiming that they were operating on a tip given to them by two nightclub doormen, the officers pinned him against a wall and called for back-up when Burke accused them of unlawful arrest. Eventually, after being pushed to the ground in the ensuing struggle to apply handcuffs, Burke was pepper sprayed in the face and taken to a police station, where he was charged with threatening bodily harm, resisting arrest, escaping custody, and causing a disturbance (Rankin et al. 2002b). Burke claimed that while at the police station he was denied access to liquid to flush out his eyes and that he was eventually forced to use water from a holding cell toilet to relieve the irritation (ibid.). The investigation would later show that no drugs were found on Burke, no drugs were found in the area where he was arrested, and no drugs were found on his companion (ibid.). Later he would launch a $2 million civil suit against the Toronto Police Service (TPS) for malicious prosecution, negligence, assault, and human rights violations. At the time of writing, the suit is pending.

Burke's complaint came to public attention as part of an investigative series in October 2002 by the *Toronto Star* on racial profiling and the TPS (Rankin et al. 2002a, 2002b). Using the service's own database of arrest profiles from 1996–2002, researchers correlated arrests against a number of variables, including race (based on police descriptions of skin colour), citizenship status in Canada, occupation, age, and gender ('The Story Behind the Numbers' 2002). The TPS itself had been prevented from compiling and analysing data based on race since 1989, when Julian Fantino (at the time a police staff inspector) generated a public relations crisis when he reported to a race relations committee that based on his own accounting of arrest numbers, the problem in the Jane-Finch corridor, one of Toronto's high-crime neighbourhoods, was that 'blacks' were committing the most offences even though they accounted for a small percentage of the total population ('Racial Data a Hot Potato' 2002).

The results of the investigation were astonishing, especially given dominant performatives of Toronto as the most tolerant multicultural city in Canada, and Canada as the most tolerant multicultural country in the world:

- 'Blacks' were being ticketed at more than four times the rate of their representation in the general population for 'out-of-sight' offences, infractions that only can come to light after a traffic stop has been made; whites were underrepresented in these instances (Rankin et al. 2002a).
- 'Black' men aged between twenty-five and thirty-four were being ticketed for out-of-sight violations at more than five times the rate of their representation in the general population within the same age category (ibid.).

These initial findings for 'out-of-sight' violations were congruent with disparities found in arrests for simple drug possession, another type of offence that usually only arises *after* a suspect is stopped by police:

- 'Whites,' while accounting for 62 per cent of Toronto's population, made up 58 per cent of all drug arrests for simple possession. In comparison, 'blacks,' who comprised 8 per cent of the population, comprised 23 per cent of all drug arrests for simple possession, a marked overrepresentation (Rankin et al. 2002b).
- A 'black' person arrested for simple possession was less likely to be released at the scene than a 'white' person (62 per cent compared to 77 per cent) (Rankin et al. 2002b).
- In custody, 'black' suspects in simple drug possession arrests were twice as likely to be held for a bail hearing in comparison to 'white' suspects facing the same charge (ibid.).

According to experts in policing, these results clearly indicated a systemic pattern of racial profiling.

The law enforcement community refused to acknowledge the validity of these allegations. In an interview before the results were distributed to the public, Fantino (then the police chief) declared that racial profiling did not exist in Toronto and that the *Toronto Star* had not conducted a fair assessment of the situation. His counterinterpretation of the results was that 'we have certain communities ... that are under great stress and great distress. The ratio of population in certain areas, the type of environmental conditions that exist, the high concentration of public housing in certain areas – all are factors beyond our control that, clearly ... require a police response. Communities ... are different. They're different throughout the city' ('Fantino: "There is No Racism"' 2002).

Instead of promising to investigate the serious issues raised by the report, Fantino blamed the *Toronto Star*: 'It seems that, according to some people, no matter what honest efforts people make, there are always those who are intent on causing trouble. Obviously this (story) is going to do exactly that' (ibid.).

Fantino's remarks were mainly an attempt to deflect any concern over the behaviour of the TPS by geographing extraordinary threats into specific areas (i.e., public housing) and unnamed 'problem' communities. While he did not identify specific communities, given the context in Toronto at the time, readers would have understood these to be ethnic communities in general, and likely Caribbean-Canadian communities in particular. Fantino also attempted to discipline the boundaries of debate by implying that anyone who dared suggest that racial profiling occurred in Toronto was merely a troublemaker who was making it harder for law enforcement to protect citizens from crime.

The rank and file of the TPS also disputed the results of the report, by commissioning an alternative analysis of the data. This second analysis claimed that racial profiling did not exist and referred to the original findings as 'junk science' (Moloney 2003). When this counter-report was released, it was immediately discredited by experts in the Canadian criminological community as having no appreciation of the nuances of racism and so being rife with methodologically unsound data-set manipulations; moreover, its findings, despite all this, in fact *were* consistent with the existence of racial profiling (Levy 2003). Undeterred, the Toronto Police Association (TPA), the TPS's union, filed a $2.7 billion class action libel suit against the *Toronto Star* alleging that the special series on race and crime had damaged the reputation of every officer in the service. This suit was immediately dismissed by an

Ontario Superior Court judge, who ruled that 'the stories cannot "be reasonably understood" to state or even hint "that every member of the service is a racist or a bigot" ... The whole thrust of the articles is that the evidence suggests that racial profiling occurs and that steps must be taken to identify the causes and remove them' (Tyler 2003).

Despite these setbacks, the TPA steadfastly maintained that it had not engaged in any practices that needed to be reassessed with regard to its members' treatment of visible minorities.

In December 2003 the Ontario Human Rights Commission (OCHR) released a report which argued that racial profiling did happen in Ontario in a wide range of institutions and agencies (beyond the police) and that the practice was negatively affecting people's lives (Simmie 2003). Organizations, agencies, and areas explicitly identified as potentially having a problem with racial profiling included the following: police services across the province, the criminal justice system, all levels of the education system, the Canada Customs and Revenue Agency, private security companies, private business establishments (e.g., restaurants, bars, malls, clubs, stores, theatres, and casinos), airports, and airport security services (2003, 67). Defining racial profiling as 'any action undertaken for reasons of safety, security or public protection, that relies on stereotypes about race, colour, ethnicity, ancestry, religion, or place of origin ... rather than on reasonable suspicion to single out an individual for greater security treatment,' the provincial probe heard testimony from more than four hundred individuals who related experiences that met this classificatory criterion (Simmie 2003).

Having heard all this testimony, the OHRC put forward numerous recommendations with the goal of ending racial profiling:

- A Racial Diversity Secretariat should be established to monitor and report on racism in Ontario.
- All organizations and agencies entrusted with public security and safety should monitor their activities to prevent racial profiling, and develop and/or modify their practices, policies, and training accordingly.
- All organizations that have or are alleged to have had problems with racial profiling must acknowledge that it does exist.
- Government officials in Ontario must take action to combat racial profiling.

- All organizations that serve the public in Ontario must have a zero tolerance policy towards racial profiling.
- The economic effects of racial profiling need to be examined when analysing economic costs and productivity issues.
- There should be ongoing communication between organizations and institutions with the communities they serve to facilitate solutions to racial profiling.
- Police services across the province should install cameras in police vehicles to monitor interactions between officers and the public.
- All police officers and private security guards should wear clearly displayed name badges (OHCR 2003, 67–73).

Unfortunately, despite initial hopes that this report would spur governments at all levels in Canada to confront racial profiling, the issue remains largely unaddressed.

Selling Fear, Buying Security, and Constructing Canada

A diverse body of literature has been examining the prevalence of what has been referred to as the 'culture of fear' in many Western societies (Glassner 1999; Massumi 1993; Beck 1992). The Canadian body politic, like many other political communities around the world, has been warned of a growing gamut of looming threats, including transnational organized crime, terrorism, resource wars, global warming, air pollution, infectious diseases, illegal migration, computer viruses, weapons of mass destruction, and cultural penetration by global Others. Engin Isin (2004) has argued that these threat discourses have been instrumental in the production of 'neurotic citizens,' a collectivity whose political paralysis is made possible through the proliferation and management of anxiety by state structures.

Although they may not manifest themselves as fantastically in Canada as in other comparable societies, the Canadian body politic is afflicted with a range of threat neuroses that have made a growth in securitization possible and helped entrench it in already securitized locales. At the same time, there has been a concomitant move to marginalize in and/or exclude from the public policy agenda an alternative series of security concerns, including racial profiling, domestic violence, child poverty, corporate crime and corruption, police corruption, and the plight of Canada's indigenous peoples. For example, though it pledged to eliminate child poverty in Canada by 2000 when elected in 1993, the Liberal government's record on this issue area was abysmal, with research showing that at best, levels of child poverty in Canada have returned to about one in ten children, the same level as 1989 (Jackson 2004, 43).

More and more resources (over $7.7 billion to date) are being directed towards the recently formed Department of Public Security and Emergency Prepardness (DPSEP), whose domestic security mandate, in covering everything from disaster relief coordination to counterterrorism, exceeds that of the Department of Homeland Security in the United States. This new 'superministry' has incorporated six existing agencies, including Correctional Service of Canada, the National Parole Board, the RCMP, the Canadian Security and Intelligence Service, the Office of Critical Infrastructure and Emergency Preparedness, and the Canadian Firearms Centre; it has also created the Canadian Border Services Agency, which combines personnel formerly involved in customs, border inspections, immigration intelligence, and deportations.

Public opinion polls have shown strong support for large increases in military spending, including the procurement of heavy equipment such as helicopters, submarines, and other advanced war-fighting technology. A Canadian Institute of International Affairs and Pollara public opinion poll in April 2004 showed that there were only two areas in foreign policy where a majority of Canadians supported increased levels of spending: fighting terrorism at home (54 per cent) and national defence (53 per cent) (Pollara 2004, 14). The Harper government has substantially increased military spending; even so, critics have argued that Canada's security needs require overall spending to double as a percentage of GDP.

At the same time, the popular Canadian imagination envisions a society in which criminal violence is increasing. This, even though the federal government's own data show that the overall crime rate in Canada is in sharp decline (Statistics Canada 2004b). According to Statistics Canada data, the overall rate of Criminal Code offences (excluding traffic offences) declined from 8,136.5 per 100,000 in 1998 to 7,589.8 per 100,000 in 2002. The violent crime rate dropped from 979.1 in 1998 to 965.5 in 2002. Overall, crime rates are at their lowest levels since the late 1970s (Statistics Canada 2004a). However, seizing the opportunity presented by the popular imagination, law enforcement has continued to lobby for more resources and more uniformed officers by implying that a failure to provide both will result in social catastrophe.

The discursive representation of understaffed and underpowered law enforcement agencies in Canada has resonated with the public and with policymakers, even though many police forces across the country are already commanding a huge percentage of discretionary municipal spending. For example, in the spring of 2004, the Police Services Board and Toronto City Council approved a $679 million financial plan for the TPS. Chief Fantino complained that this was far too little to provide adequate safety services for the public, yet he failed to mention that this marked an increase of over $50 million from the previous year – an 8 per cent increase in a city facing a severe budgetary crisis and social service cutbacks (*Budget Blues* 2004).

Moreover, the City of Toronto's own budgetary report revealed that law enforcement spending in the city represented 58 per cent of discretionary (i.e., non-critical infrastructure) spending, dwarfing the total amount of municipal funds devoted to public health (even in the aftermath of SARS), public libraries, community centres, public transit, and environmental conservation combined (City of Toronto 2004, 48). Not even a series of corruption scandals that implicated the head of the TPA and other union officials, disbanded an entire plainclothes division, and required a multiyear investigation by the RCMP into criminal activities undertaken by the TPS drug squad, shook the belief of law enforcement and the Canadian body politic that the 'real' security threats are illicit drugs, marijuana grow-ops, ethnic criminal organizations, bikers, illicit drug production laboratories, and foreign terrorists.

Jacques Derrida (1995) has argued that the concept of illicit drugs 'supposes an instituted and an institutional definition: a history is required, and a culture, conventions, evaluations, norms, an entire network of intertwined discourses, a rhetoric, whether explicit or elliptical' (1995, 229). In a social environment where the public has become hypersensitive to notions of threat, where security and liberty have been discursively constructed as an economy rather than as complimentary, where it is still considered possible to become totally invulnerable to the myriad risks of the contemporary global moment, and where the United States continues to explicitly and implicitly discipline (with varying degrees of success) Canadian conceptions of the politically possible, illicit drugs are both a lightning rod for and a reflection of *the* dominant Canadian notion of security and hegemonic performatives of Canadian identity.

Although moves towards marijuana decriminalization are deployed within discourses of Canadian nationalism to performatively represent Canada as a socially progressive state, it is important to keep in mind that in 2002 there were still over 93,000 drug arrests in Canada, with only one-third of these being for trafficking, importation, or production (Statistics Canada 2004a). From a longitudinal perspective, the arrest rate for drug offences in Canada by 2004 had reached a twenty-year high (Powell 2004, A5). Nearly seventy thousand of the total number of arrests were marijuana related, and 72 per cent of these were for simple possession (ibid.). The age group most frequently charged were youths aged eighteen to twenty-four, followed by youths aged twelve to seventeen. Even claims that Canada had adopted a medicalized harm reduction approach to drug use with its series of drug strategies stood in stark contrast to data from the Canadian Centre for Justice Statistics indicating that the total number of police arrests for marijuana had jumped by 80 per cent since 1992 (ibid.). These numbers illustrate that policing priorities seem to be at odds not only with public attitudes towards marijuana, but also with their own representations of the most substantial threats posed to society by organized crime, illicit drug trafficking, illicit drug production, and terrorism. The power/relations that have made this possible are crucial to understanding what security can mean in Canada and the processes of securitization in Canadian society.

The Canadian medical community has continued to prescribe drugs at a record rate, with over 361 million prescriptions filled in 2003 (Canada NewsWire 2004). Retail prescriptions had grown 7.9 per cent over the previous year – the largest annual increase for the decade. The monetary value of the prescription market was estimated at $15.9 billion, which amounted to a mean of eleven prescriptions per Canadian at an average retail price of $44 per prescription (ibid.). Antidepressant prescriptions rose over 10.1 per cent despite a series of class action suits in North America, growing concerns over the side effects, and well-known evidence of the development of dependencies and problems with withdrawal (ibid.). Hormones were the third most prescribed class of medications even though a series of long-term studies has shown that hormone replacement therapy in women significantly increases the risks of heart disease and cancer (ibid.). Ritalin, an amphetamine with numerous side effects, continues to be prescribed to more than 200,000 children in Canada who have been diagnosed with Attention Deficit Disorder (ADD) or Attention Deficit Hyperactivity Disorder (ADHD) (CBC Winnipeg 2003).[1] Yet the Canadian

Medical Association does not counsel its members to avoid prescribing these medications. Instead, it continues to advise against medical marijuana by claiming that there is no scientific proof that its medical benefits outweigh its potential costs. Given this incongruency, it is imperative to expose the 'aspiration to power' that lies behind these claims about drugs and the types of knowledge and experience that are disqualified within this regime of truth (Foucault 2003e, 10).

Viewing illicit drugs as a problematique that draws the attention of various institutionalized sites of power concurrently reveals the multiple forms that power can assume in contemporary society. We can see the sovereign power over death that sanctions the utilization of physical punishment, violence, and the aggrandizement of the state as a negative force. We can see the disciplinary and governmental forms of power over life that manage the ways in which people *must* live by harnessing the legal and medical realms to promote public and individual 'health.' We can see the power of security to identify threats, calculate risks, and respond in ways that pass the limits of law and/or convention. We have also seen a power of control that establishes networks that survey, track monitor, restrict, and regulate societal flows. While these have been traditionally portrayed as separate types of power – and in some strands of contemporary social theory as following an exclusive evolutionary trajectory – the issues of illicit drugs demonstrate that the full palette operates simultaneously, sometimes at various sites, sometimes at the same sites, sometimes in opposition, and sometimes in conjunction, as the art of government.

Writ large, the case studies examined in this project have been humble attempts to begin the process of mapping out all of these contours of the social contexts, relations of power, discursive formations, representational practices, narratives, and commonly held meanings that have shaped Canadian understandings of (inter)national security and identity. In other words, genealogies of illicit drugs help reveal what Canada understands itself to be and what it claims it needs to actively defend itself against. Previous chapters have shown that interpretation is *central* to these processes; dominant understandings of illicit drugs are not innate to the substances themselves, nor can one naturally derive such understandings from what are taken as their probable effects. Through discourse, meaning has been assigned to subjects and objects, and to the contexts in which they have been constituted, through mutual multidirectional interaction. More important, the case studies reveal that meaning is always arbitrary and contestable. For example, there were no objective reasons to make raves a site for securitization in Canadian society; and racial profiling is not viewed as a security issue independent from *dominant* understandings of what security is, what it must be provided against, and who is entitled to its benefits. In this way, security is inseparable from broader ethico-political issues in the Canadian body politic about negotiating difference. Yet these moments of negotiation are central to our understanding of ourselves and our own identities.

Return of the Dragon

In the introductory chapter it was argued that 'chasing the dragon,' a slang term for smoking opium, is an excellent metaphor through which to read the intricacies of Canadian responses to illicit drugs. Drugs, like dragons, have been subject to competing perceptions within popular discourses (or mythologies), which have positioned them along a spectrum whose polar extremes are guarded by sacred gatekeepers of transcendental experience at one end and, at the other, by insidious enemies intent on destroying *the* civilized characteristics that constitute Canadian society.

As previous chapters have shown, some communities and individuals in Canada have seen illicit drug use as an activity that can strengthen interpersonal bonds across a range of social relationships and that in some cases can improve the quality of life for those suffering from debilitating medical conditions. Yet for most of the past hundred years, the hegemonic understanding has constructed illicit drugs as threats to *the* Canadian way of life and the values that are constitutive of it. Moreover, within this matrix of threat, illicit drug use has not been repressed so much as managed as a problem with biological, cultural, criminal, and medical dimensions.

From these sites, illicit drugs are viewed as a danger not just for explicit reasons relating to their supposed chemical effects, but more important, because of what they are said to represent: attempts by Others to defile the Canadian body politic. As foreign modes of being, illicit drugs have historically been classified as deviant, inferior, and distinctly *un*-Canadian. Canadian identity and security, though, are not just 'made in Canada.' Already established global discourses of race, culture, civilization, and danger are mobilized within these debates about what it means to be Canadian, what threatens the Canadian Self, and what therefore must be secured. This contributes to a feedback loop that further concretizes specific representations. At various times over the past hundred years, performatives and performances around illicit drugs have been initiated to distinguish 'Canadian' attributes from those of the 'criminal addict,' the 'Chinese opium smoker,' the 'Negro peddler,' the 'Somali,' and even the 'American.' And it has been discourses of security and identity that have created these threats and enemies.

Thus, the substances, those who use them, and the spaces in which it is claimed they are exclusively produced/used have been subject to a series of securitizations that have marginalized specific individuals and entire communities in the employment of technologies of discipline and social control generated by the processes of governmentality and biopolitics. There are numerous strategies for dealing with difference, such as acceptance, understanding, management, tolerance, rejection, denial, and elimination. As has been shown in the case studies considered here, from management onwards, all of these strategies involve various degrees of securitization, both overt and covert.

Most notably within these domains, practices have included monitoring, confinement, quarantine, and isolation. All of these have constituted attempts to remove illicit drugs and their users from the sanctified space of the Canadian body politic. Beyond physical actions, these practices and the technologies that are central to them also 'create the knowledge of [national identity], create a fact of [national identity],' by inscribing a spatial–temporal sphere with particular characteristics through their associated discourses (Winichakul 1994, 15). But the vision of nationhood that these performatives and performances put forward 'is an imagined sphere with no given identity or essence; it is a cultural construct' (ibid.). Thus, Canadian identity remains arbitrary and contradictory.

For example, even with the securitization of illicit drugs, their production, distribution, and consumption remains prevalent throughout the Canadian body politic. In 2003 a *Forbes Magazine* report estimated that illicit marijuana production alone is about a $7 billion-a-year agricultural industry in Canada, eclipsing both cattle ($5.63 billion) and wheat ($1.73 billion) (forbes.com 2003). Still, despite the lack of success of the counternarcotics campaign (as judged by its own internal standards), its practices are made possible by discourses that deploy a range of disciplinary knowledge in security, criminology, and medicine to constitute the boundaries that divide the Canadian Self from the foreign Other, a process that legitimizes their inevitable ethico-political content.

Security and identity have also intersected in terms of how the Canadian body politic has understood the practices of dragon slaying – that is, Canada's policies on illicit drugs. That Canada is a progressive country on the leading edge of social reform is a long-standing performative that been interpreted as embodying Canadian responses to illicit drugs. From the early construction of a global illicit drug control regime to recent policies with respect to medical marijuana and decriminalization, Canada's reactions to illicit drugs have contributed to the Canadian (inter)national sense of Self. This has allowed Canada to maintain that it is a society of moral, hard-working, chaste, healthy, sane, and civilized individuals compared to various racialized Others.

Canada has also claimed that its policies on illicit drugs mark it as essentially different from its close contemporaries. Initially, this country contrasted itself against its European peers, whose roles in the global drug trade were presented as an indication of their immorality. With contemporary popular discourses representing the United States as increasingly extremist and fundamentalist with respect to its security policies and social outlook, medical marijuana and decriminalization are understood by many Canadians as reflecting the inherent superiority of Canada in terms of permitting individual choice over the body and limiting social control. But as has been shown in this analysis, the performative has not been matched by its performances. Social control is not absent in Canadian illicit drug policy; rather, at key moments it has been able to assume more sophisticated and hidden forms, thus demonstrating the productive dynamics of existing power/relations.

A Canadian War on Drugs?

The notion that Canada is fighting a 'war on drugs' is most often perceived as hyperbole. Given that Canada has publicly taken a harm reduction approach to illicit drug use, that discursively it has made use of a more measured rhetoric, that it has developed a less punitive system of legal penalties, and that it has not adopted the militarized aesthetic of the United States, it is perhaps an exaggeration to claim that a Canadian 'war on drugs' has been underway for at least two decades. To a large degree, this is so: Canada does not have an

American-style 'war on drugs.' But this does not mean that Canada is not engaged in its own 'war on drugs.'

In understanding the modern state and the juridical notion of sovereignty, Foucault (2003e) has argued that a belief in the embeddedness of war in society (i.e., battles, massacres, conquests made possible in the theoretical 'state of nature') played, and continues to play, a central role in the disciplinary and regulatory systems of governance and its associated discourses (2003e, 50).[2] From this foundation he argues that 'law is not pacification, for beneath the law, war continues to rage in all the mechanisms of power, even in the most regular. War is the motor behind institutions and order. In the smallest of its cogs, peace is waging a secret war ... peace itself is a coded war. We are therefore at war with one another; a battlefront runs through the whole of society, continuously and permanently, and it is this battlefront that puts us all on one side or the other. There is no such thing as a neutral subject. We are all inevitably someone's adversary' (ibid., 50–1).

The practices of the Canadian state in response to illicit drugs have contributed to the reproduction of an adversarial social system in which particular classifications of people who reside in Canada are denied the potential political benefits of being part of the Canadian body politic. These are the victims of practices such as racial profiling, police brutality, political marginalization, cultural rejection, and cultural assimilation – practices that are (para)sites in the Canadian 'war on drugs.' In this sense, these practices are constitutive of a battleground located in a much larger theatre in which Self and Other have contested the boundaries of 'Canadianess' and clashed over their potential extension.

The role of law in this struggle has been made possible by constellations of power/relations that have been constituted through discourse and dominant regimes of truth. As a disciplinary practice, legal sanctions against illicit drugs have been a means to expel those considered dangerous to the Canadian body politic – for example, Chinese-Canadian opium smokers in the 1920s – or to deny entrance to newcomers whose cultural practices (such as chewing khat) are perceived as beneath Canadian social mores. Within the confines of the Canadian body politic, the law also serves as a mechanism to restrict alternative forms of cultural expression (e.g., rave); and in unison with scientific discourse, it constructs the boundaries that 'separate' medicine from quackery.

Contemporary punishments under the law pale in comparison to their historical predecessors. That said, legal prohibitions not only expose people to extensive intrusion on their private lives and lifestyles in the name of public security, leaving them vulnerable to the coercive power of the state security apparatus, but also potentially mark them with the current equivalent of the scarlet letter: a criminal record. As discussed above, law enforcement continues to proactively pursue possession arrests, while Canadian prosecutors are beginning to apply new legislation enacted to fight organized crime and terrorism, whether these involve outlaw bikers or compassion clubs. A criminal record in Canada continues to cripple one's opportunities for employment, besides compromising access to key services. Moreover, in today's world, states have increasing access to cyberinformation (e.g., national security databases and information systems), and a large part of the Canadian population is being entered into the machinery of a global panopticon, which has been emboldened by a series of wars against drugs, terror, and illegal migration. Once classified as a problem within this security architecture, there is no clear way to be removed from this information network and to de-escalate the authoritative perceptions of threat that construct oneself as a specific type of political actor: the dangerous individual. For example, U.S. criminal databases (which are fully integrated with Canada's) do not acknowledge Crown pardons granted in Canada for past criminal activities. The Canadian state may forgive an individual for transgressions within Canadian sovereign space and remove his or her criminal record from the Canadian database; the United States does not recognize the pardon, so the record remains on file permanently.

Beyond a War on Drugs?

Popular performatives of Canadian identity continue to assign Canadian illicit drug policy a prominent place in defining Canada as a socially progressive state. These articulations have only been reinforced by reactions from the United States, both positive and negative, which have catalysed a particular sense of the Canadian Self as a distinct and sovereign entity that can look down disdainfully at its southern neighbour. But when we peer beneath this veneer at the power/relations that are constitutive of these performatives, an equally plausible interpretation of the contemporary politics of identity in Canada is that we are experiencing a case of the emperor's new clothes. Medical marijuana and the decriminalization of pot have not lived up to their promise as progressive social policies. Yet for the Canadian public, the mere appearance of these policies within discourses has been enough to sustain the notion that there has been a substantial transformation in mechanisms of control in Canadian society. Moreover, the case of rave shows that overly aggressive reactions in Canada are even downplayed by the communities *that are their targets* as less intrusive on liberty than American policies.

Notions of multiculturalism, pluralism, diversity, and tolerance of difference have long been embedded in Canadian performatives of the Self. Again, though, these performatives are not politically neutral; they mask a history of Canada that has demonstrated, and continues to demonstrate, a marked intolerance for cultural practices and social communities that are considered to be 'too different.' Various practices and people have been coded as 'uncivilized' and/or 'dangerous.' And these classifications have made these cultures and communities subject over the past hundred years to an assortment of technologies of violence, from race riots to racial profiling.

Because these problems are so ingrained in the relationships between Self and Other, and between the Canadian body politic and the state, and even in competing modes of contemporary thinking that transcend the issue of illicit drugs, there are no easy answers to the issues raised by this book. There is no silver bullet that will initiate critical transformations towards more progressive social policy and the lessening of state-imposed managerial control over the body politic and individual bodies. Thus, critics must resist the temptation to assign all responsibility for the current configurations of power to specific individuals such as William Lyon Mackenzie King, Emily Murphy, C.H.L. Sharman, or Julian Fantino. It can be argued that certain moral entrepreneurs in their respective social contexts conducted themselves irresponsibly and even unethically, but they were all acting within a far more extensive grid of intelligibility that not only made possible particular understandings, problematiques, and policies, but also *legitimated* them. Thus, criticisms *must* extend beyond individuals to dominant meanings, representations, discourses, bodies of knowledge, and modes of thinking, as well as to their constitutive power/relations.

This approach to criticism provides a list of targets that is more extensive but also more elusive and resilient. Critical modes of thinking are imbricated within the dominant understandings of those things which they wish to contest and critique. Even as critics, our notions of possibility are shaped by context. With regard to illicit drugs, this has paralysed alternative conceptualizations of the legitimate boundaries of freedom of the individual body beyond those offered by the medical and law enforcement communities. This is the paradox that ensnared Canadian rave culture when it tried to free itself from state control. This is also the disciplinary mechanism that has recently bound discussions of Canadian social policy to inevitable benchmark comparisons with the United States, thereby allowing anything not perceived to be as extreme as American policy to be defined as progressive within Canada. When we let the United States serve as our benchmark, we are setting the bar far too low. This has greatly stunted the space for a radical rethinking of the Canadian body politic to emphasize social inclusion, intersubjective understanding, and responsibility and accountability to our Others.

However, rather than lamenting and cursing the impossibilities of the current social and political context and the impracticality of criticism, we must recognize the limits of contemporary modes of thinking as a crucial first step towards significant transformation:

> Criticism (and radical criticism) is utterly indispensable for any transformation. For a transformation that would remain within the same mode of thought, a transformation that would only be a certain way of better adjusting the same thought to the reality of things, would only be a superficial transformation. On the other hand, as soon as people begin to have trouble thinking things the way they have been thought, transformation becomes at the same time very urgent, very difficult, and entirely possible. So there is not a time for criticism and a time for transformation; there are not those who do criticism and those who have to transform, those who are confined within an inaccessible radicality and those who are obliged to make the necessary concessions to reality. As a matter of fact, I believe that the work of deep transformation can be done in the open and always turbulent atmosphere of a continuous criticism. (Foucault 2003d, 172)

It is my sincere hope that I have made Canadian security and identity as interpreted through the issue of illicit drugs in Canada extraordinarily difficult for the reader to think about in relation to any prior certainties. It is the undermining of certitude about what is at stake in discussions of illicit drugs that can potentially unlock the ethical dimension central to successfully chasing the dragon and positively encountering the Other within these security issues, and in those that extend beyond this social domain. There are no definite answers here, only an expanse of choices that represent vastly different assessments of ethical responsibility and accountability in our social worlds of mutual vulnerability.

Appendix: The Progression of Canadian Drug Law – Key Events*

1850s   Chinese immigrants brought to Western Canada to fill labour shortages.

1870   First opium den opened in Vancouver.

1876–1908   Thousands of pounds of opium imported into Canada.

1879   In Vancouver, Chinese merchants must pay the city a $500 fee to deal in opium.

1880   Chinese constitute 20% of the population in British Columbia.

1883   Three opium production factories are operational in Victoria. *American Pharmaceutical Association* releases a report stating that drug use is rampant throughout American society though particularly concentrated in Chinese immigrant and African-American communities.

1884   B.C. government imposes an annual $10 tax on all Asians in the province and prohibits them from buying provincial Crown land.

---

*The following information has been collected from Boyd (1984, 1988), Chapman (1979), Erickson and Oscapella (1999), Giffen, Endicott, and Lambert (1991), Green (1979), Mosher (1999), Murray (1987), Solomon and Green (1988), Trasov (1962), and Senate Special Committee on Illegal Drugs (2002b, c, d, e).

1885   The Federal Royal Commission on Chinese Immigration proposes a $50 head tax on Chinese entering the country (enacted the same year).

1891   More than ten opium dens estimated to be operating in the Canadian West.

1901   Head Tax raised to $100.

1904   Head Tax raised to $500.

1907   Anti-Asian riot in Vancouver.

1908   British and Chinese reach the 10 per cent solution, which is supposed to eliminate the international opium trade.
In July, Canada passes the Anti-Opium Act, which:
  1 prohibits the importation of opium without proper authorization;
  2 limits the use of opium to medicinal purposes; and
  3 sets a maximum prison term of three years and/or a $1,000 fine.
Proprietary or Patent Medicine Act is passed.

1909   Canada is invited to the first meeting of the International Opium Commission in Shanghai.

1911   Canada passes the Opium and Narcotic Drug Act:
  1 Cocaine, opium, morphine, and eucaine are scheduled to restrictions in use.
  2 Any alkaloid, by-product, or drug preparation can be added to the schedule if it is deemed to be in the public interest. No evidence or debate is required (this provision still exists today).
  3 Police are given new search powers and the power to confiscate prohibited drugs.
  4 A reverse onus is placed on cases of simple possession (i.e., the burden of proof falls on the accused) and mens rea is not required for conviction of possession.
  5 Maximum sentence of one year and/or maximum fine of $500.

1912   International Opium Convention signed by Canada. This convention is imposed on non-signatories by the Treaty of Versailles (1919).

1918   U.S. Senate files an official complaint with the Canadian government about drug trafficking (shortages occur in the U.S. from the implementation of the Harrison Narcotic Act).

1919   Amendments are made to the 1911 Act.
The Department of Health is established.

1920   Amendments are made to the 1911 Act:
1 The minimum fine is now $200, the maximum $1,000.
2 The Opium and Narcotics Branch of the Department of Health, in concert with the recently constituted (for this purpose) Royal Canadian Mounted Police, begins antidrug work.

1921   Amendments to the 1911 Act bring tougher sentencing possibilities (up to seven years if indicted, eighteen months for a summary conviction).
Chinese constitute less than 6 per cent of the population of British Columbia.

1922   Amendments to the 1911 Act increase police search and seizure powers and add whipping as a penalty, as well as deportation for aliens charged with drug offences.
From 1922 to 1944 (when the last immigrants were deported for drug offences), 1,082 Chinese (82 per cent of the total) are deported; 163 Americans are deported (13 per cent); and 68 'others' (5 per cent) are deported.
From 1922 to 1930, 7,096 persons are convicted under the Opium and Narcotic Drug Act, 69 per cent of whom are Chinese Canadians.

1923   Marijuana is added to the 1911 schedule of prohibited drugs; no reason is given.
The Chinese Exclusion Act is passed.
Searches and orders of forfeiture are extended to vehicles in which drugs might be found.

The right to appeal summary convictions for drug offences is eliminated.

People found guilty of summary convictions are given a criminal record.

All narcotic prescriptions now require physician approval for renewal.

1924   Alberta amends its Insanity Act to include drug addiction.

1925   Tougher requirements for physicians dispensing narcotics are added to 1911 Act.

Judges are allowed to add forced labour to summary sentences for simple possession.

1928   Passing of the Act Respecting Sexual Sterilization in Alberta gives legal sanction for the sterilization of drug users.

1929   Legal loopholes remaining in 1911 Act are closed through definitional and procedural changes.

Police officers are issued lifetime writs of assistance, which allow them to enter private dwellings suspected of containing drugs without requiring a warrant.

1931   Canada plays a significant role in the drafting of the Geneva Convention for Limiting the Manufacture and Regulating the Distribution of Narcotic Drugs, to which it becomes a party.

1932   Medicines are permitted to contain small amounts of certain prohibited drugs, including cannabis.

Ten more psychoactive substances are added to the prohibited schedule, including coca leaf and synthetic drugs.

1938   Cannabis and opium poppy cultivation are prohibited unless authorized by the Department of Health.

1954   Possession for the purposes of drug trafficking is defined so that the burden of proof falls on the accused (guilty until proven innocent).

Maximum prison sentence is increased from seven years to fourteen years; whipping and deportation remain as punishments.

1955   Special Committee of the Senate on the Traffic in Narcotic Drugs is created; it estimates that there are 3,212 drug addicts in Canada, of whom only twenty-six are under the age of twenty.
The committee concludes that drug addiction is a symptom of individual character weaknesses that lead to criminality. It rejects government-sponsored treatment facilities on this basis; instead, it advocates that addicts be segregated from the general population in prisons. It also recommends tougher sentencing provisions.

1961   Narcotic Control Act replaces the Opium and Narcotic Drug Act:
   1 Importing and exporting prohibited drugs is now subject to a minimum sentence of seven years and maximum twenty-five-year prison sentence.
   2 The trafficking penalty is raised from fourteen to twenty-five years.
   3 Whipping as a punishment is repealed.
   4 Repeat drug offenders can now be placed in preventative detention indefinitely if charged with a drug offence. For first-time offenders, preventative detention cannot last longer than ten years.
   (These measures are passed by Parliament but never proclaimed.)
   5 Ninety-two drugs and derivatives comprising fourteen major classes are placed on the prohibitive schedule.
The Food and Drug Act is passed to regulate the distribution and use of barbiturates and amphetamines.
The Single Convention on Narcotic Drugs creates the modern international drug control system.

1969   An amendment to the Food and Drug Act adds LSD, DET, and STP as restricted substances:
   1 Possession is prohibited.

2 The maximum prison term for possession is three years and/or a fine of $5,000.

3 Penalties for simple possession are reduced from seven years to a maximum of one year for summary convictions.

The Le Dain Commission of Inquiry into the Non-Medical Use of Drugs is formed (1969–73) with the mandate to:

1 find information on the non-medical use of drugs in Canada;

2 report on the state of medical knowledge of the effects of drugs;

3 report on the motives for the non-medical use of drugs; *and*

4 find ways the federal government can act to reduce the problems associated with the non-medical use of drugs.

At the height of its mandate, the Le Dain Commission employs one hundred people.

1973   The Le Dain Commission releases its report on cannabis, which recommends:

1 retaining existing penalties for trafficking and importing/exporting cannabis;

2 repeal of prohibitions against the simple possession of cannabis and its cultivation for personal use;

3 where possible, that fines be imposed in lieu of imprisonment;

4 that trafficking not include giving small amounts of cannabis without exchange of value; *and*

5 that the burden of proof on persons charged with possession for the purposes of trafficking be reduced.

1974   Bill S-19, an amendment to the Food and Drug Act, which would reduce most penalties for cannabis possession, is proposed but not passed in the House of Commons.

1973–88   Despite promises by both Liberal and Progressive Conservative governments, cannabis laws remain unchanged.

1987   Canada ratifies the Convention on Psychotropic Substances (1971).

A decision by the Supreme Court of Canada in *R. v. Smith* declares a minimum seven-year sentence for importing or exporting to be unconstitutional (cruel and unusual punishment). This leads to the repeal of the mandatory minimum.

Canada launches a National Drug Strategy to educate the public about substance abuse, enhance the availability of treatment and rehabilitation, energize enforcement and control, coordinate national efforts, and cooperate with international organizations to promote a balanced approach to the drug problem.

1988   Canada becomes a party to the United Nations Convention on Illicit Traffic in Narcotic Drugs and Psychotropic Substances (passed by Parliament in 1990).

Bill C-61, designed to combat laundering of the proceeds of crime, is passed by Parliament.

1991   Canada joins the Inter-American Drug Abuse Control Commission (CICAD).

1992   The National Strategy to Reduce Impaired Driving and the National Drug Strategy are merged, launching a second phase, called 'Canada's Drug Strategy.'

1993   Bill C-85, an attempt to unify the Food and Drug Act with the Narcotic Control Act, dies when the 34th Parliament is dissolved before it can be tabled.

1995   Bill C-8 (a retabling of Bill C-85) is passed (in effect June 1996):

   1 In combining substances covered by the previous two acts, five schedules of drugs are created, including narcotics (opium, cocaine), cannabis, stimulants, prescription medications, and other substances as well as a schedule of precursor substances, subject to regulation.

   2 Over 150 substances are covered by the act, including khat.

   3 Maximum sentences for possession range from three years (for stimulants) to seven years (for narcotics).

4 Maximum sentences for trafficking and export/import range from six months for prescription medications to life imprisonment for narcotics and cannabis (over 3 kg).

5 Maximum sentences for production range from three years for prescription medications to life imprisonment for narcotics.

6 Any property declared by the court to be offence related is subject to forefeiture.

7 Inspectors are granted the power to enter any place that holds an authorization or licence to deal in controlled substances or precursors at any reasonable time.

The bill is known as the Controlled Drug and Substance Act (CDSA).

1998   Canada's Drug Strategy unveils its revamped seven-component framework:

1 Research and knowledge development.

2 Knowledge dissemination.

3 Prevention programming.

4 Treatment and rehabilitation.

5 Legislation, enforcement, and control.

6 National coordination.

7 International cooperation.

James Wakeford launches a legal challenge to the prohibition on marijuana possession based on provisions contained with Section 56 of the *CDSA* for medical exemptions. His challenge is successful and is considered the legal precedent for medical marijuana in Canada.

2000   In July 2000, the Ontario Court of Appeal rules in *R. v. Parker* that the *CDSA* sections on marijuana potentially force those suffering from illness to have to choose between effective treatment and arrest. Thus, the court gives Ottawa a year to change its laws to allow for the medical use of cannabis. Furthermore, the court threatens to strike down all marijuana possession laws if the federal government fails to comply.

2001   An Auditor General's Report finds Canada's Drug Strategy to be ineffective. Weaknesses identified in the report include a lack of information on drugs and drug use, a lack of clear objectives, and a lack of information on results. Furthermore, despite the advocation of a harm reduction approach, it finds that nearly 90 per cent of the $500 million annual budget is being dedicated to supply reduction (i.e., law enforcement).

In response to *R. v. Parker*, Marihuana Medical Access Regulations (MMAR) are instituted by the federal government. The program will immediately fall under scrutiny for its demanding criteria, barriers to access, and barriers to supply.

2002   Nine patients in the MMAR program sue for access to government supplies of marijuana.

The government begrudgingly agrees to supply patients with its crop once it can guarantee the quality.

The Senate Special Committee on Illegal Drugs issues its final report, which recommends that marijuana possession be legalized.

In its final report, the Parliamentary Special Committee on the Non-Medical Use of Drugs recommends that marijuana possession be decriminalized.

2003   Decisions reached in two court cases, *R. v. Hitzig* and *R. v. JP*, cause sections of the CDSA relating to marijuana possession to be unenforceable from May to October as the federal government makes changes to the MMAR. Thus, for several months there are no possession prohibitions in Canada for small amounts of marijuana.

Quickly, the federal government introduces legislation to decriminalize the possession of marijuana (under 15 grams). The Parliamentary session ends before the bill can be passed.

In August, the federal government releases its first crop of medical marijuana. Users complain that it is unsafe and of poor quality.

In October the Ontario Court of Appeal recommends

changes to the MMAR that would make it constitutional. In addressing concerns over access to medical marijuana, the ruling brings the existing criminal prohibition into force again.

In December, the Supreme Court finds 6–3 in favour of the constitutionality of laws against simple marijuana posses- sion. The Court also rules 9–0 in favour of the constitu- tionality of laws against possession of marijuana for the purposes of trafficking.

2004   Data released by Statistics Canada show that arrests for marijuana possession continue to increase.

2007   Decriminalization legislation still has not been passed by the House of Commons.

Health Minister Tony Clement announces the launch of a tough new antidrug strategy.

A UN report reveals that marijuana use in Canada is four times the global rate.

Marijuana arrests in Canadian cities increase by 20 to 50% over the previous year.

Notes

Chapter 1

1 For a visual representation of the insert, go to absolutad.com/absolut _lists/ads/pictures/?id=2299&_s=ads.

2 According to Canada's Drug Strategy, the estimated total monetary cost of alcohol consumption in 1992 (the last year for which these data are available) was $7.52 billion. Illicit drugs were estimated at $1.37 billion (Health Canada 1998, 28).

3 I am thankful to the reviewer who made this point to me.

4 There is a great deal of literature that puts forward these themes of Canadian identity. For examples, see Lipsett (1990); Berton (1982); Granatstein (1998); Hillmer and Granatstein (1994). For further explorations of Canadian identity, see Angus (1997); Smith (1994); Keohane (1997); Mathews (1988); Manning (2000); Strong-Boag et al. (1998); Reitz and Breton (1994); Littleton (1996); Watson (1998); Clift (1989); Thomas (2000); and Satzewich (1992).

5 For further analysis of the problems with the traditional discursive/extra-discursive dichotomy, see David Campbell's discussion of Laclau and Mouffe (1998, 6–7).

6 Foucault has argued that 'whenever, between objects, types of statement, concepts, or thematic choices, one can define a regularity (an order, correlations, positions and functionings, transformations), we will say, for the sake of convenience, that we are dealing with a discursive formation' (1972, 38).

7 Power/relations is being used rather than the conventional power relations, to highlight that power necessitates relations and that relations are necessarily imbued with power.

8   Foucault's analysis here omits a potentially fascinating avenue of inquiry into *parrhesia*'s role in the reproduction of social asymmetries of power that entrenched the hegemony of male citizens and the subordination of women, slaves, and aliens.

9   More traditional acts of *parrhesia* do occasionally occur. For example, the 'whistleblower,' a person who exposes the deceptions and cover-ups of governments and corporations, seems in many respects similar to the *parrhesiastes* of old.

10   Appendix I contains a more detailed time line of Canadian drug law.

11   It could be argued that Karl Deutch's pioneering work on security communities and the international society work of E.H. Carr and Hedley Bull are the exceptions to the rule here.

12   For examples, see Ruggie (1993); Peter Katzenstein (1996); Adler and Barnett (1998); Finnemore and Sikkink (1998, 2001); and Haas and Haas (1995, 2002).

13   I am in debt to Elizabeth Dauphinée for bringing this point, in this form, to my attention.

14   For Derrida, play can be said to be operational in the absence of a nodal point that 'arrests and grounds' the signs (e.g., concepts), which can potentially assume the role of 'nodal points' to orient meaning (Derrida 1978, 289).

15   See Martel (2006); Alexander (1990); Murray (1987); Green (1979); Chapman (1979); Mosher (1999); Trasov (1962); Solomon and Green (1988); and Boyd (1984).

16   See Boyd (1984); Giffen, Endicott, and Lambert (1991); Tooley (1999); Whitaker (1969); Alexander (1990); and Martel (2006).

17   See Campbell (1998); Oren (2000); Bonura (1998); and Sparke (1998).

Chapter 2

1   See Booth (1991); Krause and Williams (1996, 1997); Tickner (1995); Sylvester (1994); and Christie (2003) for examples of this kind of work.

2   See Griffith (1993/4); Krasna (1999); Liotta (2002a, 2002b); Smith-Windsor (2002); and Homer-Dixon (1994).

3   The work done by Buzan, Waever, and de Wilde (1998) has been labelled the Copenhagen School of International Relations, in honour of the institutional home of the authors at the time of writing.

4   Objectification refers to instances in which the dominant interpretation of an event is naturalized within a particular social context so that it is no longer seen as an interpretation but rather as an objective truth.

5 For example, Butler's own work (1990, 1999) looks at how the category of sex is constantly disciplined to maintain an inelastic binary of the male body and the female body.

6 For the sake of consistency at this time, I am using the term Self here. Butler's primary concern is the 'body' and how the conceptual dichotomy established between gender (construction) and sex (material) leaves the 'matter' of sex untheorized. She argues that treating sex as a given 'presupposes and consolidates the normative conditions of its own emergence' (1999, 239). In later chapters I will explore the politics of the human body as a site for security practices and foreign policy in the Canadian context.

7 See transcripts from the Television Broadcast to the American People, 11 September 2001, and President Bush's Address to the Republican Party of Florida Majority Dinner, 21 June 2002, for examples of how these have been deployed.

Chapter 3

1 The Netherlands, another privileged member of the global system and favourite target of American disapproval for its internal illicit drug policies, was also mentioned in the Determination with regard to the production of MDMA (ecstasy).

2 According to Presidential Determination 2003–14, 'one of the major reasons that major drug transit or drug producing countries are placed on the list is the combination of geographical, commercial, and economic factors that allow drugs to transit or be produced despite the concerned government's most assiduous enforcement efforts' (White House 2003).

3 The term geonarcotics was coined by Ivelaw L. Griffith (1993/4) who argued that the post–Cold War world would be increasingly defined by 'relations of conflict and cooperation among national and international actors that are driven by the narcotics phenomenon' (1993/94, 33).

4 See also the discussion of David Campbell (1998) in chapter 2.

5 The masculine possessive is being used deliberately to reflect the gendered construction of objective social science.

6 For more detailed discussions of the 'war on drugs' and its foreign policy/Foreign Policy practices, see Campbell (1998, 169–89); Grayson (2003); Dalby (1997, 13–15); Walker (1993/4); Bollinger (1994); Chepesiuk (1999); Fischer (1998); Flynn (1994); Friman (1996); Johns (1992); Szasz (1974); and Walker (1996).

7 By intelligence foundation, I am referring to both actual information that

was used and the institutional sites from which data were collected, such as the Federal Bureau of Investigation, the Central Intelligence Agency, the Drug Enforcement Administration, and the Department of State.

8 For discussion of the certification process, see http://www.state.gov/www/global/narcotics_law/1998_narc_report/policy98.html and Bewley-Taylor (1998).

9 Walker (1997) has made the argument that 'the claims about political realism that still echo in discussions about security serve as a crucial reminder that accounts of imminent historical transformation are invariably overdone and that claims about alternatives [e.g., geonarcotics] are very likely to express a continuing, even if veiled, commitment to those practices that are supposedly obsolete' (1997, 71).

10 The following arguments on panopticism and discipline borrow heavily from Grayson (2003a).

11 This is explored in more detail in chapter 4.

12 Colonel Sharman was involved in international drug negotiations from 1927 to 1958.

13 Chapter 5 will show how far away Canada was from adopting a medical approach that would have significantly differed from the dictates of the global control regime.

14 In the early 1990s, Klepak (1993/4) observed that unnoticed by many in Canada, NORAD's resources were increasingly being diverted to combating the drug trade. More important, he argued that 'while this change of task fitted well with the United States' perspective on the trade as a security issue, it was not in fact compatible with Canadian views' (1993/4, 82–3). Yet relatively little discussion of this issue took place within Canadian security discourses at the time.

15 For more discussion of law enforcement dissatisfaction in Canada, see MacCharles (2003a, 2003c); Canadian Professional Police Association and Canadian Association of Chiefs of Police (2003); Lawton (2003); Avery (2003); Canada NewsWire (2002a, 2003a); Babbage (2002); Millar (2001); and Gillespie (2004).

16 Consider Drache (2004) for an in-depth discussion of North American Homeland Security and Canada's roles within it.

17 For discussions of American perspectives on other aspects of the Canada–U.S. security relationship, including the war on terrorism, homeland security, national missile defence, and Gulf War II, see Harper (2002a, 2003); Fraser (2003); Walkom (2003); Morris (2003); Toughill (2003); Thompson (2003); Cordon (2003a, 2003b); Thorne (2003); Canadian Press

(2003b); Whittington (2003a); Canadian Press (2003d, 2003e, 2003f); Dabrowski (2003); Carmichael (2003); Stefaniuk (2003); Axworthy (2003); Babbage (2003); Crane (2003); Bonnell (2003); Canadian Press (2003l); Ferguson (2003); Elliot (2002); MacCharles (2002); Thompson (2002a, 2002b, 2003a, 2003b); Canadian Press (2002a, 2002b, 2002c); Cheadle (2002); Panetta (2002); Griffiths (2002); and Cotroneo (2002).

18 Stairs and colleagues (2003) clearly delineate between interests, which they argue are central to Foreign Policy, and values, which are tangential.

19 See Grayson (2004) for a critical discussion.

Chapter 4

1 Actual statistics on the number of persons arrested on khat-related charges, the number of persons found guilty of khat-related charges, and the number of persons incarcerated on khat-related charges are not available. The lack of detailed statistics about drug offences in Canada was one of the primary complaints in the Auditor General's Report (2001) on Canada's drug strategy.

2 See Frankenberg (1993, 1997); McLaren (1994); and Goldberg (1994).

3 For a more detailed discussion of the practices of representation, see Doty (1996, 10–11).

4 See Section 38, clause C, of the Immigration Act of 1910. Along with the imposition of a series of progressively larger 'Head Taxes,' this clause helped dramatically reduce the number of immigrants to Canada from China and Japan (Mackey 2002, 33).

5 Examples can be found in the William Lyon Mackenzie King microfiche archive at the National Library in Ottawa.

6 See also Boyd (1984); Solomon and Green (1988).

7 Originally the Opium and Drug Act was passed at the urging of police, who claimed that they could not enforce the prohibition of the opium trade if possession were not also illegal.

8 For a similar argument with respect to Sikhs and turbans, see Arnold (2003).

9 This observation opens the possibility for an interesting genealogical account of the relationship between Christianity and science in terms of the their respective amenability to work together in the imposition of social controls.

10 Apparatuses can be defined as groupings of heterogenous elements into common networks to define and regulate targets constituted by a mixed economy of power and knowledge (Rabinow and Rose 2003, xvi).

11 Cathinone was added in 1993. Today, persons caught with khat leaves in the United States are charged with possessing a material or preparation containing a Schedule I substance, the most controlled (and punishable) schedule, which includes LSD, MDMA, marijuana, and heroin. Interestingly, the status of the khat plant itself remains legally ambiguous in the United States.

12 See Associated Press (1993); and 'Khat Smuggler from Etobicoke' (1995, A36).

Chapter 5

1 For more details on the reticence of the federal government, see 'Double-Talk on Weed' (2002); Canadian Press (2002e); 'Pot Policy Unsteady' (2002); 'Listless Confusion' (2003); 'Why Is Ottawa So Afraid of Pot?' (2003); Abbate (2002); Abraham (2002b); Canadian Medical Association (2001a, 2001b, 2001c); Beeby (2003a, 2003b, 2003c); Bueckert (2002a, 2002b; 2003a, 2003b, 2003c, 2003d); Health Canada (2003a, 2003b); Damuzi (2002b); Faulkner (2002a, 2002b); Fayerman and Kennedy (2003); Gifford-Jones (2002); Gordon (2003); Habib (2003); Hawthorn (2002); Howard (2002); Jackson (2002); Jacobs (2002a, 2002b); Laghi (2002a, 2002b, 2002c, 2003a, 2003b, 2003e); Landry (2003); McLellan (2002); Medusers (2002, 2003); Necheff (2002); Nuttall-Smith (2003); Pearson (2002); Picard and Abraham (2002); Robinson (2003); Rubec and Trace (2002); CBC News Online (2002); Tyler (2002a, 2002b); and Zollman (2003).

2 See Giffen, Endicott, and Lambert (1991) for a full discussion of this case and its context.

3 A burgeoning interest in public health was catalysed by the alarming number of men rejected for military service during the First World War due to previously undiagnosed medical conditions (Cassel 1994, 283).

4 A detailed examination of the bureaucratic structure of the early drug law enforcement network and histories of all of its parts are beyond the scope of this chapter. For an exhaustive discussion, see Giffen, Endicott, and Lambert (1991).

5 According to Giffen and colleagues (ibid.), these letters appear in the file archive for these reports.

6 Marijuana was added after the Minister of Health's simple assertion 'there is a new drug in the schedule,' with no further explanation of the matter (Boyd 1984, 129).

7 As illustrated earlier, typologies of drug users did exist that distinguished between criminal users and professional (or medical) users. The

important thing to note is that professional users were usually considered to be an extremely small segment of the subpopulation. One notable exception to this interpretation was provided by the Ontario Minister of Health, who on the advice of the Alcoholism and Drug Addiction Research Foundation of Ontario opposed the 1961 federal legislation that would require compulsory confinement for drug users on the basis that 'the greater problem really exists among decent law abiding people, [and] this emphasis [on confinement] ... will drive much of the ... problem underground and make it more difficult to handle' (Giffen, Endicott, and Lambert 1991, 393).

8 At the time, limited sentencing options led to half of all cannabis possession offenders being imprisoned; see Erickson (1992, 245).

9 Perhaps sardonically, the article was titled 'Discipline and Caring Are the Keys to the Mounties' Greatness.'

10 Convictions for other illicit drugs during this time period rarely numbered more than a thousand per year (ibid., 246).

Chapter 6

1 Erickson (1992) has presented evidence that shows the number of illicit drug users was actually falling during this period.

2 According to the Senate Special Committee on Marijuana, only $101.5 million was actually allocated because of federal government budget cuts (Senate 2002c, 238).

3 For a discussion of *Wakeford*, see the beginning of chapter 5.

4 For more details, see CMA (2001a, 2001b, 2001c).

5 In this same editorial, the CMA expressed its support for a medical marijuana licensing regime. By July 2001 the CMA had publicly voiced its strong opposition to medical marijuana access (CMA 2001b).

6 This legislation was not introduced into Parliament before the end of session and has not been introduced in subsequent sessions.

7 For more details, see 'Decriminalization Useless to Medical Users – No Legal Supply' (2002); Canadian Press (2002e); 'Suit Aims to Force Ottawa to Supply Medical Pot' (2002); 'Giving a Graceless Okay to Medical Marijuana' (2003); 'Ottawa to Sell Marijuana to Patients' (2003); Arnold and Vinnick (2002); Beeby (2007); Bergman (2003); Brautigam (2003); Health Canada (2003c); Cohen (2003); Gordon (2003); Jacobs (2002b); McCarten (2002); McLellan (2002); Samyn (2002); British Columbia Compassion Club Society (2002); and Vallis (2003).

8 See the following for more information: Beeby (2003a); Cheney (2002);

Kennedy (2002); Laghi (2003b); Loome (2003); Lunman and Laghi (2003); and O'Neil (2002a, 2002b).

Chapter 7

1 It should be noted that at his family's request, Allen Ho was not publicly identified in the media at the time of his passing. His name was published only with the commencement of the inquest into his death in the spring of 2000.
2 At the municipal level, the City of Toronto had added ninety-seven drug enforcement officers by May 1989 at a cost of $6 million (Morris 1989a, C7). At the provincial level the Ontario Anti-Drug Secretariat was created with an annual budget of $39 million (Solomon 1995).
3 Throughout this chapter, rave will be used as a noun, verb, and adjective (often interchangeably) in an attempt to capture all of its dimensions.
4 The American military establishment as an institution has been virulently antirave. For example, it was instrumental in having leading venues in the United States (such as Nation in Washington, D.C.) shut down after reports began to surface that military personnel were attending raves and consuming ecstasy.
5 Jungle is a musical fusion of high-speed break beats, hip-hop, dancehall reggae, massive bass lines, and dub.
6 For a discussion of the shootings, see Canadian Press (2002a, 2002b).
7 Alig and his 'club kid' following gained fame after pulling numerous publicity stunts in the New York City area and being featured on tabloid television shows like *Geraldo*. For more details on club kids, rave in New York, Michael Alig, and the murder, see St James (1999); Owen (2003); and the feature film *Party Monster* (2003), written and directed by Fenton Bailey and Randy Barbato.
8 I am not claiming that previous treatments of rave had not appeared in popular Canadian media. For example, in 1995 the Canadian run of *Life Magazine* published an article titled 'A Full Moon Rave: It's Three AM and There's a Party Going On: Do You Know Where Your Teenagers Are?' (1995). Canadian medical journals had also been aware of rave as far back as 1995 (see *Journal of the Addiction Research Foundation* 1995).
9 *Tribe Magazine* was published on a monthly basis for over ten years in Toronto, providing comprehensive coverage of the Canadian rave and dance music scene. *Tribe* continues to operate as a community message board that can be accessed at tribe.ca. Forums range from music genres, to politics, to event listings and reviews.

10 All attendees were asked to donate a non-perishable food item for
    Toronto's Daily Bread Foodbank. A one-day record for donations was set
    over the course of iDance.

11 See chapter 2 for more details on covert securitization.

12 In 'Chemical Drug Trends,' a presentation package distributed at the
    Canadian Association of Chemical Distributers' 17th Annual Meeting in
    2003, the RCMP attempted to causally link poly-drug use with homosex-
    uality and HIV transmission.

13 Preventing the distribution of precursor chemicals used in the production
    of these substances has also been framed in terms of proliferation. See the
    RCMP/DEA joint report 'Chemical Drug Diversion and Synthetic Drug
    Manufacture' (2001).

14 For discussions on the marketing potential of rave, see Allossery (2000);
    Potter (2000); and Cohen (2000).

15 *The Globe and Mail* reported in 1993 that Chemistry, a Toronto rave pro-
    motion company, was distributing flyers which stated that 'the scene has
    gone commercial, been bastardized, and generally gotten f–ked up.
    That's why we've reluctantly decided to pack it all in' (Parsons 1993, A1).
    Consider also Luciano (1999) and Rushkoff (1999).

16 The Rave Act was passed in the U.S. House of Representatives and
    Senate as a rider attached to the 'Amber Alert' legislation on child kid-
    napping. The Rave Act extends the scope of the 'crack house' statute to
    apply to concert and entertainment events so that organizers and venue
    owners can be found liable for the drug use of their patrons. The
    CLEAN-UP Act proposed to make it a crime (punishable by nine years in
    federal prison) for an event to be promoted if an organizer 'knows or rea-
    sonably ought to know' that illegal drugs will be sold or consumed'
    (EM:DEF 2004). This section was eventually eliminated from the Act
    when it passed in 2005. See Blashill (1999); Cloud (2001); Eliscu (2001);
    Eliscu (2003); and Werde (2001) for discussions of U.S. public policy and
    raves.

Chapter 8

1 These side-effects include increased heart rate, increased blood pressure,
   nausea, loss of appetite, insomnia, bizarre and/or aggressive behaviour,
   paranoia, stroke, heart failure, psychological dependence, malnutrition,
   amphetamine psychosis, kidney damage, and lung problems (CBC Winnipeg 2003).

2 War should be interpreted here as social conflict in all of its many facets,
   not solely (or even at all) as pitched battles between competing armies.

References

Academic

Adams, Michael. 1997. *Sex in the Snow: Canadian Social Values at the End of the Millennium*. Toronto: Penguin Canada.

Adler, Emanuel. 1997. 'Seizing the Middle Ground: Constructivism in World Politics.' *European Journal of International Relations* 3, no. 3: 319–63.

Adler, Emanuel, and Michael Barnett. 1996. 'Governing Anarchy: A Research Agenda for the Study of Security.' *Ethics and International Affairs* 10: 63–98.

– eds. 1998. *Security Communities*. Cambridge: Cambridge University Press.

Adler, Emanuel, and Peter M. Haas. 1992. 'Epistemic Communities, World Order, and the Creation of a Reflective Research Program.' *International Organization* 46, no. 1: 367–90.

Agamben, Giorgio. 1999. *Homo Sacer: Sovereign Power and Bare Life*. Trans. Daniel Heller-Roazen. Stanford: Stanford University Press.

Alexander, Bruce K. 1990. *Peaceful Measures: Canada's Way Out of the War on Drugs*. Toronto: University of Toronto Press.

Allen, Richard. 1975. 'The Social Gospel and the Reform Tradition in Canada 1890–1928.' In Samuel D. Clark, J. Paul Grayson, and Linda M. Grayson, eds., *Prophecy and Protest: Social Movements in Twentieth-Century Canada*, 45–61. Toronto: Gage.

Angus, Ian. 1997. *A Border Within: National Identity, Cultural Plurality, and Wilderness*. Montreal and Kingston: McGill-Queen's University Press.

Ashley, Richard K. 1986. 'The Poverty of Neorealism.' In Robert Keohane, ed., *Neorealism and Its Critics*, 255–300. New York: Columbia University Press.

Austin, J.L. 1962. *How to Do Things with Words*. Oxford: Oxford University Press.

Arnold, Samantha. 2003. '"Sikh-ing" Diversity in the Canadian Forces: A Research Agenda.' In Kyle Grayson and Christina Masters, eds., *Theory in Practice: Critical Reflections on Global Policy*, 153–62. Toronto: York Centre for International and Security Studies.

Bannerji, Himani, ed. 1993. *Returning the Gaze: Essays on Racism, Feminism, and Politics*. Toronto: Sister Vision.

Bartholomew, R.E. 2000. 'Dancing through Time.' *Canadian Medical Association Journal* 163, no. 9: 1132.

Beck, Ulrich. 1992. *Risk Society: Towards a New Modernity*. London: Sage.

Beier, J. Marshall. 2001. 'Postcards from the Outskirts of Security: Defence Professionals, Semiotics, and the NMD Initiative.' *Canadian Foreign Policy* 8, no. 2: 39–49.

Berger, Carl. 1970. *The Sense of Power: Studies in the Ideas of Canadian Imperialism, 1867–1914*. Toronto: University of Toronto Press.

Berton, Pierre. 1982. *Why We Act Like Canadians*. Toronto: McClelland and Stewart.

Bewley-Taylor, David R. 1998. 'Certification Meets NAFTA: More Schizophrenia in the Misguided War.' *International Journal of Drug Policy* 9: 417–26.

Blackwell, Judith C., and Patricia G. Erickson, eds. 1988. *Illicit Drugs in Canada: A Risky Business*. Scarborough: Nelson Canada.

Bollinger, Lorenz, ed. 1994. *De-Americanizing Drug Policy: The Search for Alternatives for Failed Repression*. Frankfurt: Peter Lang.

Bonura Jr, Carlo J. 1998. 'The Occulted Geopolitics of Nation and Culture: Situating Political Culture within the Construction of Geopolitical Ontologies.' In Gearoid Ó Tuathail and Simon Dalby, eds., *Critical Geopolitics*, 86–105. London: Routledge.

Booth, Ken. 1991. 'Security and Emancipation.' *Review of International Studies* 17, no. 4: 313–26.

– 1997. 'Security and Self: Reflections of a Fallen Realist.' In Keith Krause and Michael C. Williams, eds., *Critical Security Studies*, 83–120. Minneapolis: University of Minnesota Press.

Booth, Martin. 1996. *Opium: A History*. New York: Simon and Schuster.

Boyd, Neil. 1984. 'The Origins of Canadian Narcotics Legislation: The Process of Criminalization in the Historical Context.' *Dalhousie Law Journal* 8: 102–36.

– 1988. 'Canadian Punishment of Illegal Drug Use: Theory and Practice.' In Judith C. Blackwell and Patricia G. Erickson, eds., *Illicit Drugs in Canada: A Risky Business*, 301–13. Scarborough: Nelson Canada.

– 1991. *High Society: Legal and Illegal Drugs in Canada*. Toronto: Key Porter.

Burchell, Graham, Colin Gordon, and Peter Miller, eds. 1991. *The Foucault Effect: Studies in Governmentality.* Chicago: University of Chicago Press.

Butler, Judith. 1990. *Gender Trouble: Feminism and the Subversion of Identity.* New York: Routledge.

– 1999. 'Bodies That Matter.' In Janet Price and Margrit Shildrick, eds., *Feminist Theory and the Body*, 235–45. London: Routledge.

Buzan, Barry, Ole Waever, and Japp de Wilde. 1998. *Security: A New Framework for Analysis.* Boulder: Lynne Rienner.

Campbell, David. 1993. *Politics without Principle: Sovereignty, Ethics, and Narratives of the Gulf War.* Boulder: Lynne Rienner, 1993.

– 1998. *Writing Security: United States Foreign Policy and the Politics of Identity.* 2nd ed. Minneapolis: University of Minnesota Press.

– 1999. 'Contra Wight: The Errors of a Premature Writing.' *Review of International Studies* 25: 317–21.

Carstairs, Catherine. 2006. *Jailed for Possession: Illegal Drug Use, Regulation, and Power in Canada, 1920–1961.* Toronto: University of Toronto Press.

Cassel, Jay. 1994. 'Public Health in Canada.' In Dorothy Porter, ed., *The History of Public Health and the Modern State*, 132–64. Amsterdam: Rodopi.

Chapman, T.L. 1979. 'The Anti-Drug Crusade in Western Canada 1885–1925.' In David Bercuson and L.A. Knafla, eds., *Law and Society in Canada in Historical Perspective*, 100–21. Calgary: University of Calgary.

Chepesiuk, Ronald. 1999. *Hard Target: The United States War against International Drug Trafficking, 1982–1997.* Jefferson: McFarland.

Christie, Ryerson. 2003. 'Human Security and Identity: A Securitization Perspective.' In Kyle Grayson and Christina Masters, eds., *Theory in Practice: Critical Reflections on Global Policy*, 117–34. Toronto: York Centre for International and Security Studies.

Clift, Dominique. 1989. *The Secret Kingdom: Interpretations of the Canadian Character.* Toronto: McClelland and Stewart.

Connolly, William E. 1989. 'Identity and Difference in Global Politics.' In James Der Derian and Michael J. Shapiro, eds., *International/Intertextual Relations: Post Modern Readings of World Politics*, 323–42. Lexington: Lexington Books.

Cook, Ramsey. 1985. *The Regenerators: Social Criticism in Late Victorian Canada.* Toronto: University of Toronto Press.

Dalby, Simon. 1997. 'Contesting an Essential Concept: Reading Dilemmas in Contemporary Security Discourse.' In Keith Krause and Michael C. Williams, eds., *Critical Security Studies*, 3–32. Minneapolis: University of Minnesota Press.

– 1998. 'Geopolitics and Global Security: Culture, Identity, and the "Pogo

Syndrome.'" In Gearoid Ó Tuathail and Simon Dalby, eds., *Critical Geopolitics*, 295–313. London: Routledge.

Dauphinée, Elizabeth. 2003. 'International Interventions, Discourses of Representation, and the Production of Subordinated Sovereignties.' In Kyle Grayson and Cristina Masters, eds., *Theory in Practice: Critical Reflections on Global Policy*, 223–38. Toronto: Centre for International and Security Studies, York University.

Der Derian, James. 1995. 'The Value of Security: Hobbes, Marx, Nietzsche, and Baudrillard.' In Ronnie Lipschutz, ed., *On Security*, 24–45. New York: Columbia University Press.

Derrida, Jacques. 1978. 'Structure, Sign, and Play in the Discourses of the Human Sciences.' In Alan Bass, ed., *Writing and Difference*, 278–94. Chicago: University of Chicago Press.

– 1982. 'Differance.' In Alan Bass, ed., *Margins of Philosophy*, 1–27. Chicago: University of Chicago Press.

– 1995. 'The Rhetoric of Drugs.' In Elisabeth Weber, ed., *Points ...: Interviews, 1974–94*, 228–54. Stanford: Stanford University Press.

Dillon, Michael. 1995. 'Sovereignty and Governmentality: From Problematics of the "New World Order" to the Ethical Problematic of the World Order.' *Alternatives* 20, no. 3: 323–68.

Doty, Roxanne Lynn. 1996. *Imperial Encounters: The Politics of Representation in North–South Relations*. Minneapolis: University of Minnesota Press.

– 2000. 'Desire All the Way Down.' *Review of International Studies* 26, no. 1: 137–39.

Drache, Daniel. 2004. *Borders Matter: Homeland Security and the Search for North America*. Toronto: Fernwood.

'Drug Taking a Powerful Undertow to Rave Wave.' 1995. *Journal of the Addiction Research Foundation* 24, no. 2: 9.

Edkins, Jenny. 2002. 'Forget Trauma? Responses to September 11.' *International Relations* 16, no. 2: 243–56.

Erickson, Patricia G. 1992. 'Recent Trends in Canadian Drug Policy: The Decline and Resurgence of Prohibitionism.' *Daedalus* 121, no. 3: 239–68.

Erickson, Patricia G., and Eugene Oscapella. 1999. 'Cannabis in Canada – A Puzzling Policy.' *International Journal of Drug Policy* 10: 313–18.

Fairclough, Norman. 1992. 'Discourse and Text: Linguistic and Intertextual Analysis within Discourse Analysis.' *Discourse and Society* 3, no. 2: 193–217.

Ferguson, Kennan. 1996. 'Unmapping and Remapping the World: Foreign Policy as Aesthetic Practice.' In Michael J. Shapiro and Hayward R. Alker, eds., *Challenging Boundaries: Global Flows, Territorial Identities*, 165–92. Minneapolis: University of Minnesota Press.

Finnemore, Martha, and Kathryn Sikkink. 1998. 'International Norm Dynamics and Political Change.' *International Organization* 52, no. 4: 887–917.

– 2001. 'Taking Stock: The Constructivist Research Program in International Relations.' *Annual Review of Political Science* 4: 391–416.

Fischer, Benedikt. 1998. 'Prohibition as the Art of Political Diplomacy: The Benign Guises of the "War on Drugs" in Canada.' In Eric L. Jensen and Jurg Gerber, eds., *The New War on Drugs: Symbolic Politics and Criminal Justice Policy*, 157–75. Cincinnati: Anderson Publishing.

Flynn, Stephen. 1994. 'World Wide Drug Scourge: The Expanding Trade in Illicit Drugs.' In Steven L. Spiegel and David J. Pervin, eds., *At Issue: Politics in the World Arena*, 443–57. New York: St Martin's Press.

Forbes, E.R. 1975. 'Prohibition and the Social Gospel in Nova Scotia.' In Samuel D. Clark, J. Paul Grayson, and Linda M. Grayson, eds., *Prophecy and Protest: Social Movements in Twentieth-Century Canada*, 62–86. Toronto: Gage.

Foucault, Michel. 1972. *The Archaeology of Knowledge and the Discourse on Language*. New York: Pantheon.

– 1977a. *Discipline and Punish: The Birth of the Prison*. Ed. Alan Sheridan. New York: Pantheon.

– 1977b. 'Truth and Power.' In Colin Gordon, ed. *Power/Knowledge*, 109–33. New York: Random House.

– 1984a. 'The Body of the Condemned.' In Paul Rabinow, ed., *The Foucault Reader*, 170–8. New York: Pantheon.

– 1984b. 'Nietzsche, Genealogy, History.' In Paul Rabinow, ed., *The Foucault Reader*, 76–100. New York: Pantheon.

– 1984c. 'Panopticism.' In Paul Rabinow, ed., *The Foucault Reader*, 206–13. New York: Pantheon.

– 1990. *The History of Sexuality: An Introduction*. Vol. 1. New York: Random House.

– 2001. *Fearless Speech*. Ed. Joseph Pearson. Los Angeles: Semiotext(e).

– 2003a. 'The Birth of Biopolitics.' In Paul Rabinow and Nikolas Rose, eds., *The Essential Foucault: Selections from Essential Works of Foucault, 1954–1984*, 202–7. New York: New Press.

– 2003b. 'Governmentality.' In Paul Rabinow and Nikolas Rose, eds., *The Essential Foucault: Selections from Essential Works of Foucault, 1954–1984*, 229–45. New York: New Press.

– 2003c. 'Questions of Method.' In Paul Rabinow and Nikolas Rose, eds., *The Essential Foucault: Selections from Essential Works of Foucault, 1954–1984*, 246–58. New York: New Press.

– 2003d. 'So Is It Important to Think?' In Paul Rabinow and Nikolas Rose, eds., *The Essential Foucault: Selections from the Essential Works of Foucault, 1954–1984*, 170–3. New York: New Press.

– 2003e. *Society Must Be Defended: Lectures at the College De France, 1975–1976.* Trans. David Macey. New York: Picador.

Frankenberg, Ruth. 1993. *White Women, Race Matters: The Social Construction of Whiteness*. Minneapolis: University of Minnesota Press.

– ed. 1997. *Displacing Whiteness: Essays in Social and Cultural Criticism.* Durham: Duke University Press.

Friman, Richard. 1996. *Narcodiplomacy*. Ithaca: Cornell University Press.

Fukuyama, Francis. 1992. *The End of History and the Last Man*. New York: Avon.

Gasché, Rodolphe. 1986. *The Tain of the Mirror: Derrida and the Philosophy of Reflection*. Cambridge, MA: Harvard University Press.

George, Jim. 1994. *Discourses of Global Politics: A Critical (Re)Introduction to International Affairs*. Boulder: Lynne Rienner.

Giffen, P.J., Shirley Endicott, and Sylvia Lambert. 1991. *Panic and Indifference: The Politics of Canada's Drug Laws*. Ottawa: Canadian Centre on Substance Abuse.

Giffen, P.J., and Sylvia Lambert. 1988. 'What Happened on the Way to Law Reform?' In Judith C. Blackwell and Patricia G. Erickson, eds., *Illicit Drugs in Canada: A Risky Business*, 345–69. Scarborough: Nelson Canada.

Glassner, Barry. 1999. *The Culture of Fear: Why Americans Are Afraid of the Wrong Things*. New York: Basic.

Goldberg, David Theo. 1994. 'Introduction: Multicultural Conditions.' In David Theo Goldberg, ed., *Multiculturalism: A Critical Reader*, 1–41. Oxford: Blackwell.

Gong, Gerrit W. 1984. *The Standard of 'Civilization' in International Society*. Oxford: Oxford University Press.

Granatstein, J.L., ed. 1993. *Canadian Foreign Policy: Historical Readings*. Rev. ed. Toronto: Copp Clark Pittman.

– 1998. *Who Killed Canadian History?* Toronto: HarperCollins.

Granatstein, J.L., and Norman Hillmer. 1991. *For Better or for Worse: Canada and the United States to the 1990s*. Toronto: Copp Clark Pitman.

Gray, James H. 1972. *Booze: The Impact of Whiskey on the Prairie West*. Toronto: Macmillan.

Grayson, Kyle. 2003a. 'Discourse, Identity, and the U.S. "War on Drugs."' In Margaret E. Beare, ed., *Critical Reflections on Transnational Organized Crime and Corruption*, 145–70. Toronto: University of Toronto Press.

– 2003b. 'Securitization and the Boomerang Debate: A Rejoinder to Liotta and Smith-Windsor.' *Security Dialogue* 34, no. 3: 337–43.

– 2004. 'Branding "Transformation" in Canadian Foreign Policy: Human Security.' *Canadian Foreign Policy* 11, no. 2: 41–68.

Green, Melvyn. 1979. 'A History of Canadian Narcotics Control: The Formative Years.' *University of Toronto Faculty of Law Review* 37: 42–79.

Griffith, Ivelaw L. 1993/4. 'From Cold War Geopolitics to Post–Cold War Geonarcotics.' *International Journal* 49 (winter): 1–36.

Haas, Peter M., and Ernst B. Haas. 1995. 'Learning to Learn: Improving International Governance.' *Global Governance* 1, no. 3: 255–84.

– 2002. 'Pragmatic Constructivism and the Study of International Institutions.' *Millenium* 31, no. 3: 573–601.

Hansen, Lene. 1997. 'A Case for Seduction? Evaluating the Poststructuralist Conceptualization of Security.' *Cooperation and Conflict* 32, no. 4: 369–97.

– 2000. 'The Little Mermaid's Silent Security Dilemma and the Absence of Gender in the Copenhagen School.' *Millenium* 29, no. 2: 285–306.

Heeler, Mark. 2003. 'Theorizing the Global Organized Crime Threat: A Perspective from the 1990s.' In Kyle Grayson and Cristina Masters, eds., *Theory in Practice: Critical Reflections on Global Policy*, 15–40. Toronto: Centre for International and Security Studies, York University.

Hillmer, Norman, and J.L. Granatstein. 1994. *Empire to Umpire*. Toronto: Copp Clark Longman.

Hollis, Martin, and Steve Smith. 1990. *Explaining and Understanding International Relations*. Oxford: Clarendon Press.

Homer-Dixon, Thomas. 1994. 'Environmental Scarcities and Violent Conflict.' *International Security* 19, no. 1: 5–40.

Hopf, Ted. 1998. 'The Promise of Constructivism in International Relations Theory.' *International Security* 23, no. 1: 171–200.

Huntington, Samuel. 1996. 'The Clash of Civilizations? The Next Pattern of Conflict.' *Foreign Affairs* 72, no. 3: 22–48.

– 2004. 'The Hispanic Challenge.' *Foreign Policy* 141 (March–April).

Inden, Ronald B. 2001. *Imagining India*. Bloomington: Indiana University Press.

Isin, Engin. 2004. 'The Neurotic Citizen.' Unpublished paper.

Jackson, Andrew. 2004. 'Income Inequality and Poverty: The Liberal Record.' *CanadaWatch* 9, nos. 3–4: 42–4.

Jenkins, Philip. 1999. *Synthetic Panics: The Symbolic Politics of Designer Drugs*. New York: New York University Press.

Johns, Christina Jacqueline. 1992. *Power, Ideology, and the War on Drugs: Nothing Succeeds Like Failure*. New York: Praeger.

Kaplan, Robert. 2000. *The Coming Anarchy: Shattering the Dreams of the Post–Cold War*. New York: Vintage.

Katzenstein, Peter J., ed. 1996. *The Culture of National Security: Norms and Identity in World Politics*. New York: Columbia University Press.

Katzenstein, Peter J., Robert O. Keohane, and Stephan D. Krasner. 1998. 'International Organization and the Study of World Politics.' *International Organization* 52, no. 4: 645–85.

Kent, Heather. 2002. 'Medical Marijuana Crusader Wins Judge's Praise.' *Canadian Medical Association Journal* 172 (25 July): 00–00.

Keohane, Kieran. 1997. *Symptoms of Canada: An Essay on the Canadian Identity*. Toronto: University of Toronto Press.

Klein, Andy. 2001. 'Everything You Wanted to Know about "Memento."' archive.salon.com/ent/movies/feature/2001/06/28/memento_analysis.

Klein, Bradley. 1997. 'Conclusion: Every Month Is 'Security Awareness' Month.' In Keith Krause and Michael C. Williams, eds., *Critical Security Studies*, 359–68. Minneapolis: University of Minnesota Press.

Klepak, Hal. 1993/4. 'The Impact of the International Narcotics Trade on Canada's Foreign and Security Policy.' *International Journal* 49 (winter): 66–92.

Krasna, Joshua S. 1999. 'Testing the Salience of Transnational Issues for International Security: The Case of Narcotics Production and Trafficking.' *Contemporary Security Policy* 20, no. 1: 42–55.

Kratochwil, Friedrich. 1993. 'The Embarrassment of Changes: Neo-Realism as the Science of Realpolitik without Politics.' *Review of International Studies* 19, no. 1: 63–80.

Krause, Keith, and Michael C. Williams. 1996. 'Broadening the Agenda of Security Studies: Politics and Methods.' *International Studies Review* 40: 229–54.

– eds. 1997. *Critical Security Studies*. Minneapolis: University of Minnesota Press.

Kubálková, Vendulka. 2001. 'A Constructivist Primer.' In Vendulka Kubálková, ed., *Foreign Policy in a Constructed World*, 56–76. Armonk: M.E. Sharpe.

Liotta, P.H. 2002a. 'Boomerang Effect: The Convergence of National and Human Security.' *Security Dialogue* 33, no. 4: 473–88.

– 2002b. 'Converging Interests and Agendas: The Boomerang Returns.' *Security Dialogue* 33, no. 4: 495–8.

Lipset, Seymour Martin. 1990. *Continental Divide: The Values and Institutions of the United States and Canada*. New York: Routledge.

Littleton, James, ed. 1996. *Clash of Identities: Essays on Media, Manipulation, and Politics of the Self*. Toronto: Canadian Broadcasting Corporation.

Luciano, Gerry. 1999. 'Quality of "Love" Drugs at Raves Is Declining, and So Is Rave Culture.' *Journal of Addiction and Mental Health* 2, no. 6: 3.

Mackey, Eva. 2002. *The House of Difference: Cultural Politics and National Identity in Canada*. Toronto: University of Toronto Press.

Manning, Erin. 2000. 'Beyond Accommodation: National Space and Recalcitrant Bodies.' *Alternatives* 25, no. 1: 51–74.

Marez, Curtis. 2004. *Drug Wars: The Political Economy of Narcotics*. Minneapolis: University of Minnesota Press.

Martel, Marcel. 2006. *Not This Time: Canadians, Public Policy, and the Marijuana Question*. Toronto: University of Toronto Press.

Massumi, Brian. 1993. *The Politics of Everyday Fear*. Minneapolis: University of Minnesota Press.

Mathews, Robin. 1988. *Canadian Identity: Major Forces Shaping the Life of a People*. Ottawa: Steel Rail.

McAllister, William B. 1992. 'Conflicts of Interest in the International Drug Control System.' In William O. Walker III, ed. *Drug Control Policy: Essays in a Historical and Comparative Perspective*. 143–66. University Park: Pennsylvania State University Press.

– 2000. *Drug Diplomacy in the Twentieth Century*. London and New York: Routledge.

McCall, Tara. 2001. *This Is Not a Rave*. Toronto: Insomniac.

McLaren, Peter. 1994. 'White Terror and Oppositional Agency: Towards a Critical Multiculturalism.' In David Theo Goldberg, ed., *Multiculturalism: A Critical Reader*, 45–74. Oxford: Blackwell.

McSweeny, Bill. 1999. *Security, Identity, and Interests: A Sociology of International Relations*. Cambridge: Cambridge University Press.

Mitchinson, Wendy. 1988. 'Reasons for Committal to a Mid-Nineteenth Century Ontario Insane Asylum: The Case of Toronto.' In Wendy Mitichinson and Janice Dicken, eds., *Essays in the History of Canadian Medicine*. Toronto: McClelland and Stewart.

Morris, Kelly. 2003. 'Concern over Research Awakens Ecstasy Neurotoxicity Debate.' *Lancet: Neurology* 2, no. 11: 650.

Mosher, Clayton. 1999. 'Imperialism, Irrationality, and Illegality: The First Ninety Years of Canadian Drug Policy.' *New Scholars, New Visions* 3: 1–40.

Murphy, Emily. 1922. *The Black Candle: Canada's First Book on Drug Abuse.*
Toronto: Thomas Allen.

Murray, Glenn. 1987. 'Cocaine Use in the Era of Social Reform: The Natural
History of a Social Problem in Canada, 1880–1911.' *Canadian Journal of Law
and Society* 2: 29–43.

– 1988. 'The Road to Regulation: Patent Medicines in Canada in Historical
Perspective.' In Judith C. Blackwell and Patricia G. Erickson, eds., *Illicit
Drugs in Canada: A Risky Business*, 72–87. Scarborough: Nelson Canada.

Mutimer, David. 1997. 'Reimagining Security: The Metaphors of Proliferation.' In Keith Krause and Michael C. Williams, eds., *Critical Security
Studies*, 187–222. Minneapolis: University of Minnesota Press.

– 1998. 'Reconstituting Security: The Practices of Proliferation Control.' *European Journal of International Relations* 4, no. 1: 99–127.

Nigg, Joe. 1995. *Wonder Beasts: Tales and Lore of the Phoenix, the Griffin, the
Unicorn, and the Dragon.* Englewood: Libraries Unlimited.

Ó Tuathail, Gearoid. 1996. *Critical Geopolitics.* Minneapolis: University of
Minnesota Press.

– 1998. 'Postmodern Geopolitics? The Modern Geopolitical Imagination and
Beyond.' In Gearoid Ó Tuathail and Simon Dalby, eds., *Critical Geopolitics*,
16–38. London: Routledge.

Ó Tuathail, Gearoid, and Simon Dalby. 1998. 'Introduction: Rethinking
Geopolitics: Towards a Critical Geopolitics.' In Gearoid Ó Tuathail and
Simon Dalby, eds., *Critical Geopolitics*, 1–15. London: Routledge.

Ó Tuathail, Gearoid, Simon Dalby, and Paul Routledge, eds. 1998. *The Geopolitics Reader.* London: Routledge.

Oren, Ido. 2000. 'Is Culture Independent of National Security? How
America's National Security Concerns Shaped "Political Culture"
Research.' *European Journal of International Relations* 6, no. 4: 543–73.

Owen, Frank. 2003. *Clubland: The Fabulous Rise and Murderous Fall of Club
Culture.* New York: St Martin's Press.

Rabinow, Paul, and Nikolas Rose. 2003. 'Introduction: Foucault Today.' In
Paul Rabinow and Nikolas Rose, eds., *The Essential Foucault: Selections from
Essential Works of Foucault, 1954–1984*, vii–xxxv. New York: New Press.

Reitz, Jeffrey G., and Raymond Breton. 1994. *The Illusion of Difference: Realities
of Ethnicity in Canada and the United States.* Winnipeg: C.D. Howe Institute.

Reynolds, Simon. 1999. *Generation Ecstasy: Into the World of Techno and Rave
Culture.* New York: Routledge.

Rieder, Michael J. 2000. 'Some Light from the Heat: Implications of Rave
Parties for Clinicians.' *Canadian Medical Association Journal* 162, no. 13:
1829–30.

Royle, Nicholas. 2000. 'What Is Deconstruction?' In Nicholas Royle, ed., *Deconstructions: A User's Guide*, 1–13. New York: Palgrave.

Ruggie, John Gerard. 1993. 'Territoriality and Beyond: Problematizing Modernity in International Relations.' *International Organization* 47, no. 1: 139–74.

– 1998. 'What Makes the World Hang Together? Neo-Utilitarianism and the Social Constructivist Challenge.' *International Organization* 52, no. 4: 855–85.

Samuels, Raymond. 1997. *National Identity in Canada and Cosmopolitian Community*. Kanata: Agora Cosmopolitan.

Satzewich, Vic, ed. 1992. *Deconstructing a Nation: Immigration, Multiculturalism, and Racism in '90s Canada*. Halifax: Fernwood.

Savas, Daniel. 2001. 'Public Opinion and Illicit Drugs: Canadian Attitudes Towards Decriminalizing the Use of Marijuana.' Vancouver: Fraser Institute.

Shapiro, Michael J. 1989. 'Textualizing Global Politics.' In James Der Derian and Michael J. Shapiro, eds., *International/Intertextual Relations: Post Modern Readings of World Politics*, 11–22. Lexington: Lexington Books.

Silcott, Mireille. 1999. *Rave America: New School Dancescapes*. Toronto: ECW.

Smith, Allen. 1994. *Canada an American Nation? Essays on Continentalism, Identity, and the Canadian Frame of Mind*. Montreal and Kingston: McGill-Queen's University Press.

Smith, Linda Tuhiwai. 1999. *Decolonizing Methodologies: Research and Indigenous Peoples*. London: Zed Books.

Smith, Malcolm, ed. 1977. *The Dragon: Charles Gould and Others*. London: Wildwood House.

Smith, Steve. 1996. 'Positivism and Beyond.' In Ken Booth, Steve Smith, and Marysia Zalewski, eds., *International Theory: Positivism and Beyond*, 1–44. Cambridge: Cambridge University Press.

Smith-Windsor, Brooke A. 2002. 'Terrorism, Individual Security, and the Role of the Military: A Reply to Liotta.' *Security Dialogue* 33, no. 4: 489–94.

Solomon, Robert R. 1988. 'Canada's Federal Drug Legislation.' In Judith C. Blackwell and Patricia G. Erickson, eds., *Illicit Drugs in Canada: A Risky Business*, 117–30. Scarborough: Nelson Canada.

– 1995. 'Perspectives on Privatization/Alcohol Deregulation.' Alcohol Policy Network [accessed 7 April 2004]. www.apolnet.org/resources/rp_pri2.html.

Solomon, Robert R., and Melvyn Green. 1988. 'The First Century: The History of Non-Medical Opiate Use and Control Policies in Canada, 1870–1970.' In Judith C. Blackwell and Patricia G. Erickson, eds., *Illicit Drugs in Canada: A Risky Business*, 88–116. Scarborough: Nelson Canada.

Sparke, Matthew. 1998. 'Outsides inside Patriotism: The Oklahoma Bombing and the Displacement of Heartland Geopolitics.' In Gearoid Ó Tuathail and Simon Dalby, eds., *Critical Geopolitics*, 198–223. London: Routledge.

St James, James. 1999. *Disco Bloodbath: A Fabulous but True Tale of Murder in Clubland*. New York: Simon and Shuster.

Stairs, Denis, David Bercuson, Mark Entwistle, Jack Granatstein, Kim Richard Nossal, and Gordon Smith. 2003. 'In the National Interest: Canadian Foreign Policy in an Insecure World.' Calgary: Canadian Defence and Foreign Affairs Institute.

Strong-Boag, Veronica, Sherrill Grace, Avigail Eisenberg, and Joan Anderson, eds. 1998. *Painting the Maple: Essays on Race, Gender, and the Construction of Canada*. Vancouver: UBC Press.

Sylvester, Christine. 1994. *Feminist Theory and International Relations in a Post-Modern Era*. Cambridge: Cambridge University Press.

Szasz, Thomas. 1974. *Ceremonial Chemistry: The Ritual Persecution of Drugs, Addicts, and Pushers*. Garden City: Doubleday.

Thomas, David M., ed. 2000. *Canada and the United States: Differences That Count*. 2nd ed. Peterborough: Broadview Press.

Tickner, J. Ann, ed. 1992a. *Gender in International Relations: Feminist Perspectives on Achieving Global Security*. New York: Columbia University Press.

– 1992b. 'Man over Nature: Gendered Perspectives on Ecological Security.' In J. Ann Tickner, ed. *Gender in International Relations: Feminist Perspectives on Achieving Global Security*. 97–126. New York: Columbia University Press.

– 1995. 'Re-Visioning Security.' In Steve Smith and Ken Booth, eds., *International Relations Theory Today*, 175–97. University Park: Pennsylvania State University Press.

Tooley, Jennifer. 1999. 'Demon Drugs and Holy Wars: Canadian Drug Policy as Symbolic Action.' Masters thesis, University of New Brunswick.

Trasov, C.E. 1962. 'History of the Opium and Narcotics Drug Legislation in Canada.' *Criminal Law Quarterly* 4: 274–82.

Vitalis, Robert. 2000. 'The Graceful and Generous Liberal Gesture: Making Racism Invisible in American International Relations.' *Millennium* 29, no. 2: 331–56.

Wald, Priscilla. 2000. 'Imagined Immunities.' In Jodi Dean, ed., *Cultural Studies and Political Theory*, 189–208. Ithaca: Cornell University Press.

Walker III, William O. 1991. *Opium and Foreign Policy: The Anglo-American Search for Order in Asia, 1912–1954*. Chapel Hill: University of North Carolina Press.

– 1993/4. 'The Foreign Narcotics Policy of the United States since 1980: An End to the War on Drugs?' *International Journal* 49 (winter): 37–65.

– ed. 1996. *Drugs in the Western Hemisphere: An Odyssey of Cultures in Conflict*. Wilmington: Jaguar Books.

Walker, R.B.J. 1992. 'Gender and Critique in the Theory of International Relations.' In V. Spike Peterson, ed., *Gendered States: Feminist (Re)Visions of International Relations Theory*, 179–202. Boulder: Lynne Rienner.

– 1997. 'The Subject of Security.' In Keith Krause and Michael C. Williams, eds., *Critical Security Studies*, 61–82. Minneapolis: University of Minnesota Press.

Walt, Stephen. 1999. 'Rigor or Rigor Mortis? Rational Choice and Security Studies.' *International Security* 23, no. 4: 5–48.

Waltz, Kenneth. 1979. *Theory of International Politics*. Reading: Addison-Wesley.

Watson, William. 1998. *Globalization and the Meaning of Canadian Life*. Toronto: University of Toronto Press.

Weber, Cynthia. 1998. 'Performative States.' *Millenium* 27, no. 1: 77–95.

– 1999. *Faking It: US Hegemony in a 'Post-Phallic' Era*. Minneapolis: University of Minnesota Press.

Weldes, Jutta, Mark Laffey, Hugh Gusterson, and Raymond Duvall. 1999. 'Introduction: Constructing Insecurity.' In *Cultures of Insecurity: States, Communities, and the Production of Danger*, 1–33. Minneapolis: University of Minnesota Press.

Wendt, Alexander. 1992. 'Anarchy Is What States Make of It: The Social Construction of Power Politics.' *International Organization* 46, no. 2: 391–425.

– 1999. *Social Theory of International Politics*. Cambridge: Cambridge University Press.

Whitaker, Reginald. 1969. *Drugs and the Law: The Canadian Scene*. Toronto: Methuen.

Williams, Michael C., and Keith Krause. 1997. 'From Strategy to Security: Foundations of Critical Security Studies.' In Keith Krause and Michael C. Williams, eds. *Critical Security Studies*. 33–60. Minneapolis: University of Minnesota Press.

Winichakul, Thongchai. 1994. *Siam Mapped: A History of the Geo-Body of a Nation*. Honolulu: University of Hawaii Press.

Media

'12 at Concert Face Drug Charges.' 1988. *Toronto Star*, 9 August, A6.

Abbate, Gay. 2002. 'Sick People Have Right to Use Pot, Lawyer Argues.' *Globe and Mail*, 20 September. medicalmarihuana.ca/dissension.html.

Abraham, Carolyn. 2002a. 'Medicinal-Marijuana Harvest on Hold.' *Globe and Mail*, 22 April. www.medicalmarihuana.ca/delay.html.

– 2002b. 'Medicinal-Pot Users Fuming over Delays.' *Globe and Mail*,
  22 December. www.medicalmarihuana.ca/delay.html.
Ainsworth, Lynne. 1988a. 'Parents Want Schools to Stress Drug Education.'
  Toronto Star, 26 May, A6.
– 1988b. 'Wrong Attitude Killed Benji, Expert Says.' *Toronto Star*, 3 June, H10.
Allossery, Patrick. 2000. 'Marketers Waiting for the Right Time to Hit Rave
  Scene: Well Targeted Promotions Will Be Well Received.' *Financial
  Post–National Post*, 4 December, C4.
Anderssen, Erin. 2002. 'Would Softer Pot Laws Stir Wrath of US?' *Globe and
  Mail*, 13 July. www.medicalmarihuana.ca/meddling.html.
Arnold, Tom, and Jeff Vinnick. 2002. 'Ottawa Probes Marijuana's Effect on
  Pain.' *National Post*, 10 October. www.medicalmarihuana.ca/study.html.
Associated Press. 1993. 'Toronto Man Held in Buffalo Drug Bust.' *Associated
  Press Wire*, 30 April.
Avery, Roberta. 2003. 'Chiefs Balk on Gun Registry.' *Toronto Star*, 25 January,
  A7.
Axworthy, Lloyd. 2003. 'A Canadian Alternative to the Bush Doctrine.'
  Toronto Star, 30 March, F5.
Babbage, Maria. 2002. 'Illicit Drug Legalization Lashed by Police Group.'
  Toronto Star, 25 August, A8.
– 2003. 'Liberal Stance Will Make It Tougher to Avoid New Border Measures
  Says Alliance.' *Canadian Press*, 27 March.
Baillie, Andrea. 2003. 'McLellan to Examine If Drug Shortages a Result of
  Cross-Border Trade.' *Canadian Press*, 30 October.
Bali, Mohamed. 1997. 'Chewing Khat: Reflections on the Somali Male Food
  and Social Life.' *Maroodi Jeex* 6 (September–November). http://storm
  .prohosting.com/~mbali/bali09.htm.
Barnes, Allan, and Leslie Papp. 1988. 'Kindergarten Anti-Drug Education
  Good Idea If Done Right, Experts Say.' *Toronto Star*, 18 October, A12.
Barutigam, Tara. 2003. 'Court Hears Appeal That Could Alter Pot Possession
  and Distribution Laws.' *Canadian Press*, 29 July. www.medicalmarihuana
  .ca/appeal.html.
Beeby, Dean. 2003a. 'Ottawa's Marijuana Maven Puts Breaks on Distribution
  Proposal: Documents.' *Toronto Star*, 15 January. www.medicalmarihuana
  .ca/scandal.html.
– 2003b. 'Health Canada Considers Abandoning Highly Potent Marijuana
  Strain.' *Canadian Press*, 20 April. www.medicalmarihuana.ca/failure.html.
– 2003c. 'Health Canada Set to Release Users' Manual for Medical Marijuana.' *Canadian Press*, 20 July. www.medicalmarihuana.ca/manual.html.

– 2007. 'Mind-Blowing Mark-Up for Medicinal Pot.' *Toronto Star*, 16 April. http://www.thestar.com/article/203446.

Bennett, Samantha. 2003. 'It's Not Just the Weather That's Cooler in Canada.' *Pittsburgh Post-Gazette*, 30 July.

Bergman, Brian. 2003. 'Just Say "Yes."' *Maclean's*, 3 March. www.medical marihuana.ca/inaction.html.

Bilodean, Paul. 1988. 'LSD "Trip" Can Panic the First Time User Pharmacologist Says.' *Toronto Star*, 19 May, A10.

Blashill, Pat. 1999. 'Dark Side of the Rave: Drug Deaths and Police Crackdowns Threaten the National Rave Scene.' *Rolling Stone*, 11 November, 27–8.

Bonnell, Greg. 2003. 'US "Disappointed" Canada Not Supporting War against Iraq, Says Ambassador.' Canadian Press, 25 March.

'Boy, 14, Disappears During Rock Concert.' 1988. *Toronto Star*, 16 May, A1.

Brautigam, Tara. 2003. 'Marijuana Now Sold, Taxed and Distributed by Canadian Doctors.' Canadian Press, 26 August. www.medicalmarihuana.ca/dispense.html.

Brown, Barbara. 2003. 'Pot Laws May Go up in Smoke.' *Hamilton Spectator*, 28 July. www.medicalmarihuana.ca/appeal.html.

'Budget Blues.' 2004. Pulse24.com. www.pulse24.com/News/Top_Story/20040402-009/page.asp. (Last accessed April 2004)

Bueckert, Dennis. 2002a. 'McLellan Prescribes Clinical Trials for Medical Marijuana.' *Halifax Herald*, 23 April. www.medicalmarihuana.ca/trials.html.

– 2002b. 'Medical Marijuana Program Thrown for a Loop When US Refused to Supply Seeds.' Canadian Press, 7 May. www.medicalmarihuana.ca/seeds.html.

– 2003a. 'Critics Give Government Plan to Sell Medical Pot Mixed Reviews.' Canadian Press, 9 July. www.medicalmarihuana.ca/comply.html.

– 2003b. 'Doctor Resigns from Health Canada Advisory Committee.' Canadian Press, 15 July. www.medicalmarihuana.ca/resignation.html.

– 2003c. 'Government Gets Nowhere on Pot Research.' *Halifax Herald*, 9 July. medicalmarihuana.ca/notrials.html.

– 2003d. 'Health Canada Agrees to Provide Pot Long-Term: Patients Protest.' Canadian Press, 8 December.

– 2003e. 'Turmoil Continues in Offices of Medical Pot as Director Quits.' Canadian Press, 16 July. medicalmarihuana.ca/resignation.html.

Burnett, Thane. 2003. 'Pot Exemptees Left at Mercy of Black Market.' *Toronto Sun*, 15 January. medicalmarihuana.ca/scandal.html.

'Canada Helping Our American Ally.' 2003. Editorial, *Toronto Star*, 26 March, A30.

Canada NewsWire. 2002a. 'The Canadian Police Association Holds Its 8th National Lobby Day.' 12 March.

– 2002b. 'Don't Legalize Marijuana: National Association of Professional Police.' 8 September.

– 2003a. 'The Canadian Police Association Holds Its 9th National Lobby Day.' 11 March.

– 2003b. 'New Statistics Canada Study Shows Decline in Firearms Homicide Rates Continues.' 1 October.

– 2004. 'IMS Health Canada–Retail Prescriptions Grow at Record Level in 2003.' 25 March.

'Canadian Marijuana Reform Concern to US.' 2002. *Globe and Mail*, 13 May. www.medicalmarihuana.ca/meddling.html.

Canadian Press. 1988. 'Watch for Signs of Drugs, Parents Told.' *Toronto Star*, 30 May, C2.

– 2000a. 'Custom Officials Seize 1,000 Kilograms of Khat at Toronto Airport.' 23 April.

– 2000b. 'Downtown Club Shooting.' 4 March.

– 2000c. 'The Fatal Shooting of a Bouncer at a Downtown Rave Club Has Left Neighbouring Businesses Shaken and One Considering Closing Down.' 5 March.

– 2001. 'Party Continued after Man Stabbed to Death at All Night Toronto Rave.' 5 February.

– 2002a. 'MSNBC's Pat Buchanan Calls Canada "Soviet Canuckistan" for Stand on Targeting.' 31 October.

– 2002b. 'US Ambassador Says Canada Must Beef Up Military in "a Very Dangerous World."' 28 October.

– 2002c. 'US Ambassador Says More Legislation Needed to Help Police Fight Terror.' 17 January.

– 2002d. 'Minister Uncomfortable with Pot Issue.' 19 August. www .medicalmarihuana.ca/revoke.html.

– 2002e. 'Nine Sick Canadians Plan to Sue Federal Government for Access to Marijuana.' 21 May. www.medicalmarihuana.ca/lawsuit.html.

– 2003a. 'Canada Has Not Been Asked to Cooperate in Missile Defence, Says Chrétien.' 29 April.

– 2003b. 'Canada Must Boost Homeland Security to Help Mend Relations with US: Manley.' 21 April.

– 2003c. 'Canada Rethinks Medical Marijuana Laws.' 27 April. www .medicalmarihuana.ca/dutch.html.

- 2003d. 'Canada's First Cannabis HIV/Aids Study Suspended.' 19 June. www.medicalmarihuana.ca/notrials.html.
- 2003e. 'Canada's New Marijuana Law Will Worsen US Problems, American Official Says.' 22 August.
- 2003f. 'Cellucci "Grossly Undiplomatic," Says Passionate Canadian Nationalist.' 4 April.
- 2003g. 'CEOs Propose Joint Canada–US Border Management to Battle Terrorism, Smuggling.' 13 January.
- 2003h. 'Court Makes Pot Possession Illegal Again.' 7 October.
- 2003i. 'Decriminalizing Marijuana Could Mean Border Slowdowns: US Ambassador.' 2 May.
- 2003j. 'Health Department Eases Restrictions on Access to Medical Marijuana.' 8 December.
- 2003k. 'Ontario Court Strikes Down Ottawa's Pot Laws.' *Globe and Mail*, 9 January. medicalmarihuana.ca/unconstitutional.html.
- 2003l. 'Ottawa Must Move Quickly on Border Security Issues, Ontario Official Says.' 3 March.
- 2003m. 'US Consul General Weighs in on Marijuana Crossing over Border.' 25 September.
- 2003n. 'US Government Tells Illinois That Canadian Drugs May Not Be Safe.' 7 November.
- 2003o. 'Washington Says Firms Shouldn't Be Allowed to Continue Selling Canadian Drugs.' 20 November.
- 2004. 'US Government Says Minnesota Review Shows Canadian Internet Drugs Dangerous.' 13 February.

Canadian Professional Police Association and Canadian Association of Chiefs of Police. 2003. 'Open Letter to the Prime Minister of Canada Concerning Bill C-38: Decriminalization of Marijuana.' Canada News Wire, 21 October.

Carmichael, Amy. 2003. 'Howe Institute: US Need for Energy Security Puts Canada in Power Position.' Canadian Press, 1 April.

CBC News Online. 2002. 'Federally Approved Marijuana Growers Must Wait and See.' 12 August. www.medicalmarihuana.ca/conflict.html.

CBC Winnipeg. 2003. 'Ritalin on the Rise.' http://winnipeg.cbc.ca/archives/ritalin/index2.html.

Cheadle, Bruce. 2002. 'Canadians Generous after 9–11 But Not in Defence Budget, Says US Ambassador.' Canadian Press, 3 September.

Cheney, Peter. 2002. 'Flin Flon Pot Escape Fiery Fate.' *Globe and Mail*, 18 November. www.medicalmarihuana.ca/burned.html.

Cleverly, Bill. 2003. 'US Fear over Liberalized Pot Laws Unwarranted, Argues

Islander.' *Victoria Times Colonist*, 6 May. www.medicalmarihuana.ca/ meddling.html.

Cloud, John. 2001. 'Ecstasy Crackdown: Will the US Use a 1980s Anti-Crack Law to Destroy the Rave Movement?' *Time* (Can. ed.), 9 April, 50–2.

Cohen, Shawna. 2000. 'Fitting In: The Fine and Subtle Art of Marketing to Young Rave Partiers.' *Marketing Magazine*, 3–10 January, 17.

Cohen, Tom. 2003. 'Canadian Patients Get Government Marijuana.' Associated Press, 27 August. www.medicalmarihuana.ca/dispense.html.

Contenta, Sandro. 'Something to Chew on Yemeni Style: Khat Leaves Are King in This Improverished Land, Where Booze Is Illegal and Munching's the Thing.' *Toronto Star*, 24 March, B3.

Cordon, Sandra. 2003a. 'NORAD Could Be in Jeopardy If Canada Doesn't Join Missile Defence: Cellucci.' Canadian Press, 2 May.

– 2003b. 'Ottawa Reconsidering Controversial US Missile Defence Program.' Canadian Press, 28 April.

Cotroneo, Christian. 2002. 'US Envoy Backs "Smart" Border: Technology Will Aid Flow of Goods, Cellucci Says.' *Toronto Star*, 27 February, E3.

'Council Should Lift Ban on Legal Raves.' 2000. *Toronto Star*, 27 July, A26.

'A Crack Regiment Is on Trial.' 1993. *Western Report*, 7 June, 23.

Crane, David. 2003. 'US Ambassador Guilty of Misleading Canadians.' *Toronto Star*, 27 March, B2.

Crawford, Trish. 1999. 'Somalis Complain of Police Searches.' *Toronto Star*, 3 May, B3.

Cudmore, James. 1999. 'Rave Drug GHB Doesn't Mix Well: Toronto Club Goers Increasingly End Up in Hospital.' *National Post*, 9 March, B4.

Dabrowski, Wojtek. 2003. 'Protests across Canada Continue as Activists Rage against US-Led War in Iraq.' Canadian Press, 5 April.

Damuzi, Reverend. 2002a. 'Canadian Med-Pot Clubs under Attack.' *Cannabis Culture Magazine*, 22 November. www.medicalmarihuana.ca/raids.html.

– 2002b. 'Official Med-Pot Producer Claims His Buds Are Dank and Pure but Patients Have Yet to Get Them.' *Cannabis Culture Magazine*, 10 May. www.cannabisculture.com/articles/2399.html.

– 2003. 'Black Tuesday for Canadian Cannaphiles.' *Cannabis Culture Magazine*, 7 October.

'A Day of Chewing Khat.' 1990. *Toronto Star*, 9 December, H3.

'Decriminalization Useless to Medical Users – No Legal Supply.' 2002. *Eye Weekly*, 19 December. medicalmarihuana.ca/decriminalize.html.

DeMara, Bruce. 2000. 'Ravers Rally for Freedom to Dance.' *Toronto Star*, 25 July, B3.

DeMara, Bruce, and Paul Moloney. 2000. 'Council Votes to Suspend Raves: Urging Move, Chief Cites Heavy Drug Use.' *Toronto Star*, 11 May.

'Do Your Kids Rave? Talk to Your Kids about All Night Dance Parties/ Raves.' 2001. *Oakville Today*, 12 July.

'Double-Talk on Weed.' Editorial, *National Post*, 21 August. www .medicalmarihuana.ca/stall.html.

Duncanson, John, and Tracy Huffman. 2004. 'Source: Police Shielded Drug Dens.' *Toronto Star*, 24 April, A1.

'Easing Border Tensions.' 2003. Editorial, *Toronto Star*, 20 April, A12.

'"Educate Yourself, Get Involved," Jury Tells Parents.' 1988. *Toronto Star*, 13 August, A8.

Egan, Kelly. 2002. 'Retired Lawyer Tackles the Law on Driving under the Influence of Drugs.' *Ottawa Citizen*, 11 December. www.medicalmarihuana .ca/lawchange.html.

Eliscu, Jenny. 2001. 'The War on Raves: Rave Promoters Busted in Wave of Drug Crackdowns at Dance Clubs around the US.' *Rolling Stone*, 24 May, 21–2.

– 2003. 'Senate Just Says No to Clubs: New Anti-Rave Legislation Threatens Concert Industry.' *Rolling Stone*, 21 April.

Elliot, Louise. 2002. 'McCallum Lashes Out at Bush over Defence Spending at NATO Summit in Prague.' Canadian Press, 20 November.

'Fantino: "There Is No Racism. We Do Not Do Racial Profiling."' 2002. *Toronto Star*, 19 October, A14.

Fatah, Tarek. 2001. 'Police Crackdown on Somali "Khat" Smacks of Racism.' *Toronto Star*, 25 July, A23.

Faulkner, Vern. 2001. 'Problems over Pot.' *Saanich News*, 21 November. www .medicalmarihuana.ca/young.html.

– 2002a. 'Medicinal Marijuana User Takes Ottawa, Province, and College of Physicians to Court.' *Saanich News*, 28 August. www.medicalmarihuana .ca/young.html.

– 2002b. 'Pot Smoker Claims He Has Been Discriminated Against.' *Saanich News*, 30 January. www.medicalmarihuana.ca/young.html.

Fayerman, Pamela, and Mark Kennedy. 2003. 'BCMA Head Decries Federal Marijuana Shipments to Doctors.' *Victoria Times Colonist*, 10 July. www .medicalmarihuana.ca/distribution.html.

Ferguson, Rob. 2003. 'Martin Cool to Security Perimeter.' *Toronto Star*, 14 January, A6.

'Fewer Are Using Drugs Now, Students Say.' 1988. *Toronto Star*, 19 May, A10.

Fidelman, Charlie. 2001. 'Police to Crash the Party.' *Montreal Gazette*, 12 August.

Fiorito, Joe. 2000. 'You Do the Math: 911 Calls Show Drop: Chief Fantino's Push to Get Tough Doesn't Match Stats.' *National Post*, 12 May.

forbes.com. 2003. 'Cannabits.' www.forbes.com/maserati/146tab.html.

Fraser, Graham. 2003. 'US Will Protect Itself, Says Ambassador.' *Toronto Star*, 5 December, A3.

Freed, Dale Anne. 2001. 'Teen Bought Ecstasy at Club Shortly before He Died.' *Toronto Star*, 10 July.

Freeze, Colin. 2003. 'Pot Possession Not Illegal, Judge Rules.' *Globe and Mail*, 3 January. www.medicalmarihuana.ca/possession.html.

Friendly, Michael. 2002. 'Analysis of Toronto Police Database: Drug Charges Data and Highway Traffic Act Data.' *Toronto Star*, 19 October.

'A Full Moon Rave: It's 3am and There's a Party Going On: Do You Know Where Your Teenager Is.' 1995. *Life*, August, 20–4.

Gifford-Jones, W. 2002. 'The Doctor Game.' *Winnipeg Free Press*, 2 October. www.medicalmarihuana.ca/smokescreen.html.

Gillespie, Elizabeth. 2003. 'US Drug Czar Claims Canada Is Too Lax Prosecuting Drug Crimes.' Canadian Press, 11 September.

Gillespie, Kerry. 2004. 'The High Price of Law and Order.' *Toronto Star*, 21 February, B4.

Giradet, Edward. 1992. 'A Forgotten Face of War.' *US News & World Report*, 4 May, 38–41.

Givens, Robin. 1998. 'Khat Ban Racist, Ignorant.' *Toronto Star*, 27 September, E5.

'Giving a Graceless Okay to Medical Marijuana.' 2003. *Globe and Mail*, 10 July. www.medicalmarihuana.ca/distribution.html.

'How Far Will MPs Go to Torpedo a Bill?' 2003. *Globe and Mail*, 20 August, A14.

Goar, Carol. 2003. 'It's About War, Not Loyalty, Sir.' *Toronto Star*, 28 March, A28.

Gordon, Mary. 2003. 'Medical Marijuana Can Be Distributed.' *Toronto Star*, 9 July. medicalmarihuana.ca/comply.html.

Gorrie, Peter. 2003. 'Now, They Don't Like Our Marijuana Plan.' *Toronto Star*, 10 May, H3.

Green, Sarah. 2000. 'Mother Blames Raves.' *Toronto Sun*, 18 May.

Griffiths, Frank. 2002. 'A New Vision of North America … And Denmark Should Play a Role in Defending It.' *Toronto Star*, 24 May, A25.

Haans, Dave. 1998. 'Wrong-Headed Laws Give Drug Lords Power.' *Toronto Star*, 27 September, E5.

Habib, Marlene. 2003. 'Ottawa Appeals Judge's Marijuana Ruling.' *Toronto Star*, 4 January. www.medicalmarihuana.ca/possession.html.

– 2004. 'Toronto's Image as Safe Place to Visit at Risk after Violent Weekend: Chief.' Canadian Press, 23 February.

Harding, Katherine. 2000a. 'Council Expected to Lift Rave Ban.' *Toronto Star*, 3 August, B4.

– 2000b. 'Council Lifts Ban on Raves.' *Toronto Star*, 4 August, B1.

Harper, Tim. 2002a. 'Bush to Allies: Boost Military.' *Toronto Star*, 21 November, A1.

– 2002b. 'Potency of Government Marijuana Questioned: McLellan Said to Be Misrepresenting Rock's Weed Crop.' *Toronto Star*, 16 May. www.medical marihuana.ca/blame.html.

– 2003. 'Martin Tackles Iraq Contract Dispute.' *Toronto Star*, 11 December, A1.

Harper, Tim, and Valerie Lawton. 2003. 'Canadians Face Drug Shortages, US Warns.' *Toronto Star*, 31 October, A3.

Hartley, Norman. 1971a. 'New Drug Accords to Be Delayed for National Debate, Munro Says.' *Globe and Mail*, 2 March, 5.

– 1971b. 'UN Convention on Drugs End Quiet Controversy in Canada.' *Globe and Mail*, 3 March, 35.

Hawthorn, Tom. 2002. 'Marijuana "Pharmacist" Wins Praise for His Work.' *Globe and Mail*, 11 July. www.medicalmarihuana.ca/discharge.html.

Hirave, Hassan. 1996. 'New Drug Finds a Home in Metro: Potentially Violent Trade in Khat Arrived Along with Influx of Somali Refugees.' *Toronto Star*, 2 January, A13.

Howard, Robert. 2002. 'Medical Marijuana: Health Minister Ducking the Issue.' *Hamilton Spectator*, 23 September. www.medicalmarihuana.ca/avoidance.html.

Hundley, Tim. 1992. 'Yemen Makes a Habit of High Living.' *Toronto Star*, 20 July, A3.

'How to Stall on Medicinal Marijuana.' 2002. *Globe and Mail*, 21 August. www.medicalmarihuana.ca/stall.html.

Jackson, Marni. 2002. 'Smoke Out the Politicians.' *Globe and Mail*, 26 August. www.medicalmarihuana.ca/backtrack.html.

Jacma, Farah. 1998. 'Feeble Law Hasn't Stopped Trade in Khat.' *Toronto Star*, 5 September, E5.

Jacobs, Mindelle. 2002a. 'Hysteria Still Reigns on Pot Laws.' *Edmonton Sun*, 22 September. www.medicalmarihuana.ca/patients.html.

– 2002b. 'Ottawa's Not a Very Good Drug Dealer.' *Edmonton Sun*, 23 April. www.medicalmarihuana.ca/trials.html.

James, Royson. 1988. 'Petition Urges Tougher Laws against Drugs.' *Toronto Star*, 12 July, NR6.

Jones, Frank. 1988. 'Let's Not Deny Link between Rock Music, Drugs.' *Toronto Star*, 30 May, C2.

Jones, Vernon Clement. 2001. 'Cultures Clash on Streets over Canada's Ban on Khat.' *Toronto Star*, 27 July, F5.

– 2002. 'Charter Allows Use of Pot, Civil Suit Says.' *Globe and Mail*, 24 May. www.medicalmarihuana.ca/lawsuit.html.

Kari, Shannon. 2002. 'Health Canada Hires Scientist Developing Alternative to Drug to Outline Weed's Dangers.' *Ottawa Citizen*, 28 October. www .medicalmarihuana.ca/biased.html.

– 2003a. 'Crown Presses Case against "Pot Club."' *Ottawa Citizen*, 29 January. www.medicalmarihuana.ca/noregulations.html.

– 2003b. 'Judge Allows Marijuana Ruling to Stand.' *Ottawa Citizen*, 11 June. www.medicalmarihuana.ca/rogin.html.

– 2003c. 'Judge Tells Feds to Provide Legal Pot.' *Ottawa Citizen*, 10 January. www.medicalmarihuana.ca/unconstitutional.html.

– 2003d. 'Medical Marijuana Appeal Weak – Judge.' Canada.com, 13 March. www.medicalmarihuana.ca/weakcase.html.

– 2003e. 'Ontario Has No Marijuana Laws, Ottawa Concedes.' *Vancouver Sun*, 7 June. www.medicalmarihuana.ca/rogin.html.

Kennedy, Mark. 2002. 'Canada's First Crop of Officially Sanctioned Medical Marijuana Contains a Rainbox of Potencies and Purities.' *Ottawa Citizen*, 8 May. www.medicalmarihuana.ca/badcrop.html.

Keung, Nicholas. 2000. 'Attack Drugs Not Dancing, Chow Says: Councillor Warns against Banning Raves.' *Toronto Star*, 22 May.

'Khat Crackdown Alarms Somalis.' 1999. *Toronto Star*, 5 May, B2.

'Khat Smuggler from Etobicoke Fined $7000.' 1995. *Toronto Star*, 14 October, A36.

Kingstone, Jonathan. 2000. 'Fantino Asks PM to T.O. Rave: Asks Chretien to See "Kids ... High on Drugs."' *Toronto Sun*, 5 May.

– 2001.'Rave Teen Dies after Taking Pills.' *Toronto Sun*, 9 July.

Klein, Naomi. 2000. 'How to Radicalize a Generation.' *Globe and Mail*, 10 May.

Knox, Jack. 2003. 'Legal-Pot Crusaders Bond Financially.' *Victoria Times Colonist*, 15 February. www.medicalmarihuana.ca/incompetence.html.

Laframboise, Donna. 2000. 'The Sky Isn't Falling.' *National Post*, 16 May.

Laghi, Brian. 2002a. 'First Clinical Pot Trial to Use US Stash.' *Globe and Mail*, 10 October. www.medicalmarihuana.ca/smokescreen.html.

– 2002b. 'Rock Planned to Release Pot, Letter Says.' *Globe and Mail*, 18 September. www.medicalmarihuana.ca/dissension.html.

– 2002c. 'Split Emerges over Releasing Marijuana.' *Globe and Mail*, 21 August. www.medicalmarihuana.ca/conflict.html.

– 2003a. 'MDs Will Dispense Marijuana.' *Globe and Mail*, 10 July. www .medicalmarihuana.ca/distribution.html.

– 2003b. 'Medical Pot Firm Mulls Legal Action over Delays.' *Globe and Mail*, 26 April. www.medicalmarihuana.ca/ppslawsuit.html.

– 2003c. 'MP Group Sought US Help to Derail Pot Bill.' *Globe and Mail*, 19 August, A1.

– 2003d. 'Not Leaning on US to Halt Marijuana Bill.' *Globe and Mail*, 20 August, A7.

– 2003e. 'Ottawa to Appeal Marijuana Ruling.' *Globe and Mail*, 11 February. www.medicalmarihuana.ca/incompetence.html.

Landry, Frank. 2003. 'Government Pot Ready.' *Winnipeg Sun*, 11 January. www.medicalmarihuana.ca/scandal.html.

Larsen, Dana. 1999. 'Cops Pull Khat's Leash.' *Cannabis Culture Magazine*. July–August. www.hempbc.com/library/hparchive/copspullkhatsleash .html.

Lawton, Valerie. 2003. 'Liberals among Bills Harshest Opponents.' *Toronto Star*, 28 May, A6.

Layton, Jack. 2003. 'Why We Must Change Voting System.' *Toronto Star*, 29 August, A25.

Lee-Shanok, Phillip. 2000. 'Fantino: It's Not Raves, It's the Drugs.' *Toronto Sun*, 17 May.

Levy, Harold. 2003. 'Police Rebuttal Called Flawed: Racial Profiling May Exist: Report Sociologist's Approach Slammed.' *Toronto Star*, 10 June, A1.

Levy, Sue-Ann. 2000. 'Rave Suspension Causes Waves.' *Toronto Sun*, 12 May.

'Licensed Marijuana Factory Opens.' 2002. Canada.com, 30 September. www.medicalmarihuana.ca/factory.html.

Lightstone, Michael. 2003. 'Pot Access up to Courts – Senator.' *Halifax Herald*, 22 February. www.medicalmarihuana.ca/inaction.html.

'Listless Confusion.' *Winnipeg Free Press*, 3 January. www.medicalmarihuana .ca/possession.html.

Ljunggren, David. 2003. 'Pot Growers' Sentences Too Lenient, Fantino Says.' *Toronto Star*, 23 August, A18.

Loome, Jeremy. 2003. 'Special Delivery! Feds Begin Mailing Marijuana.' *Edmonton Sun*, 10 July. www.medicalmarihuana.ca/distribution.html.

Lunman, Kim, and Brian Laghi. 2003. 'Ottawa's Pot Grower Will Supply Patients.' *Globe and Mail*, 9 July. www.medicalmarihuana.ca/comply.html.

MacArthur, John. 2003. 'Medical Marijuana Patient Refused Access to Gov't Meetings.' Medwire, 28 January. www.medicalmarihuana.ca/sacked.html.

MacCharles, Tonda. 2001. 'Powers of Arrest Are Not Clear: Police.' *Toronto Star*, 2 November, A6.

– 2002. 'We're Both at Risk, Powell Tells Canada: Border Dominates the Discussion.' *Toronto Star*, 15 November, A7.

– 2003a. 'Easier Wireless Snooping Worries Watchdogs.' *Toronto Star*, 7 August, A6.

– 2003b. 'Ottawa Battles to Regain Control of Reefer Madness.' *Toronto Star*, 20 January. www.medicalmarihuana.ca/noregulations.html.

– 2003c. 'Police Chiefs Slam "Flawed" Pot Bill.' *Toronto Star*, 4 November, A22.

Makin, Kirk. 2003. 'Ottawa's Pot Rules Unconstitutional, Court Rules.' *Globe and Mail*, 7 October.

Matas, Robert. 2002a. 'Joint Operations Flourishing.' *Globe and Mail*, 27 April. www.medicalmarihuana.ca/homegrown.html.

– 2002b. 'Pot Factory to Be First in Canada, Group Says.' *Globe and Mail*, 30 September. www.medicalmarihuana.ca/factory.html.

Maychak, Matt. 1988. 'Drug Training Recommended for Guards at Rock Concerts.' *Toronto Star*, 18 October, A12.

McCarten, James. 1999. 'Province, Police Team up to Crack Down on Rave Parties.' *Canadian Press*, 3 November.

– 2002. 'Medical Marijuana Advocates Go to Court to Fight Ottawa's Rules on Pot.' *Canadian Press*, 19 September. www.medicalmarihuana.ca/dissension.html.

McCulloch, Sandra. 2003. 'His Pot's Legal, but So Is His Eviction.' *Victoria Times Colonist*, 17 June. www.medicalmarihuana.ca/eviction.html.

McLellan, Anne. 2002. 'Re: Medical Marijuana Plan Still on Track, Health Minister Says.' *National Post*, 29 August. www.medicalmarihuana.ca/mclellanltr.html.

McNeil, Donald G. 2003a. 'Report of Ecstasy Drug's Great Risks Is Retracted.' *New York Times*, 6 September.

– 2003b. 'Research on Ecstasy Is Clouded in Errors.' *New York Times*, 2 December.

Millar, Cal. 1988. 'Kids Obtain Drugs Easily Police Admit.' *Toronto Star*, 21 May, A16.

– 2001. 'Police Can't Fight Drug Use by Themselves, Fantino Says.' *Toronto Star*, 11 September, B3.

Millar, Cal, and Catherine Porter. 2004. 'Drug Squad Fallout Rages: Chief Faces Heat Amid Corruption Allegations.' *Toronto Star*, 21 January, B1.

Moloney, Paul. 2000. 'Ravers to Give City Demo.' *Toronto Star*, 14 July, F7.

– 2003. 'Police Attack Star's Race Articles, Police Chief's Race Response Gets Crowd's Full Attention.' *Toronto Star*, 21 February, A1.

Moore, Oliver. 2003. 'US Brings Anti-Pot Message to Ottawa.' *Globe and Mail*, 8 July, Online. www.globeandmail.com/servlet/story/RTGAM.20030708 .wmari0708/BNstory/National.

Morris, Chris. 2003. 'US Envoy Lauds Canada for Assistance.' *Toronto Star*, 9 September, A16.

Morris, Nomi. 1988a. 'Benji No "Druggie" Despite LSD Trip Say Friends Shocked at Teen's Death.' *Toronto Star*, 21 May, A1.

– 1988b. 'Benji's Friend Relives Drug Trip under Hypnosis.' *Toronto Star*, 5 August, A6.

– 1988c. 'Benji's Mom Begs for Way to Stop "Blatant" Dealing of Drugs in Metro.' *Toronto Star*, 19 July, A6.

– 1988d. 'Community Rallied to Aid Benji Search.' *Toronto Star*, 19 May, A10.

– 1988e. 'Drug Culture Bared at Probe.' *Toronto Star*, 13 August, A8.

– 1988f. '"It's Everyone's Problem," Benji Jury Says Declare War on Drugs Ontario Told.' *Toronto Star*, 13 August, A1.

– 1988g. '"No Evidence" for Arrest, Officer Says.' *Toronto Star*, 9 August, A6.

– 1988h. 'Use Common Sense in Plan to Fight Drugs, Jurors Urged.' *Toronto Star*, 11 August, A16.

– 1988i 'Young Rock Fan Found Drowned.' *Toronto Star*, 19 May, A1.

– 1989a. 'Are Students Heeding Word: Dope Isn't Cool?' *Toronto Star*, 7 May, C7.

– 1989b. 'Benji's Folks Fight to Reach Other Parents.' *Toronto Star*, 7 May, C7.

'Nations United in Good Cause: The Conference for the Abolition of the Opium Trade.' 1909. *The Globe*, 8 May, 8.

Necheff, Julia. 2002. 'Medical Marijuana Plans Remain Active.' Canadian Press, 27 August. www.medicalmarihuana.ca/backtrack.html.

Nuttall-Smith, Chris. 2003. 'Ottawa's Marijuana Stash Sitting on the Shelf Wrapped in Red Tape.' CanWest News Service, 22 July. www.medicalmarihuana.ca/rescind.html.

Oh, Susan 2000. 'Rave Fever: Raves are All the Rage but Drugs Are Casting a Pall over Their Sunny Peace-and-Love Ethos.' *Maclean's*, 24 April, 38–13.

O'Neil, Peter. 2002a. 'BC Pot Growers Blast $6 Million Waste: Ottawa Ignored Expert Advice, Cannabis Community Says.' *Vancouver Sun*, 11 May. www .medicalmarihuana.ca/flinflonflop.html.

– 2002b. 'Senator Tells Feds to Buy BC Bud.' *Vancouver Sun*, 10 May. www .medicalmarihuana.ca/bcmarijuana.html.

Orwen, Patricia. 1988. 'Views Differ on Success of Drug War.' *Toronto Star*, 21 May, A1.

'Ottawa to Sell Marijuana to Patients.' 2003. *Halifax Herald*, 10 July. www
.medicalmarihuana.ca/distribution.html.

Page, Shelley. 1988a. '7 Arrested on Drug Charges at Heavy Metal Rock
Concert.' *Toronto Star*, 21 May, A1.

– 1988b. 'Drugs and Heavy Metal Music Are a Bad Mix for Some Teens.'
Toronto Star, 22 May, A1.

Panetta, Alexander. 2002. 'Open Border Is Key to North America Suceeding
in Global Economy: Premiers.' Canadian Press, 26 August.

Papp, Leslie. 1988a. 'Counsellors Say They're Fighting an Uphill Battle.'
Toronto Star, 21 May, A16.

– 1988b. 'Kids Have Lots of Money to Get High.' *Toronto Star*, 21 May, A16.

Parsons, Charlotte. 1993. 'They Only Come Out at Night: Rave Is on the
Rise: Is the Underground Selling Its Soul?' *Globe and Mail*, 9 October,
A1.

Pearson, Craig. 2002. 'MDs Refuse to Prescribe Medicinal Pot.' *Windsor Star*,
31 October. www.medicalmarihuana.ca/refusal.html.

Picard, Andre. 2007. 'Clement Plans "Plain Truth" Anti-Drug Campaign.'
Globe and Mail. http://www.theglobeandmail.com/servlet/story/LAC
.20070821.CMA21/TP/Story/National.

Picard, Andre, and Carolyn Abraham. 2002. 'Ottawa Shelves Medicinal Pot:
Uneasy McLellan Backs Off Plan to Supply.' *Globe and Mail*, 20 August.
www.medicalmarihuana.ca/revoke.html.

'Police Chiefs Push for Undercover Powers: Want Anti-Gang Bill to Fight
Crime.' 2001. *Toronto Star*, 23 August, A7.

Porter, Catherine. 2002. 'US Drug Idea Stirs Fears Here: Senate Bill Seen
Threatening Canada's Supply.' *Toronto Star*, 20 July, F3.

'Pot Policy Unsteady.' 2002. *Kitchener-Waterloo Record*, 22 August. www
.medicalmarihuana.ca/conflict.html.

'Pot Prescriptions Leave Doctors Cold.' 2003. *Victoria Times Colonist*, 25 July.
www.medicalmarihuana.ca/rescind.html.

Potter, Greg. 2000. 'Party Boy: Meet Vancouver's Premier Rave Promoter.' *BC
Business Magazine*, July, 134–40.

Powell, Betsy. 2000. 'Drugs, Death, and Dancing.' *Toronto Star*, 7 May.

– 2001. 'Dancers Rant for Raves: Promoters Say Cost of Policing Destroys
Scene.' *Toronto Star*, 29 August.

– 2004. 'Pot Busts Jump Despite Decriminalization Intent: Increase Related to
Arrests for Pot Possession.' *Toronto Star*, 24 February, A5.

Pron, Nick. 2004. 'Veteran Officers Face 40 Charges: Took Law into Their
Own Hands Says RCMP, Grim Chief Fantino Insists Problem Is "Isolated,"
"Confined."' *Toronto Star*, 8 January, A1.

Pugsley Fraser, Amy. 2003a. 'Good News for Claiming Pot.' *Halifax Herald*, 17 April. www.medicalmarihuana.ca/deductions.html.

– 2003b. 'No Tax Break for Marijuana.' *Halifax Herald*, 16 April. www .medicalmarihuana.ca/expenses.html.

Quinn, Jennifer. 2000. 'Chief Says It's His Call on Policing Raves.' *Toronto Star*, 28 July, B5.

'Racial Data a Hot Potato.' 2002. *Toronto Star*, 26 October, B4.

Rankin, Jim. 2000. 'Raid Leaves Painful Memories: Man Accuses Drug Squad of Beating Him Viciously.' *Toronto Star*, 27 November, B1, B5.

Rankin, Jim, Jennifer Quinn, Michelle Shephard, John Duncanson, and Scott Simmie. 2002a. 'Police Target Black Drivers: Star Analysis of Traffic Data Suggests Racial Profiling.' *Toronto Star*, 20 October, A8.

– 2002b. 'Singled Out: Star Analysis of Police Crime Data Shows Justice Is Different for Blacks and Whites.' *Toronto Star*, 19 October, A1.

Raphael, Mitchel. 2002a. 'Afraid of Rave? Remember Rock? Reaction of the Press Fuelled by Fear of the Unknown.' *National Post*, 19 April.

– 2002b. 'Ravers Say Security Requirements "Unreasonable."' *National Post*, 25 October.

Rayner, Ben. 2000a. 'Detroit All the Rave: Techno Music's Birthplace Shows T.O. There's Nothing to Fear.' *Toronto Star*, 29 May.

– 2000b. 'Toronto Just Keeps Ranting About Raving: But Detroit Embraces the Sub-Culture with a Weekend Festival Supported by the City.' *Toronto Star*, 13 May.

– 2001. 'Bustin' a Move or Two.' *Toronto Star*, 3 September, E2.

– 2002a. 'Corporations Have Joined the Party – So What?' *Toronto Star*, 9 February, J3.

– 2002b. 'Rave Culture Celebration Cancelled.' *Toronto Star*, 17 July, D1.

Rosenberg, Debra. 1997. 'Death of the Party: GHB Is a Hot Drug in the Nightclub and Rave Scenes, but This Cheap High Can Bring Fatal Lows.' *Newsweek*, 27 October, 55.

Rubec, Stephanie, and Susy Trace. 2002. 'Anne "Stalling" on Pot.' *Edmonton Sun*, 21 August. www.medicalmarihuana.ca/revoke.html.

Rupert, Jake. 2003. 'Messy Marijuana Law Tries Courts, Police.' *Ottawa Citizen*, 29 June. www.medicalmarihuana.ca/rogin.html.

Ruryk, Zen, and Antonella Artuso. 2000. 'Raves History, Lastman Says: Mayor Wants Council to End City-Sanctioned Parties.' *Toronto Sun*, 4 May.

Rush, Curtis. 2004. 'Four Officers Face Corruption Charges: All Four Linked to Deceased Car Dealer.' *Toronto Star*, 8 January, A1.

Rushkoff, Douglas. 1999. 'Rave against the Machine [Commercialization of Rave Culture].' *This Magazine*, November–December, 37–39.

Rusk, James. 2000. 'Councillors Resist Making Hasty Move.' *Globe and Mail*, 4 May.

– 2001. 'More Could Die If Raves Stifled, Official Warns.' *Globe and Mail*, 29 August.

Samyn, Paul. 2002. 'Feds Shelve Medical Marijuana.' *Winnipeg Free Press*, 23 April. www.medicalmarihuana.ca/trials.html.

Segal, Adam. 2001. 'Unknown.' *Toronto Star*, 9 July.

Sharrif, Ali. 1996. 'Khat on a Hot Fed List: Ottawa Is Moving in on the Somali Community's Leafy Stimulant.' *Now Magazine*, 8–14 August. www.nowtoronto.com/issues/15/49/News/feature2.html.

Shephard, Michelle, and Tracy Huffman. 2000. 'Ottawa Asked to Deal with Raves: Chief Seeks Drug Education, Faults Parents.' *Toronto Star*, 7 May.

Simmie, Scott. 2003. 'Racial Profiles Harm Ethnics: Report.' *Toronto Star*, 8 December, A19.

Smith, Graeme. 2000. 'Rave Fans Dance for the Cause.' *Toronto Star*, 2 August, B1.

'Somalia: Death by Looting.' 1992. *The Economist*, 18 July, 41.

'St Mike's Study Probes Role of Medical Pot.' 2002. *Toronto Star*, 10 October. medicalmarihuana.ca/study.html.

Stanleigh, Sean. 2000. 'Peace Rave Rally Was a Seminal Event.' *Toronto Star*, 4 August, B4.

Stefaniuk, Walter. 2003. 'You Asked Us: War on Iraqis Divides Callers.' *Toronto Star*, 1 April, B2.

'Strangers in a Strange Land.' 1992. *US News and World Report*, 21 December, 60–6.

'The Story Behind the Numbers.' 2002. *Toronto Star*, 19 October. http://www .thestar.com/NASApp/cs/ContentServer?pagename=thestar/Layout/ Article_Type1&c=Article&cid=1035 025238759&call_page=TS_ RaceAndCrime&call_pageid=4935301156&call_pagepath=GTA/Race_ and_Crime&col =4935301113.

'Suit Aims to Force Ottawa to Supply Medical Pot.' 2002. Torstar News Service, 22 May. www.medicalmarihuana.ca/lawsuit.html.

Swainson, Gail. 1988. 'Police Seek $6 Million, 90 Officers for Anti-Drug Fight.' *Toronto Star*, 13 August, A8.

Tchir, Jason. 2001. 'A Mother's Anguish: Raves Are Not for Teens: Mom of OD Kid.' *Toronto Sun*, 10 July.

Thomas, Sandra. 2003a. 'Medical Marijuana a Potential Headache for Landlords.' *Vancouver Courier*, 16 June. www.medicalmarihuana.ca/eviction.html.

– 2003b. 'Vancouver Tenant Tending Legal Grow-Op.' *Vancouver Courier*, 11 June. www.medicalmarihuana.ca/eviction.html.

Thompson, Allan. 2002a. '"No Country Is Exempt in the War against Terrorism," Ashcroft Tells Canada.' *Toronto Star*, 8 November, A1.

– 2002b. 'US Envoy Urges Joint Screening.' *Toronto Star*, 12 November, A7.

– 2003a. 'Canada Invited to Help Police Iraq.' *Toronto Star*, 18 April, A1.

– 2003b. 'Ottawa Eyes US Missile Defence Plan.' *Toronto Star*, 29 April, A4.

– 2003c. 'US Won't Wait Long: McCallum.' *Toronto Star*, 9 May, A7.

Thompson, Elizabeth. 2003. 'Cigarette Girls and Boys Spark Debate: Justice Minister's Office Says Practice Is Disappointing as It Targets Young People.' *Montreal Gazette*, 1 October.

Thorne, Stephen. 2003. 'Canada Offers Planes, Police, and Advisors to Help in Post-War Iraq.' Canadian Press, 29 April.

Toughill, Kelly. 2003. 'US-Canada Relationship "Pretty Much" Normal Again, Envoy Says.' *Toronto Star*, 21 June, A25.

Tracey, Scott. 2002. 'Medical Marijuana Rules Rile City Man.' *Guelph Mercury*, 20 September. www.medicalmarihuana.ca/patients.html.

Tuck, Simon. 2003. 'Tobacco Giant Creates New Marketing Arms: Critics Say Moves Aim to Skirt Tough Anti-Smoking Laws.' *Globe and Mail*, Investor Section. http://www.globeinvestor.com/servle...ws?back_url=yes.

Tyler, Tracey. 2002a. 'Ottawa Back-Peddling on Pot, Critics Believe.' *Toronto Star*, 18 September. www.medicalmarihuana.ca/dissension.html.

– 2002b. 'Patients Take Pot Fight to Court.' *Toronto Star*, 24 May. www.medicalmarihuana.ca/lawsuit.html.

– 2003. 'Police Lawsuit against the *Star* Dismissed: Officers' Union Sought $2.7 Billion.' *Toronto Star*, 25 June, A1.

Tyler, Tracey, and Karen Palmer. 2003. 'Judge Strikes Down Rules on Access to Medical Pot.' *Toronto Star*, 10 January. www.medicalmarihuana.ca/unconstitutional.html.

Vallis, Mary. 2003. 'McLellan, Pharmacists to Discuss over-the-Counter Marijuana Sales.' *National Post*, 19 August. www.medicalmarihuana.ca/pharmacists.html.

van Rijn, Nicolaas, and Dale Ann Freed. 2004. 'Payoffs, Sexual Favours at Heart of Police Probe.' *Toronto Star*, 19 April, A2.

Van Wageningen, Ellen. 2003. 'Pot Law Fight Predicted.' *Windsor Star*, 10 December.

Vasil, Adria. 2003. 'Smoking Out Big Tobacco.' *NOW Magazine*, 16–22 October. www.nowtoronto.com/issues/2003-10-16/news_feature.php.

'Viagra Finds Favour with Ravers.' 2000. *Toronto Star*, 22 May, A6.

Walkom, Thomas. 2003. 'Security Ties to US Key to Arar Saga.' *Toronto Star*, 7 October, A21.

Wallace, Bruce. 1992. 'The Cry of a Dying People.' *Maclean's*, 7 September, 20–4.

Wanagas, Don. 1988. 'Watch for Signs of Drugs, Parents Told.' *Toronto Star*, 30 May, C2.

– 2000a. 'City Councillors Oppose Ban on Supervised Raves: Disagree with Lastman.' *National Post*, 6 May.

– 2000b. 'Council Puts Temporary Ban on City-Run Raves: Minority Warn That City's Reversal Could Increase Drug Use.' *National Post*, 11 May.

– 2000c. 'Fantino behind Mel's About-Face: Mayor Changes Tune on Raves after New Chief Appointed.' *National Post*, 10 May.

– 2000d. 'Father Julián Missed His Calling: Toronto's New Police Chief Spends a Lot of His Time Preaching.' *National Post*, 13 May.

Werde, Bill. 2001. 'The Fight for the Right to Party.' *Urb*, July–August, 118–31.

White, Tarina. 2002. 'Court Gives Medical Pot Crusader a Break.' *Oak Bay News*, 19 July. www.medicalmarihuana.ca/discharge.html.

Whittington, Les. 2003a. 'Border Exemption "Big Win" Manley Says.' *Toronto Star*, 18 April, A4.

– 2003b. 'Economy at Risk in US Tiff, Beatty Says.' *Toronto Star*, 29 March, F4.

'Why Is Ottawa So Afraid of Pot?' 2003. *Victoria Times Colonist*, 10 July. www.medicalmarihuana.ca/comply.html.

Williams, James. 1914. 'Negro Cocaine Fiends, New Southern Menace.' *New York Times*, 11 February.

Wright, Lisa. 1988a. 'Education Needed on Substance Abuse.' *Toronto Star*, 31 May, A18.

– 1988b. 'Task Force Advisor Seeks Immediate Action on Drugs.' *Toronto Star*, 30 September, A6.

Xavier, David. 2001. 'Police Were Just Doing Their Jobs in Somali Drug Bust.' *Toronto Star*, 25 July, A23.

Yakabuski, Konrad. 1988. '200 Join Search for Missing 14-Year-Old.' *Toronto Star*, 18 May, A16.

Yelaja, Prithi. 2001. 'Somali "Tempers Boiling" after Police Drug Bust.' *Toronto Star*, 24 July, B4.

Yourk, Darren, and Kim Lunman. 2002. 'Quebec Judge Throws out Pot Case.' *Globe and Mail*, 19 December. www.medicalmarihuana.ca/victory.html.

Zollmann, Paul. 2003. 'Deathly Ill Don't Care About Experts' Views.' *Ottawa Citizen*, 22 July. www.medicalmarihuana.ca/rescind.html.

Government and Other Primary Sources

Auditor General. 2001. 'Illicit Drugs: The Federal Government's Role.' Ottawa: Government of Canada.

Basrur, Sheela V. 2000. 'Drug Prevention and Harm Reduction Strategies of Toronto Public Health in Regards to Raves.' Toronto: Medical Officer of Health.

British Columbia Compassion Club Society. 2002. 'Letter to Health Minister Anne McLellan from BCCCS.' 6 November. www.medicalmarihuana.ca/sabotage.html.

Bureau for International Narcotics and Law Enforcement Affairs. 1999. 'International Narcotics Control Strategy Report 1998.' Washington, D.C.: U.S. Department of State, 1999.

Canada. 1988. 'Action on Drug Abuse: Making a Difference.' Ottawa.

– 1996. Controlled Drug and Substances Act. Ottawa.

Canadian Association of Chiefs of Police. 2003. 'Open Letter to the Prime Minister of Canada Concerning Bill C-38: Decriminalization of Marijuana.'

Canadian Bar Association. 1996. 'Canadian Bar Association Joins Protest against Bill C-8.' *Canadian HIV/AIDS Policy and Law Newsletter* 2, no. 4. www.aidslaw.ca/publicationsdocEN.php?ref=557.

Canadian Medical Association. 2001a. 'Letter From Canadian Medical Association to Health Minister Allan Rock.' Ottawa. www.medicalmarihuana.ca/cmajulyltr.html.

– 2001b. 'Marijuana: Federal Smoke Clears a Little.' *Canadian Medical Association Journal*, 15 May. www.medicalmarihuana.ca/cma.html.

– 2001c. 'Open Letter to CMA Members.' Ottawa: Canadian Medical Association. www.medicalmarihuana.ca/problems1.html.

Canadian Medical Protection Agency. 2001. 'What to Do When Your Patients Apply for a Licence to Possess Marijuana for Medical Purposes.' Canadian Medical Protection Agency. www.cmpa-acpm.ca/cmpapd02/cmpa_docs/english/resource_files/infosheets/common/2001/pdf.

City of Toronto. 2004. 'City of Toronto 2004 Budget Launch.' Toronto.

Coroner's Inquest into the Death of Allen Ho. 2000. 'Jury Recommendations Concerning the Death of Allen Ho.' Toronto.

CISC (Criminal Intelligence Service Canada). 2002. 'Annual Report on Organized Crime in Canada 2002.' Ottawa.

Drug Analysis Section (RCMP). 2002. 'Drug Situation in Canada – 2001.' Ottawa: RCMP.

DEA (Drug Enforcement Administration). 2001. 'Club Drugs: An Update.' Washington, D.C.: Drug Enforcement Administration.

– 2002. 'Drug Intelligence Brief: Khat.' Washington, D.C.: Drug Enforcement Administration.

EM:DEF. 2004. 'Clean-up Meth Act of 2003.' Electronic Music Education and Defence Fund. www.emdef.org/hr834.

306   References

Federal Research Division, Library of Congress. 2003. 'Nations Hospitable to
    Organized Crime and Terrorism.' Washington, D.C.: Library of Congress.
General Accounting Office. 1997. 'Drug Control: Long Standing Problems
    Hinder US International Efforts.' Washington, D.C.: General Accounting
    Office.
Health Canada. 1998. 'Canada's Drug Strategy.' Ottawa: Office of Alcohol,
    Drugs, and Dependency.
– 2000. 'Straight Facts About Drugs and Drug Abuse.' Ottawa.
– 2003a. 'Health Canada News Release.' 8 December. Ottawa.
– 2003b. 'Marihuana Medical Access Regulations.' Ottawa.
– 2003c. 'Reply to Medusers Petition.' 24 January.
House of Commons. 2002. Special Committee on Non-Medical Use of Drugs.
    'Policy for the New Millenium: Working Together to Redefine Canada's
    Drug Strategy: Report of the Special Committee on Non-Medical Use of
    Drugs.' Ottawa.
Kalix, Peter. 1986. 'Chewing Khat.' Geneva: World Health Organization.
Khat Habit Awareness in Toronto Project. 1998. 'A Preliminary Review of the
    Social, Economic, and Health Effects of Khat Use in Toronto.' Toronto: City
    of Toronto.
Le Dain Commission (Commission of Inquiry into the Non-Medical Use of
    Drugs). 1970. *Interim Report*. Ottawa.
– 1973. *Final Report*. Ottawa.
Legislative Assembly of Ontario. An Act to Promote Public Peace and Safety
    by Regulating Late-Night Dance Events (Rave Act). 1st Session, 37th Legis-
    lature, Ontario, 49 Elizabeth II, Bill 73.
Looney, Lt.-Gen. Bill. 2002. 'ESC Members Restricted from Attending
    "Raves."' Hanscom, MA: Hanscom Air Force Base.
Medusers. 2002. 'Press Release: Stakeholder Advisory Committee on Medical
    Marihuana.' www.medicalmarihuana.ca/meeting.html.
– 2003. 'The Medusers Petition to the Stakeholder Advisory Committee,
    Office of Cannabis Medical Access, Health Canada.' www.medical
    marihuana.ca/sacked.html.
NORML (National Organization for the Reform of Marijuana Laws). 2003.
    'Weekly Press Release: Canada's Supreme Court Rules 6–3 in Favor of
    Continuing Marijuana Prohibition.'
OHRC (Ontario Human Rights Commission). 2003. 'Paying the Price: The
    Human Cost of Racial Profiling.' Toronto.
Ontario Police Chiefs Association. 2002. 'Press Release: Ontario Police Chiefs
    Oppose the Legalization of Marihuana.'
Pollara. 2004. 'Canadians' Attitudes toward Foreign Policy.' Toronto: Cana-
    dian Institute of International Affairs.

Royal Canadian Mounted Police. 2001. *Designer Drugs and Raves.* 2nd ed. Vancouver.

RCMP Criminal Intelligence Directorate and DEA Intelligence Division. 2001. 'Chemical Diversion and Synthetic Drug Manufacture.'

RCMP Drug Awareness Service. 2003. 'Chemical Drug Trends: British Columbia.' Vancouver.

Robinson, Gregory. 2003. 'Letter of Resignation to Health Minister Anne McLellan.' medicalmarihuana.ca/resignation.html.

Senate. 1955. Special Committee on the Traffic of Narcotic Drugs in Canada. 'Traffic in Narcotic Drugs in Canada.' Ottawa.

Senate. 2000. Special Committee on Illegal Drugs. 'Proceedings of the Special Commitee on Illegal Drugs.' Ottawa.

– 2002a. 'Cannabis: Our Position for a Canadian Public Policy: Report of the Senate Special Committee on Illegal Drugs (Summary Report).' Ottawa.

– 2002b. 'Cannabis: Our Position for a Canadian Public Policy: Report of the Senate Special Committee on Illegal Drugs (Volume 1: Parts I and II).' Ottawa.

– 2002c. 'Cannabis: Our Position for a Canadian Public Policy: Report of the Senate Special Committee on Illegal Drugs (Volume 2: Part III).' Ottawa.

– 2002d. 'Cannabis: Our Position for a Canadian Public Policy: Report of the Senate Special Committee on Illegal Drugs (Volume 3: Part IV and Conclusions).' Ottawa.

– 2002e. 'Cannabis: Our Position for a Canadian Public Policy: Report of the Senate Special Committee on Illegal Drugs (Volume 4: Appendices).' Ottawa.

Statistics Canada. 2003. 'Canada's Enthnocultural Portrait: The Changing Mosaic (2001 Census: Analysis Series).' Ottawa.

– 2004a. *Crimes by Type of Offence.* www.statcan.ca/english/Pgdb/legal02.htm.

– 2004b. *The Daily (July 24): Crime Statistics.* www.statcan.ca/Daily/English/030724/d030724a.htm.

TDSC (Toronto Dance Safe Committee). 1999. 'Toronto Dance Safe Committee Protocol for the Operation of Safe Dance Events.' Toronto.

– 2000. Press Release: City of Toronto Endangers Young Citizens. 10 May.

U.S. Department of Justice and the Solicitor General Canada. 2001. 'United States–Canada Border Drug Threat Assessment.' Washington, D.C.: National Drug Intelligence Center.

White House. 2003. 'Presidential Determination No. 2003-14.' Washington, D.C.

Index